THE POLITICS
OF STATES
AND URBAN
COMMUNITIES

HUGH L. LeBLANC
D. TRUDEAU ALLENSWORTH
The George Washington University

HARPER & ROW, PUBLISHERS
New York, Evanston, San Francisco, London

The Politics of States and Urban Communities

Copyright © 1971 by HUGH L. LEBLANC and D. TRUDEAU ALLENSWORTH

Printed in the United States of America. All rights reserved. No part of this book may be used or reproduced in any manner whatsoever without written permission except in the case of brief quotations embodied in critical articles and reviews. For information address Harper & Row, Publishers, Inc., 49 East 33rd Street, New York, N.Y. 10016.

Standard Book Number: 06-043885-1

Library of Congress Catalog Card Number: 70-148451

CONTENTS

PREFACE   vii

1. The Study of State and Local Governments   1
2. Power Allocations in the Federal System   17
3. Political Participation   42
4. Political Parties at the State Level   70
5. The Politics of the State Executive   92
6. Politics of State Legislatures   118
7. Courts in the Political Process   147

8. Governing Communities: Form, Influence, and Public Policy   173
9. Governmental Decentralization in Metropolitan Areas   202
10. Metropolitan Reorganization Strategies   219
11. Politics and Power Structures in the City   244
12. Suburban Politics   264
13. The Politics of Finances   284
14. The Politics of Public Education   312
15. The Politics of Law Enforcement   336
16. Urban Housing   359
17. City and Regional Planning   392
18. Urban Transportation   412
19. Poverty and Community Politics   435

INDEX   453

PREFACE

This book is about politics in states and their communities. If politics is the "authoritative allocation of values in society," then we are obliged to discuss more than the forces at play within the political system. We must relate them to the public policies which emerge as outputs of the political system. To adequately explain the influences upon public policy, no narrow view of the political process is possible. The social and economic environments in which our political institutions operate must also be considered as important variables that shape the character of our public policies. This point of view we have tried to convey in the organization of our text. The first twelve chapters provide the broadly conceived setting for the process of politics as it takes place within states and communities. The remaining seven chapters discuss the forces affecting contemporary issues of public policy.

Any work that is a collaboration must entail a division of labor. The responsibility of each of the authors was assigned on the basis of his teaching and research interests. Hugh L. LeBlanc wrote chapter one, the chapters treating politics at the state level, and those covering the politics of law enforcement, education, and finances. Don Allensworth wrote the chapters on federalism and politics at the local level, and those discussing urban housing, urban transportation, city and regional planning, and poverty programs.

As any text writer knows, however, our product is not ours alone but depends upon the scholarship of those who have provided the research findings that give us a clearer understanding of politics at state and community levels. The list of our indebtedness is too long to acknowledge here, but we hope our footnoting will indicate those who provided valuable insights to us. We must, of course, accept full responsibility for any errors of fact or interpretation. However, since this effort is a joint undertaking, each of the authors can cheerfully blame the other for any shortcomings that appear.

Hugh L. LeBlanc
Don Allensworth

THE POLITICS
OF STATES
AND URBAN
COMMUNITIES

1. THE STUDY OF STATE AND LOCAL GOVERNMENTS

Until recently the study of state and local governments has been neglected by the discipline of political science. It is difficult to assign precise causes for this phenomenon. Perhaps it is the transcendent importance of problems grappled with by the national government that commands the attention of scholars and the general public alike. Perhaps also the political scientist's methodologies were not equal to the challenge of comprehending patterns in the bewildering array of state and local forms and processes. Whatever the causes, until the last decade and a half the literature on state and local governments has lacked the richness and imagination shown in the study of national government and politics.

1

ROLE IN GOVERNANCE

Despite dire predictions to the contrary, the responsibilities of state and local governments have not shrunk as the national government has expanded the scope of its powers and activities. Occurring as it did during wars and depression, the growth of centralized authority has been visible and dramatic. The incredible list of bills acted on by Congress in the first 100 days of the New Deal inspired a nation beset by economic woes which threatened the collapse of its political institutions. Taking advantage of the troubled times, Franklin D. Roosevelt employed federal powers in a way his predecessor would not have conceived to be either legally or morally right. The President's critics foresaw dire consequences to American society in the changes that were wrought. Indeed, the effects of New Deal actions on the patterns of federalism have been widespread; but this should not obscure the fact that the states and their subdivisions not only have retained their vitality as governmental units but also are expanding their activities at a rate that suggests that reports of their demise, like that of Mark Twain's death, have been premature and greatly exaggerated. Figures 1.1 and 1.2 present graphic evidence that Washington has not supplanted the statehouse and city hall in serving the domestic needs of today's population.

Deducting the amounts spent on present and past wars, the federal budget shrinks to two-thirds of combined state and local expenditures. The aggregate budgets of states and their subdivisions provide a useful shorthand to convey the importance of their undertakings. But it does not suggest the intimate ways in which their activities affect the lives of their citizens. Most school children receive their instruction in local public schools, and those who continue their education will more likely than not attend a state-supported institution. Behavior that threatens a breach of peace or poses a threat to another's person or property is regulated by state law and enforced by both state and local police officials. Care of the poor, the aged, the blind, the mentally ill, and other classes of unfortunates is still a major responsibility of state and local government despite the efforts of private humanitarian organizations and the federal government. Regulation of marriage as well as matters of wife and child support, rights of inheritance of widows and children, and child neglect and abuse are entrusted to state governments. Water, sanitation, streets, and sidewalks are provided the urban dweller by cities and local authorities. Urban transit systems are either municipally owned or closely regulated by city or state governments. Corporations are chartered, business and trades are regulated, and entry

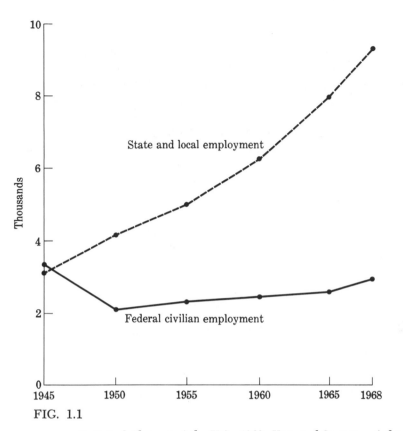

FIG. 1.1

SOURCE: *Statistical Abstract of the U.S., 1969; Historical Statistics of the U.S., 1965* (Washington, D.C.: U.S. Government Printing Office).

into the professions is licensed by state and local governments. It is hard to conceive of any aspect of our daily lives that is not affected in some way by the activities of state governments or their political subdivisions.

We tend to overlook what state and local governments do—unless a teachers' strike threatens to close the public schools, money is lost in a state-regulated savings and loan institution, a house is burglarized, land is rezoned for commercial development near a subdivision of single-family dwellings, a child is sought for adoption, or any of a host of common occurrences bring us into contact with state and local officials. Because their responsibilities are commonplace does not mean that they are unimportant. A moment's reflection will show that state and local

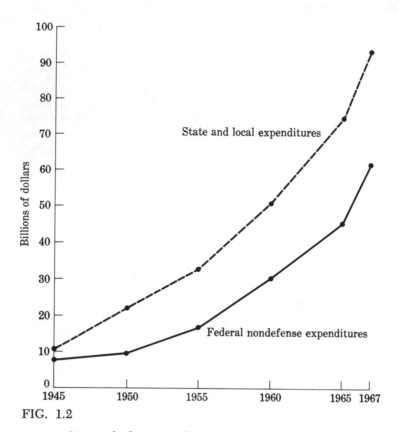

FIG. 1.2

SOURCE: *Statistical Abstract of the U.S., 1969; Historical Statistics of the U.S., 1965* (Washington, D.C.: U.S. Government Printing Office).

units of government affect very closely the quality of life that we enjoy in mid-twentieth-century America.

Although conceding the importance of state and local governments, some nevertheless argue that the activities undertaken are relatively noncontroversial and do not present issues over which people disagree. Thus the argument is often made that there is neither a Republican nor a Democratic way to pave a street. But who is to make the determination that streets should be paved (more likely resurfaced) in the first place, particularly if there is a shortage of funds and a need as well for additional school classrooms? Or what section of the city is going to have its chuckholes repaired following a hard winter? What route will be selected for an expressway to move traffic more rapidly in and out of the city? Such questions often produce conflict among groups and interests within a city.

Political conflict, of course, does not have to be partisan conflict. It is true that the Republican and Democratic parties do not take sides on all public issues and may even attempt to suppress some that would divide their own supporters. Yet since parties are not the only groups that contest public issues, the allegation that there is neither a Republican nor a Democratic way of doing things is beside the point. Other interest groupings may have a stake in what government does and will act to see that their interests are promoted or protected. Indeed, struggles among groups and interest constellations that do not follow partisan lines may be the most important conflict in the politics of some states and communities.

There is one additional point we wish to emphasize in regard to the responsibilities of state and local governments because it is a persistent theme throughout this book. Placing decision-making in the hands of professionally qualified personnel does not insure that the "right" decision will be made. What is implicit in the argument that there is no partisan way to pave a street is the belief that governmental problems can be solved best by those possessing technical expertise. The basic fallacy of this assumption is that professional judgment alone can be relied upon in distinguishing priorities among community needs. The expert in any one line possesses those amounts of human frailty and wisdom with which most of us are endowed. His personal convictions, prejudices, biases, and hunches meld together with his professional judgment as he acts upon political problems. What city manager of today, for example, would allege that governing a city is more of a science and less of an art? How many will say, at least in their private conversations, that they stay clear of "politics" as counseled in the code of ethics of the International City Manager's Association? Perhaps handing to the professionally qualified a large share of decision-making is the ideal "best" way of running a city, but it does not preclude the possibility that some will find their government inadequate to their needs.

Recognition that government cannot be "depoliticized" by a reliance on professional expertise or the views of those upon whom convention bestows civic or other virtues is peculiarly important today. The traditional authority exercised by most of society's institutions—family, school, church, and government—is being challenged. No matter what might be their claim to conventional wisdom, today's leaders are finding that their leadership role is not universally accepted and that their counsel is not always heeded. Moral and ethical codes that governed personal conduct in the past are being reinterpreted and new standards erected. A new generation of youth has become increasingly restive under the older, more confining morality and is striking out on its own. Perhaps without a keen sense of the ethic of responsibility, they nevertheless are making their voices heard on social and political problems. What all of this means insofar as the study of state and local governments is concerned is that no area of public decision-making can be demarcated as "out of politics" because what should be done appears well settled. It means further that a politician's professional and personal background must be investigated, insofar as this is feasible, to uncover the motivations behind his official acts. The more one understands the sources of influence on public policy, of whatever sort, the better he understands politics.

VARIETY IN STATES
AND COMMUNITIES

State and local governments are similar in many of their outward characteristics. All states have a governor to act as chief executive, a legislature to pass laws, and a court system to interpret and apply state constitutions and statutes. Although more variety is found in the structure of local governmental units, most cities are governed under mayor-council or city manager plans. A board or commission remains the principal public agency in counties, although some with more urban characteristics employ a manager or elected executive to direct county affairs. States and their political subdivisions operate within the framework of a common national culture and heritage which defines certain values and norms generally subscribed to by officials at all governmental levels. Thus in the abstract, at least, majority rule and minority rights are considered part of the fundamental rules governing American political practices.

Since we take for granted many of our democratic processes and institutions, to speak of similarities among state and local governments does not advance the level of analysis. What of the differences? How important are they to governance? And can we offer explanations of why the politics of some states differ from that of others? An answer to these questions must be sought to guide us in the analyses we shall make in the later chapters of this book.

States and communities differ in important ways. Although part of a common heritage, states are also influenced by their own peculiar regional or state histories. The populations of states and communities differ in terms of their size and the mix contained of rich and poor, white and nonwhite, and the number and kinds of ethnic strains. The physical features of a state vary from mountainous terrain, rolling countryside, flat plains, to desert land. The largest state, Alaska, is more than 539 times the size of the smallest, Rhode Island, yet the population of Rhode Island is greater. The economies of states such as California are well developed and diversified, with a mixture of both agriculture and manufacturing industries. Other states are industrially advanced but without diversification, such as Michigan whose economy is dominated by the automotive industry. Montana relies heavily on mining and ranching to support its population. Some southern states are still dependent on an agrarian economy, and many of their manufacturing industries are classed as nondurable (generally considered less desirable than durable manufacturing because the capital investment is usually lower and the labor employed is unskilled and paid at a low rate). Other variations are shown in Table 1.1 for selected states.

A state's physical, economic, and social characteristics are an interlocking set of variables which in their sum influence the workings of its politics. Geography and physical features, for example, will shape its economy. Is its land rich and fertile enough to support a prosperous agriculture? Is it endowed with mineral resources of oil, gas, iron, or coal? Is it close enough to urban concentrations which can serve as a market for its products? Availability of resources and markets is a measure of a state's economic assets. They determine the state's basic industries (those that create new wealth) which, in turn, support the activities of service and trade occupations which also provide for the needs of the population.

The adverse effects of limited physical resources on a state's economy are not easily overcome. Sections of Appalachia have experienced difficulty in recent years because mining industries have either been automated or closed as mineral resources have been depleted. Unemployment and underemployment is widespread. At the same time, the mountainous terrain makes agriculture a marginal undertaking, and the lack of labor skills and transportation difficulties prevent the easy replacement of mining industries by manufacturing enterprises. Although a target of federal aid because of its depressed economic areas, Appalachia has stubbornly refused to yield the prosperity longed for by its leaders.

A state's economic structure conditions its social structure. The number of job opportunities will determine, in part, where and how people live. Thus the more industrially advanced states will support large urban populations which are manufacturing centers. The skills demanded in manufacturing occupations and the service and trade professions they support place a premium on educational achievement and are rewarded by relatively high salaries and wages. It is no accident that the more industrialized states show a higher median family income and a higher median education.

The link between economic life and social fabric was nowhere better

TABLE 1.1
A Comparison of Physical, Social, and Economic Characteristics in Selected States

	CALIF.	COLO.	MAINE	MINN.	MISS.	N. MEX.	NEW YORK	N. DAK.	U.S. AVERAGE
Physical size (1000 sq. miles)	158.7	104.2	33.2	84.1	47.7	121.7	49.6	70.1	—
Population in thousands (1968)	19,300	2,043	976	3,647	2,344	1,006	18,078	627	—
Per capita income (1968)	$4,012	$3,371	$2,857	$3,318	$2,057	$2,695	$4,133	$2,808	$3,412
Median education (1960)	12.1	12.1	11.0	10.8	8.9	11.2	10.7	9.3	10.6
Percent urban (1960)	86.4	73.7	51.3	62.1	37.7	65.7	85.4	35.2	69.9
Percent nonwhite (1960)	8.0	3.0	0.6	1.2	42.3	7.9	8.9	2.0	11.4
Percent foreign stock (1960)	25.4	14.9	23.3	25.6	1.3	8.4	38.6	30.0	19.0
Percent employed in manufacturing (1960)	24.1	15.8	33.2	19.5	19.2	7.5	28.6	3.7	27.1
Percent employed in mining (1960)	0.5	2.0	0.1	1.2	0.8	6.1	0.2	0.8	1.0
Percent employed in agriculture (1960)	4.8	8.0	5.6	15.2	22.2	7.4	1.9	34.5	7.0

SOURCES: U.S. Bureau of the Census, *City and County Data Book 1967; Statistical Abstract 1969.*

demonstrated than in the post–Civil War industrial boom which went far in transforming American society. The demand for cheap labor attracted immigrants to this country, literally by the millions. Those that came at the turn of the century were not the familiar English, Irish, Germans, and Scandinavians, but Italians, Poles, Czechs, Slovaks, and Russian and Eastern European Jews. They settled in the large cities of the East and Midwest and found employment in the mineral and manufacturing industries that had been nurtured by rich iron and coal resources. Crowded into ghettos, oftentimes resented by the Yankee stock, they nevertheless found their way into the American class structure; and when they did, they exerted an enormous leveling influence on American society.

Both the economic and social characteristics of a state shape its politics, by creating particular kinds of groups which place particular demands upon government. A state's economic resources will determine its fiscal capacity and thus its ability to respond to the demands made. A heavily urbanized state with a large working class composed of nonwhite and foreign stock elements, for example, will likely receive demands for generous workmen's compensation and unemployment insurance plans, a variety of welfare measures, strong educational systems, projects to rejuvenate the cities' physical plants, progressive laws dealing with minority rights and interests, and similar programs. The more rural agricultural states experience less of a demand for parks and playgrounds, sanitation systems, urban renewal programs, or other governmental services which can only increase state or local taxes.

Indeed, socioeconomic groupings within a state will determine basic life styles which shape attitudes toward government and, as a consequence, partisan preferences. The urban dweller has come to depend upon government to provide him with a host of services. He may not like everything that government does, but he realizes that the absence of governmental activity provides no solution to problems of depressed economic conditions, slums and ghettos, or unhealthy living conditions. If among lower economic groups, he often turns to the Democratic party as the party more likely to use governmental power to correct social and economic ills.

On the other hand, the resident in rural areas and small towns has historically been less dependent upon governmental services that extend beyond the provision of basic necessities. The farmer depends upon the elements for the success of his endeavors and is more inclined to believe in a natural order of things. Feeling closer to nature, he is skeptical about the intrusion of government in what he believes are private matters. Inclined to independence and self-reliance, his partisan preferences are for the party whose governmental responses to economic and social issues are more restrained. Thus the traditional support of the Republican party has come from the so-called "out-state" areas.

We do not wish to oversimplify the patterns of a state's political interests or suggest that population groups can be easily characterized as to their voting preferences. Yet to ignore the influence that social and economic systems have on a state's politics is unacceptable political analysis. If the central task of political science is to explain why power configurations develop as they do and how they influence public policies, the environment in which political actors operate, as we elaborate below, must be considered part of the over-all political system.

THE ANALYSIS OF STATE
AND LOCAL POLITICS

Given the variations among state and local political systems, the task of the political scientist is a formidable one. To describe the differences among state and local units is easy enough; to offer explanations for the patterns that develop is the challenge. Although largely descriptive in the past, the more recent literature of state and local government has contributed importantly to our theoretical knowledge of the political process. And, paradoxically, part of the reason for the advances is the variability found among the states. By studying the many state and local governments, the student can hope to isolate those elements of the political system that appear to exert the greatest influence on policy outcomes, the end product of the political process. For example, if one wishes to determine if personal wealth within a state has important influences on a state's expenditure budget, he may compare per capita expenditures among the fifty states with per capita personal income. To insure that any positive relationship he finds is not spurious, he may wish to control for factors such as the level of party competition. Thus for the more wealthy states, he may compare those with strong and competitive parties against those in which partisanship is weak. If he finds that party competition affects state budgets, he knows that by itself the personal income factor is an inadequate predictor. It is through such comparative analyses, made possible by variations among state and local governments, that we can make generalizations which help explain why states enact the laws they do.

The state of our knowledge is not so complete that we can offer explanations for all political occurrences. Nor can we fit all of the generalizations we can make into an over-all theory of politics. Yet since such a general theory is the ultimate goal of political scientists, we must continue to devise ways in which political problems may be fruitfully analyzed. Through our analyses additional generalizations can be made and synthesized into broader theories which explain more of political behavior. Although an explanation of political analysis is not the primary concern of this book, we nevertheless believe that some basic ideas and analytic concepts must be presented so that the reader may know how we approach our subject matter. He may also wish to use them for his own interpretations of state and local politics.

The first point we wish to make clear is that our objective is to describe and explain political phenomena rather than to construct ethical or moral criteria to judge political acts and events. Such a statement requires explanation. We do not maintain that our professional and ethical values have not dictated the choice of the materials we cover later in this book. Such a position would be absurd and would leave us open to the charge made by metaphysicians that those who are more empirically oriented in their political analyses do not distinguish between the trivial and the politically relevant. However, as the reader can judge, the questions to which we seek answers are those that must be asked if one is to know not only who governs in states and communities but also who *should* govern. Thus we believe (and this is a value judgment) that an empirically supported explanation of how our political systems operate is the first step toward making wise moral choices.[1]

To say that we will not offer moral guidance in evaluating political actions is not to suggest that such judgments can be avoided in the real world of politics. Nor do we maintain that political philosophers who are concerned with the "oughts" of politics are engaged in a meaningless exercise. Indeed, shorn of value questions, political scientists would not know what questions they should address themselves to. In the interests of practicality, therefore, we have allowed ourselves some flexibility in discussing political behavior. For example, on a number of occasions we have singled out for special discussion public policies that have a peculiar impact upon Negroes. Now the obvious reason for this is that the economic and social conditions of Negroes, as an empirical fact, have presented moral questions to white, middle-class Americans. It is the fact of the moral issues that has influenced our judgment to include separate discussions of Negro rights and opportunities. Furthermore, we do not shrink from offering explanations of political behavior we believe to be empirically supported even though the findings themselves may be judged by some to involve moral issues. Thus the evidence that crime rates are highest in the slum-ridden sections of a central city is too well established for us to ignore. If we infer from this that crime rates will remain high until attacked at their root cause, that is, the slums that

[1] See the discussion in Robert Dahl, *Modern Political Analysis* (Englewood Cliffs: Prentice-Hall, 1963), p. 106.

breed crime, we are immediately involved in the controversial issue that has been labeled as "crime in the street." Some believe that such a socio-logical explanation of criminal activity can only lead to coddling of crimi-nal elements. Yet the author who avoids judgments to which his evidence fairly leads him must write a sterile work. We have taken care to exclude as nearly as possible our own value preferences in analyzing the political data presented. If our choice of words conveys our feelings, we hope at least that, in the context of our writing, value premises can be distin-guished from political facts.

The focus of our study will always be on the politics of states and their communities. It is necessary, therefore, that we convey as precisely as possible our use of the term "politics." Today most writers agree at least that politics involves relationships of power or influence. Thus in one of the most widely quoted definitions, Lasswell states that "the study of politics is the study of influence and the influential."[2] Some writers dis-tinguish influence from power; according to this usage, power, not influence, implies the reliance on sanctions (rewards or punishment) to induce desired behavior in others. We shall use the two terms inter-changeably. What must be stressed is that power (influence) involves a relationship (when one person or group influences the behavior of another person or group) and that relationship is the basic unit of politi-cal analysis.

To view politics as a set of interactions or relationships has analytical utility, because it helps us avoid some of the common errors made in the study of politics. For example, we may distinguish potential power from its actual exercise. Undoubtedly, some people have more political re-sources at their command than others. Yet if those resources are not translated into political power, they have little impact on the behavior of others. The fact is that some people are more skilful in the use of re-sources at their command than others, or they use more of them to gain political ends. If we focus on the relationships that exist, then we avoid the assumption that power is exercised by those who merely possess political resources, particularly the most visible kind such as wealth and status.

A second error that can be avoided by examining power relationships is the assumption that individuals influential in one area of political activity are equally influential in other areas. We are more likely to find some differentiation among the individuals and groups interested enough to use the political resources at their command in given issues of public policy. Of course, some, such as governors or mayors, may attempt to

2 Harold Lasswell, *Politics: Who Gets What, When, How* (New York: Meridian Books, 1958), p. 13.

wield influence over a broad spectrum of public decisions. The pattern that exists, and it will vary from state to state and from city to city, is revealed by systematic study.

We stress these aspects of power early because of the widely held popular view, supported by some students of politics, that a social and economic elite govern in their own interests at all levels of government. We do not discount the possibility that such a ruling class does govern in some communities. We simply wish to guard the reader against thinking in a stereotypical fashion about the influence of wealth and status in American society. If a power elite composed of the business and financial leaders does rule, it can be revealed by an empirical analysis of the relationships they have with political leaders.

Although the basic unit of political analysis, not all power relationships will be considered political. We shall focus on the set of power relationships that are basically "oriented toward the authoritative allocation of values for a society."[3] Values are authoritatively allocated *for a society* only by legal governments. There are many reasons why an individual will accept values as authoritatively binding (self-interest, loyalty, tradition), but the principal reason why governmental decisions are accepted as authoritative is that, if all else fails, they can be enforced by the threat of legal sanctions. All individuals and groups within society must accept the decisions reached by governments or be subject to the penalties and sanctions that apply to those who disobey the laws. The decisions of no other groups are similarly binding for society as a whole. The values articulated by some private groups may be accepted as authoritative and binding upon their members but not to those who do not belong. For our purposes, then, politics may be defined as a competition or struggle for power to control the decisions of government.

Two consequences flow from our definition of politics. The first is the obvious fact that politics cannot be confined to a study of formal or legal relationships of government. The structure and procedures of governmental institutions are, of course, important to the study of politics. But so are the organizations and operations of groups outside of government, particularly political parties and private interests. We are interested in nongovernmental groups insofar as their actions may influence the public policies adopted within a state or community. Although some political scientists believe that the internal operations of "private governments" (private organizations) should be separately studied to advance our understanding of power relationships generally,[4] we believe such an undertaking would be too diffuse for a textbook presentation. When we

[3] David Easton, *A Framework for Political Analysis* (Englewood Cliffs: Prentice-Hall, 1965), p. 50.
[4] Dahl, *op. cit.*, p. 6.

treat private groups separately, it is always with an eye toward how they influence the decisions reached by "legal governments."

The second consequence of our definition is that we necessarily are referring to a set of power relationships that exist within a political system. The concept of a political system provides further focus for our analysis of political struggles as they influence the authoritative allocation of values in society. It conveys the idea of interdependent and interacting elements that in their sum can be separately identified and studied. To say the system can be separately identified does not mean that it is a self-contained unit. On the contrary, state and local political systems are obviously subsystems of the national political system. American national government thus becomes part of the external environment which may lend support, create demands, or place stress on the system. The relationships, which are shown schematically in Fig. 1.3, are intended to represent a political system rather than to suggest an approach to political analysis we invariably follow.

Figure 1.3 may be interpreted in the following way. The external environment will create demands and lend support to the political system. Since state systems are part of a national political system, they

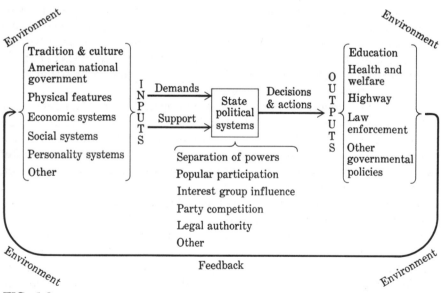

FIG. 1.3

SOURCE: Adapted from David Easton, *A Framework for Political Analysis* (Englewood Cliffs, N.J.: Prentice-Hall, 1965), p. 112.

operate under the general set of rules that characterize the American political style—whose values are in part institutionalized in electoral systems, deliberative assemblies, independent courts and voluntary associations. The American national government may influence the workings of state systems in more precise ways, as when the Supreme Court invalidates a state literacy test for voting, or Congress authorizes the appointment of federal examiners to enroll Negro voters. The actions of the federal government may be viewed as exogenous to the state political system but nevertheless influential in its operations.

Social and economic systems will also generate demands or lend support to the political system, as we discussed earlier. For example, a state with sizable manufacturing interests will support a large class of industrial workers. Probably organized into trade unions, the workers will bring pressures to improve workmen's compensation or extend unemployment compensation coverage. The pressures they bring are demands on the political system which may be expressed in their votes for political officers, representations made to members of the executive and legislative branches, or negotiations with party leaders. The demands made by labor may be opposed by employer associations, taxpayers' leagues, or other groups. The conflicts entailed are the power struggles that are the stuff of politics. As the conflict is reconciled, it results in certain actions (or a decision not to act) which create the public policies that allocate values authoritatively in society. The outputs of the political system then become part of its general environment and may affect the type of further inputs that are made.

Although our illustration depicts a state political system, the concept is useful as well in portraying local political systems. State government then becomes a part of the external environment in which the local system operates. Or we may focus on part of a political system and analyze it in terms of input demands and support. We do this in the case of the legislative system (subsystem) because it conveys more realistically the influences on legislative behavior. The advantage of the systems concept is that it avoids treating government in narrow legalistic terms and yet at the same time delimits the area of useful analysis.

One final word is in order to describe the approach we take in the pages that follow. There apparently is an irresistible temptation among textwriters (or their publishers) to characterize their approach in such shorthand terms as institutional, behavioral, structural-functional, or whatever. Aside from the fact that these descriptive terms are imprecise, one wonders whether an author can afford to be less than eclectic in the selection of methodological approaches he draws on for his materials. It seems to us that, no matter what methodology one prefers to utilize in his research, he must borrow from any writer whose analysis provides a better understanding of the political processes of state and local govern-ments. This involves a judgment on our part. Since we believe that the intellectual commitments (theory building, quantification of data when possible, value-free research) of those described as behaviorists has produced new insights into the workings of political systems, we borrow heavily from their findings. The selection of materials may carry some of the flavor of this approach, which does not disturb us, since it reflects the contemporary mood of the discipline. Yet it should be made clear that the insights gleaned from more traditional writers have helped us immensely in interpreting our data and analyzing the political process in areas where systematic research has not been developed.

2. POWER ALLOCATIONS IN THE FEDERAL SYSTEM

As this is a text on state and local government we shall approach federalism and intergovernmental relations from the perspective of the state and local communities. Federalism usually covers the subject matter that treats relations among, and the relative assignments of functions to, somewhat independent governmental systems operating as segments of a more general political system. The terms "federalism" and "intergovernmental relations" can be used more or less interchangeably even though, technically speaking, there are certain kinds of intergovernmental relations that need not directly involve federalism—that is, relations between governments at the same level.

A number of principles and sets of institutions depict the character of the American political system, and one of these principles calling for a particular arrangement of governments is federalism. Federalism is especially important to students of state and local government because its use, in this nation, makes it a key determinant of the formal authority theoretically available to state and local units. This is so because the Constitution of the United States, which incorporates the federal principle, in effect makes certain general functional assignments to the various governments in the country. Federalism, then, establishes the broad framework within which state and local governments, as well as the national government, must operate.

In this light, federalism shapes American democracy, allowing for the existence of numerous governments with different geographical and functional area responsibilities. At last count there were well over 80,000 governments in our political system, and these units elect over 500,000 governing board and executive officials. This means that the American system is a territorial democracy which is not the same as a pure majoritarian or a Rousseauean/Jacobin government.[1] No single majority or single government rules in the American federal system. A national majority may rule in the national government; but this government is just one element of a broader federal structure, restricted in authority to powers found in the Constitution.[2] The actual nature of the federal system makes difficult a reconciliation between the reality of politics in the United States and the ideals of majoritarianism embedded in the theory of democratic government.

THE PHILOSOPHY AND HISTORICAL ROOTS
OF AMERICAN FEDERALISM

One cannot determine the philosophical premises of American federalism simply by reasoning through the advantages and disadvantages of various kinds of governments which might be used by a society and then, referring to our system. This cannot be done because this nation's system of federalism has deep historical roots which largely accounted for our adoption of the federal principle.

[1] Daniel J. Elazar, *American Federalism: A View from the States* (New York: Crowell, 1966), pp. 48, 214. The political system of this country has other features that distinguish it from a pure majoritarian democracy (separation of powers, constitutional protection of minority rights, and judicial review, for example).
[2] Alexander Hamilton carefully and methodically demonstrated in the early years of the operation of the new national government that these powers may be viewed in the most general of senses, which interpretation carved out a rather significant role for the national government. The spirit of the Hamiltonian interpretation has been accepted by the national government, including the national judiciary.

Historical conditions in fact appear to have been considerably more responsible for our use of federalism than is commonly assumed. Federalism did not come about even originally because the citizens or their representatives *thought* in the abstract that it was a good idea; it developed essentially as a result of political realities facing a new nation. Intellectually, we often today compare and contrast the federal with the unitary system as a means of explaining the peculiar benefits of federalism, when in reality, from a historical standpoint, the only real alternatives the country had after it cut the British ties in 1776 were confederation and federation. Some, perhaps many, of the delegates attending the Philadelphia convention which produced our Constitution undoubtedly favored a unitary government—for instance, Alexander Hamilton proposed what amounted to a strong unitary state—but such a political system was not even remotely politically feasible in 1787. Our initial use of a confederation (Articles of Confederation) as the governing process in the nation is suggestive of how far leaders were from ever seriously considering seeking the approval of the American people for a unitary system. In a unitary government all powers would reside in a central unit.

Our first national political experiment then was a confederation, adopted after the American Revolution and at a time when there was a prevailing sense of fear of centralized authority; this fear stemmed mainly from the experience of the colonists under the British Crown. Consequently, Americans created a system under the Articles of Confederation that provided for a weak and heavily dependent central government and that allowed for the continuation of the virtually unrestricted sovereign state governments. The Articles lodged all central power in a legislative body legally and politically dominated by the state governments in their corporate capacities. The national government had only the most limited authority to resolve differences between the states, and furthermore had no executive branch where central authority might be concentrated. What this meant was that any student of American government interested in the political system at that time had to turn to the states, which had the supreme authority. The early states placed virtually all governmental power in a legislative body, which normally appointed both a governor and the judiciary. The original governors did not usually possess the veto and were surrounded by a council; and state legislatures were mostly bicameral in structure.

The convention called by the Congress in 1787 was significantly constrained by political forces, the most important of which was the existence of sovereign and democratic state governments who would not sit idly by if efforts were made to abolish them. Still, many in the states recognized certain problems under the confederation, including trade barriers among the states, the absence of justice across state boundaries, the lack of a uniform currency, inadequate protection of western lands, and a degree of general instability. Further, the more conservative and monied classes were stirred by the oppressive fiscal and economic policies of the more undisciplined state legislatures. The states had not uncommonly enacted measures making currency worth less than it had been (when debts had been incurred) and making it hard, if not impossible, for some creditors to collect. All of this tended to undermine confidence in the country's early economic system and served to inhibit economic growth. Such policies were assumed to be in response to the pressures and interests of popular majorities who controlled a number of legislatures (property restrictions to voting and holding office, widely used in the states at that time, apparently were not sufficient to bar radical legislative action). Shay's Rebellion in Massachusetts in 1786, a revolt of radicals against the high-tax policies of the conservative government in that state, so disturbed conservatives that a movement was on to change the form of government in the nation.

A constitution was formulated by representatives of the states in the Philadelphia convention, sent to the states for their consideration and consent, and ratified by the required number of states through the mechanism of state conventions called expressly for that purpose. The approved document is to this day the fundamental law of the United States. The new Constitution divided powers between the national and state governments, building on the concept of dual sovereignty. Under the new document both the national and state governments were restricted; and national powers were specifically listed while state powers were initially assumed to be reserved—a point later made explicit with the adoption of the first ten amendments, or Bill of Rights. From the beginning, then, some powers were delegated to the central government by the fundamental law and others by implication to the states—or as Daniel Webster so aptly put it later, the national government was given specific and limited functions while the states had general and residual authority, with neither being considered primary.

The changes that became part of the new system were not minor. There was a meaningful shift of political power as well as a redistribution of legal authority between the levels of government with the new Constitution. Under the new government, for example, national authorities had an independent base, to be contrasted with their precarious position in the old government. Certainly, the state governments had lost their previously institutionalized and nationally recognized exclusive sovereign status; and the whole superstructure of the national government, but especially the protected judiciary and a potentially powerful independent executive, posed a major challenge to the future autonomy of the states and their dominant legislative bodies. Clauses in the new Constitution giving Congress the right to make all laws "necessary and proper" for carrying out the listed powers, proclaiming the Constitution and national legislation (that consistent with the Constitution) to be the supreme law of the land, and granting the Congress the seemingly unlimited power to tax to provide for the general welfare[3] made unclear, at best, precisely what powers were reserved to the states.

Philosophically, the Founding Fathers believed the federal system, as embodied in the Constitution, to have numerous advantages. Some functions were assumed to be within the sphere of national government authority and others within the province of state governments, with economic, defense, and international affairs falling in the first category and with such matters as the supervision of agriculture and the administration of intrastate justice being the proper concern of local authorities. Further, both national and local representation was provided, permitting balance in the legislative processes. Probably the overriding philosophical rationale for the inclusion of the federal principle in the Constitution, however, was essentially political in nature. And this was the fear that the Founding Fathers had of factious dominance of the state governments and of the policies of the dominant factions. As explained, the states could not be abolished; thus, the only alternative was to superimpose a new political system on top of them and thereby effectively curtail their power.

To the Founding Fathers a faction was a group composed of a minority or the majority that works against the rights of others or against the permanent and aggregate interests of the whole. In the 1780s, the faction that proved most troublesome was the majority interest which orchestrated action in so many of the early state legislatures. As Madison argued in *Federalist* Number 10, by extending the size of the republic (another way of saying, establishing an independent national government), one makes it more difficult for such a faction to control. This is so because a larger republic encourages the expression of a number of viewpoints and the interaction of several or many interests, and consequently the impact of a single majority faction will be less on policymakers. By containing popular forces through the creation of a strong

---

[3] It is highly instructive to note that the authors of the *Federalist* papers (the publication that explained the proposed Constitution), chided the critics of the proposed government for suggesting that the Article I, Section 8 clause which authorizes taxation for the general welfare was not limited by the congressional powers specified in that section (their point being that this clause gave unlimited power to the national government). The *Federalist* papers held that this clause was merely a general statement, qualified and conditioned by the specific powers which followed. To a considerable extent, the fears of the critics proved to be well founded as the Supreme Court has upheld independent federal government action based on this clause.

central authority, one makes it easier for government to resist policies of the more radical elements in the society. Specifically, there is less of a likelihood that paper money, debt abolition, and property redistribution policies will prevail in the national government than in the states. In sum, the American political system was established along federal lines because one of the strong motives of the nation's leaders was to prevent an over-powering majority from making the final decisions for the nation. And the philosophy by which this was justified must be considered one of the more sophisticated, well-reasoned, and practical contributions ever made to political theory.

CLASSICAL THOUGHT AND FEDERALISM

In the general sense, classical political theory is significantly concerned with the question of the assignment of power and authority to different levels of government within a single political society, although most classical political philosophers do not address the matter directly. For example, in the light of the Aristotelian conception of the nature of human associations, one would likely conclude that a unitary system with a single government, be it democratic (polity), monarchical, or aristo-cratic, is best. Aristotle's doctrine of the fulfilment of individual ideals in successively broader collective environmental settings, beginning with the family and culminating in the city-state, would probably lead one to reject federalism as the basic principle by which to structure a political system—although Aristotle would certainly permit subordinate or inferior units to exist. On the other hand, the essential individualism advanced by such classical theorists as Hobbes or Locke, or even our own Jefferson, might very well cause one to embrace the federal (or even confedera-tion) principle. This would be so because the foundation of this classical liberal philosophy is the dignity and worth of the individual (as opposed to the state or the organization), encouraging one to prefer the location of government powers as close to the individual as possible (that is, in local units), where government can be easily checked and observed (inci-dentally, Hobbes' individualism did not lead him to favor any form of federalism; it actually led him in the opposite direction).

The classical conservative, who emphasizes the whole as opposed to the part and society not the individual, is likely to be a friend of a unitary system (in the modern era, Edmund Burke is such a conservative). It must be noted, however, that seldom are conditions so simple or clear-cut that the philosophical positions of a conservative or liberal will always fall on one side or the other on this matter. So many variables and considera-tions are usually involved in structuring government power that the positions of various schools of thought may become reversed or unpredictable. Such variables would include *who* (what party of what philosophical persuasion, for example) is going to control under one as opposed to another system, or what the *policy consequences* of alternative systems will in all probability be. In fact, the truth of the matter is that it was the particular groups that controlled state legislatures and the *public policy* of these groups that caused the Founding Fathers to propose the system they did in the Constitution. The theory of federalism in this case was in reality a justification for a shift in political power, which the Founding Fathers knew was necessary if any change in public policy was to be effected. As if often the case, political theory here provided the rationale for political change.

THE "CLOSENESS" OF
GOVERNMENT TO THE CITIZENS

Before looking at the specific nature of the American federal system as it works today, it is instructive to examine the matter of the relationship of the government to the people. As indicated, a central feature of federalism is that it allows for the division of responsibilities. This division in turn permits the use of local governments for local activities. Typically, Americans have at least in their own minds structured the political system along hierarchical lines, with the local government (city, town, and so forth) at the bottom and the national government at the top. One of the assumptions associated with the hierarchical structure is that the government that is local is closer to the people than the government that is on the top.

Actual behavior on the part of American citizens, however, does not bear out this assumption. We do not argue with the fact that Americans *perceive* the system in these terms, but we cannot find significant evidence to support its being translated into practice. For instance, American voters are more likely to participate in the selection of officers of the national government than they are in local and state elections. In fact, the "lower" one goes in the hierarchy, the less the turnout on the part of the voters. Thus, voters do not *act* as though local government is closer to them, although they may still *think* that it is. Furthermore, it appears that the greatest interest by citizens is not in local government or local affairs, but in national government and national affairs. It is undoubtedly true that the average citizen is more likely to be familiar with his national senator or representative than he is with his local councilman or state delegate. And, in all probability, the electorate knows more about Vietnam or national tax proposals than it does about local sewer and planning policies.

Another point should be made in discussing which government is closer to the people. Grodzins believes that matter to be quite complex and to contain several dimensions. He states that in determining closeness the following considerations must be taken into account:[4]

1. Provision of services

2. Participation

3. Control

4. Understanding

5. Communication

6. Identification

In other words, an individual or group may feel close to a particular government in terms of any one or more of these factors. Unless closeness is so broken down, it is not sufficiently clear to allow a precise comprehension of its meaning. So, for example, in a practical sense one may be close to a government that he can influence, but remote in some other respect, such as the provision of services. It is also possible that one may identify with one government because of mass media attention but have more control over another unit or level of government. Furthermore, in the light of the interest-group nature of our system and the fact that such groups will often identify with one agency or functional area in government, we should take into account the fact that it is possible to be close (in any number of ways) to one service or area in government and not another.

POWER ASSIGNMENTS
IN THE FEDERAL SYSTEM

Constitutionally speaking, the American federal system has two levels: the national and state. Each level, of course, has a government and its own political system, with the government referring to the formal institutions established by the constitution, by law, or by regulation, and the political system meaning the government plus the various extragovern-

[4] Morton Grodzins, "Why Decentralization by Order Won't Work," in Edward C. Banfield (ed.), *Urban Government* (New York: Free Press, 1961), p. 125.

mental forces (parties and interest groups, for example) which impact upon and affect the direction of the government. From a constitutional point of view, local governments are part of the state government and their political systems part of the state system. Thus, while the states are not subordinate to the national government, the local governments, seen in these terms, are subordinate to the state government. Another way of putting it is that this country has a federal system composed of national and state governments, while state governments are organized internally along unitary lines.[5]

However, in practice, there are generally assumed to be three levels of government in the federal system, with local governments enjoying considerable political and legal independence from states. In fact, given the political nature of things, a city or other local government may determine the actions that will be taken by state governments or even on occasion by the federal government (a case in point being Chicago). A purely constitutional analysis then of the location of authority would overlook many important political as well as legally sanctioned facts of life.

Before looking into specific functional assignments, let us review in general the theoretically possible divisions of power in the federal system and discuss which division describes our system best. Using the two-level constitutionally prescribed standard, the following patterns might characterize the federal system:

1. Power centralized in the national government

2. Power dispersed to state governments

3. National and state governments dominant in separate spheres

4. Shared or similar powers assigned to both levels of government

Because of the number of variables involved it is not an easy task to determine which of the four categories most closely approximates reality. Further, any conclusions reached would have to be related to a particular period of time. Nevertheless, several observations can be made. In a

[5] There are two important legal schools of thought on the relationship of local government to state government. One, upheld by the Supreme Court of the United States, is that municipal corporations are creatures of the state and that the state has total power over municipalities—this reasoning is sometimes referred to as the Dillon rule, which stemmed from a decision of the Iowa State Supreme Court, whose chief justice at the time was John F. Dillon [City of Clinton v. The Cedar Rapids and Missouri River Railroad Co., 24 Iowa 455 (1868)]. A contrary view holds that local government is a matter of absolute right which may not be taken away by the state [see opinion of Judge Thomas M. Cooley in People v. Hurlbut, 24 Mich. 44 (1871)].

theoretical constitutional sense, we would have to say that the state and national governments are dominant in their respective spheres, with the state governments handling general matters within their borders (possessing the police power,[6] for instance) and the national government responsible for interstate and international functions (number 3). We can eliminate possibility number 2 almost by definition, as it is more reflective of a confederation than a federation. What this means is that, for reasons already mentioned plus the tax resources of the national government, this country has been moving toward either a system of shared powers (number 4) or a dominant national system (number 1). The most popular professional view has it that because of the many shared powers in the domestic area our system can best be described as cooperative federalism or creative federalism. Others consider this characterization to be perhaps a euphemism for a unitary system,[7] and generally see a trend toward an increasing national role. Next, we shall examine some studies and perceptions concerning where power is located in general in the federal system and what the trends have been on this matter.

Professor William Riker has reviewed a number of functions such as public safety, transportation and communication, and resources at four periods throughout American history (1790, 1850, 1910, 1964) to see if there were any shifting responsibilities between the levels of government in the performance of these activities.[8] Using a system of mathematical weighting, Riker compared these functions in terms of the degree of involvement of the national and state governments for each period and concluded that there had been a progressive rise in the participation of the national government in general in the functional areas examined, that this rise had taken place at the expense of the states, and that there had been a notable decline in the sharing of functions. In addition, another study showed that the prestige of the national government, possibly because of its growing power, is high among local government professionals—in fact, the national government is ranked higher on this standard than the states.[9] This attitude is not necessarily found among members of the general public, although it appears to be somewhat prevalent among lower socioeconomic status persons and professional-administrative personnel at all levels of government.

[6]   The police power commonly refers to a government's general regulatory authority, in this country, a power of the states; but, more broadly, it includes the right of a government to take action to promote the general health, safety, morals, and welfare of the people.

[7]   Anwar Syed, *The Political Theory of American Local Government* (New York: Random House, 1966), p. 153.

[8]   William H. Riker, *Federalism* (Boston: Little, Brown, 1964), pp. 81–84.

[9]   Municipal Manpower Commission, *Governmental Manpower for Tomorrow's Cities* (New York: McGraw-Hill, 1962), p. 164.

Furthermore, the national government has expanded its financial and consequently its program and standard-setting involvement in state and local governments. For example, in 1902, national government grants to state and local governments amounted to $7 million—or 0.7 percent of all state-local expenditures. This grant figure has escalated sharply since 1902, and, by 1969, it was close to $20 billion, representing between 15 and 20 percent of all state and local government expenditures. At the state government level alone, federal grant-in-aid funds account for approximately 20 to 25 percent of total spending.

Some accounts of national government expenditures compared to state and local expenditures picture the state and local governments of this country expanding faster than the national government in the domestic area. Such accounts do not entirely give the proper impression because they often use figures from the 1930s on (when the national government base was relatively high), exclude military-defense expenditures in the national government (such expenditures are important, more or less permanent, and have significant domestic effects, especially at the community level), do not include all national government domestic spending (that part not included in normal budgetary totals), and overlook the point that the national government is one unit while there are 80,000 subnational units (thus, even though subnational governments are spending more money than the national government is on domestic matters, or if state and local units' expenditures are increasing more rapidly than national government domestic spending, the leverage of a single government is greater than that of numerous, divided units).

Many see increasing centralization as a contemporary characteristic of our federal system. State and local government officials, for instance, view the degree of centralization that exists today, whatever in reality it may be, as unhealthy. As can be seen in Table 2.1, the majority of state and local officers who have an opinion believe that the governmental system of the United States is becoming too centralized. Certain categories of state and county officials are most concerned over centralization of government; only large-city mayors and city managers in the population class 50,000 to 250,000 (as well as, it might be added, professors) do not concur with the predominant viewpoint.

Looking at the relative positions of the levels of government from the state and local side, one can point to a number of recent developments that have served to bolster state and local governments. For example, many state governments are beginning to adopt a new "urban" image, with the creation of new agencies and programs concerned with mounting urban and metropolitan problems. States such as New York, New Jersey, Connecticut, Rhode Island, Massachusetts, Pennsylvania, Maryland, and California have been particularly active in this respect. From

TABLE 2.1
*Views of State and Local Government Officials
and Others on Centralization of Government
in the U.S.*

	Question: Do you believe that government in the U.S. is becoming too centralized?		
	YES	NO	NO ANSWER
State government	4	3	2
Governors			
Attorneys general	6	1	2
Budget officers	4	3	8
Legislative leaders	19	5	4
County government (by population)			
Below 10,000	2	2	1
10,000–50,000	10	1	3
50,000–250,000	15	4	1
250,000 and over	21	11	8
Mayors (by population of city)			
Below 10,000	1	1	1
10,000–50,000	13	6	4
50,000–250,000	8	4	2
250,000 and over	3	4	1
City managers (by population of city)			
Below 10,000	30	20	12
10,000–50,000	39	20	10
50,000–250,000	4	9	5
250,000 and over	3	2	1
School board officials	23	22	16
Professors and others	14	28	14
Totals	219	146	95

SOURCE: Subcommittee on Intergovernmental Relations of the Committee on Government Operations, U.S. Senate, *The Federal System as Seen by State and Local Officials* (Washington, D.C.: U.S. Government Printing Office, 1963), p. 183.

1966 to 1968, thirteen states established urban affairs offices to advise localities in a variety of fields, to perform certain planning functions, and in some cases to carry out program responsibilities.[10] New York now has a new Urban Development Corporation, a state urban redevelopment and renewal agency.[11] A number of states have developed comprehensive statewide planning programs (not to be confused with economic

[10] Page L. Ingraham, "State Agencies for Local Affairs," *Municipal Year Book 1968* (Washington, D.C.: International City Managers Association, 1968), pp. 44–45.
[11] Interestingly, one critic sees this agency as a threat to local autonomy. See Duane Lockard (ed.), *Governing the States and Localities* (London: Macmillan, 1969), pp. 426–428.

development, a long-time activity of state governments), often a staff function performed in the office of the governor;[12] and many states have added, or expanded, low-cost housing programs in the last few years. Maryland has established a transit agency to develop a mass transit system for Baltimore and has advanced funds to its Washington suburbs to assist in the preparation of the national capital region's mass transit program. Ten other states now aid local governments in the urban transit area; California and New York provide significant help to localities for mass transit purposes.

It has not been too long ago that localities in this country could look only to Washington for assistance in these functional areas. Local governments themselves moved into a variety of new fields in the 1960s, including manpower training and social planning. Whether these developments will have any effect on the distribution of power throughout the federal system will not be known for some time.

The American public has considerable confidence in subnational governments, and this should certainly provide some psychological satisfaction if nothing else in state capitals. A recent national public opinion poll revealed that the American people feel that the state governments spend tax dollars more wisely than does the national government, and this view was particularly popular among the higher socioeconomic strata and Republicans.

One might continue along this line of reasoning and point out that even with a shift in power and decision making in the federal system from the states to the national government, much influence is still exerted by people and interest groups in states and communities and by state and local government administrators and officials. Thus, if one concedes that in a number of functional areas the ultimate decision is made in Washington, when previously such a decision was made in states or localities (or more likely, not made at all), one does not necessarily concede that interests outside Washington have had no influence on the central authorities. In fact, decisions by the national government affecting state and local communities often are made on the basis of pressure, knowledge, and expertise coming from officials and private sources at the state and local levels. The political and administrative feedback and influence from the field is not an inconsiderable force in the policy-making and execution processes of the national government. Particularly receptive to state and local pressures are the Congress of the United States (especially the House) and any number of administrative bureaucracies in Washington.

[12] In 1960, thirty-one states had no formal statewide planning program. By 1968, all but four states had such a program. See David K. Hartley, "State Planning," *The Book of the States 1968–1969* (Chicago: Council of State Governments, 1968), p. 431.

Finally, President Richard M. Nixon's New Federalism is designed to strengthen the position of state and local governments in the federal system. The central features of this New Federalism are a shifting of responsibilities to states and localities and the channeling of federal tax revenues to state and local governments. The President, in outlining his domestic program to the American people, said that the centralization of power in Washington characteristic of the past third of a century has produced a "bureaucratic monstrosity, cumbersome, unresponsive, and ineffective."[13] The politics of federalism as well as the future prospects for states in the federal system are discussed later in the chapter.

A second way of explaining power allocations in the federal system is to examine particular patterns of influence or control by the levels of government in specific functional areas—that is, function by function (rather than in general). For each function considered, theoretically any one of the following patterns could be found:

1. Power in or dominance by the national government

2. Power in or dominance by the state government

3. Power in or dominance by the local government

4. Some combination of the above, to include:
   a. Both national and state governments exercising power
   b. Both national and local governments exercising power
   c. Both state and local governments exercising power
   d. All three levels exercising power

Examples of each of these possibilities will be reviewed in the light of actual assignments of authority in selected functional areas. We do not use the terms "cooperative" or "competitive" (such terms are commonly employed to explain relationships in the federal system) in examining any of the combinations of functional assignments for two reasons: (1) in each of the areas the authors are familiar with where two or more governments are responsible for a single function, there is *both* cooperation and competition between the governments (the reasons for cooperation are obvious, and competition exists in part because of organizational enhancement drives); and (2) whether a relationship is cooperative or competitive must in the final analysis be a matter of judgment—although it appears to us that in published documents, conferences of government officials, and many professional circles, there is a tendency to describe what in reality is often competition as cooperation. In any event, we shall

[13] Address to the Nation, August 8, 1969.

refer to a situation in which more than one government is involved in the same function as simply that and not use the more subjective cooperative or competitive concepts. Further, in discussing the functional assignments at the state and local levels, we shall review the typical organizational patterns found in state and local government.

Foreign affairs and military defense functions are virtually the exclusive responsibilities of the national government. At the same time state governments do have national guard units and civil defense programs; and state and local governments may influence the posture of the national government in both the defense and foreign relations areas. The old-age retirement program, commonly known as social security, is an exclusive function of the national government, but this activity clearly affects welfare expenditures in state and local governments. The regulation of interstate business is another example of a function that belongs in the first category.

Functions that are controlled principally if not exclusively by state governments in this country would include workmen's compensation, a program covering payment of workers injured on the job, which is administered by a state workmen's compensation commission or by a department of labor (or labor and industry or industrial relations);[14] the licensing of many occupations and professions, which is found administratively dispersed in a number of independent boards in state government (a recent trend has been the consolidation of certain administrative and related activities of independent licensing boards into a department of licensing and regulation); mental institutions or state hospitals, which may be located in a department of mental health, mental hygiene, public health, health and welfare, social services, institutions, or hospitals; and the regulation of intrastate public utilities, such as electric, gas, railway, bus, truck, oil pipe, and other companies—an administrative responsibility of a state public utilities, public service, corporation, or railroad commission.

Local governments are the dominant units in the federal system in several areas of public responsibility, including elementary and secondary public education, police and law enforcement, fire protection, code administration (building, housing, plumbing, electrical, fire, and the like), zoning, subdivision regulation administration, and comprehensive physical planning. Education is a function of a local school board which normally operates the education system through an independent school district government, although some general-purpose local governments (cities, counties, and so forth) are responsible for public schools. Police

14 U.S. Department of Labor, *Workmen's Compensation: The Administrative Organization and Cost of Administration* (Washington, D.C.: U.S. Government Printing Office, 1966), pp. 4–8.

and law enforcement will be located administratively in a police or public safety department—and fire in an agency with that name or a public safety department. The latter three activities are found in various kinds of administrative structures in local government. In the case of code administration the particular agency with the responsibility varies somewhat by the code involved. Sometimes a department of buildings will include many if not all of a community's code enforcement activities. A new trend has been the assignment of several housing, urban renewal, building, and land-use related functions to a department of community development (Baltimore, Maryland, and Dade County, Florida, are examples). Other code enforcement agencies may include licenses and inspections, health, urban renewal, and the office of fire marshal or fire department. Code development and enforcement is part of the states' police power, but this authority is nearly always delegated to localities (a few states—New York, New Jersey, and Ohio—have state building codes). The most important of the codes are the building and housing codes, covering housing construction and maintenance-occupancy respectively. Zoning and subdivision control are found in different administrative agencies at the local level, but it is safe to say that the planning commission or department will usually have some authority over both (often, the planning agency administers the subdivision regulations and advises elected officials on the zoning ordinance and its application). Zoning refers to the regulation of lot size, population density, building height and bulk, and the nature of land-use permitted (for example, residential, industrial, and commercial). Subdivision control is concerned with regulating the development of large tracts of land to assure the provision of streets, parks, school sites, and other public and private facilities. Comprehensive physical planning of future land-use in communities is almost universally a function of a planning commission or department. Both the national and state governments provide assistance to localities in some or all of these areas. The national government now has grant programs in education, law enforcement, codes, and planning, and through its various aid activities influences zoning and subdivision administration.

Some functions are not clearly the exclusive or primary responsibility of one or another level of government. Programs in both the national and state governments, performed jointly or separately, are unemployment compensation, interstate and state highways, forestry, fish and wildlife, agricultural assistance and regulation, and regional economic development. State governments have unemployment compensation programs, mainly, it would appear, because of the inducement provided by national legislation, and both the national and state governments have important responsibilities in this area. At the state level, unemployment compensation will usually be in an employment security department or commission or a labor or labor and industry department. Interstate and state highways are partly financed by federal funds (90 percent of the costs of interstate and 50 percent of the expense of state highways are borne by the national government); state responsibilities in this area are charged to a highway or roads department or commission (and, in a few cases, a department of transportation). The national and state governments separately operate forests, many times for multipurpose use. The administration of this function will be found in a state department of forestry, forests and parks, conservation, or natural resources. Through special funds administered by the U.S. Department of Interior, the national government advances money to states for fish and wildlife purposes, including the acquisition of land and bodies of water. State departments or commissions of fish and/or game, conservation, wildlife, or natural resources will handle this kind of activity. Various agricultural functions are performed at both the national and state levels, and, with the exception of a few joint assignments usually dominated by the national government, are performed independently of each other. State and local soil conservation and related federally assisted agricultural activities are heavily influenced if not controlled by the U.S. Department of Agriculture. A state department or board of agriculture is responsible for most functions in this area, although other departments are likely to be involved in some agricultural matters as well. Beginning with the Appalachian Regional Development Act of 1965, several new regional commissions have been established in some parts of the United States to assist in the achievement of regional economic development objectives. These commissions are controlled jointly by the state and national governments, even though the federal government recently moved to bring these agencies more directly under national supervision (the Department of Commerce, specifically), partly because of their somewhat independent political status and therefore their leverage over federal officials and funding sources. The commissions cover a geographical area encompassing several states, and only the state governments in this area are, of course, commission members. The sections of the country selected for this special treatment have been underdeveloped and/or depressed areas, primarily rural in character.

In some urban functional areas the pattern of relations in the federal system is one described as "national-local." In these cases the national and local governments exercise primary responsibility, normally with the national government providing the funds and setting the standards of operation and the local government executing or carrying out the program. In none of these programs does the national government provide 100 percent of the funds, as local cost-sharing is always required at some point or another in each program, but the way in which the local share is often computed—that is, contributions need not always be of a cash variety—may make the federal cash input higher than it would appear. Examples falling in this category are urban renewal, public housing, the community action program, and model cities. All of these activities are explained in detail elsewhere in this book and therefore will be only briefly reviewed here. Urban renewal and public housing are administered locally, on the average by independent agencies—in the case of housing, usually by a special district government—with reasonably close links to general-purpose governments; the community action program is operated mostly outside of local government (or any government for that matter) by private nonprofit corporations—a minority of local governments with such programs within their boundaries, including, for example, Chicago and Pittsburgh, directly control the community action program; and model cities is a function of city (and, in a few cases, county) government. All four of these programs are concerned with the urban poor—even though urban renewal has not worked out that way— and all but the community action program are organizationally in the U.S. Department of Housing and Urban Development at the national level. As implied earlier in the chapter, state governments have not been significantly stirred by the special conditions of low-income sections of urban and metropolitan areas; and for this reason, states have not participated to any extent in any of these program fields.

A variation within the national-local arrangement is a relationship or functional assignment involving national and metropolitan units. The national government makes planning, research, and program implementation funds available to certain agencies operating on a metropolitan-wide scale. Also, the national government has, in effect, delegated some authority to some such organizations. The metropolitan agencies may be technically classed as part of state or local governments, as special districts, or they may be private in legal base; and they include metropolitan planning commissions and councils of governments. In this category metropolitan agencies will perform certain functions under the general supervision of the national government—this is the way if often works in practice even though it may not be legally described as such.

Local-state activities include general relief (welfare), licensing and regulation of intrastate business, and higher public education. General relief assistance is made available to the needy poor by state and local governments through state and community welfare (or social services or health and welfare) departments. Business (other than public utilities) licensing and regulation is the responsibility of state departments of commerce, banking, and insurance and, commonly, local departments of licenses and inspections. Other departments and agencies may have some authority over business, and the organizational assignment will depend somewhat on the area of business being regulated. State-supported universities and colleges almost always enjoy considerable independence from the general processes in state government, although they are technically part of that government. Thirty-nine of the fifty states have central coordinating boards which attempt to provide a broader framework within which the individual state colleges' and universities' and the states' (as a whole) interests may be seen. Local governments now operate community and junior colleges and in some instances regular four-year institutions.

A vast number of functions are currently being performed jointly or independently by all levels of government; and, as suggested in part, some of the programs mentioned previously are becoming responsibilities of levels of government in addition to those primarily involved at present. Health, air and water pollution, much of welfare, parks and recreation, civil defense, food and drug regulation, and manpower are illustrations of functional areas now administered by all levels of government either directly or indirectly (through grants-in-aid). There is no particular logic behind many of these assignments, and mostly it appears that the programs have been developed on a piecemeal basis, designed to meet a special need or in response to a particular pressure. This last statement, which characterizes virtually the entire intergovernmental relations area, is the topic of the next section.

INTERGOVERNMENTAL RELATIONS STRATEGY

The federal Advisory Commission on Intergovernmental Relations was created in 1959 to study and analyze intergovernmental relations and to make recommendations. The commission has issued numerous reports and made literally hundreds of suggestions as to how intergovernmental arrangements should be structured for maximum productivity. In 1955, another federally sponsored group—the Commission on Intergovernmental Relations (known as the Kestnbaum Commission), an *ad hoc* organization—similarly studied this important field, published a number of documents, and recommended courses of action to lend some rationality to intergovernmental affairs.

Nevertheless, to this day the national government does not have a unified intergovernmental relations strategy. It would be erroneous to assume that any single study commission or other group or individual could superimpose such a strategy on the entire national government, and perhaps we do not have a strategy because some apparently assume a solution can be achieved through this method—that is, rational study and the publication of findings and recommendations. The absence of a unified intergovernmental relations strategy cannot be attributed to a lack of knowledge or to a lack of understanding of the various programs which characterize relations among the national, state, and local governments. At least it cannot be attributed to this alone, or even primarily to this. Basically, no such strategy exists because of the large number of competing, conflicting, and overlapping public and private interests which have much to say about what is done in particular programs at particular levels of government at particular times. The conflict over the question of whether federal aid should be channeled directly to cities or through states between the representatives of local governments (such as the National League of Cities and the United States Conference of Mayors) on one hand, the the representatives of state governments (Council of State Governments and the National Governors Conference) on the other is one illustration of the reason for the emergence of an inconsistent federal policy on intergovernmental relations. The Congress of the United States responds differentially to the pressures of such organizations, depending on the program and the sense of urgency displayed by the organizations. For example, the Eighty-eighth Congress passed 16 federal grant-in-aid programs; seven provided for funds to be given to states, six permitted funds to be granted either to states or to local governments, and three authorized grants only to local governments.[15] In 1968, the Juvenile Delinquency and Safe Streets acts provided that money be made available through states, and the Intergovernmental Relations Act of that same year delegated certain authority to state officials and agencies, seemingly elevating the importance and role of state government in the eyes of Congress. Yet, the model cities and community action program, both crucial domestic efforts authorized by the national Congress in the mid-1960s, are operated only by local governments or local units (with few exceptions), with little or no state involvement. Congress has even flirted with another strategy—as reflected in the Demonstration Cities and Metropolitan Development Act of 1966 (sections 204 and 205)—in which federal dollars and authority are given to metropolitan organizations.

Although these inconsistent strategies have been designed by the national Congress, it would appear that little could be gained by shifting the responsibility over intergovernmental relations to the executive branch of the national government. For, within that branch, regardless of which party is in control, there is considerable disagreement on precisely what pattern of intergovernmental relations should prevail or be promoted by Washington. For example, the Department of Housing and

---

[15] Elazar, *op. cit.*, p. 210.

Urban Development has long operated on the premise that direct federal-local administration is the most desirable means by which to overcome key urban problems; therefore, that department has favored a continuation of its direct-city relationships in urban renewal, public housing, and other areas. However, within the Department of Health, Education, and Welfare, the dominant position has been that funds should be given to the state governments and through the state governments to local governments if appropriate. And this position holds for any number of health, education, and welfare activities administered by the department. The federal Office of Economic Opportunity has used a variety of means in working with and through state and local authorities, but one not found in the other two departments is its heavy reliance on nongovernment local agencies in the community action program, demonstrating but another strategy.

THE FUTURE OF STATES
IN THE FEDERAL SYSTEM

Today, as we have pointed out, there are a number of views concerning the actual nature of the role of each level of government in the American federal system. To some extent, any conclusion reached on this matter must be relative, as much of the above discussion suggests or implies.

National news commentator David Brinkley, in an Ohio university speech in the mid-1960s, held out little hope for state governments as he presided over their verbal burial. Among intellectual circles generally, particularly up to the late 1960s, there has been considerable skepticism about if not outright opposition to state governments (and, by implication, local governments) as they are constituted. The position in these circles has been that states were not created along rational geographical or other lines and, in any event, do not serve rationally defined areas at the present time. From this assumption it is but a small step to urge the development of some kind of governmental system at the state and local level that reflects more natural areas, thus allowing for the more rational allocation of powers and functions. Normally linked with this position, although not necessarily articulated, is a preference for a unitary political system, with states (if they were "permitted" to continue in existence at all) and localities serving essentially as administrative subunits of the national government. In actual practice, especially in the light of the broad interpretation by the federal judiciary of the general welfare clause of the Constitution, it would appear that the national government with its numerous federal-aid programs and abundant grant funds is well on the way to realizing the ideal advanced in intellectual circles—but it is doing so without any particular political theory or more precisely within the framework of phrases that effectively link past practices and thought to contemporary realities and desires. The Advisory Commission on Intergovernmental Relations has, we believe, served more than any other organization to legitimize the emerging practices found in the federal system, providing something of an intellectual rationale for what would be happening whether or not the commission was in operation (the commission, incidentally, serves many other purposes as well).

The 1955 Commission on Intergovernmental Relations was troubled by the degree of centralization it detected in the federal system, and attributed this centralization not to a power grab on the part of Washington but to restrictions imposed by state constitutions and general inaction in state capitals.[16] V. O. Key, Jr., in a study of the political systems of 32 northern states, explained that the party system with its direct primary and local base, separation of powers, and the nature of representation in state legislatures "incapacitates states and diverts demands for political action to Washington."[17] The Commission on Intergovernmental Relations urged changes in state constitutions to liberate the states and reverse the trend of functions being performed in Washington, although the commission did not point out how this would be accomplished in the political sense. The implication of Key's analysis would be that if one wished to reverse the centralization tendency it would be necessary to strike at the causes of centralization—that is, the party system, separation of powers, and malapportionment. In point of fact, the political parties have become considerably more centrally controlled (mainly at the national level), and as a result of the Supreme Court "one-man, one-vote" decisions (Baker v. Carr, 1962, and Reynolds v. Sims, 1964, among others), state legislatures have been reapportioned more along population lines. Further, in accordance with the spirit of the Commission on Intergovernmental Relations' recommendations, several state constitutions have been revised and "modernized" to eliminate at least some of the previous restrictions on the development of a "positivist" state and local government system. Yet, centralization appears to be continuing.

If one is truly serious about changing present trends in intergovernmental relations and, as many contemporary conservatives put it, "returning powers to state and local governments," then it is necessary to examine the political roots of the entire governmental system in the country. In general, governments do what they do because of pressures—

[16] The Commission on Intergovernmental Relations, A Report to the President for Transmittal to the Congress (Washington, D.C.: U.S. Government Printing Office, 1955), chap. 2.
[17] V. O. Key, Jr., American State Politics: An Introduction (New York: Knopf, 1956), p. 267.

pressures from the outside and pressures from the inside. If the pressures are strong enough and if money is available or can be secured through some means or another, action will be taken. Normally, the bringing of pressure effectively to bear on governments at any level, including either the legislative or executive branches or committees or agencies therein, requires the creation of organizations of interests and often coalitions of like-minded organizations. Organizations or coalitions that *want* something from their government will search for units, agencies, and committees that are likely to be most receptive to their demands and urge action. In recent years in this country the interests that have asked that certain action be taken in the domestic political sphere have been patently more successful in Washington than in state capitals or local governments. Part of the reason is economic or fiscal—that is, state and local governments do not seem to have access to the kind of tax resources that the national government does in its progressive income tax and various trust funds. But, more importantly, the political system has simply dictated that pressures exerted at the national level for positive government activity will be more successfully translated into public policy. For *political* reasons, the national government has been able to find revenue sources and constitutional bases for taking certain action—often in spite of the fact that these revenue sources were new and thought by many in the light of previous Supreme Court decisions or the intent of the Founding Fathers to be unconstitutional (the social security taxes on employers for unemployment compensation or on workers and employers for old-age retirement purposes are examples). Many times state governments have not been able to find revenue sources or constitutional bases because interests have not successfully caused them to do so. Therefore, changing state constitutions, for example, will not necessarily change the political interest structure of states, and it is the latter change that must be made if states are "to assume their proper role." Given this analysis, a desire to "return" power to states or localities must in fact be a preference to see a function be placed in more conservative hands—or more broadly to have an activity of government eliminated, cut back, or operated under a more conservative pressure system.[18] And this is true regardless of what states rights advocates themselves may believe when they propose such a shift.

[18] A conservative pressure system would be one in which there would be a high value placed on economy in government and the principle of private property. Thus, a conservative pressure system would work toward keeping all government expenditures low and assuring that public policy would be based on private marketplace demands and dictates. An example of this type of public policy would be a restrained zoning policy—that is, one in which government policy more or less responds to market requirements. Furthermore, outside the routine and generally accepted areas of government responsibility, major public expenditures would be "permitted" or even encouraged in functional areas that facilitate the operation of the private market (expenditures for highways and sewers, for example).

Another point has some relevance to this discussion: the national government is a single institution operating over a larger territory than states and local governments. It would seem reasonable under these circumstances that like-minded interests would organize and lobby in such a way that would permit the action desired to affect as many of their constituents as possible and in the most permanent manner. This would appear to lead interests wishing something from their government to the national government which most closely meets these criteria. Why, for instance, should labor unions work for minimum wages in fifty jurisdictions when practically the same objective can be achieved by bringing pressure on *one* government? Why should Negroes place their major emphasis on securing open housing legislation city by city or state by state when virtually the same goal can be attained by one enactment of one government—that is, the government in Washington? Why should the private building industry press each state legislature for a policy that pumps capital into the homebuilding market when this end can be served by a decision in a single government? Or why should airport and airline interests lobby in states for airport and airways assistance if the same objective can be achieved nationwide by cornering one set of national officials?

In effect, what is being said here is that whatever we have in our federal system—that is, whether or not it is centralized, or whether or not too much power rests with Washington—will continue to be in that system and to characterize that system in the years to come. Whatever trends exist today will probably be extended tomorrow, for without restructuring our interest group system—or at least "making" some interests less influential (those asking for positive government action) and others more influential (those opposing all such action)—or restructuring our political system by broadening substantially the boundaries of subnational governments, little change can be expected. By not making these modifications (and, incidentally, they are not easily manipulated into existence), and by concentrating on removing state and local government restrictions, at best we merely open the door to more active state and local governments without in any way affecting the behavior of the national government—in other words, you make it more possible for all governments to do more. In view of such reasoning, however, this need not necessarily be the result, and it is probable that state and local governments are only slightly or minimally affected by constitutional or other legal limitations—the real constraints, underlying constitutional or other legal limitations, are political; and by removing these legal barriers, the effect on the behavior of state and local governments will also likely be slight or minimal.

In the net, for those concerned about the future of state and local

governments in the federal system and the protection of interests associated with the current administration and policy-making processes in these
governments (those—often conservatives—benefiting from the present
system), the best strategy is to press for continued state and local
government involvement and participation in the decisions that are made
in Washington. These decisions are not likely to be "returned" to the
states and localities, and therefore state and local governments and the
interests related to them have no choice but to attempt to influence
Congress and administrative agencies in the United States government so
that national decisions will reflect state and local positions, meaning to an
extent economic and political conservatism. Another strategy is to urge
the national government to provide funds without strings—block grants,
shared revenue, or some such plan—to state and local governments,
which theoretically suggests that a somewhat different set of interests will
determine the ultimate disposition of these funds than if the national
authorities dictated the precise use of the money. As matters stand now,
the adoption of this strategy by the national government would, in effect,
normally strengthen the position of the more conservative interests in the
political system and weaken the liberals. Perhaps this is why the AFL–
CIO and other similarly inclined groups have either opposed or are
skeptical about such a plan, and why the Republican party has been one
of its strongest proponents.

3. POLITICAL PARTICIPATION

THE CITIZEN VOICE
IN GOVERNMENT

It is basic to achieving a democratic society that government respond
to the wishes and needs of the people. But how is government to know
what are the expectations of its citizens? Classical democratic theory
envisages an informed and alert citizenry who make known their views
by participating in the processes of government. Active participation,
however, signifies more than the simple act of voting. The citizen must
also work for causes and candidates, contributing time, energy, and
money. He has to be alert to the covert workings of political parties,

interest groups, and government officialdom, lest the public weal be subverted out of a concern for selfish interests. Above all else, classical theory sees democracy as a government *of the people.*

Yet from what survey research tells us about popular involvement in politics, our citizens scarcely measure up to the standards set by classical theory. Participation for most consists of casting a vote on election day. The voting decision will be made, in all probability, without listening to both sides of the campaign communications. Indeed, the voter will likely be unaware of the public record of the incumbent, should he be running, except in the most vague and general way. He probably receives some exposure from the news media, particularly television, concerning major political races. He may engage in informal discussions concerning political events and the qualifications and merits of particular candidates. One cannot denigrate the significance of this type of political participation: it is important. But more active involvement in political affairs is limited to a small minority, as Table 3.1 indicates.

TABLE 3.1
Popular Participation in Politics,
1952 and 1956[a]

	1952	1956
"Do you belong to any political club or organizations?"	2%	3%
"Did you give any money or buy tickets or anything to help the campaign for one of the parties or candidates?"	4%	10%
"Did you go to any political meetings, rallies, dinners, or things like that?"	7%	7%
"Did you do any other work for one of the parties or candidates?"	3%	3%

[a] Entries are proportions of total samples answering affirmatively.
SOURCE: Angus Campbell, Philip E. Converse, Warren E. Miller, and Donald E. Stokes, *The American Voter* (New York: Wiley, 1960), p. 91.

How then do we square what survey research tells us about citizen involvement with the widely held conviction that we live in a free society in which the government does respond to the broad needs of its citizens? The most impressive studies that provide clues to an answer have been analyses made of community power structures. Although directed at local governments, we may usefully draw analogies to apply to state political systems as well.

In his study of New Haven, Robert Dahl distinguished *Homo Civicus* from *Homo Politicus*.[1] *Homo Civicus* has many demands placed upon his time, and he becomes absorbed in problems of earning a living, caring for his family, and seeking recreational outlets during his leisure time. He quite typically perceives little satisfaction from engaging in political activity and allocates few of the resources at his command toward this end. "*Homo Civicus* is not, by nature, a political animal."[2] *Homo Politicus*, on the other hand, does receive gratification from political activity and is willing to allot a large share of his time and resources to gain political power. In other words, a small minority of activists, because of their commitment to politics, participate fully in political affairs. It is they who are directly involved in making decisions on questions of public policy.

If only a small number of citizens are sufficiently motivated and skillful to wield large amounts of power and influence in our society, it is important to identify who they are. Are they members of a social and economic elite who control government covertly in their own interests? Some believe so; yet the evidence appears to point otherwise. One must not confuse potential influence with its exercise. Since most do not use fully the resources at their command for political purposes, they have little direct influence on public issues. This is often the case with the social and economic elites. Even should they express an interest in political affairs, they are unlikely to express a concern as a class for more than limited segments of public policy.

Onē must also distinguish the types of resources that can be translated into political power and influence. Since under an elective system one must appeal to the citizen-body to obtain important positions of power in government, the skills and resources required of the politician are not derived simply from wealth and position. They include time, energy, charisma, popularity, ability to evoke identification on the basis of ethnic or religious kinship, and similar resources. The very diversity of resources is likely to insure a diversity of leadership. Rather than a cohesive elite governing in their own interests, the more typical system is one characterized by competing elites drawn from a variety of social classes and demographic groups. The nature of the state's political and cultural environment, of course, will impose limits on political competition. In the South and elsewhere, a Negro seeking statewide office may be handicapped in his electoral bid. A Catholic running for governor is unlikely to

[1] Robert Dahl, *Who Governs* (paperbound ed.; New Haven: Yale University Press, 1961), pp. 223–226.
[2] *Ibid.*, p. 225.

fare well in fundamentalist regions of the nation. Other racial, religious, or ethnic minorities may be similarly disadvantaged in seeking political office. Still, it would be unfair to assert the covert control of C. Wright Mill's power elite. There might be bias in the system, but there is also competition.

The fact that elites compete for power is critical in the American system of politics. For the competition must inevitably involve large numbers of the population. It is through appeals for popular support that the citizen becomes involved in the calculus of decision-making. His participation is indirect. But those who engage directly in the formulation of public policy cannot be unmindful of the consequences of their actions. Perhaps political leaders overestimate the visibility of their public records. Yet they may be more sophisticated than we surmise, realizing that the impact of their performance will converge into a public image that will enhance or hinder their chances of electoral success. It is for this reason that the interests of broad segments of the citizen-body cannot be ignored.

What we are saying is that, by the nature of government in modern society, only the few can rule. If this is not in accord with classical theories of democracy, perhaps what is required is a redefinition of democracy, as Schattschneider argues, so that it shall not be abandoned "before we have found out what it is."[3] Herein lies the nub of the present-day controversy over democratic theory. Some argue that the citizen is not powerless because he is not involved directly in the day-to-day decisions of government. The importance of the citizen's role, they argue, should be judged by the significance, not the number, of decisions he makes. Thus the vote, the most common form of political participation engaged in by the average citizen, should not be undervalued. It determines which group of competing leaders and organizations will control the government.

On the other hand, some believe that a redefinition of democracy that takes into account the passive role of the citizen-body deprives democratic theory of its normative significance.[4] There is a danger that, in attempting to make democratic theory equate with political practice, democratic revisionists become "sophisticated apologists" for the existing political order. The citizen-role is reduced to responding to public policies after the fact, in election contests, and no longer encompasses the prescription of more active involvement.

[3] E. E. Schattschneider, *The Semi-Sovereign People* (New York: Holt, Rinehart & Winston, 1960), p. 136.
[4] See Jack L. Walker, "A Critique of the Elitist Theory of Democracy," *The American Political Science Review*, LX (June, 1966), 285–295, and the response of Robert A. Dahl, "Further Reflections on 'The Elitist Theory of Democracy,'" *American Political Science Review*, LX (June, 1966), 296–305.

If, indeed, those interested in developing empirical theory would also claim that their generalizations (for example, voter surveys showing low citizen involvement) were also prescriptive of what ought to be, we would express vigorous disagreement based on our own value commitments. We do not believe that most empiricists have this objective. At the same time, we urge the reader to retain a skepticism toward political findings purporting to describe the nature of man (his political apathy), which in fact may be a product of the structure of society's institutions and the reluctance of the political leadership to encourage broader participation. Starting with such a skeptical attitude, one may then proceed to the needed task of developing normative theory that takes into account realistically the "kinds and degrees of constraint that have to be treated as fixed by the conditions of man and society."[5]

VOTING AS PARTICIPATION

Since voting is the most accessible means for the citizen to influence the course of public policy, the turnout on election day is important. Turnout is facilitated or retarded by the legal requirements imposed on those who would exercise the franchise. But even in states with the least rigid systems of voter qualifications, some eligible voters do not go to the polls. That some citizens do not choose to vote is basically related to their membership in social groups, but, at times, it is an expression of the value the individual places on the act of voting. To understand why some vote and others do not is the subject which we explore below.

The Legal Setting

Responsibility for determining voter eligibility under the United States Consitution rests with state governments, subject to the provisions of the Fifteenth, Nineteenth, and Twenty-third amendments prohibiting the denial or abridgement of the vote because of race, color, previous condition of servitude, sex, or the payment of a poll tax. More recently, Congress relied on the equal protection and enforcement clauses of the Fourteenth Amendment to lower the voting age to 18 for both national and state elections. Even the bill's partisans conceded that the legislation raised serious constitutional issues and hoped for a speedy court test.[6]

---

[5] Robert A. Dahl, "Further Reflections on 'The Elitist Theory of Democracy,'" *American Political Science Review*, LX (June, 1966), 305.
[6] While the manuscript was in press, the Supreme Court upheld the Congressional action lowering the voting age in national elections to 18 that invalidated some of the provisions for eligibility in state elections. (*U.S.* v. *Arizona*, 91 Sup. Ct. 260 (1970)). State governments must now ponder whether they should lower the voting

If the legality of the congressional action is cloudy, so too are the consequences unclear of enfranchising an estimated 11 million youthful Americans. No empirical evidence has been assembled to suggest that lowered age requirements have altered the political balance in those states (Georgia and Kentucky, 18; Alaska, 19; and Hawaii, 20) where 21-year-old eligibility has been abandoned. It is safe to assume, on the basis of survey evidence, that the partisan attachments of the young are not so strong as those of older age groups; the young are more likely to disregard party labels and vote on the basis of candidate or issue appeals. What is difficult to predict is the direction their vote will take. Many equate the young with the college youth and believe that the "old" politics will be shattered by the onslaught of more selfless and enlightened voters. Indeed, the college youth more than his noncollege counterpart is likely to exercise his franchise. What must not be overlooked, however, is that there are fewer 18- to 20-year-olds who are enrolled in college than are not. And as to the voting predilections of the young, it must be recalled that support for the candidacy of George Wallace came disproportionately from the under-30 age group.[7] The fact is that it is too early to judge the consequences of adding such large numbers to the voting rolls.

Other legal requirements for voting may be conveniently grouped together for our purposes to establish the ease with which a voter may establish his eligibility and actually cast his vote. Voting and registration practices that, the President's Commission on Registration and Voting Participation argued, affect the size of the turnout are summarized below.[8]

1. Registration Systems

    All but four states require the voter personally to establish his eligibility to vote. In a few states he must periodically revalidate his eligibility to enable election officials to purge the rolls of those who have moved or are deceased. The most convenient system for the voter is one in which he needs to register but once, either by mail or at some suitable place in his precinct, without having to journey to the county courthouse. The commission felt that keeping registration open until at least one month before election time would add to the voting rolls because of the interest engendered by political campaigns.

---

age in state elections on their initiative in order to avoid confusion in election administration.

[7] Philip E. Converse, Warren E. Miller, Jerrold G. Rusk, and Arthur C. Wolfe, "Continuity and Change in American Politics: Parties and Issues in the 1968 Election, "*The American Political Science Review,* LXIII (December, 1969), 1103.

[8] *Report of the President's Commission on Registration and Voting Participation* (Washington, D.C.: U.S. Government Printing Office, 1963), chaps. 1 and 3.

2. Residence Requirements

All states provide for residence requirements in state and local elections to insure that the voter has had some time to appraise local issues and to prevent the importation of voters from other communities. The commission thought residency requirements exceeding six months in the state and thirty days in the county or city were burdensome.

3. Literacy Requirements

Nineteen states still require literacy tests in English to establish eligibility for voting. Although once used as a means for discouraging Negro voting in the South, literacy tests that are applied discriminatorily today may cause the appointment of federal examiners to enroll Negroes under terms of the Voting Rights Act of 1965. Further, under terms of the Civil Rights Act of 1964, no literacy test may be required of anyone who has completed a sixth-grade education. The tests that remain are, presumably, designed to insure that the voter possesses the minimal level of literacy believed necessary to make an electoral choice. Yet, as the commission argued, information is available from sources other than the printed word. Suffrage is a right of every citizen, the commission continued, no matter what his formal education or material wealth. It recommended the abolition of all literacy tests.

4. Absentee Voting

All states provide for absentee balloting by members of the armed forces. Most states provide for civilian absentee balloting, but mere absence during business or vacation travel is inadequate to establish eligibility in 16 states—that is, the travel must be proved essential or a regularly scheduled business trip. The commission recommended the extension of absentee balloting to anyone away from home on election day as well as to anyone who, because of physical handicap or incapacitation, finds it difficult to vote.

5. Election Day Procedures

Polling places that remain open only for short periods of time outside of normal hours discourage voter turnout. Similarly, providing too few polling places and/or inadequate facilities causes lines to build up which often make voters unwilling to wait to cast their ballots. The commission recommended that sufficient facilities be provided at each polling place to avoid overcrowding and that polls be kept open 12 hours or more.

Burdensome election and registration laws, independently of socioeconomic influences, undoubtedly keep potential voters from the polls.[9] Indeed, the fact that the voting turnout in election contests in the United

[9]   See the excellent article by Stanley Kelley, Jr., Richard E. Ayres, and William G. Bowen, "Registration and Voting: Putting First Things First," *American Political Science Review*, LXI (June, 1967), 359–379.

States is lower than in other western democracies can be ascribed in large part to the more demanding registration practices in this country. At the same time, the variations in voting requirements found among the states are not unrelated to their political and social environments. For example, most of the southern states have restrictive election laws, which helps explain why the turnout in the South has been lower than in other parts of the country. The reason for the restrictive laws is the preference of the political leadership for low participation, particularly by Negro voters. Active discouragement of Negro voting, in turn, reflects the historic importance of racial issues in southern states. Thus, we may conclude that election laws reflect the political and social systems of a state while recognizing that the restrictive laws themselves affect turnout. The lesson that may be learned is that those in power may devise election laws to construct a turnout that gives them partisan advantage. Such a strategy may be easier in areas of one-party control but probably is not unknown to the political leadership elsewhere.

The Special Case of Black Voting

The right of Negroes to vote free of legal obstruction has been more of a problem in the South than elsewhere. Casting about for a way to disfranchise the Negro short of physical intimidation, southern leaders found their answer in the political monopoly maintained by the Democratic party. If the Democratic party is construed to be a private, voluntary association without public responsibilities, then nothing in the Fourteenth or Fifteenth amendments prevents its leaders from restricting membership to those of the Caucasian race. And if only members can participate in its primaries, then those excluded have no real choice of who is to govern. Until the recent past, winning the Democratic nomination has been tantamount to winning office in the South. Thus the birth of the so-called "white primary," the most effective of the legal devices resorted to by southerners to block black voting.

The white primary was doomed by the Court's decision in U.S. v. Classic.[10] A primary election could be cloaked with a public character, the Court said, if state election laws made it an integral part of the state's electoral machinery or, more importantly, if participation in it was the only effective way of choosing the state's leadership. Once the primary took on public responsibilities then the prohibitions of the Fourteenth and Fifteenth amendments would apply. In a series of decisions the Court put an end to the legal façade that Negroes were not denied

[10] 313 U.S. 299 (1941).

the vote because they were prevented from entering the primary of the Democratic party.[11]

The white primary was not the only legal dodge resorted to by southerners. A test of literacy was used in some states that only white voters seemed capable of passing. Registration forms became uncommonly complex and were scrutinized carefully for any errors in their completion. The registration office was open to new voters in some communities for only a limited period and, if lines stretched outside the courthouse doors, the registrar of voters saw no special need for haste. Sometimes two registered voters were required to testify to the good moral character of the aspiring voter, but from whom could a Negro in the rural South turn to for such a testimonial? And so the story went. The black found not only legal obstacles to voting, but economic and social pressure as well. He was the victim of a social, political, and economic system that did not die easily.

Practices were not the same everywhere in the South. In 1961, the U.S. Commission on Civil Rights found a denial of the right to vote because of race in only eight southern states—Alabama, Florida, Georgia, Louisiana, Mississippi, North Carolina, South Carolina, and Tennessee.[12] In Florida, North Carolina, and Tennessee discriminatory practices were limited to isolated counties. It was the states of the Deep South, with their large Negro populations, that resisted to the last the right of blacks to vote. Although Negro registration increased, progress was lamentably slow. There matters stood until the historic Voting Rights Act of 1965 (given a five-year extension by the Congress in 1970).

The great advance of the 1965 act for the Negro is that he no longer has to fight a costly court battle to establish his claim to vote and then rely on compliance by state and local officials. The act provides that the Attorney General can request the appointment of federal examiners to enroll Negroes in any state or county where less than 25 percent of their number are registered or, if a literacy or good character test is in effect, where less than 50 percent of blacks are enrolled voters. Only if Negroes are registered at figures greater than the act's provisions is intervening court action now required to prove discrimination. Table 3.2 compares Negro and white registration before and after passage of the act.

The way now has been opened for the Negro to participate in southern politics. One measure of the change was the election in 1968 of Charles Evers as mayor in the small, rural city of Fayette, Mississippi. A victory for a black in rural Mississippi simply could not have been anticipated

---

[11] *Smith* v. *Allwright*, 321 U.S. 649 (1944); *Rice* v. *Elmore*, 333 U.S. 875 (1948); *Terry* v. *Adams*, 345 U.S. 461 (1953).
[12] U.S. Commission on Civil Rights, *Voting* (Washington, D.C.: U.S. Government Printing Office, 1961), p. 22.

TABLE 3.2
*Voter Registration by Race Before
and After Passage of the Voting
Rights Act of 1965*

STATE	PREACT REGISTRATION	POSTACT REGISTRATION[a]	PREACT PERCENT OF VOTING AGE POPULATION REGISTERED	POSTACT PERCENT OF VOTING AGE POPULATION REGISTERED
Alabama				
Nonwhite	92,737	248,432	19.3	51.6
White	935,695	1,212,317	69.2	89.6
Arkansas				
Nonwhite	77,714	121,000	40.4	62.8
White	555,944	616,000	65.5	72.4
Florida				
Nonwhite	240,616	299,033	51.2	63.6
White	1,958,499	2,131,105	74.8	81.4
Georgia				
Nonwhite	167,663	332,496	27.4	52.6
White	1,124,415	1,443,730	62.6	80.3
Louisiana				
Nonwhite	164,601	303,148	31.6	58.9
White	1,037,184	1,200,517	80.5	93.1
Mississippi				
Nonwhite	28,500	263,754	6.7	59.8
White	525,000	665,176	69.9	91.5
North Carolina				
Nonwhite	258,000	277,404	46.8	51.3
White	1,942,000	1,602,980	96.8	83.0
South Carolina				
Nonwhite	138,544	190,017	37.3	51.2
White	677,914	731,096	75.7	81.7
Tennessee				
Nonwhite	218,000	225,000	69.5	71.7
White	1,297,000	1,434,000	72.9	80.6
Texas				
Nonwhite	2,939,535[b]	400,000	53.1[b]	61.6
White		2,600,000		53.3
Virginia				
Nonwhite	144,259	243,000	38.3	55.6
White	1,070,168	1,190,000	61.1	63.4

[a] Figures for Alabama, Georgia, Louisiana, Mississippi, and South Carolina are for 1967; all other state figures are for 1966.
[b] Percentages and totals by race are not available.
SOURCE: U.S. Commission on Civil Rights, *Political Participation* (Washington, D.C.: U.S. Government Printing Office, 1968), pp. 12–13.

before 1965. Yet not all of the black's political problems will evaporate now that the main legal obstacles to voting have been cleared from his path. He still is found in great numbers among those social and economic groupings that survey research associates with nonvoting. And although his race might be a majority in some southern counties, he is everywhere a minority within the state. Any strategy devised for Negro candidates in statewide races must include an appeal for substantial white support. If racial issues polarize the electorate into white and black camps, the minority black is scarcely better off than before. On the other hand, because of the political leverage that he now has, his vote may be appealed to by rival white candidates who see it as the only way to electoral success. One can speculate that an electoral strategy of white candidates appealing to black voters will appear first in the rimland South where it would constitute less of a political hazard. In the heartland South, where racial tensions remain high, white candidates may be more cautious in making overt appeals for Negro support.

Social and Economic Correlates of Voting

Few aspects of voting behavior have been better documented than the relationship that exists between social and economic characteristics and voting turnout. The explanation is quite logical. An individual's life situation shapes his attitudes and beliefs. Those brought up and living in similar environments tend to share common goals and attitudes and exhibit similar patterns of behavior. Thus the following generalizations may be made about voting turnout:

1. Persons of low income tend to vote less than persons of middle income. However, high-income groups do not vote significantly more than middle-income groups. Once a certain threshold is reached, income ceases to be a relevant factor affecting turnout.

2. Turnout is positively related to education. Those with a college education are more likely to vote than those with a high-school education; they, in turn, are more likely to vote than those with a grade-school education.

3. Voting turnout varies with occupational classes. Professional, managerial, and other white-collar occupations show the highest rate of voter turnout. Skilled and semiskilled workers turn out in greater numbers than farmers. Unskilled workers have the poorest record of voting participation.

4. Persons of high socioeconomic status (a factor combining income, education, and occupation) tend to vote more than those of low socioeconomic status.

5. Voting is greater among middle-age groups than among either the younger or older groups.

6. Men tend to vote more than women, a fact notable in democracies other than our own.

7. Individuals who belong to organizations are more likely to vote than those who eschew organizational ties.

8. Large metropolitan areas generally have a higher vote turnout than small towns and cities which, in turn, report a higher turnout than rural areas.

What is perhaps more interesting than the descriptive differences between voters and nonvoters are the explanations that have been offered for the variations in turnout.[13] A high turnout can be expected from individuals who are affected by government policies, possess the necessary information to perceive the effects of those policies, are subject to group pressures that urge political participation, and are not subject to cross-pressures that weaken their resolve to support a particular party or candidate. Upon reflection, one can understand how the social and economic characteristics of an individual are likely related to whether government policies strongly affect him, or whether he is in a position to perceive the effects and act upon them with like-minded associates.

Factors of Psychological
Involvement

Although the individual's social environment is likely to affect his attitude toward the voting process, there nevertheless remains an individual predisposition toward political participation, which remains remarkably stable for a given person and cannot be explained solely in terms of his physical and social environment. Indeed, if membership in social, economic, and political organizations offered all of the explanation of individual behavior, an analysis of voting would be made immeasurably more simple. The fact is that social and economic correlates of voting reflect only central tendencies and cannot be used to predict individual behavior. Thus the lower economic groups vote less than the upper income voters; yet some who are poor do vote and some who are rich do not. One cannot hope to explain all of the reasons relating to individual difference in participation, but two factors of psychological involvement offer a partial explanation. These have been characterized by the University of Michigan Survey Research Center as a citizen's sense of civic duty and his sense of political efficacy.[14]

[13] Seymour M. Lipset, *Political Man* (Anchor Books ed.; Garden City: Doubleday, 1963), pp. 190–191.
[14] Angus Campbell, Philip E. Converse, Warren E. Miller, and Donald E. Stokes, *The American Voter* (New York: Wiley, 1960), pp. 103–107.

Voting in America has long been considered the citizen's duty. When the individual accepts this societal norm as his own, he is much more likely to vote than one who does not feel similarly obliged. The Survey Research Center found that only 13 percent of those who had a low sense of civic duty actually voted, while 85 percent of those with a high sense of civic duty cast a ballot in the 1956 Presidential election.

A second measure of psychological involvement is the attitude of the citizen toward the efficacy of casting a vote. To some, the world of politics appears too removed and complex to be affected by whether they cast their ballot. It matters little, they say, whether one votes—politics will be the same. Those whose sense of political efficacy is low are less likely to vote (52 percent turnout) than those who believe they can influence the workings of government (91 percent turnout).

We introduce the concepts of civic duty and political efficacy because they are not unrelated to the question of alienation in American society today. If alienation were solely a question of political apathy (that is, a lack of interest in or indifference to public issues), the quality of the existing political order would not be so forcefully called into question. Indeed, the political leadership might very well interpret even widespread apathy as a sign of contentment with the status quo. But alienation signifies a rejection of the political order and a feeling of powerlessness accompanied by strong feeling over public issues; it poses a much more visible challenge. Since the alienated feel intensely about political issues, they may transfer their feeling to political movements not within the traditional mainstream of American politics. Thus some believe that the civil riots in our cities are an expression of political discontent and have their root cause in the ghetto Negro's feeling of powerlessness and frustration. The appeal of George Wallace, others believe, is to groups who also feel alienated, but by the social forces that have changed the America they once knew. For these reasons, we wish to draw attention to the importance of investigating the psychological dimensions of voter involvement. The politics of deference and status, the sense of how one's group or class is treated and its values respected, may become increasingly important in the 1970s.

The Influence of Party

The role played by political parties in a state also affects voting turnout. In states whose elections are contested by strong and competitive parties, voting turnout is usually high. The reasons are not hard to find. The political party remains yet the most effective device for mobilizing support within the general electorate. Through their organizational efforts, parties generate an interest among the voters in the campaign and in the election outcome. The fact of a close struggle is newsworthy itself, since the outcome will determine who will govern. The more people hear of the battle, the more they perceive what the stakes are, the more likely they will turn out. It is the function of party workers to insure that their cause is known and supported by major groupings of voters.

One may also presume that vigorous party competition is accompanied by loyal partisans for each side. This in itself is associated with factors of psychological involvement likely to result in a high voting turnout. Research has shown that strong party identifiers are more likely to have an interest in a campaign and in the election outcome than weak party identifiers and independents.[15] This evidence flies in the face of popular notions of the independent voter as an informed person who carefully weighs the evidence before committing himself to party or candidate. The independent, or weak party identifier, is likely less knowledgeable and less involved in public affairs and, as a consequence, less likely to vote than the partisan voter.

Variations Among the States

Although the discussion has been based mainly on research directed at Presidential elections, we feel that the correlates of voting turnout apply as well to state and local elections. To demonstrate in a crude way the applicability of our assertion, we have constructed Table 3.3 which is based on voting turnout in gubernatorial elections. States are compared in terms of selected political, economic, and social characteristics. The best predictor of voting turnout is probably the level of party competition maintained but party competition, in turn, is a shorthand term that reflects a variety of social and economic factors within a state that contribute to the nature of its political conflict.

THE NATURE OF
POLITICAL INTEREST GROUPS

We have seen how the average American is not highly involved in political affairs and commonly confines his political participation to the act of voting. That the citizen's involvement in politics is low does not necessarily mean that his interests go unnoticed. It does mean that his potential influence must be mobilized through organizational efforts if his interests are to be more effectively represented. The political party is the principal agency for mobilizing majority support within the citizen body; but it is not the only instrument for organizing citizens for political

[15] *Ibid.*, pp. 142–145.

TABLE 3.3
Selected Economic, Social, and Political Characteristics Compared to Voter Turn-out, by State Rankings

(1) AVERAGE PERCENTAGE PARTICIPATING IN GUBERNATORIAL ELECTIONS, 1962–69		(2) MEDIAN EDUCATION 1960		(3) PER CAPITA PERSONAL INCOME 1967		(4) PERCENTAGE POPULATION RESIDING IN SMSA's,[a] 1965		(5) INDEX OF PARTY COMPETITION[b]	
1. Utah	77.5	1. Utah	12.2	1. Conn.	3,978	1. Mass.	97.3	1. Neb.	.5000
2. Wash.	71.9	2. Alaska	12.1	2. N.Y.	3,824	2. Calif.	90.2	2. Mont.	.4875
3. W.Va.	71.6	2. Calif.	12.1	3. Alaska	3,752	3. N.J.	87.3	3. N.J.	.4861
4. Ind.	71.4	2. Colo.	12.1	3. Ill.	3,752	4. Conn.	85.9	4. Colo.	.4800
5. Mont.	71.1	2. Nev.	12.1	5. Calif.	3,697	5. N.Y.	85.1	5. Conn.	.4697
6. Ill.	71.0	2. Wash.	12.1	6. N.J.	3,679	6. R.I.	82.9	6. Calif.	.4586
7. Del.	70.4	2. Wyo.	12.1	6. Nev.	3,679	7. Md.	80.7	7. Ore.	.4585
8. N.Dak.	69.7	8. Idaho	11.8	8. Del.	3,635	8. Hawaii	80.4	8. Pa.	.4426
9. S.Dak.	68.1	8. Ore.	11.8	9. Mass.	3,533	9. Ill.	79.6	9. Ind.	.4360
10. R.I.	67.0	10. Kan.	11.7	10. Md.	3,423	10. Nev.	79.5	10. Nev.	.4285
11. Mass.	66.6	11. Mass.	11.6	11. Wash.	3,389	11. Pa.	79.1	11. Mass.	.4266
12. Idaho	66.5	11. Mont.	11.6	12. Mich.	3,387	12. Ohio	76.9	12. Wash.	.4206
13. Mich.	66.3	11. Neb.	11.6	13. R.I.	3,324	13. Utah	76.7	13. Mich.	.4199
14. N.H.	64.8	14. Ariz.	11.3	14. Hawaii	3,242	14. Mich.	76.5	14. Utah	.4135
15. Mo.	64.7	14. Hawaii	11.3	15. Ohio	3,204	15. Ariz.	71.4	15. Ill.	.4104
16. Wyo.	64.3	14. Iowa	11.3	16. Ind.	3,188	16. Del.	70.4	16. Del.	.3975
17. Minn.	62.5	17. N.Mex.	11.2	17. Pa.	3,176	17. Colo.	70.2	17. R.I.	.3896
18. Vt.	61.4	18. Del.	11.1	18. Wis.	3,152	18. Tex.	69.4	18. N.Y.	.3849
19. Iowa	61.1	19. Conn.	11.0	19. Ore.	3,090	19. Fla.	66.1	19. Ohio	.3812
20. Wis.	60.2	19. Me.	11.0	20. Iowa	3,087	20. Wash.	63.6	20. Wis.	.3798
21. Conn.	60.1	21. Fla.	10.9	21. Minn.	3,079	21. Mo.	61.9	21. Iowa	.3795
22. Hawaii	59.9	21. N.H.	10.9	22. Colo.	3,077	22. Ind.	60.5	22. Wyo.	.3767

23.	Neb.	59.7	21.	Ohio	10.9	23.	Neb.	3,064	23.	Ore.	59.8	23.	Alaska	.3751
24.	Pa.	59.2	21.	Vt.	10.9	24.	Kan.	3,052	24.	La.	53.8	24.	Minn.	.3750
25.	Colo.	58.8	25.	Ind.	10.8	25.	N.H.	3,031	25.	Va.	53.1	25.	Idaho	.3723
26.	Calif.	58.1	25.	Mich.	10.8	26.	Mo.	3,003	26.	Minn.	52.7	26.	Hawaii	.3684
27.	Kan.	57.8	25.	Minn.	10.8	27.	Wyo.	2,964	27.	Ala.	49.5	27.	Ariz.	.3396
28.	Ore.	57.8	28.	N.Y.	10.7	28.	Fla.	2,834	28.	Ga.	48.1	28.	Me.	.3373
29.	N.Mex.	56.6	29.	N.J.	10.6	29.	Vt.	2,804	29.	Wis.	48.0	29.	N.H.	.3152
30.	Alaska	55.8	30.	Ill.	10.5	30.	Va.	2,801	30.	Okla.	47.8	30.	W.Va.	.3002
31.	Me.	54.3	31.	Md.	10.4	31.	Mont.	2,773	31.	Tenn.	47.6	31.	Mo.	.2946
32.	N.C.	53.1	31.	Okla.	10.4	32.	Tex.	2,747	32.	Neb.	41.3	32.	N.M.	.2888
33.	N.J.	52.9	31.	S.Dak.	10.4	33.	Ariz.	2,715	33.	Kan.	40.7	33.	Kan.	.2866
34.	N.Y.	52.5	31.	Tex.	10.4	34.	Me.	2,632	34.	S.C.	36.5	34.	N.Dak.	.2832
35.	Ohio	50.1	31.	Wis.	10.4	35.	Okla.	2,621	35.	Ky.	35.7	35.	S.Dak.	.2745
36.	Nev.	49.9	36.	Pa.	10.2	36.	S.Dak.	2,613	36.	Iowa	34.4	36.	Vt.	.2693
37.	Ariz.	49.2	37.	R.I.	10.0	37.	Utah	2,609	37.	N.C.	32.1	37.	Md.	.2584
38.	Okla.	47.3	38.	Va.	9.9	38.	Idaho	2,567	38.	W.Va.	31.2	38.	Ky.	.2463
39.	Ark.	46.0	39.	Mo.	9.6	39.	Ga.	2,552	39.	N.H.	30.5	39.	Okla.	.2140
40.	Fla.	45.2	40.	N.Dak.	9.3	40.	N.Dak.	2,515	40.	Me.	29.2	40.	N.C.	.1395
41.	Ky.	44.9	41.	Ala.	9.1	41.	N.Mex.	2,479	41.	Ark.	28.4	41.	Va.	.1344
42.	Md.	42.5	42.	Ga.	9.0	42.	La.	2,456	42.	N.Mex.	28.4	42.	Fla.	.1312
43.	Tex.	35.7	43.	Ark.	8.9	43.	N.C.	2,425	43.	Mont.	23.6	43.	Tenn.	.1309
44.	Miss.	32.6	43.	Miss.	8.9	44.	Ky.	2,417	44.	Idaho	14.3	44.	Ark.	.0905
45.	Ala.	30.0	43.	N.C.	8.9	45.	Tenn.	2,367	45.	S.D.	13.7	45.	Tex.	.0544
46.	La.	29.9	46.	La.	8.8	46.	W.Va.	2,323	46.	Miss.	10.8	46.	Ala.	.0471
47.	Tenn.	29.4	46.	Tenn.	8.8	47.	S.C.	2,181	47.	N.Dak.	10.6	47.	La.	.0388
48.	Va.	28.8	46.	W.Va.	8.8	48.	Ala.	2,167	48.	Alaska	0.0	48.	Ga.	.0371
49.	S.C.	26.2	49.	Ky.	8.7	49.	Ark.	2,095	49.	Vt.	0.0	49.	S.C.	.0341
50.	Ga.	24.4	50.	S.C.	8.7	50.	Miss.	1,900	50.	Wyo.	0.0	50.	Miss.	.0328

a Standard Metropolitan Statistical Areas.

b See Chapter 4, p. 76 for the definition of competitiveness; the index used in this table is the absolute value of the deviation from .5000 subtracted from .5000. The range of competitiveness is from .0000 (least competitive) to .5000 (most competitive).

action. The political interest group is a force that competes with, and at times supplants, the political party in influencing decisions made on public policy.

Political interest groups have not been treated kindly in the literature of political science, at least until recently. Beginning with Madison in *Federalist* paper Number 10, writers have warned of their divisive influences and covert machinations. Such descriptions are undoubtedly accurate in depicting the activities of some organized groups. Yet few would consider an organization such as the League of Women Voters a sinister influence on the workings of state and local government. The fact of the matter is that, regardless of their merit, interest groups are a vital part of the political process. We are indebted to David Truman and others who have drawn attention to the importance of groups and groupings in an analysis of American politics.

A basic thesis of those who have emphasized the group basis of politics is that the individual is less influenced by society in his attitudes and behavior than he is differentially by the groups in society. Thus the Negro child brought up under ghetto conditions of the inner city will scarcely adopt the same set of values as the white child born in a middle-class suburban community. The environments of others may not be so sharply distinguished, but the differences that do exist, for example, allow us to discuss political behavior in terms of broad social and economic characteristics.

The group theory of politics has been attacked in that it does not adequately explain the cohesiveness of society. If the group is pre-eminent in inculcating values, then politics becomes an uncontrolled conflict among competing groups; yet we know the conflict is channeled within the boundaries set by societal "rules of the game." This problem need not bother us. Let us agree that the role of political institutions and culture has been understated by the group theorists. Nevertheless, within our political culture, there is still room for differences over the appropriate course of public policy to follow. At this level, the role of groups in influencing behavior must be accepted.

Perhaps it is the case that primary groups, particularly family, school, and neighborhood, affect the attitudes and behavior of the individual the most. Such behavior, however, may be only remotely related to political activity. For this reason, we shall focus on groups organized to mobilize political resources to influence the decisions of government—that is, political interest groups.

Formal organization is not essential to the existence of an interest group, but it does reflect an advanced stage of its development through increased interaction of its members. The frequency of interaction largely determines the significance of the group in influencing individual behavior. The interaction does not have to be a face-to-face relationship, but can include any form of communication. From the contacts and relationships of the group's members emerge common attitudes and norms of behavior and a common frame of reference for viewing political events. Thus an interest group is ". . . any group that, on the basis of one or more shared attitudes, makes certain claims upon other groups in the society for the establishment, maintenance, or enhancement of forms of behavior that are implied by the shared attitudes."[16] If the claims are placed upon the institutions of government, the interest group becomes a political interest group.

Whether a group is influential in asserting its claims upon government is dependent upon a number of complex factors. According to David Truman, they may be grouped as follows:[17]

1. The group's strategic position in society:
   a. Status or prestige of the group in society
   b. Standing of group activities when measured against societal "rules of the game"
   c. Extent to which government officials are formally or informally "members" of the group
   d. Usefulness of the group as a source of technical or other information

2. The internal characteristics of the group:
   a. Degree and appropriateness of group organization
   b. Degree of cohesion of group members
   c. Skills of the group's leadership
   d. Size of group membership
   e. Financial resources of the group

3. The role of governmental institutions:
   a. Structure and operating procedures of governmental agencies
   b. Effects of the group life of the governmental agency itself

Interest Groups in State and
Local Politics

What we have said thus far has been largely theoretical and applies to interest groups generally. Let us now be more specific in the role played by interest groups in state and local politics. That role is conditioned by the capacity of state and local governments to advance or retard the aims and objectives of the groups organized within their jurisdictions, and the ability of the groups to gain access and exercise influence on the decision-

[16] David B. Truman, *The Governmental Process* (New York: Knopf, 1951), p. 33.
[17] *Ibid.*, pp. 506–507.

makers of government. The first depends upon the distribution of powers among governmental levels; the second is related to characteristics of the group itself and its relative position *vis-à-vis* other groups with whom it is competing for political power.

That the powers of the national government have expanded considerably over the private sector of society is a commonplace. It would be an error to assume, however, that the expansion has taken place at the expense of powers at the state and local level. Although it is true that the growth in promotional and regulatory powers of the nation has changed the direction of pressure brought by a variety of interest organizations from state to national level, or offered them alternatives of strategy, the powers of state and local governments have increased apace or swifter than those of the national government. As governmental power has been increased, so too has the activity of interest groups been stepped up to protect their well-being.

Nowhere is the growth of state and local governmental powers seen more clearly than in the rise in the level of expenditures. Revenue demands to meet rising expenditures fall differentially upon various groups in society, which have more than passing interest in the incidence of the tax base. Although the national government's business regulatory activities are widespread, the states continue important in granting corporate charters and regulating banks, savings and loans firms, and insurance companies; some states have so-called "blue laws" regulating the sale of commodities on Sunday; state agencies license doctors, lawyers, barbers, beauticians, and a host of other professions and trades; state agricultural departments license slaughterhouses and provide meat and commodity inspection and grading; and the list could continue. Whether it is the activity of state officials in considering right-to-work laws, revisions in workmen's compensation and unemployment compensation programs, or the cooperative endeavor of state and national agencies in health and welfare programs, the power of state governments over diverse fields is broad enough to insure that organized groups will respond with pressures brought to protect or promote their interests.

The power available to local governments is more limited than that of the other two governmental levels and the organized interests are different. Over the years taxing and regulating the uses of property and land have been at the heart of local governmental powers and interest groups have clustered about these activities. Thus real estate developers and contractors have expressed an interest in zoning ordinances, subdivision regulations, and building, plumbing, and electrical codes. Downtown merchants have been concerned about property tax rates, urban renewal, and plans for revitalizing the central business district. Neighborhood improvement associations have kept a watchful eye on the property tax rate and the designation of land for commercial, industrial, or other high density uses. Although these and other business groups and middle-class endeavors have been probably the most influential of interests represented in many local communities, they do not by any means cover the lists of interests represented. With a heightened political awareness and a growing strength of numbers in many of our larger cities, black groups are expressing an interest in a range of municipal policies covering schools, housing, jobs, poverty programs, law enforcement, and urban renewal. Trade unions that have organized municipal employees, church groups concerned with issues of public morality, underworld figures who need protection to sell their wares, all may be included among the interest constellations surrounding local government. The point to be made is that the power of government to affect group interests is a basic determinant of any group's political activity.

The influence that the group is able to exercise over government is a consequence of factors related to its status and prestige in society and the internal characteristics of its organization, outlined earlier. Thus it is in Montana that the Anaconda Company, the state's largest employer, has wielded political power of considerable consequence in that state's political history. The power of organized labor in industrial states of the East and Midwest is significant, as is the role of Negro groups in cities and states where they enjoy pivotal voting power. The Mormon Church in the politics of Utah, insurance companies in the state of Connecticut, oil interests in the Southwest are all illustrations of groups whose religious, economic, or political position accords their voice weight when they make their demands upon government.

The group's position in society can be established, its leadership skilful, and its resources considerable, yet it may not accomplish its objectives. Much depends upon the competition that it encounters. Competition can come from other organized interests, political parties, agencies of government, or all three. How then does one measure the "strength" of an interest group system? Does one examine the *number of interest groups* that express a concern and compete for control of public decisions? Or does one measure strength by the ability of one or more groups to *work their will* through the agencies of government? Either definition would be acceptable as long as it were made known. A precise definition is required to avoid confusion over the role played by interest groups in state politics.

According to the hornbook, interest group activity is strong where parties are weak. The reverse is also argued. Where political parties are well organized and effective, interest group activity is weak. If such a characterization is accurate, we can only surmise that "strength" is defined in terms of the power of one or more interest groups to get what they want most of the time. This is more probable when a few interests that are dominant within a state find that an alliance of forces can be mutually beneficial in pursuing their causes. Such an alliance does occur in some states whose economy is not well developed and where, as a partial consequence, two-party competition is not keen. On the other hand, the more industrially developed states are likely to support many and competing interest groups as well as two-party competition. Such an interest group system then may be designated as "weak" or "moderate." The relationships are shown in Table 3.4.

Whether organized interests are influential in gaining their objectives is not simply a matter of the competition they meet from other interest groups. Political parties often play a role envisaged by responsible party

TABLE 3.4
The Strength of Pressure Groups in Varying
Political and Economic Situations

| SOCIAL CONDITIONS | TYPES OF PRESSURE SYSTEM[a] | | |
	STRONG[b]	MODERATE[c]	WEAK[d]
Party competition	(24 states)	(14 states)	(7 states)
One-party	33.3%	0%	0%
Modified one-party	37.5%	42.8%	0%
Two-party	29.1%	57.1%	100.0%
Cohesion of parties in legislature			
Weak cohesion	75.0%	14.2%	0%
Moderate cohesion	12.5%	35.7%	14.2%
Strong cohesion	12.5%	50.0%	85.7%
Socioeconomic variables			
Urban	58.6%	65.1%	73.3%
Per capita income	$1,900	$2,335	$2,450
Industrialization index	88.8	92.8	94.0

[a] Alaska, Hawaii, Idaho, New Hampshire, and North Dakota are not classified or included.
[b] Alabama, Arizona, Arkansas, California, Florida, Georgia, Iowa, Kentucky, Louisiana, Maine, Michigan, Minnesota, Mississippi, Montana, Nebraska, New Mexico, North Carolina, Oklahoma, Oregon, South Carolina, Tennessee, Texas, Washington, Wisconsin.
[c] Delaware, Illinois, Kansas, Maryland, Massachusetts, Nevada, New York, Ohio, Pennsylvania, South Dakota, Utah, Vermont, Virginia, West Virginia.
[d] Colorado, Connecticut, Indiana, Missouri, New Jersey, Rhode Island, Wyoming.
SOURCE: Harmon Zeigler, "Interest Groups in the States," in Herbert Jacobs and Kenneth N. Vines (eds.), *Politics in the American States* (Boston: Little, Brown, 1965), p. 114.

enthusiasts—that is, they organize and control interests that rally to their banner. The idea that parties are held captive by the interests they represent will not withstand analysis.[18] Since any single organized interest represents a minority within a state, it depends more upon party to gain its goals, at least in the competitive states, than the reverse. The leadership is thus in a position to refuse demands that pose an electoral threat to the party.

One also should not ignore the role of government agencies in passing on the claims of organized interests. The political process does not consist simply of competition among private interests in which government acts as an impartial arbiter. On the contrary, public officials have their own group life with their own set of norms and rules governing acceptable behavior. The values they hold may or may not coincide with those of interests attempting to influence their decisions. Indeed, studies of both state legislatures and city councils have shown that sizable numbers of each of these bodies are either neutral or hostile toward group activities.[19] A majority of the respondents in one study of 112 councilmen from 22 cities in the San Francisco Bay Area saw politics, not as a bargaining process among competing groups, but as a search for the "common good."[20] No matter that such a vague concept as the "common good" cannot be operationally defined; it is believed in by political actors and influences their behavior. The reader should be wary of theories that suggest public officialdom can be easily manipulated against their will by covert groups working behind the scenes.

Lobbying at the State Level

To make known their views on questions of public policy, private organizations often maintain representatives to plead their causes at the state capital. One must presume that groups that hire lobbyists gain some advantage from the direct contact their representatives have with legislators and agency officials. And it is likely that such organizations are viewed as "powerful" within a state. Yet it would be a mistake to judge interest group influence on the basis of lobbying activities alone. Some organizations that wield extensive political power may be overlooked as powerful lobbies either because their activities are not as visible in the legislative halls or because their activities are more electorally oriented. In the 1963 New York legislative session important issues of civil rights

[18] Schattschneider, *op. cit.*, chap. III, particularly pp. 56–59.
[19] John C. Wahlke, Heinz Eulau, William Buchanan, and LeRoy C. Ferguson, *The Legislative System* (New York: Wiley, 1962), chap. 14; Betty H. Zisk, Heinz Eulau, and Kenneth Prewitt, "City Councilmen and the Group Struggle: A Typology of Role Orientations," *Journal of Politics*, 27 (August, 1965), 618–646.
[20] Zisk, Eulau, and Prewitt, *supra*, p. 645.

were considered, including measures affecting public accommodations and the sale of property. In a survey of New York legislators, however, no legislator suggested that civil rights groups were one of the more powerful pressure groups.[21]

The interest groups most frequently mentioned as powerful lobbies before state legislative bodies, and there are sixty such groups, include the AFL–CIO, state teachers' associations, manufacturing associations, state farm bureaus, truckers, and utilities.[22] Other groups mentioned as strong in particular states are:

Oil and gas lobbies in Alaska, California, Kansas, Louisiana, Mississippi, New Mexico, Texas, and Oklahoma

Financial institutions in New York, California, Rhode Island, and Hawaii

Insurance lobbies in Connecticut, Delaware, Massachusetts, Oregon, and Rhode Island

Gambling interests in Florida, Nevada, and New Hampshire

Liquor lobbies in Maryland, Minnesota, New Mexico, South Dakota, Wisconsin, Arizona, and Tennessee

Chambers of Commerce in Colorado, Hawaii, Indiana, Michigan, New Jersey, Utah, Ohio, and Virginia

Railroad and transportation groups in Kentucky, Minnesota, North Dakota, and Tennessee

Mining interests in Arizona, Montana, and West Virginia

Local public officials in Arkansas, Georgia, Oklahoma, Pennsylvania, and Wisconsin

Fishing industries in Alaska

Government employees in Hawaii

REA Co-ops in South Dakota and North Carolina

As we have suggested earlier, a state's peculiar economic and social make-up together with the power of government to influence a group's well-being, determine the type and number of groups that band together

---

[21] Wayne L. Francis, *Legislative Issues in the Fifty States: A Comparative Analysis* (Chicago: Rand McNally, 1967), p. 42.
[22] *Ibid.*, pp. 41–42.

to protect or promote their interests. Yet no single interest group will express a concern for the range of subjects dealt with by state legislatures. Nor will there always be a conflict among competing interests over legislative policies. One can get some idea of the issues that either elicit group interest or produce group conflict from Table 3.5.

Table 3.5 may be interpreted in the following way: Most legislative issues that attracted the interests of organized groups produced conflicts among them. The notable exception was education. Although state education associations express a considerable concern over school bud-

TABLE 3.5
*Pressure Group Interest and Pressure
Group Conflict in the Policy Areas*

PRESSURE GROUP INTEREST (IRV)[a]	POLICY AREAS	RANK	POLICY AREAS	PRESSURE GROUP CONFLICT (IRV)[a]
.80	Civil rights	1	Labor	.69
.78	Agriculture	2	Liquor	.65
.78	Labor	3	Business	.63
.75	Liquor	4	Civil rights	.59
.73	Gambling	5	Gambling	.56
.72	Education	6	Water resources	.52
.69	Business	7	Agriculture	.50
.65	Water resources	8	Taxation	.48
.63	Taxation	9	Social welfare	.42
.62	Social welfare	10	Apportionment	.38
.60	Land	11	Constitutional revision	.33
.50	Highways-transportation	12	Local government	.33
.47	Finance	13	Education	.32
.47	Constitutional revision	14	Highways-transportation	.32
.45	Elections-primaries-conventions	15	Administration	.30
.45	Apportionment	16	Land	.30
.42	Local government	17	Courts-penal-crime	.27
.39	Administration	18	Elections-primaries-conventions	.27
.39	Health	19	Finance	.27
.35	Courts-penal-crime	20	Health	.17
.59	IRV	ALL RESPONSES	IRV	.42

[a] The letters IRV, Issue Respondex Value, refer to the percentage of responses from legislators who perceived pressure group interest or conflict on important bills before the 1963 legislative sessions of the fifty states.

SOURCE: Wayne L. Francis, *Legislative Issues in the Fifty States: A Comparative Analysis* (Chicago: Rand, McNally, 1967), p. 29.

gets and other educational policies, they seldom encounter an antieduca-
tion lobby. At the same time, the relative absence of interest group
conflict does not signify the absence of other types of conflict. For
example, financial and elections-primaries-conventions issues rank rather
low on interest group conflict but often produce heated contests within a
legislature among contending parties or regions of a state. Thus the Table
3.5 can also be considered as evidence that political interests are not
represented alone by privately organized groups that make representations to their legislative leaders.

If one examines the lists of lobbyists who are required to register
under state law, he may reach the conclusion that the state legislator is
overwhelmed by their sheer numbers. Although we do not wish to denigrate the role of the lobbyist, the numbers themselves are misleading if
they convey the notion of full-time lobbyists, well trained and experienced in their tasks, assiduously seeking to advance the cause of the
group to whom they have been committed over the years. If lobbying in
Oklahoma is not atypical, and there is some evidence to think it is not,
then the pattern of state lobbying is quite different from what we have
suggested.[23] Patterson found that nearly one half of the lobbyists he
interviewed had undertaken that role for the first time with the legislative
session under study. Over 60 percent of the lobbyists devoted half or less
of their time to lobbying activities. Furthermore, it is not uncommon to
find a lobbyist serving several masters who are likely to change from year
to year.[24]

If lobbying is not as professional an occupation as we have come to
expect, what of the techniques used by state operatives? Douglass Cater
makes much of the change that has occurred in lobbying activities in
Washington. Although the old-style lobbyist has not disappeared, the
modern-day lobbyist avoids the more crude techniques that involve the
exchange of money for legal fees, speeches, or whatever. According to
Cater, the smart lobbyist,

> . . . by skillful intrusions into the communications system . . . strives not
> only to waken general public sympathy for his cause but also to coagulate
> support among other interest groups. Thus sustained, he turns his attention
> to the policy-making process. He knows he can be most effective by being
> helpful, by being timely, and, not least, by being accurate. According to the
> testimony of lobbyists themselves, the cardinal sin is to supply faulty infor-
> mation which puts a trusting policy-maker in an exposed position.[25]

[23] Samuel Patterson, "The Role of the Lobbyist: The Case of Oklahoma," *Journal of Politics*, 25 (February, 1963), 91.
[24] Harmon Ziegler, "Interest Groups in the States," in Herbert Jacob and Kenneth N. Vines (eds.), *Politics in the American States* (Boston: Little, Brown, 1965), p. 130.
[25] Douglass Cater, *Power in Washington* (Vintage ed.; New York: Random House, 1965), p. 209.

There is some evidence that the new lobby has not taken hold in the state capitals. In his study of lobbying in Washington, Lester W. Milbrath reported the comments of two lobbyists with prior experience at the state level:[26]

> Lobbying is very different before state legislatures; it is much more individualistic. Maybe this is the reason they have more bribery and peddling of influence in state legislatures than in Congress. Most state legislators take it as a part-time job and don't have the feeling that their future and career is tied up with it, certainly not to the extent that this is true of members of Congress. It is easier to get a bill through a state legislature than through Congress too.
>
> • • •
>
> In the state legislatures, lobbying is definitely on a lower plane. The lobbyists are loose and hand out money and favors quite freely. Lobbyists exercise influence on the regulatory agencies at the state level, too. Here in Washington, however, no man is a real power in himself.

The reasons for the difference in lobbying techniques cited by Milbrath relate to the character of the state legislative process.[27] Lawmaking at the state capitals is a more informal process in which the individual legislator is easily accessible. The lawmaker seems to have less concern for establishing a professional reputation or of making a career out of his legislative job. Because service in the legislature is viewed as a part-time undertaking, the legislator seldom establishes a second home at the state capital or has access to satisfactory office facilities which would ease the personal and professional requirements of fulfilling his job. He then becomes more susceptible to the blandishments of entertainment or the offers of technical and clerical assistance made by the lobbyist. Not all succumb, but apparently enough do to create an unfavorable impression of lobbying techniques at the state level.

POLITICAL PARTICIPATION
AND DEMOCRATIC GOVERNANCE

We may now pull together the several threads that have run through this chapter to respond to the question "To what extent may it be said that the broad interests of the citizen body are represented by the decision-makers of government?" No single answer to such a basic question is

---

[26] Lester W. Milbrath, *The Washington Lobbyists* (Chicago: Rand McNally, 1963), p. 302.
[27] *Ibid.*, pp. 302–304.

likely to satisfy all of our readers. Yet we feel that it is possible to isolate the major differences of views held by political commentators on the subject and desirable to state our positions on them.

The findings of survey research are sufficiently clear to conclude that the average citizen is not highly involved in political undertakings. The act of voting is the single most important role he performs. Differences exist, however, over the importance to be attached to the voting decision. We believe that any decision that ultimately determines who will govern is of major significance. At the same time, we recognize as valid the arguments of those who suggest that our election contests often place in contention nominees of political parties whose labels convey no precise meaning to the majority of voters. Nevertheless, a choice is provided the voter. We attach importance to the fact that two sets of political leaders are competing to control the offices of government. The continued tenure of incumbent officers will depend upon currying popular favor, and this is one way the interests of broad segments of the citizen body are represented.

The activity of interest groups is a second way that citizen interests may be brought to the attention of public officials and is both supplementary to and dependent upon the influence of the ballot box. Given the vagueness of electoral mandates and the inherent impossibility of participation by all affected by a governmental decision, like-minded individuals—whether doctors, teachers, sanitation workers, veterans, contractors, or students—frequently band together and have their representatives speak for their interests and thus help shape the character of public debate. The fact that the top officials in government got there through popular election insures broadly based interests some degree of access to the decision-makers.

The difficult question which is often raised is the extent to which rank-and-file members actively participate in the policy-making of their organizations. The answer is seemingly straightforward. Michel's "iron law of oligarchies" is widely accepted as applying to organizations generally. Yet the implications of Michel's "law" are not so clearly seen. The focus of his study of European socialist parties was on their democratic *procedures* and not the *substance* of their goals.[28] This is an important distinction. It is still possible for rank-and-file interests to be represented in an organization that lacks internal democracy. Clark Kerr comes to a similar conclusion in discussing trade-union government in the United States.[29] The appropriate test of union "democracy," he argues, is the responsiveness of

[28] Betty H. Zisk (ed.), *American Political Interest Groups: Readings in Theory and Research* (Belmont, Calif.: Wadsworth, 1969), editor's introductory comments to chap. 3, p. 84.

[29] Clark Kerr, "Unions and Union Leaders of Their Own Choosing," in Zisk, *supra*, p. 116.

the leadership to membership desires and not the extent to which the membership participates in the decisional processes. We are inclined to accept the view that interest groups operating at the state and local level respond in varying degrees to the desires of those whom they purport to represent.

Even though it may be conceded that electoral decisions and interest group activity help shape public decisions, there are those who nevertheless believe that the tolerable limits of change in public policy are channeled within very narrow bounds. Thus the argument is made that the dominant elements in society determine, in effect, what the debate on public policy is to be over. The control that is suggested, at least by the more careful analysts, is not the covert machinations of a power elite; rather it is a more subtle thing, akin to Carl Friedrich's "rule of anticipated reactions." The politically active become socialized to what is permissible policy. Yet this is a tenuous kind of control which may be broken as new values replace old within the general population.

No objective observer will argue that state and local political systems equate with conventional ideals of democratic society. Indeed, survey research that shows the more politically active are better educated, receive greater income, and enjoy a higher status than the noninvolved suggests the bias of the systems. But we question whether the panacea is in greater participation by the citizen-body. The evidence is convincing that a limited number of political activists will continue to bear the burden of political activity, even in democratic societies. If this is accurate, then it suggests where one must focus his attention to insure that the system does not become rigid and unresponsive to major elements of American society. At the very least, there must be an opportunity for individuals from diverse ethnic, social, and economic backgrounds to enter the political stratum to plead their causes; and there must be a free and open network of communications so that what goes on in government can be widely disseminated and responded to by the politically active.

4. POLITICAL PARTIES AT THE STATE LEVEL

Perhaps the most fundamental issue in politics is the appropriate relationship between man and his government. In democratic societies government is presumed responsive to the needs, mood, and sentiments of the populace. The difficult problem, taking for granted that the political system has the accompaniment of institutions associated with democratic practice—electoral processes, deliberative assemblies, voluntary associations, and the like—is to provide a link between governors and governed that is rationally ordered. Providing such a rational linkage, some believe, is a major function of political parties.

Research has shown that the American voter has relatively little specific knowledge about the issues in political campaigns. He is unlikely to have listened to both sides of the campaign discussion, and weighed them, before making up his mind as to how he will cast his vote. If survey literature on the subject is accurate, how does one make sense out of the electoral processes? How can one argue that public officials are accountable to the voting public in any rational sense? The question is an intriguing one, and there are several possible answers discussed elsewhere. For the moment, though, we wish to focus on the role played by the political party.

In the classic two-party model of politics, the answer to the question posed above is simple and straightforward. The role of the party is to organize the electorate in support of its candidates and its program. The party adopts a platform, selects candidates for office, and backs its choices in the general election. The successful party then organizes the government in order to deliver on the promises made during the campaign. The manner in which the party is capable of meeting its platform commitments and campaign pledges then adds content to the meaning of the party label, and the process is repeated. A corporate image of the party emerges over time, so that the broad policy stances of each party can be identified and distinguished from that of the other. The voter comes to believe that one party rather than the other best serves his interest when in power. Thus he does not have to know a great deal about the individual qualifications of those who bear the party label to which he is committed. Should he become disenchanted with a particular party, he may change his allegiance; but a basic change in party attachment, not merely a vote for a candidate of the opposite party, is usually the product of substantial social, economic, or political upheaval in the country. Although the linkage provided is imprecise and vague, it is nevertheless argued that the system is basically a rational one. The party label, because its "meaning" is established by what the party does when it is in power, serves to orient the voter in making his electoral choices.

No one would contend that American parties have developed ideological positions comparable to European socialist and communist parties. Marxist parties in particular have developed a *Weltanschauung* which extends well beyond what Americans consider to be political. Yet some believe that American parties are not without their ideological content. Frank Sorauf argues effectively that the ideology implicit in both American parties is of great consequence because it sets the limits of political debate.[1] Broadly, the commitment of both parties is to capitalistic democracy signified by acceptance of our basic political, economic, and social institutions. Changes in public policy must come from within exist-

---

[1] Frank Sorauf, *Political Parties in the American System* (Boston: Little, Brown, 1964), p. 63.

ing institutions rather than an attack upon them. Those who do not seek change through orthodox channels are, by definition, extremists, on the fringe of the system.

Yet the fact that both parties subscribe to the same political ideology, however loosely it is articulated, does not mean that policy stands taken by the parties are indistinguishable. Parties at the national level can and have taken different positions on questions of taxation, business regulation, social justice, farm price supports, the level of government spending, the promotion and regulation of labor organizations, and other issues which are not negligible in their impact. The policy stands taken by each party reflect the interests of the electorate they have come to depend on for support. Seymour Martin Lipset argues: "The differences between the social bases of the two major parties which have held up for more than a century and a half suggest that those who believe in the Tweedledee-Tweedledum theory of American politics have been taken in by campaign rhetoric and miss the underlying basis of the cleavage."[2]

Yet if parties at the state level are to meet the role assigned them as brokers between people and their government, several conditions must be met. First, the political system must be sufficiently independent of external forces that the parties can be organized around state interests and offer meaningful alternatives of state policies. Second, the parties must be competitive so that the chances of victory for the minority party are not hopeless. Third, the parties must be sufficiently cohesive in backing a party program when in power that they have identifiable policy postures. Fourth, the programs of each party must be reasonably different from that of the other party. And fifth, party differences must be perceived by the voter and serve as the basis for his electoral choices. The conditions we have described are those of party under the familiar responsible-party model. The extent to which the conditions are met in state practice is the question to which we must now turn.

THE AUTONOMY OF STATE PARTIES

The dispersal of power characterized by our federal system has an impact upon the party system. By creating two levels of government, the constitutional framers insured that parties would find power bases in each to sustain partisan organizations. Actually, because of the development of local communities, we have three governmental levels where parties find the patronage and perquisites of officeholding sufficient to attract their interests and support their activities. Yet the several levels of

[2] Seymour M. Lipset, *Political Man* (Anchor Books ed.; New York: Doubleday, 1963), p. 329.

party are not each independent but are intertwined in a loose configuration of power.

The most obvious reason for the linking of national, state, and local party organizations is to mobilize support for national contests, particularly the Presidency. In a country so large that diversity can be overcome only with effective political management, national leaders must turn to state and local leaders who have command of preexisting organizations that can be used to turn out the vote in large numbers. The skills and resources of state and local politicians, when united, constitute a powerful force which would be difficult if not impossible to duplicate. No Presidential candidate can afford to shun such efforts on his behalf.

The relation between national organizations and state and local organizations, however, is not a one-way street. When support is accorded a Presidential contender, some return is expected that either will enhance the political fortunes of local leaders, will improve the electoral base of their organizations, or will benefit their state or region in some fashion in terms of future public policies. The fact of the matter is that Presidential races are a cooperative undertaking in which those who participate together expect to receive mutual advantages.

To the ties apparent from the party working together for national electoral victories must be overlaid the governmental machinery of federalism. The national legislature is composed of representatives from states and districts who are elected by local constituencies with only their party as a common bond. Because of regional diversity, the goals sought by Republican or Democratic congressional delegations may vary considerably, not simply among regions, but within states as well. Although party serves as a mechanism to overcome the dispersal of power in our governmental systems, its legislative members, dependent upon a local power base, often use the federal structure to pursue divisive goals.

What this all means is that there is both unity and diversity in the American party structure. Our concern here, however, is autonomy of the state political systems. Can we expect both cooperation among levels of party in seeking victory in national elections and isolation in a party's pursuit of state objectives? The answer must be in the negative. V. O. Key, Jr., has observed: "The governmental system may be federal but the voter in the polling booth usually is not."[3]

The reason why a state's political system cannot be considered an autonomous unit of a federal system is, in the first place, the fact that voting in state elections is influenced by the tides of national elections. Candidates at the state and local levels are swept into office on the coattails of popular Presidential candidates without regard for the peculiarities of candidate qualification, party stand, or campaign issues within

3 V. O. Key, Jr., *American State Politics* (New York: Knopf, 1956), p. 33.

the states. In other words, the mobilization of support is so effective that it temporarily overcomes the separateness of the several governmental and party systems. Figure 4.1 shows the relationship between Democratic party successes at state and national levels for Presidential election years.

At the same time that national tides might propel candidates into office who otherwise may have had little hope for electoral success, the conditions of federalism have operated in other regions to deny the minority-party candidates a chance for victory. When issues of a fundamental nature to a state or a region can be controlled only at the national level, it may require a solidarity toward the nation that affects the divisions that

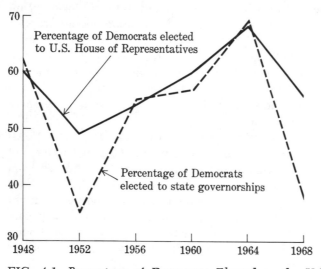

FIG. 4.1. *Percentage of Democrats Elected to the U.S. House of Representatives and to State Governorships: 1948–1968*

otherwise might occur in state politics. The states of the Confederacy, of course, have provided the most clear-cut but not the only example of this phenomenon. To protect the southern position on race relations, political contests in the South over a long period have been fought out largely within the Democratic party primary. Key maintains: "The party that functions as the sectional instrument becomes overwhelmingly dominant in state matters. The hopeless minority, although it may have a good cause locally, remains handicapped by the fact that it bears the name of the party that is the sectional enemy nationally."[4]

[4]   *Ibid.*, p. 24.

It would seem from the foregoing that a federal system seriously impedes the development of full-blown party politics within the states. Yet it would be inaccurate to assume that party systems at the state level are without vitality. Voting in state politics follows the same trend as in national elections, not because of the centripetal effect of the national campaigns alone, but because the voter wishes to see his government, no matter what level, move in the same direction. To the extent that the state parties represent interests similar to their national counterparts, one should expect a close correlation in voting between national and state elections.

Two related trends bode well for the meaningfulness of state party competition. One has been the gradual decline of the sectional politics that arose in the aftermath of the Civil War, destroyed first in the Northeast and the Midwest, and currently weakened in the South. A second trend, the increasing urbanization and industrialization of regions such as the South, provides the base for political divisions not unlike national party divisions or those experienced in other parts of the country. In other words, the nationalization of politics is being brought on by factors that can both create a two-party division at the state level and relate it to national party divisions. To the extent that such a development has occurred, one need not worry overly that national issues and candidate images interjected into state contests so obstruct the workings of local party systems that they are rendered ineffectual. On the contrary, the relationship might actually strengthen the state parties and give their label greater meaning.

States that remain primarily rural and agricultural may not divide politically in the same proportions as the more urban and industrial states. If the population of a state is relatively homogeneous, one may question whether dominance by a single party indicates irrational voting choices, particularly if there are lively contests within the primary. At the same time, the fact that a national campaign can sometimes elevate the minority party candidate into a position of power within a state provides a healthy opposition in government that may make the normal majority party more sensitive to popular needs.

THE EXTENT OF
TWO-PARTY COMPETITION

If what we have said about the autonomy of state parties is accurate, then there are no insuperable obstacles to state parties' functioning as part of a state political system. We must then turn to the second condition to be met if the two-party model is effectively to perform its brokerage role between people and their government. To what extent do parties compete on more or less equal terms for control of state government?

In attempting to measure the degree of interparty competition, several factors must be kept in mind. A state may be competitive in terms of Presidential elections and yet be dominated by one party in terms of state elections. The measure of competitiveness, then, must be restricted to state offices since we are interested in state politics *qua* state politics.

A second consideration is the time span selected for measurement. Too short a period may distort by catching a party that temporarily enjoys electoral success or suffers defeat due to forces that are transient in character. On the other hand, too lengthy a period may misrepresent competitiveness because the measures reflect conditions that are no longer applicable. For example, parties in the urban-industrial states of the North are surely among the most competitive. Yet if one's measure of competition includes the early decades of the twentieth century when the Republican party was firmly in control, today's competition would be hidden in the averages.

We shall apply an "index of competitiveness" developed by Austin Ranney to political conditions of the last twenty years. The index is based on an average of the following figures:[5]

1. The average percent of the popular vote won by Democratic gubernatorial candidates

2. The average percent of the seats in the state senate held by Democrats

3. The average percent of the seats in the state house of representatives held by the Democrats

4. The percent of all terms for governor, senate, and house in which the Democrats had control

The index may be interpreted in the following manner:[6]

.9000 or higher: one-party Democratic
.7000 to .8999: modified one-party Democratic
.3000 to .6999: two-party
.1000 to .2999: modified one-party Republican
.0000 to .0999: one-party Republican

Table 4.1 reveals that three fifths of our states maintain reasonably competitive party systems. The most obvious explanation for the number

[5] Austin Ranney, "Parties in State Politics," in Herbert Jacobs and Kenneth Vines (eds.), *Politics in the American States* (Boston: Little, Brown, 1965), p. 64.
[6] *Ibid.*

TABLE 4.1
The Fifty States Classified According to
Degree of Interparty Competition

ONE-PARTY DEMOCRATIC	MODIFIED ONE-PARTY DEMOCRATIC	TWO-PARTY		MODIFIED ONE-PARTY REPUBLICAN
Mississippi (.9672)	Tennessee (.8691)	West Va. (.6998)	Colorado (.4800)	Kansas (.2866)
South Carolina (.9659)	Florida (.8688)	Arizona (.6604)	Oregon (.4585)	North Dakota (.2832)
Georgia (.9629)	Virginia (.8656)	Hawaii (.6316)	Pennsylvania (.4426)	South Dakota (.2745)
Louisiana (.9612)	North Carolina (.8605)	Minnesota[a] (.6250)	Indiana (.4360)	Vermont (.2693)
Alabama (.9529)	Oklahoma (.7860)	Alaska (.6249)	Michigan (.4199)	
Texas (.9456)	Kentucky (.7537)	Rhode Island (.6131)	Utah (.4135)	
Arkansas (.9095)	Maryland (.7416)	Delaware (.6025)	Illinois (.4104)	
	New Mexico (.7112)	Washington (.5794)	New York (.3849)	
	Missouri (.7054)	Massachusetts (.5734)	Ohio (.3812)	
		Nevada (.5715)	Wisconsin (.3798)	
		California (.5414)	Iowa (.3795)	
		Connecticut (.5303)	Wyoming (.3767)	
		Nebraska[a] (.5000)	Idaho (.3723)	
		New Jersey (.4861)	Maine (.3373)	
		Montana (.4857)	New Hampshire (.3152)	

[a] Since Minnesota and Nebraska have formally nonpartisan legislatures, only their gubernatorial elections have been used to measure interparty competition.
SOURCE: The table is an updated version of Austin Ranney, "Parties in State Politics," in Herbert Jacobs and Kenneth Vines (eds.), *Politics in the American States* (Boston: Little, Brown, 1965), p. 65.

of one-party and modified one-party states is visually portrayed in Fig. 4.2. The distribution of Democratic and Republican one-party areas follows sectional lines that divided our national party politics in the past. Yet the sectional division does not tell all of the story. Why is it that the

☐ Two-party		⊠ Modified one-party Republican
⧄ One-party Democratic		⧄ Modified one-party Democratic

FIG. 4.2. *Level of State Party Competition*

Democratic party monopoly has persisted longer in the South than the Republican party dominance north of the Mason-Dixon line? The best answer that can be given is that the states that have been less affected by forces of change are the most likely to retain traditional party loyalties. Specifically, in the case of the southern Democratic stronghold, the reasons are threefold: (1) The immigration that hit our shores at the turn of the century and later provided such a leveling influence on American society largely by-passed the South. Dominated by a planter class whose agrarian philosophy was antithetical to industrialization, the South had no need for a cheap source of industrial labor. Blacks provided a suitable and cheap labor for its agriculture. (2) Partly as a consequence of its agricultural base, the South lagged behind the nation in urbanization. The nation became urban by census classification in 1920, the South as a region by 1960. (3) A key to southern politics has always been the peculiar importance of racial issues. An early attempt by southern Populists such as Tom Watson to portray economic issues as more important than racial divisions was unsuccessful. The South became racially polarized with the whites overlooking their own differences and accepting a planter-merchant-banker-lawyer ruling class. Table 4.2 shows differences between the South and the nation which may have political relevance.

Northern Republican sectionalism, on the other hand, did break up under the onslaught of New Deal style politics. Sectional solidarity gave way to issues based broadly along class-status lines. The heavy migration of peoples from southern and eastern Europe, urbanization and industrialization, and the deprivations imposed by the Depression combined to convince the voter that differences between the haves and the have-nots in our society held political significance. The states that fought on the Union side (or were settled by Union loyalists) and that still cling to their sectional party are once again those that have felt less keenly the winds of change. The characteristics of the modified one-party Republican states are shown in Table 4.3.

INTERPARTY DIFFERENCE
AND INTRAPARTY COHESION

If party is to realize its responsibilities, one presumes that it should be able to organize the executive and legislative branches of government, maintain reasonable cohesion in the legislative body, and develop a program or policy stance with which it may be identified and distinguished from the opposition. What we have to say must apply basically to the two-party states. Parties that dominate their states assuredly will organize both branches of government, and the central thrust of their program may even be distinguished from the opposition minority party. But they are unlikely to exhibit legislative cohesion and are more prone to engage in factional contests.

The surprising thing about the two-party states is the incidence of divided party control of government—that is, the number of times that the minority party controls cither the governor's chair or one or both houses of the legislature. Two explanations may be offered to explain this breakdown in party government. A minority party is more competitive in gubernatorial politics than for control of the legislative body. The organizational requirements to contest legislative seats throughout a state are sizable and not uncommonly outrun the resources a minority party has at its disposal. That the minority party is able to win one or both houses of the legislature may also be due to malapportionment (certainly this was a prime cause before recent Court decisions set down the principle of one-man one-vote) or simply gerrymandering. As we explain elsewhere, a

TABLE 4.2
Selected Characteristics of One-Party Democratic States, 1960

STATES	% POPULATION URBAN	% WORKFORCE IN MFG.	MEDIAN FAMILY INCOME	MEDIAN SCHOOL YEAR COMPLETED	% POPULATION NONWHITE	% POPULATION FOREIGN STOCK
Alabama	55.0	26.5	$3937	9.1	30.1	1.7
Arkansas	42.8	20.1	3184	8.9	21.9	1.9
Florida	74.0	13.1	4722	10.9	17.9	14.8
Georgia	55.3	26.3	4208	9.0	28.6	1.9
Louisiana	63.3	15.6	4272	8.8	32.1	3.8
Mississippi	37.7	19.2	2884	8.9	42.3	1.3
North Carolina	39.5	31.7	3956	8.9	25.4	1.5
South Carolina	41.2	32.0	3821	8.7	34.9	1.6
Tennessee	52.3	26.0	3949	8.8	16.5	1.6
Texas	75.0	16.3	4884	10.4	12.6	11.3
Virginia	55.8	22.4	4964	9.9	20.8	4.5
Average	53.8	22.7	4071	9.3	25.7	4.2
United States	69.9	27.1	5660	10.6	11.4	19.0

TABLE 4.3
Selected Characteristics of Modified One-Party Republican States, 1960

STATES	% POPULATION URBAN	% WORKFORCE IN MFG.	MEDIAN FAMILY INCOME	MEDIAN SCHOOL YEARS COMPLETED	% POPULATION NONWHITE	% POPULATION FOREIGN STOCK
Kansas	61.0	16.6	$5295	11.7	4.6	9.4
North Dakota	35.2	3.7	4530	9.3	2.0	30.0
South Dakota	39.3	6.6	4251	10.4	4.0	20.8
Vermont	38.5	25.0	4890	10.9	0.2	22.0
Average	43.5	13.0	4741.5	10.6	2.7	20.6
United States	69.9	27.1	5660	10.6	11.4	19.0

legislative district can be equally apportioned but, through the gerry-mander, can still unfairly prefer one party over the other.[7] The incidence of divided control is portrayed in Table 4.4.

TABLE 4.4
*Incidence of Divided Party Control
of State Governments*

CONTROL	1962		1964		1966	1968
	Ala.	Mo.	Ala.	Md.	Ala.	Ala.
	Ark.	N.M.	Alaska	Miss.	Conn.	Conn.
	Calif.	N.C.	Ariz.	Mo.	Ga.	Ga.
	Del.	S.C.	Ark.	N.Mex.	Haw.	Haw.
	Fla.	Tenn.	Calif.	N.C.	Ky.	Ky.
	Ga.	Tex.	Del.	S.C.	La.	La.
Democratic control	Haw.	Va.	Fla.	Tenn.	Miss.	Md.
of legislative and	Ky.	Wash.	Ga.	Tex.	Mo.	Miss.
executive branches	La.	W.Va.	Haw.	Utah	N.C.	Mo.
	Md.		Ind.	Va.	S.C.	N.C.
	Mass.		Iowa	W.Va.	Tenn.	R.I.
	Miss.		Ky.		Tex.	S.C.
			La.		Va.	Tex.
					W.Va.	Va.
						W.Va.
	Colo.		Idaho		Alaska	Ariz.
	Idaho		Kans.		Ariz.	Colo.
	Kans.		S.Dak.		Colo.	Idaho
	Maine				Idaho	Ill.
Republican control	Mich.				Ohio	Ind.
of legislative and	N.Y.				Pa.	Iowa
executive branches	Ohio				S.Dak.	N.H.
	Pa.				Wis.	Ohio
	S.Dak.				Wyo.	S.D.
	Utah					Vt.
	Wyo.					Wis.
						Wyo.
	Ill.		N.H.		Ill.	Del.
	Ind.		N.J.		Kans.	Kans.
Democratic governor	Iowa		Vt.		Me.	Me.
opposed by Republican	N.H.				N.H.	N.J.
legislature	N.J.				N.J.	N.Dak.
	N.Dak.				N.Dak.	Utah
	Vt.				Utah	
	Wis.				Vt.	

[7] See Chapter 6, pp. 124–125.

TABLE 4.4 (*Continued*)

CONTROL	1962	1964	1966	1968
Republican governor opposed by Democratic legislature	Ariz. Okla. Ore. R.I.	Me. Mass. Mich. Mont. N.Y. Okla. R.I. Wash.	Ark. Calif. Fla. Md. Mass. Nev. N.Mex. Okla. R.I.	Ark. Fla. Mass. N.Mex. Okla.
Democratic governor opposed by one Republican legislative chamber	Conn. Nev.	Conn. Ill. N.Dak.	Ind. Iowa	Mont.
Republican governor opposed by one Democratic legislative chamber	Mont.	Colo. Ore. Pa. Wis. Wyo.	Mont. N.Y. Oreg. Wash.	Alaska Mich. Nev. N.Y. Oreg. Pa. Wash.

It is obvious that party cannot perform its functions if it has to share control of government with its opposition. If cohesion is maintained within the legislative parties, the likely result will be frustration rather than facilitation of orderly government. Although based on only one year's legislative experience, Wayne Francis' data supports the generally accepted thesis that divided control impairs the policy-making process. His index of policy success was highest for states with competitive parties in which one party was in control of the government, and lowest for states that were competitive and in which control of government was divided.[8]

Yet it is not sufficient for the establishment of responsibile party government merely that a single party organizes the government. The party must be strong enough to write a legislative program in keeping with its traditional stand on state policies. More than this, the parties must contest state issues so that the voting public can rely on the meaning of a party label to fix the general policy postures of those who run under a given banner.

[8] Wayne L. Francis, *Legislative Issues in the Fifty States: A Comparative Analysis* (Chicago: Rand McNally, 1967), p. 55.

The data to support intraparty cohesion and interparty difference are based fundamentally on roll-call analysis which is discussed more fully in Chapter 6. It is important here to note that one must distinguish between the electoral competitiveness of parties and the competitiveness they show in contesting issues of public policy within government. The parties may contest election battles on even terms, yet the campaign rhetoric may provide few clues as to how the legislator will line up with his colleagues in support of the party program. Thus, although the contrasts are probably exaggerated, John Fenton distinguishes between what he terms "job-oriented" parties, interested only in patronage and perquisites of office holding, and "issue-oriented" parties, concerned with contemporary issues of the day.[9] Fenton describes Illinois, Ohio, and Indiana as essentially job-oriented, while Wisconsin, Michigan, and Minnesota are issue-oriented. The importance of the distinction is the meaning the party label holds for the voter in weighing his electoral decisions.

The pattern that emerges with some regularity from interstate comparisons of party competition is that the urban-industrial states of the Midwest and the East come closest to a competitive two-party model in which the parties divide on a large number of issues. Moreover, although matters of self-interest to the parties are prominent among the list of divisive issues, taxation, finance, labor, and social welfare policies are also commonly contested along partisan lines.[10] Such divisions parallel the differences between the parties nationally and suggest that the images of the parties at the two governmental levels are comparable, particularly in those states most like the country nationally.

VOTER PERCEPTIONS

The final requisite of the responsible party model is that the voter perceive the differences between the parties and identify with the one he feels best promotes his interest. The data to test for this requirement have not been fully developed because research has focused more on voter attitude toward the national parties. If the parties perform a comparable role at both governmental levels, which is often the case, then one could make analogous inferences. Such inferences lead to the conclusion that voter identification is likely to be based on interests rather than ideology, or to be vague and general as to reason.[11] Yet differences are perceived by the voter, however lacking in eloquence are the reasons cited. Perhaps

9 John H. Fenton, *Midwest Politics* (New York: Holt, Rinehart & Winston, 1966), p. 1.
10 Francis, *op. cit.*, p. 24.
11 Angus Campbell, Philip E. Converse, Warren E. Miller, and Donald E. Stokes, *The American Voter* (New York: Wiley, 1960), chap. 10.

one should not expect the average voter to articulate fluently the reasons he has identified with a party when his choice was made for him a generation ago by the circumstances into which he was born.

There are data that support the assumption that voter identification with a party makes sense in terms of the performance of the parties. At least, one can show relations between the socioeconomic make-up of a constituency and the way its legislative representative casts his vote. As we have already argued, simply proving that the electoral make-up of the parties differs is insufficient evidence that the parties act responsibly toward the electorate. One must also show that the party divisions within a legislature relate to party divisions within the electorate in terms of meaningful criteria. One of the authors attempted to correlate socioeconomic constituency factors with the stand of the parties on legislative issues in state senates.[12] Generally, in states characterized by competitive parties with high legislative cohesion, legislative-constituency relations appeared to be logical—that is, the stand taken by a majority in each party could be linked to a constituency base that made sense in terms of the conventional interpretation of who supports the Republican and Democratic parties. What this means is that where the responsible party model is most closely approximated in the states, the constituencies represented by each of the parties are relatively homogeneous and distinct from one another, and the program of each party is built with an eye toward its constituency base. The conditions for such a party system are most closely approximated in the urban-industrial states east of the Mississippi. Where such conditions apply, the evidence strongly suggests that voters will perceive differences between the parties and will vote their interests in election contests.

PARTY ORGANIZATION

In discussing the structure of political parties, a danger exists that the full significance of party will be understated. Much of the importance of party lies in the corporate image it acquires over time. It is the image that is the potent force in mobilizing support behind the party banner, attracting candidate and voter alike. The image is developed scarcely at all by the formal party structure.

Although any on-going organization must have a structure and members, they are uncommonly difficult to describe in the case of political parties. The problem lies in the several elements that make up the party

[12] Hugh L. LeBlanc, "Voting in State Senates: Party and Constituency Influences," *Midwest Journal of Political Science*, XIII (February, 1969), 33–57.

structure. The simplest to come to grips with are the committees, conventions, and caucuses usually prescribed or regulated by state statute. This element of party might be labeled as the formal party bureaucracy, although the term should not convey any elaborate organizational structure.

A second element of party is composed of the candidates and officeholders. In many senses it is the most important segment of party because its quality will have the greatest impact upon the conduct of governance. Some duplication invariably occurs between the officeholders and those who manage the party's formal structure. Nevertheless, the activities of the two are quite distinct.

The third element of party is the membership. In the strictest sense the members of a political party organization should include only those who devote a substantial portion of time to party work. This would exclude those in the electorate who merely support the candidates of a given party. Nevertheless, the following (or party-in-the-electorate, as it is sometimes called) is of consequence in determining the nature of the organization. As we contended in the last section, a party's constituency exerts a powerful force on the stand party members take on legislative issues.

The point we wish to convey is that, given the nature of the political party, one cannot neatly set down the network of relationships that exist among its several elements. We hope that the role of each element will be made clear as it is discussed in other chapters. We shall proceed now to discuss the formal party structure with the understanding that it does not convey the diffuse character of the party organization.

According to the literature of public administration, one of the common bases of organization is in accordance with the major purpose or objectives of the enterprise. In the case of American parties, winning election contests is widely considered their basic task. State laws regulating political parties reflect this notion by prescribing an organizational structure built around the electoral divisions of the state. Given this organization style, and its seasonal character, American parties are not geared to indoctrinate and educate in the manner of European socialist parties.[13] Whether American parties are simply electoral parties without programmatic content, the parties are organized as if election victories were their basic goal.

A state's formal party structure presents a bewildering array of patterns and powers. In no state is the party centralized through a formal hierarchy, although informally organized factions or cliques such as the legendary Byrd machine in Virginia may wield considerable power. The state central committee or executive committee, by whatever name, is nominally the apex of the organization. Members are selected either by

13 Maurice Duverger, *Political Parties* (New York: Wiley, 1954), pp. 23–27.

primary contests, state conventions, locally held caucuses or, on occasion, serve *ex officio* by virtue of county posts held. In addition to functions associated with the call of a state convention or related to the conduct of party primaries, the central committees issue party propaganda and may even maintain research units for this purpose. They are important in some states in two additional ways. They may endorse an official slate of candidates who then supposedly are given an advantage in running in the party's primary. The state committee may also be prominent in the selection of delegates to the national convention and in the commitment of those delegates. Still one should not exaggerate these roles since the state committeemen are probably acting as the lieutenants for the governor, United States Senator, or other officeholders.

The effective organization at the local level is the county committee, although on occasion city committees also function. The county committee is composed of party functionaries from the county's political subdivisions—precinct, ward, township, or other unit. They are sometimes appointed, sometimes selected in caucus or convention, and sometimes elected in primary contests. The local committees represent real, although declining, political power in many cities. The county chairman, through the power base of the "delivery" wards, directed the legions of the fabled political machines of days now gone. He still is important in overseeing the grass-roots campaign to get the vote out for candidates seeking office at all governmental levels. The county committee also endorses slates of candidates in primary elections and may assist in the dispensing of such patronage available when their party holds office.

What the formal hierarchy of a political party suggests in most states is the existence of an experienced coterie of political activists for whom politics is either a profession or, at least, an avocation. When grouped together in their formal capacity as members of the party bureaucracy, they may possess few important powers. Yet it would be a mistake to denigrate their role in a state's politics. Virtually no phase of party process—candidate selection, issue formulation, electioneering—escapes their attention in their role as informal managers of the corporate party. It is they to whom aspiring leaders as well as seasoned veterans must turn for advice, counsel, and support. The party professionals leave their imprint on the politics of the states in ways not seen in their official decision-making.

PARTY NOMINATIONS

One of the more important functions of political parties is the selection of candidates to compete for the offices of government. If one reflects on the social and economic diversity that characterizes the average-sized state, one can grasp the powerful organizational force exerted on the American electorate. By making their selections, the parties effectively limit the number who may realistically compete for a share of governmental power. The manner in which the parties nominate their candidates then must have important consequences to the workings of the party system and, indeed, the political system itself.

Selection of those who will bear the party label in general elections is in the hands of party professionals in most democratic countries. This was the case in the United States until the latter part of the nineteenth century, when the technique of the direct primary was first introduced. The pressure for reform of the convention system came initially from states in which a single party was dominant. How could there be popular participation if an inner core of party leaders selected candidates whose opposition in the general election was only nominal? The primary was first developed as a party device in South Carolina under "Pitchfork Ben" Tillman, but soon was in wide use in the Progressive strongholds of the West as a legal prescription. From there it spread throughout the country so that today only three states retain the convention system for making statewide nominations—Delaware, Indiana, and Connecticut. New York abandoned the convention method only in 1967.

The objective of the primary as a technique is to take control of nominations away from the political professionals and place it in the hands of the people. The movement reflected the Progressive's suspicion of the evils of partisanship and his faith in the power of the people to purify politics. The direct primary was only one of the institutional devices sought by the Progressive movement. The direct election of senators, the initiative, referendum and recall, nonpartisan elections, and city manager government later advocated for municipalities were all part of the same reform strain.

While introduction of the direct primary in areas of one-party control is easily understood, some students of politics, and probably most political professionals, would debate its need in a state with vigorous two-party competition. The argument in support of the convention system runs somewhat as follows. In order to perform adequately the functions set down in the responsible two-party model, a party must be assured that those who bear its label are truly committed to its program and traditional principles insofar as they are known. The party professionals, it is argued, are best equipped to know the qualifications of candidates and to exercise sanctions should there be a need. They know when it is necessary to compromise, are more willing to see the point of view of an opposing side and, above all, are concerned with the need for containing differences within the "family." Moreover, in a convention setting, alternative strategies for agreeing on a candidate and platform are available that are precluded in the either-or choice of a primary. Popular sentiment cannot be disregarded, since the convention delegates must be mindful of the strength of their candidates in the general electorate. And the final choice of who is to hold office is in the hands of the voter as he selects between the party nominees.

The argument of the professionals has its persuasive points. And it may be true that the quality of nominees in the convention states compares favorably with that in the primary states. Still, a great deal of trust is placed in the hands of party professionals whose decisions will affect the quality of state leadership and shape the character of public debate. Are the party activists committed to a consistent set of principles? Is the desire to accomplish program goals uppermost in the minds of convention delegates, or do matters of narrow self-interest dictate the candidate choice? That there exists a popular skepticism toward political professionals is shown in the almost total eclipse of the delegate convention as a nominating device in the vast majority of states.

The direct primary used in the nonconvention states has two basic varieties. The most commonly employed is the closed primary, so-called because of its intent to limit participation to those who are party members. The critical feature of a closed primary is the test used to determine party membership. States that require the voter to declare his affiliation at the time of registration as a basis for determining eligibility are the most effective. Those that permit the voter to declare his affiliation at the time of voting, even though subject to challenge by poll watchers, are scarcely more exclusive than the open primary. In Virginia, for example, the closed primary presents few barriers to prevent even Republican precinct workers from entering the Democratic primaries where commonly the real battle for office takes place.

In the open primary states the voter may choose without restriction which primary he wishes to cast his vote. Only in Washington, however, can he participate in the primaries of both parties. Marking his selections on a consolidated ballot, the voter in Washington may indicate his choice among the candidates offered by one of the parties for a given office, and then make a selection from the candidates offered by the other party for a second office. The voter may not express both a Republican and a Democratic choice for the same office.

The significance of the eligibility tests for voting in the primaries is in the size and composition of the turnout. In the closed primary states that effectively restrict voting to party members, the party leadership and candidates are more likely to know the electorate to whom they make their appeals. In an open primary state, or a closed primary state without rigid qualifications, the electorate is likely more fluid. Particularly if a primary battle is lacking in the opposing party, the number of voters who will cross over is unknown and the candidates will not know how to pitch their campaign appeals.

No empirical evidence points to a "raid" of a party's primary by members of the opposition party who consciously seek to nominate the weakest candidate of their opponents in order to enhance their own chance for victory in the general election. Nevertheless, voters frequently cross over in primary battles and bring with them attitudes that are scarcely representative of the general political outlook of their opposite numbers. By registering their choice, even with the best of intentions, they may embarrass a party by assisting in nominating a candidate who is not the choice of a majority of its loyal supporters or is not its most effective vote-getter in the general election.

The political professional has other reservations about the use of the primary. In order to secure the nomination, candidates may resort to rhetoric on the campaign trail that opens wounds within the state party electorate that do not heal before the general election. The bitterness of a primary battle that is allowed to spill over into the general election is a constant fear of the professional. He would much prefer to work in the smoke-filled rooms to seek accommodations that will preserve party unity.

The crux of the problem, as the professionals see it, is the control they may exercise over the nominating process. They would prefer no primary contest and, indeed, Key has found evidence to suggest that they are sometimes successful in preventing primary battles where stiff competition is faced in the general election.[14] However, the problem is not confined simply to divisions within party ranks induced by candidates vying for the nomination. A second problem concerns the strength of candidates in the statewide electorate.

Often the combined turnout in the primaries in the two-party states is far less than the turnout for the general election. Those most likely to vote in the primaries are the hard-core party supporters, the party militants. The candidates who are their choices may not meet with general approbation. Key describes the dilemma of the Massachusetts Democrats whose primaries were often dominated by the Boston Irish.[15] The candidates nominated, including James Curley following a prison sentence, had little appeal to the Yankee stock who voted in the general election. Only with the institution of a preprimary convention could the party professionals endorse a slate with a mixture of ethnic strains and a greater statewide appeal. The convention slate is marked by asterisks on the Massachusetts primary ballot.

The professional worries too about the party maverick, or candidate with an independent frame of mind, who eschews the tutelage offered by

---

[14] Key, *op. cit.*, pp. 110–111.
[15] *Ibid.*, pp. 154 ff.

the party leaders. Such a figure might have considerable popular strength and win nomination regardless of efforts by the party organization to prevent it. If elected, he need pay little heed to the counsel of the professionals to whom he owes no responsibility. At best, such a personality may breathe new life into the party. At worst, the image and tradition of the party in the minds of the voters may be eroded to the extent that future candidates have no firm base on which to campaign. Herein lies the destruction of party responsibility.

POLITICAL PARTIES, POLITICAL PROFESSIONALS, AND GOVERNANCE

The central theme of this chapter has been the role played by political parties and political professionals in supporting governance at the state level. Starting with a description of the responsible party model of politics, we attempted to show its applicability to state systems. We were not arguing that the conditions conducive to the operation of the theoretical model were everywhere in evidence among the states; indeed, the very existence of one-party areas stands as a contradiction to the idea of responsible party government. We do believe that the growth in the number of competitive states augurs well for an enhanced role of party in mobilizing majority support for governance. That the role of party at the state level is increasingly signficant in controlling access to leadership posts and in developing policy postures on state issues is viewed with approval by those who subscribe to the values implicit in the responsible party model. Indeed, in the abstract, we also are similarly convinced of its worth.

Yet one cannot accept the arguments of party professionals and responsible party enthusiasts uncritically. Their logic is compelling only if the parties are well-organized enterprises that alternate in their control of government and exhibit cohesion in support of the party program when in power. But where the party professionals are more concerned with matters of self-interest, or where the professionals have not developed a policy stance that has become identified with their party in the minds of the voters, then one may question the wisdom of enhancing their power. Participatory democracy, the cry of those who seek the "new politics," may be necessary to prevent unimaginative leaders from continuing to wield power in a manner that is unresponsive to a society rent by divisions of black and white, young and old, and the poor and the affluent. When we have emphasized the thinking of the political professionals, we meant no more than that the political party *can* be used as an effective instrument of majority government.

5. THE POLITICS OF THE STATE EXECUTIVE

It is now a commonplace that chief executives at all governmental levels have undertaken increased responsibility for the formulation of public policies. The role has been thrust on them. Rapid social change under conditions of an urban-industrial society creates tensions and unrest within the citizen-body that demand the attention of governmental authorities. The call for action cannot be answered in the leisurely pace of deliberative assemblies; it requires a show of activity that can be met, if at all, in the energy of executive action. The governor's leadership role, it is said, is not due simply to the nature of the office. It arises as well from popular expectations that a chief executive should be able to lead.

Yet for all the demands placed upon chief executives, the nature of executive power is little understood by the general public.

THE NATURE OF EXECUTIVE POWER

That confusion exists over the nature of executive power is amply illustrated by the vexing problem it has presented to the United States Supreme Court. In the decision in *Youngstown Sheet and Tube Company v. Sawyer*,[1] for example, each of the six justices in the majority felt compelled to write a separate opinion justifying his vote. Stripped to its essentials, the case seemed simple enough. The President of the United States had seized privately owned property and alleged that his action was supported by constitutional grants of executive power. Considered in the context of Anglo-Saxon law with its respect for the rights of property, the Presidential action was rather remarkable. Yet for all this, no two justices in the majority could agree why the action was invalid, while the three dissenting justices were united in their support of the Presidential seizure. If the highest judicial tribunal is uncertain of the limits of executive power, what of the populace?

Perplexity over the nature of executive power stems in part from misconceptions of the doctrine of separation of powers. Although every schoolboy learns to recite that the three branches are coordinate, there is still widespread belief that the legislative branch is superior in declaring the "public interest." This is so because it is looked upon as the representative branch, the deliberative branch, and thus having a better claim that it represents "the people," the source of power. That the legislative branch is looked upon as the highest branch springs also from the traditional distrust of executive power, which can be traced to our colonial heritage and the opposition to the royal governors as symbolic of the crown. Executive tyranny was and is feared more than the tyranny exercised by legislative assemblies.

The paradoxical fact is that chief executives on the whole, and for a variety of causes, have represented more popular forces in our body politic than legislatures, perhaps since the days of Andrew Jackson in the case of national politics, and more recently in the case of state politics. And since the executive has become the initiator of public policies, his office has become the best instrument for pursuing an innovative strategy —that is, one that seeks change or a new way of dealing with governmental problems. By the same reasoning, the legislature has become increasingly the critic or check upon executive power. Because of the many places in the legislative process that executive proposals can be

[1]   343 U.S. 599 (1952).

killed, the legislature has become the primary instrument of those pursuing a defensive strategy—one designed to preserve the status quo.

The confusion over appropriate roles to be played by the two branches arises from the basic conflict within the popular mind. Since many still distrust executive power and praise the representative character of legislative assemblies, they see no reason why executive leadership should be enhanced. At the same time that they are unwilling to equip the governor with the powers to do so, they nevertheless expect him to lead. Until gubernatorial leadership potential is brought into line with popular expectations, the governor in many states will find it difficult to satisfy his constituents.

THE FUNCTIONS OF THE GOVERNOR

The orthodox manner of discussing the functions performed by an executive is to refer to the various "hats" he wears—as party chief, legislative leader, head of the administrative establishment, or as leader of some other activity necessarily undertaken by a chief executive. This approach does have some descriptive utility but is of doubtful analytical value. In trying to provide leadership for his state, the governor does not perceive his activities as compartmentalized but rather as what he must do in order to develop a successful program for his state. If one starts with the assumption that public policy is the end of the political process, then one may divide the activities of the governor into three broad areas of operations that he must undertake to discharge his responsibilities. As described by Coleman Ransone, these are policy formulation, management, and public relations.[2]

The three functions are interrelated in practice but are nevertheless analytically distinct. Under the rubric of policy formulation, the governor endeavors to influence his legislature, lead his administration, and exert policy control over his party or, in some cases, party factions. The program he develops may or may not signify a radical departure from existing policies, but it is his program and he will be identified with it. To enact it into law and to fund it he must deal with diverse groups, both governmental and nongovernmental, and does not feel he is changing hats constantly as he arduously works to see his policies effectuated.

The governor's role in management is not easily distinguishable from that of his activities in policy formulation. They both will affect the character of his program. Yet Ransome felt that the governors themselves

[2] Coleman B. Ransone, Jr., *The Office of Governor in the United States* (University, Ala.: University of Alabama Press, 1956), Part II.

saw a distinctiveness in the two areas of operation. Policy formulation activities were more directed to the development of legislative policies, although, of course, they might involve negotiations with agency heads as well as party and legislative leaders. The management function was more directed to the successful execution of his program. The primary effort of the governors in management is not in overseeing day-to-day operations; they have neither the time nor the authority, given the dispersal of power in the typical state administrative establishment. Rather, it is a broad effort at coordination which requires bargaining, persuasion, and compromise to insure that the gubernatorial program is put into operation with a minimum of conflict or resistance on the part of the administrative agencies.

The governor's role in public relations is one designed to insure a favorable view of the chief executive and his program within the state. The governor makes public speeches, addresses radio and TV audiences, attends social and professional gatherings, answers a formidable amount of correspondence, and grants countless interviews, all mainly in the name of public-support building. Ransone quotes with approval from the Forrestal diary that ". . . the difficulty of Government work is that it not only has to be well done, but the public has to be convinced that it is being well done."[3]

One aspect of Ransone's analysis is particularly revealing. When interviewed, governors tended to describe their duties in terms of the relative importance of the tasks they performed. Thus the policy formulation and management aspects of their work were emphasized. The same priorities do not emerge in describing the relative amount of time spent on each of their major activities. The weekly schedule of the governor of New Hampshire (Table 5.1) was compiled from his activities in each of three weeks selected randomly in 1949 and is illustrative if not typical. As Ransone writes:

> Perhaps the most significant point which emerges is the amount of time which the governor spends on correspondence, telephone calls, interviews, travel, and speechmaking. While all of these may be concerned with either policy or management, they may also be classified partly as public relations. Most of the governor's correspondence and telephone calls as well as the majority of his interviews are concerned with problems which are presented by the state's citizens rather than by party leaders, legislators, or department heads. . . . This aspect of the governor's functions emerges as the most time-consuming if not the most important of his duties on the evidence presented in this section.[4]

3 *Ibid.,* p. 153.
4 *Ibid.,* pp. 137–138.

TABLE 5.1[a]
Weekly Schedule of the Governor
of New Hampshire

ACTIVITY		AVERAGE TIME SPENT IN ACTIVITY
Correspondence		9 hrs. 40 min.
Phone calls		3 hrs. 30 min.
Interviews		20 hrs.
with members of the legislature	5 hrs.	
with department heads and officers	4 hrs. 20 min.	
with citizens	4 hrs.	
with job seekers	1 hr. 20 min.	
with the press	1 hr.	
on industrial development	1 hr.	
with party leaders	1 hr.	
on state reorganization	1 hr.	
on employee reclassification study	40 min.	
on miscellaneous matter	40 min.	
Meetings		7 hrs. 20 min.
of governor's council	4 hrs.	
with state boards and commissions	2 hrs.	
on political matters	1 hr. 20 min.	
Making and writing speeches		3 hrs. 30 min.
Travel		10 hrs. 30 min.
"Dignitary" matters (Such affairs as christening *U.S. Pickerel*, bill-signing ceremonies, meeting groups of school children, acting as honored guest at various meetings.)		9 hrs.
Total time spent on week's activities		63 hrs. 30 min.

[a] Based on figures taken from "What Does a Governor Do?" *The New Hampshire Taxpayer*, XII (January, 1950), 1.
SOURCE: Coleman B. Ransone, Jr., *The Office of Governor in the United States* (University, Ala.: University of Alabama Press, 1956), p. 137.

THE GOVERNOR
AS POLICY LEADER

A critical factor in the governance of a state is the ability of the governor to pyramid power sufficient to push his program through the state legislature and give direction to his administrative establishment. The governor's ability to amass power follows no rigid pattern, but we may distinguish at least three sources of his influence: personal, extra-legal, and legal-institutional. As a political strategist, the governor draws upon his resources to fit the issues at hand. In some cases his legal authority may be clear and he need worry only about the public response to his action (for example, in vetoing an unwanted item in an appropriation bill). In other situations the governor may lack the necessary authority to act and must rely on his personal skill, backed by such support as he can command from his administrative agencies and private organizations and groups, to effect an acceptable settlement of an issue. Thus the governor confronted by a legislature organized by the opposition party must marshal his forces astutely to obtain his legislative program and establish a positive record for his administration. Obviously, no two governors will have the same amount of political resources or will use their resources to the same extent. Nevertheless, it is possible to suggest some of the factors that tend to enhance a governor's leadership potential as well as those that tend to handicap the governor in exercising a forceful leadership.

Personal Resources

Perhaps there is no more important variable affecting the governor's leadership role than the personal values, attributes, and skills he brings to the office. In the first place, his views of the office will affect the style of leadership he adopts. He may view his role as one that requires the exercise of a forceful leadership that will either lead to innovative policies in his state or will halt or reverse the direction of state policy-making. Alternatively, the governor may disdain such ambitious undertakings and see his role as an overseer or caretaker of government operations without challenging in any significant way the traditional manner of handling the public business. The role he assigns himself may be influenced also by his assessment of the political risks entailed. Thus he may believe that his political future would benefit from a successful attack on a broad range of established policies but judge that the opposition to such an attempt requires more modest moves. Whether based on abstract political doctrines or strategies designed to protect his political future, the governor's personal values will determine the extent to which he asserts himself in leading his state.

The role that the governor sees for himself as the correct and politically feasible one to undertake does not in itself determine his leadership style. He must also possess the skills and traits required to play his selected role. They are more demanding the more the leadership is assertive. Some individuals possess personal qualities that command respect, elicit trust, convey confidence, inspire large audiences, or otherwise induce others to do their bidding. Such qualities are hard to describe because they are not the same even for leaders of pronounced charisma or personal magnetism. One either has such attributes of personality or lacks them. But by building upon the qualities possessed, a governor can learn to take advantage of his leadership position.

Richard Neustadt counsels a President, in a way applicable as well to a governor, to protect both his "Washington reputation" and his public prestige.[5] By the former, Neustadt refers to the professional reputation of an executive. If he shows that he is a knowledgeable and tough-minded leader, who will not hesitate to use the powers of his office to discipline the uncooperative and favor his supporters, he may actually avoid conflicts that would weaken his position. The word will spread among those who are professionally tied to the world of the state capital that the resolve of the governor is not to be lightly taken. His friends will know that they will be protected in pursuing his policy aims, his opponents will learn that opposition is not easily forgiven.

A governor's position is made more secure if he maintains a respected public image. It becomes for him an independent source of influence, although he may draw upon this resource in enhancing his professional reputation. Both the governor and his political antagonists must weigh the public responses to their actions. Thus the governor may capitalize upon his popular support to see his legislative program through, counter the moves of an agency head who has challenged his authority, or thwart the efforts of an interest group that has opposed his program.

Both to enhance his professional reputation and to build a desirable public image, according to Neustadt, the executive must be conscious of the choices he makes.[6] The goals toward which a governor works, what he says and does, to whom he speaks and when, a decision to remain silent, all involve choices that may affect his general reputation. He must make his choices with an awareness that they affect his personal power stake. He has no other means of building the reputation he desires that rests entirely in *his* hands.

Extralegal Resources

The governor possesses an inherent advantage over his competitors in striving for leadership in his state. His office is the most prominent position in state government and is awarded on the basis of a statewide, popular contest. Because what the governor says and does can influence the course of public policy within a state, his actions and remarks are reported by the news media. Already more visible to the public than lesser political figures, the governor becomes even better known as he

[5]   Richard E. Neustadt, *Presidential Power* (New York: Wiley, 1960), particularly chaps. 4 and 5.
[6]   *Ibid.,* p. 107.

grapples with the problems confronting his administration. In the hands of an able tactician, the ability to attract an audience is a political resource of no little significance. At the very least, it means that the governor has an opportunity to justify the stands he has taken on issues of major importance to the state. If the explanations of his official conduct meet with general approbation, the governor finds himself with a firm electoral base which will enhance his leadership potential.

The fact that the governor can have his voice heard with little difficulty does not insure the credibility of what he has to say. And if the electorate is badly divided over an issue on which he must take a stand, he may desire at times a lower public profile. His adeptness at knowing not only what to say but when it is best to remain silent may determine whether he emerges politically unscathed from the conflict. Yet few governors view public attention as unwanted, accepting the adage that it is better to be attacked than ignored. They apparently sense that the average citizen is less attentive to issues than personality images, and it is to their advantage to have their name a household word.

Because the general public is often uninterested in the debate over governmental policies, the governor cannot confine his efforts at marshaling political resources to his public relations activities. He must also attempt to draw strength from other political groups that have a stake in what the state government does. Thus he has probably depended upon his party, or factions within it, to get elected in the first place. He will continue to seek partisan aid in putting his program through the state legislature, managing the program that has been enacted, and continuing his electoral success. Yet the extent to which he may rely on partisanship to gain his ends varies widely among the states. In the competitive states with well-organized parties, the governor trades heavily on his partisan ties. In the one-party states, and states whose partisanship is not finely drawn, the governor has a more difficult time in establishing an effective grouping of partisan leaders to do his bidding.

Even if conflict over public policies within the state has followed well-established partisan lines in the past, the governor does not always find the party faithful anxious for his leadership. He may find that he presides over an organization so rent by personal, factional, or regional rivalries that it poses a severe test of his leadership skill. Indeed, if his leadership is sufficiently challenged, he may adopt a lofty, nonpartisan stance of placing principle above party. Yet it is the atypical governor who is unwilling to negotiate with his party's leaders to gain their support for the considerable agenda he must address.

The governor turns, not alone to his party, but to interest group leaders as well in seeking political support. Some will have been already identified with the fortunes of the governor's party and he will experience little difficulty in bringing them into his camp. Others may not have so distinctly associated themselves with partisan affairs and the governor must determine their usefulness to him in building his political support. Politics is not a one-way street. Enlisting the aid of interest organizations is accomplished ordinarily at the price of *quid pro quo* agreements. No governor can avoid such negotiations with the principal political actors of the state. Yet no governor wishes to be merely the captive of the leadership whose support he has solicited. He wishes to preserve his options by having others depend upon him in gaining their objectives. The skill of a governor may be measured in large measure by his ability to command the fealty of interest group and party leaders without undermining the policy objectives to which he is committed.

Legal-Institutional Resources

The formal authority possessed by the governor is not an accurate measure of the political influence he may exercise. As we have discussed, the governor relies on personal traits and skills and appeals to private groups and organizations to enhance his leadership potential. Nevertheless, the governor's legal authority and his formal relations to administrative agencies affect his leadership in important ways. It is his formal position and the legal and administrative authority to which he is entitled that the governor must ultimately trade on in inducing others to follow his lead. It is because he is governor that he can take advantage of the personal skills and nongovernmental support that are his. To strip him of his authority would reduce him to the position of any other private bargainer.

The potential for using formal authority as a political resource depends upon the extent to which it is concentrated in the hands of the governor rather than dispersed among his subordinates or shared with the legislative branch. Legal and institutional deficiencies of the state executive have been recorded in countless numbers of state reorganization reports with a monotonous regularity and are easily available to the interested student. Some of the more important are described below.

1. Most governors share executive power with a host of elected subordinates—a secretary of state, an attorney general, a treasurer, an auditor or comptroller, and a superintendent of education are among the most common. Table 5.2 shows the offices. Many of the subordinates enjoy a longer tenure than the governor because those who choose to seek additional terms are more likely to be reelected.[7] Since they have their own power base, elected subordinates may be and often are disinclined

[7] Joseph Schlesinger, "The Structure of Competition for Office in the American States," *Behavioral Science*, V (July, 1960), 208.

TABLE 5.2
*Number of States with Elected
Executive Officials*

Governor	50		
Attorney general	42	University regents	7
State treasurer	40	Mining commissioner	5
Secretary of state	39	Tax commission	3
Lieutenant governor	38	Highway commissioner	2
State auditor	30	Board of equalization	1
Superintendent of education	26	Printer	1
Public utilities commission	14	Railroad commission	1
Agriculture commission	11	Fish and game commission	1
Controller	10	Corporation commission	1
Board of education	10	Commissioner of charities	1
Insurance commissioner	8	Secretary of internal affairs	1
Land commissioner	8	Adjutant and inspector general	1

SOURCE: Thomas R. Dye, *Politics in States and Communities* (Englewood Cliffs: Prentice-Hall, 1969), p. 171.

to accept the leadership of the governor in matters that affect their department.

2. The number of officers reporting to the governor combined with a lack of a rational organization of state functions makes effective management difficult. Some of the offices are frozen into the state constitution, and administrative reform is either difficult or unlikely. Although more recent agencies commonly have been established by legislative statute, many states have followed the practice of creating new organizations as new problems have become isolated rather than finding a department to which the activity is functionally related. The consequences have been administrative structures nothing short of chaotic.

3. The existence of boards and commissions given statutory authority for particular functions makes the governor's authority unclear—for example, boards of health, boards of welfare, agricultural commissions, highway commissions, and similar agencies. The confusion is compounded when they are legislatively appointed commissions, which is the case in some states. Not only is gubernatorial control imprecise; the agencies are difficult to coordinate because, by their nature, plural executives are a cumbersome administrative arrangement.

4. Restrictions exist in many states on the removal power of the governor, even where his power of appointment is clear-cut. In contrast to federal practice, many state officials serve for fixed terms of office and not at the pleasure of the governor. As a consequence, they can be removed by the governor only for legal cause and not for a disagreement

over policy issues, much like the protection afforded members of independent regulatory commissions of the federal government.

5. In 22 states the governor faces legal restrictions on his length of service, preventing him from building power over time and with experience. In 15 states he cannot succeed himself in office; in seven states, he cannot serve more than two consecutive terms of office. Combined with the defeat ratio of those seeking reelection, the average governor has a tenure somewhat under five years.

The governor, of course, is specifically designated as chief executive in most state constitutions, and the title is more than a nominal one. He is equipped with legal and administrative powers that, although pale in comparison to Presidential authority, are nevertheless important political resources. Some of the more significant sources of his authority are summarized below.

1. The governor commonly has the power to appoint the heads of many key state administrative agencies. Many of the elected subordinates (secretary of state, treasurer) have relatively little political implications for the governor. These positions are the traditional offices of state government and are commonly provided for in the constitution. Offices of more recent origin are often legislative creations and their heads are not uncommonly appointed by the governor. Thus most governors appoint the heads of their labor, health, welfare, revenue, highways, and budget agencies. Even should restrictions be placed on his removal power, at least some governors follow the simple expediency of demanding an undated letter of resignation from his appointee.

2. The so-called executive budget—that is, a budget prepared by an agent of the governor—is in widespread use today. Since all governmental programs, insofar as they can be expressed in financial terms, are highlighted in the preparation of the budget, the budget agency has considerable potential as a vehicle for gubernatorial control and commonly is called the chief administrative arm of the executive by students of administration. For his power to be effective, however, the governor must have a sure control over an agency that is adequately staffed, and he must have flexibility in distributing revenue sources among state expenditure demands. As Anton has shown, these conditions are not always met in practice.[8] In some states the governor must share his formal budget making authority with other state officials. But the problem extends well beyond the formal distribution of power. Often compelled to submit his first budget only shortly after election, he is not in a position to master such a complex undertaking with a firmness that will enhance his professional reputation. Since first impressions are

[8] Thomas J. Anton, "Roles and Symbols in the Determination of State Expenditures," *Midwest Journal of Political Science,* XI (February, 1967), 31–33.

important for the governor who is around for a short tenure, he may be unfairly characterized as inept because of the situation into which he is thrust. Even if the governor should work arduously at his task, he may be hamstrung by the sizable number of earmarked taxes and special funds. According to one source, over 50 percent of total expenditures are financed from special funds in three-fifths of our states.[9] What is left in the general fund is often taken up by major state expenditures (welfare, health, education) that leave the governor little room for experimentation. Nevertheless, few governors would be willing to forego the budgetary authority they possess.

3. In 49 states the governor possesses a veto power over legislative proposals. With but a few exceptions he possesses an item veto in regard to appropriations measures—that is, he may strike individual items in an appropriation measure rather than facing the alternative of signing a bill in its entirety or rejecting it in its entirety. The peculiar importance of the governor's veto power is its effectiveness. It is not uncommon to find a large number of bills passed in the closing weeks of a legislative session, the so-called legislative logjam. The significance of the practice of making maximum use of the waning days of a legislative session is that the legislature, particularly if under a legal time limit, will have adjourned before it receives back a gubernatorial veto. Under such circumstance, the veto becomes absolute by default. The actual power of the veto, of course, varies among the states in the size of the majority that can override and the length of time available to the governor to peruse the bill before it takes effect without his signature. It must also be remembered that the veto is primarily a defensive weapon and is not useful in helping the governor mobilize support for his legislative program except as a bargaining device.

4. The modern-day governor is not without political and administrative aides, although one should not presume that his personal staff approaches the specialization of White House personnel. The number and type of assistants aiding the governor varies with the size of the state, the character of its problems, and the personal predilections of the governor. In the smaller states the governor's office may consist of no more than one professional assistant and a handful of stenographers and typists. Large states such as California and New York have a more complex organization which may appear to be a small-scale model of the White House staff. Whatever the size of the staff, at least three jobs are performed by the personal aides:[10] (a) The governor must be assisted in maintaining

[9] Tax Foundation, Inc., *State Expenditure Controls: An Evaluation* (New York: Tax Foundation, Inc., 1965), p. 74, quoted in Anton, *supra*, p. 32.
[10] The Council of State Governments, *Reorganizing State Government* (Chicago: The Council of State Governments, 1950), p. 31.

friendly relations with state legislators, interest group leaders, citizen organizations, and party officials. The task must be performed by someone who has the governor's confidence and shares his political views. (b) The governor needs assistance in directing and coordinating the administrative agencies. The task is more internally directed and involves advising and consulting with state officialdom concerning gubernatorial policies and interests. (c) Someone must act as a personal aide to the governor, scheduling his appointments, answering his telephone, greeting his visitors, and generally protecting his time from unwanted or unnecessary interruptions. These are the minimal functions of the governor's office whether or not performed by separate aides. In the larger offices special assistants may be assigned responsibility for press relations, speechwriting, patronage, research, program-planning, requests for pardons and reprieves, legal advice on pending legislation, or advising the governor in respect to particular policies such as urban affairs or minority rights. The importance of the personal aides as alter egos for the governor cannot be overstressed given the amount of time he must spend on dignitary matters, the signing of countless bills and documents, and in being visible to the public.

An Assessment of Formal Powers

Attempts have been made to find patterns in the possession of formal powers by the governor. By assigning numerical ratings to the strength of a governor's veto, appointive, and budgetary powers, and his tenure potential, Joseph Schlesinger constructed the index of gubernatorial authority shown in Table 5.3. The indexes were then compared to state social and economic indicators.

What emerges from an analysis of the Schlesinger ratings is the relationship that exists between the large urban-industrial states and the strength of a governor's formal powers. A similar relationship also exists between urban-industrial states and strong two-party competition as we discuss elsewhere. Does this mean, then, that the governors of those states are in a better position to attack the problems confronting them because of a pyramiding of power? The answer must be yes. One has only to speculate what decision-making would be like if power were further dispersed in a large state of considerable complexity and diversity. At the same time, one cannot assume that decision-making is more orderly and manageable in those states than elsewhere, for the obvious reason that the problems faced are more acute and their solution more vexing than those of more simple social and economic structures.

The possession of formal powers by the governor, as we have emphasized earlier, is not necessarily an accurate indication of the real power exercised by the governor. Wayne Francis found, for example, that no significant relationship existed between the formal powers possessed by a governor based on the Schlesinger scale and whether the governor actively pressed for legislation deemed important by the legislators.[11] Nor did he find a significant relationship between the centralization of legislative decision-making, sometimes but not necessarily directed from the governor's office, and the index of formal powers.[12] Despite the absence of significant correlations, however, one cannot assume that formal powers are worthless, unless the classification itself does not reflect actual conditions within a state—that is, a governor is rated strong on budgetary powers, for example, when in actual fact he shares the power with a legislative committee. What complicates the relationship

TABLE 5.3
*A Combined Index of the Formal Powers
of the Governors*

	BUDGET POWERS	APPOINTIVE POWERS	TENURE POTENTIAL	VETO POWERS	TOTAL INDEX
New York	5	5	5	4	19
Illinois	5	5	5	3	18
New Jersey	5	5	4	4	18
Pennsylvania	5	5	3	4	17
Virginia	5	5	3	4	17
Washington	5	4	5	3	17
California	5	3	5	4	17
Maryland	5	5	4	2	16
Missouri	5	4	3	4	16
Oregon	5	4	4	3	16
Utah	5	3	5	3	16
Wyoming	5	3	5	3	16
Montana	5	2	5	4	16
Alabama	5	3	3	4	15
Connecticut	4	4	5	2	15
Ohio	5	4	4	2	15
Tennessee	5	5	3	1	14
Kentucky	5	4	3	2	14
Michigan	5	4	2	3	14
Minnesota	5	4	2	3	14
Nevada	5	2	5	2	14
Colorado	4	1	5	4	14
Idaho	1	5	5	3	14
Louisiana	4	2	3	4	13
Oklahoma	5	1	3	4	13

[11] Wayne L. Francis, *Legislative Issues in the Fifty States: A Comparative Analysis* (Chicago: Rand McNally, 1967), p. 76.
[12] *Ibid.*, p. 77.

TABLE 5.3 (*Continued*)

	BUDGET POWERS	APPOINTIVE POWERS	TENURE POTENTIAL	VETO POWERS	TOTAL INDEX
Iowa	5	3	2	2	12
Nebraska	5	3	2	2	12
Wisconsin	5	2	2	3	12
Georgia	5	1	3	3	12
Massachusetts	5	1	2	4	12
Indiana	3	5	3	1	12
Arkansas	5	2	2	2	11
South Dakota	5	2	1	3	11
New Mexico	4	3	1	3	11
Kansas	4	2	2	3	11
Maine	4	1	4	2	11
New Hampshire	5	1	2	2	10
Rhode Island	4	3	2	1	10
North Carolina	4	2	3	1	10
Vermont	2	4	2	2	10
Arizona	2	3	2	3	10
Delaware	1	1	4	4	10
West Virginia	1	3	3	1	8
Florida	1	2	3	2	8
Mississippi	1	1	3	2	7
South Carolina	1	1	3	2	7
Texas	1	1	2	3	7
North Dakota	1	1	2	3	7

SOURCE: Joseph Schlesinger, "Politics of the Executive," in Herbert Jacobs and Kenneth Vines (eds.), *Politics in the American States* (Boston: Little, Brown, 1965), p. 229.

are the interests competing with the governor in the exercise of political power. Only when power can be effectively marshaled through gubernatorial leadership and the congruent interests of party and pressure groups in the state will effective decision-making emerge. This is the task, of course, of political leadership.

Even with the centralization of power, however, policy conflicts may be reconciled no easier. As Francis observes, the consequence may be centralization of conflict and no better assurance of policy success.[13] Nevertheless, one may speculate that more centralized decision-making insures a bargaining relationship among competing interests in a more orderly and less erratic fashion than one in which a greater number of power centers are involved. This was the conclusion of Samuel Beer in

[13] *Ibid.*, p. 80.

comparing British and American political systems, the former characterized by greater centralization.[14] Obviously no American state approaches the centralization of the British parliamentary system, but one may believe the comparison is descriptive of the nature of conflict.

THE GOVERNOR AS
MANAGEMENT LEADER

The governor's role in managing the executive agencies is really an extension of his role as policy leader. It can best be understood by viewing policy formulation as the first phase of the policy processes which is typically directed toward securing a legislative program. The second phase of the policy processes involves the direction and coordination of the program enacted. By viewing policy-making as a process involving both the formulation and management of programs, one avoids the suggestion, discussed below, that the execution of programs does not involve policy questions. At the same time, by considering the several phases of policy-making, one can discuss the separate problems confronting the governor as he attempts to run his state. This we do below in discussing how well the governor is able to direct and control his administrative establishment.

Political Values in Administrative
Operations

That the governor should be firmly in control of his executive agencies has not always been administrative dogma. On the contrary, as Herbert Kaufman shows, values of representativeness and neutral competence preceded the quest for executive leadership in the administrative processes of the past.[15] Each of the three values has been dominant in particular periods of our history but never so completely as to suppress the other two.

Representativeness was the original value to be highlighted in the early state governments. It took on two tangible forms: legislative dominance in state affairs and widespread use of the electoral principle. In the immediate postrevolutionary period, the governor was selected by the legislature in ten states. He was scarcely considered more than a

14 Samuel Beer, "Group Representation in Britain and the United States," *The Annals of the American Academy of Political and Social Sciences,* CCCXIX (September, 1958), 130–140.
15 Herbert Kaufman, "Emerging Conflicts in the Doctrines of Public Administration," *American Political Science Review,* L (December, 1956), 1057–1073. The paragraphs which follow are based on the Kaufman article.

figurehead and ceremonial leader in any state. And with the spread of the franchise, more and more positions were filled by popular election. The long ballot and short tenure of office was a characteristic feature of state government by the Jacksonian era. Even the advent of the so-called "spoils system" could be viewed as the triumph of the representative principle, inasmuch as it assured access to government by those who had formerly been denied entry into government circles.

It soon became evident that a government operated under a long ballot, the spoils system, and a dominant legislature was prey to the avarice of political bosses and other corrupting forces, not the least of which were the industrial empires that flourished in the post–Civil War era. Since existing governmental institutions were susceptible to corruption, reform sentiment began to stress professional competence for government officeholders to free them from partisan or interest associations. Through merit systems of personnel selection and the creation of independent boards and commissions, the administration of governmental affairs was to be protected from "political" intervention. The rationale was found in the familiar politics-administration dichotomy.[16]

Just as a reaction set in against government organized under the representative principle, so too was a cry raised against government that pursued the ideal of neutral competence. A continuation of the two earlier philosophies resulted in a splintering of the administrative establishment that was both costly and inefficient as independent commissions and elected agency heads followed their separate ways without effective coordination. Now the reformers said there was a need for order that could be supplied only by strengthening the hand of the chief executive over the administrative establishment. The executive budget, the administrative reorganization movement designed to produce a rational administrative structure, and increases in the staff of the chief executive, all became elements of the executive leadership model of administrative organization.

The differing views of students of administration over how government should be run are not based solely on differences concerning structural values. On the contrary, as Kaufman argues, the divisions among the ranks of scholars and practitioners are reinforced by their differing concepts of political—that is, program—values. The executive leadership model draws its support from contemporary liberal thinkers who stress the need for executive energy in keeping pace with society's ever-growing problems. Those who believe that the government has expanded too far already are likely to prefer the advantage in protecting the status quo found in the legislative processes. And still others remain skeptical toward administrative involvement in either legislative or executive politics and prefer to emphasize the professionalism of career civil

16 See below, pp. 109–111.

servants. Kaufman may be correct that the incompatibility of the several values "can only produce gulfs in the realm of ideas and confusion in proposals for governmental reform."[17]

The Nature of the State Bureaucracy

A governmental bureaucracy presents peculiar problems for governance in a democratic society. On the one hand, as the scope of governmental tasks increase, the necessity of maintaining a professional and career-minded civil service also rises. On the other hand, as the professional bureaucracy undertakes an increasing share of decision-making, it raises the fundamental question of maintaining its responsiveness to the citizen-body. How does one reconcile the needs of expertise, acquired through systems of merit selection and continued by guarantees of job tenure, and the needs of representation, traditionally provided by election to office and alternation in power?

A simplistic solution was provided by the early students of administration who even yet exert a considerable influence on our thinking. Frank Goodnow may be used as a representative thinker for our purposes. Goodnow rejected the concept of the tripartite division of governmental powers into executive, legislative, and judicial functions.[18] He argued that all of government could be divided into two basic functions: the making of public policy, which is the realm of politics; and the execution of public policy, which is the realm of administration. This division is commonly referred to as the politics-administration dichotomy.

The significance of the assertion of the dichotomy to responsible government is this. The notion arose that once public policy had been agreed upon, the remaining task was simply one of determining the most economical and efficient way of executing that policy. At the same time, it was widely felt that the execution of public policy was subject to scientific study; that is, one could determine the principles of organization and canons of administrative behavior which, if followed, would result in the goals of administration, economy and efficiency in operations.

Regardless of what Goodnow intended, the politics-administration dichotomy soon gave rise to the proposition that the makers of public policy should be popularly elected and representative of the electorate, presumably, the chief executive and the legislature. By the same reasoning, those who merely execute the public will were to be appointed on the basis of their expertise, presumably, the bureaucrats, and their performance would be judged only on the basis of the efficiency with which they discharged their duties. The rationale of the politics-administration

---

[17] Kaufman, op. cit., p. 1058.
[18] See the analysis of Goodnow in Dwight Waldo, The Administrative State (New York: Ronald, 1948), pp. 106–111.

dichotomy is carried to its extreme under the city manager form of municipal government, where even the chief executive, the city manager, is viewed as a technician, serving an indefinite term of office and responsible, not to the electorate, but to the city council which theoretically evaluates his performance only on the basis of his professional competence.

Now there are flaws in this rather naive theory of governance. The basic misconception is in the belief that those who make public policy can be neatly separated from those who execute public policy. In the real world of government it is just not the case. If it were, controlling the bureaucracy would present no problem; bureaucratic performance would be measured against the so-called principles of scientific management.

The problem of responsiveness occurs because policy-making and policy-execution are intertwined in government. Without too much elaboration, some of the more obvious ways in which the bureaucrats influence policy are:

1. Even though they may not have authority to make formal policy decisions, the advice of career officials is sought. They are the experts, and the weight of expertise is a powerful force. The actual possession of power—that is, the ability to influence the behavior and attitudes of others—does not have to follow formal, hierarchical lines. The bureaucrats, through their expertise, possess nonhierarchical sources of influence.

2. Because of the complexities of modern industrial society, legislative policies often must be stated in rather broad and necessarily vague terms. The fleshing out of that policy must devolve to the experts and technicians—that is, the bureaucrats. Sometimes the delegation is so broad that the rules and regulations promulgated have the force and effect of law. Whether with the force of law or not, the power to make decisions that influence public policy is delegated to career officials.

3. Even should the guidelines of public policy handed down be explicit, the manner in which they are enforced, lax or zealous, even-handed or prejudiced, is going to determine the actual character of public policy.

Broadly speaking, state government has two types of executives in the administrative establishment—the political executive and the career official. The political executive is appointed by the governor and owes his allegiance only to the governor. He must be committed to the gubernatorial program in all of its partisan and personal implications. By adhering to the governor's goals in the discharge of his administrative duties, the political executive is indirectly accountable to the electorate.

The career official, on the other hand, is the classic civil servant, theoretically capable of serving any master, regardless of his political partisanship. He is a repository of expertise on how to deal with governmental problems. He provides continuity to the state system, insuring a smooth flow of the day-to-day operations of government, regardless of changes in partisan control.

Yet if the career official also exercises important responsibilities in decision-making that influence the course of public policy, how is he held accountable? The answer is complex and perhaps not entirely satisfactory. The state legislature plays a role because it gives the bureaucrat his job and supplies him with money. Interest groups play a role because they attempt to influence those who have power to advance or threaten their interests, and, increasingly, that power is in the hands of administrative officials. The courts play a role because they are available to protect the individual from an overzealous application of the law or rules and regulations. The elected department heads play a role because they are accountable to an electorate and have responsibilities for departmental control. But it is on the governor and his associates and advisors that the more important responsibilities devolve, if for no other reason than that the governor is the one person whom the public holds accountable for the conduct of state government.

The Limits of Gubernatorial Control

The governor may be popularly thought to be the administrative leader of his state, and the literature of public administration may subscribe to the executive leadership model as its central theme, but the evidence we have today seems to suggest that such notions of gubernatorial influence are greatly exaggerated. A systematic attempt to probe the question of administrative control of executive agencies was undertaken by Deil S. Wright.[19] Surveying 933 department and agency heads from all fifty states, Wright elicited responses to specific questions concerning agency controls and the preferences of the state executives for particular types of control. The results are shown in Table 5.4.

What is immediately striking about the responses is the number of department heads who felt the legislature rather than the executive exercised greater control over their agency. That the evaluation was not based solely on legal considerations of authority is suggested by the tendency of the legislature more than the governor to cut agency budget requests. Who deprives an agency of money in the budgetary cycle is likely to be keenly perceived by those affected. That legislative control is so highly visible to department heads is all the more remarkable considering the limited time the typical state legislature is in session. Perhaps it is the case that legislative oversight by interim committees or off-duty legis-

[19] Deil S. Wright, "Executive Leadership in State Administration," *Midwest Journal of Political Science*, XI (February, 1967), 1–26.

TABLE 5.4
*Attitudes of American State Executives
on Political Relationships*

	PERCENTAGES[a] ($N = 933$)
"Who exercises greater control over your agency's affairs?"	
Governor	32
Each about the same	22
Legislature	44
Other and n.a.	2
	100
"Who has the greater tendency to reduce budget requests?"	
Governor	25
Legislature	60
Other and n.a.	15
	100
"Who is more sympathetic to the goals of your agency?"	
Governor	55
Each about the same	14
Legislature	20
Other and n.a.	11
	100
"What type of control do you prefer?"	
Governor	42
Independent commission	28
Legislature	24
Other and n a.	5
	100

[a] Tabled percentages may not add to 100 because of rounding.
SOURCE: Deil S. Wright, "Executive Leadership in State Administration," *Midwest Journal of Political Science,* XI (February, 1967), 4.

lators is not so discontinuous as one might surmise from a reading of the formal sessions.

The preferences of agency heads would seem to substantiate the Kaufman thesis that the value of executive leadership is dominant today—that is, preferred by more—but not to the exclusion of support for neutral competence and representativeness. Substantially more respondents preferred gubernatorial control than legislative control, which is not too surprising since the governor is generally viewed as more sympathetic to agency goals. Yet a surprising number of department heads preferred the insulation from the normal political and administrative controls offered by the independent commission. The fact that administrative practice is not in accord with administrative preference suggests that the conflict involved is not simply one over structural values to be contested by students of administration, but involves political forces outside of government who are interested in what effect structural change may have on state policies.[20]

A second question concerning the relationship of legal powers to gubernatorial control of administrative agencies was also addressed by Wright. The findings shown in Table 5.5 tend to confirm our own judgment of the role of formal authority expressed earlier. In states where the governor's legal powers are strong-to-moderate, his control over agency affairs is generally greater than in states where the governor's legal powers are weak-to-very-weak. Nevertheless, this does not mean the "strong" governor is the master of his administrative house; it simply suggests that he has a better chance to compete with his legislature for administrative control. The conclusion is inescapable that the conventional political science literature has oversold the role of the governor as chief administrator.

The fact is that decision-making within the executive branch has not been effectively centralized in most state governments. The operating independence of administrative agencies provides the vehicle through which separatist tendencies may be expressed. Why is this the case when the central thrust of most state reorganization proposals points to the need for a unified executive? The answer requires the identification of the several forces that combine to resist general government controls:[21]

1. It is typically the case that agency heads see plainly the need for executive integration—so long as it does not touch upon their own autonomy. The desire for independence in their operating roles must be considered an innate characteristic of most administrative officials.

2. Clientele and other interest groupings often prefer to deal with an agency that is free from general government controls, sensing that their influence will be greater. Indeed, agency-clientele relationships are sometimes so close that the distinction between public authority and private power is lost. One need only mention the role of the farm bureau in state agricultural extension services, but illustrations abound among groups as diverse as teacher organizations and state boards of education and highway users and state highway departments. Frequently, the drive is not simply for structural autonomy, but for financial autonomy as well. Thus

[20] See the discussion on the relationship of political values and structural values on page 108.
[21] The list is taken from York Wilbern, "Administrative Organization" in James W. Fesler (ed.), *The 50 States and Their Local Governments* (New York: Knopf, 1967), pp. 345–352.

TABLE 5.5
Appointment Method and Perceived and Preferred Political Relationships of American State Executives

		APPOINTMENT METHOD				
		GOVERNOR ALONE	GOVERNOR WITH ADVICE & CONSENT	BOARD WITH GOVERNOR'S CONSENT	BOARD WITHOUT GOVERNOR'S CONSENT	POPULARLY ELECTED[a]
		(PERCENTAGES; NUMBER OF CASES IN PARENTHESES)[a]				
Greater control over agency affairs:	Governor	57	41	28	15	9
	Each about the same	18	26	30	30	11
	Legislature	25	33	42	55	80
		100 (131)	100 (230)	100 (89)	100 (149)	100 (124)
Greater tendency to reduce budget requests:	Governor	35	29	37	24	17
	Legislature	65	71	63	76	83
		100 (115)	100 (204)	100 (78)	100 (123)	100 (111)
Sympathy for agency goals:	Governor	80	70	66	58	33
	Each about the same	16	18	16	18	15
	Legislature	4	12	18	24	51
		100 (123)	100 (213)	100 (80)	100 (135)	100 (105)
Preferred type of control:	Governor	68	67	31	27	18
	Commission	20	17	47	53	18
	Legislature	13	16	22	20	65
		100 (126)	100 (227)	100 (87)	100 (144)	100 (114)

[a] Tabled percentages may not add to 100 because of rounding.

SOURCE: Deil S. Wright, "Executive Leadership in State Administration," *Midwest Journal of Political Science*, XI (February, 1967), p. 15.

the preference for earmarked taxes by interest organizations who have a stake in a given governmental function.

3. The growth of professionalism among the occupational groupings employed by state government makes coordination difficult under the best of circumstances. The professional subscribes to a professional code of ethics and he bases his decision on his professional expertise. Control by a generalist is resented, particularly if the professional senses that the control is "political."

4. The number of separate federal grant programs available to state governments today requires agency officials to serve two masters. Indeed, looking as they do for out-of-state funds, the state executives may express more loyalty to Washington than to their own political superiors within the state. The relationship may be all the more strong if reinforced by professional ties.

5. From time to time—when some scandal erupts in state government, for example—the public outcry is such to demand administrative reform. A not untypical reaction is to try to isolate the function from the normal play of politics by establishing an independent board composed of bipartisan members to undertake administrative responsibility. This was one of the principal causes of the plethora of independent agencies established in the late nineteenth and early twentieth century and still persists today.

6. Legislative-executive antagonisms often are reflected in a state's administrative structure. Realizing that executive unity will enhance the power of the governor, state legislatures have been reluctant to accept administrative proposals that would increase gubernatorial power over the operating agencies. Legislators believe a strong chief executive will mean a subservient legislature.

7. The nature of some administrative processes have suggested the desirability of operating independence. These are principally either of a quasijudicial nature (railroad and public service commissions) or of a quasicommercial nature (insurance and retirement systems, packaged liquor monopolies, toll road authorities). Independence is sought to insure impartiality for the quasijudicial functions and operating flexibility for the quasicommercial operations.

8. Inertia may not be an explanation of the causes of separatist tendencies in state government, but it probably is an important factor in their having persisted. Elected agency heads and independent boards acquire the respectability of time. Change represents unknown quantities and many people are comfortable with settled practices. Indeed, resistance to change is likely to be more effectively organized than is reform sentiment, as the history of constitutional revision at the state level so amply testifies.

THE VULNERABILITY OF
THE GOVERNOR

We have discussed thus far the role of the governor as leader and manager of his state. We think it is fair to assume that in those states whose societal fabric is varied and complex, the problems confronting government are both more pressing and more difficult of solution. Although the governors of the large urban-industrial states are more likely to possess greater authority than those in the more rural-agricultural states, so too are the problems greater in managing social forces in a just and orderly fashion. The governor, to whom the people look for leadership and assign responsibility for managing state affairs, may find it difficult to emerge with a record of accomplishment that is popularly recognized. If such is the case, then one might expect that he will be subject to political reprisals.

Is the political mortality rate of governors on the increase? Although we must proceed with caution in interpreting the data, the answer seems to be a qualified yes. Table 5.6 shows the percentage of governors defeated in competitive states in each decade since 1920. On the surface, it appears that the vulnerability of the governor shows an increase over the fifty-year period. Yet some of the reasons for the rise are easy to explain and do not relate to inherent difficulties of the office. Republicans seeking reelection during the twenties were both more numerous and more successful than Democratic incumbents. No one would expect otherwise with the political tide running in favor of the Republican party. However, dur-

TABLE 5.6
Incumbent Governors Defeated for Re-election
in Competitive States, 1920–1969

PERIOD	NUMBER OF INCUMBENTS RUNNING	INCUMBENTS DEFEATED	
		NUMBER	PERCENTAGE
1920–1929	40	9	22.5
1930–1939	46	15	32.6
1940–1949	56	22	39.3
1950–1959	52	15	28.9
1960–1969	44	18	40.9

SOURCE: Stephen Turett, *The Vulnerability of American Governors* (Unpublished Honors Thesis, The George Washington University, 1969), p. 12.

ing the thirties and the formation of the Roosevelt coalition, the fortunes of the Republicans seeking reelection were reversed and the defeat ratio of incumbents rose as Democrats replaced Republicans.

The pattern of external influences on gubernatorial elections becomes somewhat cloudy in the forties. A higher percentage of Democratic incumbents were defeated than Republican incumbents, despite the fact that the Democrats held the White House. Yet the Democratic party was in disarray and the Republicans captured the Congress in 1946. Perhaps national tides more than ingrained features of gubernatorial authority swelled the ranks of defeated incumbents.

The defeat ratio of incumbent governors actually dropped in the fifties. Peace and prosperity was the slogan that brought Eisenhower his second term. Republican and Democratic incumbents were almost equally successful in their re-election bids. Indeed, if one is to find statistical evidence of increasing gubernatorial vulnerability, one must seek it in the decade of the sixties. Forty percent of the incumbents have been defeated with Democratic incumbents encountering the greatest electoral resistance despite the fact that their party nationally controlled Congress throughout the decade and the Presidency until 1968.

One may speculate that the mood of a country experiencing rapid social change rents the body politic. Some are caught in the throes of rising expectations; others are fearful of the direction in which American society is heading. Both groups look to their governments to clarify their status, whether it is to preserve their hopes or to calm their fears. Governance at any level is difficult under such circumstances. The governor may or not be peculiarly ill-equipped to attack the ills of society; but ill-equipped or not, he does seem increasingly vulnerable to electoral sanctions.

6. POLITICS
OF STATE
LEGISLATURES

State legislatures are frequently described by analogies drawn from the congressional system. Not all such analogies are apt, since state legislatures follow procedures peculiar to their own needs. Nor can one assume that state practices are everywhere the same. Legislative behavior is influenced by the political and social environment in which a legislature operates. Yet it would be equally unsatisfactory to suggest that no patterns can be found among the states in their legislative systems. More than one state has been dominated by a powerful governor. More than one state has a strong partisan cast to its decision-making. Urban-rural conflict is not an uncommon feature in state legislative divisions. Nor is the pressure brought by powerful economic interests an isolated phenomenon. Our task is to describe and explain the patterns that exist and to suggest why they might be important.

Before entering a discussion of legislative politics, we must explain how we approach our subject. When anyone speaks of a state legislature, he is referring at least to the elected members of that body. As any contemporary student of politics recognizes, however, to focus only on senators and representatives to explain legislative politics would be incomplete. Influence comes from others outside the institutional context of the legislative forum—from governors and executive agencies, from political parties, from pressure groups and private organizations, from constituency interests. A more useful way to describe the structure and process of legislative politics is to refer to the legislative system. It is a broad enough term to convey the idea that individuals and groups outside of the formal institutional environment of the legislature have an important bearing on the decisions reached by the elected representatives. We seek no more technical term to invite attention to what is obvious upon reflection.

Several choices are open to us in treating legislative systems. We may view the legislature as an institution, a set of human relationships, or as a way of performing basic functions required of the political system. Without denigrating the conceptual problems involved, we feel the methodological differences are more apparent than real.[1] It seems obvious to us that formal legislative arrangements have an immediate and direct bearing upon the politics of lawmaking. It is just as obvious that a study of legislative behavior will uncover other dimensions of the legislative process. Neither approach is meaningful unless linked to the functions performed by the legislature in our society. In the pages that follow, we hope that the relationships among the institutional, behavioral, and functional aspects of legislative systems will be made clear.

THE FUNCTIONS OF
STATE LEGISLATURES

The most obvious activity of a legislative body is to pass laws that govern state affairs. Such a simple declaration, however, may conceal more than it reveals. The legislature may have relatively less influence in decisions on the content of some laws than the governor or private interests within the state. The statutes passed by the legislature may delegate considerable discretion to executive agencies to develop public policies

[1] See the discussion in John C. Wahlke, Heinz Eulau, William Buchanan, and LeRoy C. Ferguson, *The Legislative System* (New York: Wiley, 1962), pp. 3–7.

which were unknown to or unclear in the minds of the legislators. The courts may further modify the content of legislative enactments as they apply constitutional or common-law principles to statutory interpretation. Nevertheless, if we keep in mind that the legislative system is in reality a subsystem within the political system, that external forces influence the decisions reached by members of a legislative body, we may properly focus on the legislative arena and consider the passing of statutes as the most important legislative activity.

While describing lawmaking as the principal activity of legislative bodies, we must further recognize that the process itself can serve varying functions in the political system. Two students of the legislative process, Malcolm Jewell and Samuel Patterson, described the activities of the legislative system (including but not limited to lawmaking) as serving two broad purposes: the management of conflict and the integration of the polity.[2] The management of conflict is essential in maintaining the stability of a political system. The conditions of a pluralist society such as our own are bound to place groups in contention as they seek to use political power to protect or advance their interests. The legislature is peculiarly adapted as an institution to promote the compromises essential for the resolution of conflict. Yet it cannot resolve conflicts without stress developing unless the system itself is broadly supported. The legislature, in authorizing the executive to act and providing it with money, in following procedures time-honored by their legitimacy in a democratic setting, and through its representative character, provides support for the system that Jewell and Patterson label "integration of the polity."

Although we can divide legislative responsibilities into analytically distinct functions, we shall not attempt to describe them separately in the remainder of this chapter. Instead we shall focus on what we believe to be the most significant aspects of legislative behavior—those that will likely affect the performance of broader and more transcendent legislative functions. For example, in its role of conflict management through the passing of laws, to what extent are legislative bodies subservient to the will of the governor? To what extent do political interest groups influence legislative decisions? Do legislative bodies follow partisan lines in voting decisions? Do the legislative parties present recognizable alternatives to the electorate, which serve them as voting references in their choice of legislative members? To what extent may it be said that constituency interests are represented by individual legislators? Although the list is not an inclusive one, it suggests the types of questions to be asked to examine legislative performance.

[2]   Malcolm E. Jewell and Samuel C. Patterson, *The Legislative Process in the United States* (New York: Random House, 1966), pp. 8–15.

THE COMPOSITION OF
STATE LEGISLATURES

The legislators who assemble in the state capital are not simply a cross section of the state's population. They are better educated, more affluent, and represent fewer occupational groupings than the general population. In state legislators as in the Congress, lawyers are everywhere in evidence. As a group they apparently perceive lawmaking as their special province. But there are additional reasons for their prominence as well as the appearance of self-employed businessmen and farmers. The tasks of the state legislator are essentially part time and the job low-paying as Table 6.1 shows. Only a limited number of occupations afford their members an opportunity to take time off from their employment to serve in periodic legislative sessions of a few months' duration.

Although the number of Negroes winning legislative seats has increased in the past decade, they remain underrepresented in most states. Other racial, ethnic, and religious minorities fare somewhat better than the Negro, having been assimilated earlier into the American class structure, in large part through the efforts of urban political machines. For example strong contingents of legislators of southern and eastern European extraction are found in the states of the Midwest and East. Nevertheless, it is probably true that white, male, Protestant legislators of north European origin are overrepresented in our state capitals.

The question that must inevitably be asked is does it make a difference in the public policy that evolves from our legislatures? No firm answer supported by empirical evidence can be given. One may speculate that a legislature does not have to include membership from each of the social and economic groupings of a constituency in order to fairly represent it. Such reasoning may be accurate in the abstract, but those who find themselves outside the normal recruitment zone for legislative positions may be unconvinced that their interests receive equal treatment.

One study that throws some light on the issue was undertaken by David R. Derge.[3] He addressed himself to the question of whether the lawyer-legislator showed bias in his voting behavior in the Illinois and Missouri legislative assemblies. One could argue that because lawyers are a professional class with superior income and frequently serve a business and financial clientele their political loyalties lean to the "right." Yet on the basis of roll-call analysis, Derge found that lawyers acted little differently from nonlawyers on bills reflecting liberal-conservative issues. The

[3]   David R. Derge, "The Lawyer as Decision-Maker in the American State Legislature," *Journal of Politics,* XXI (August, 1959), 408–433.

TABLE 6.1
Frequency and Length of Legislative Sessions,
Length of Term and Compensation of Legislators

STATE	YEARS IN WHICH SESSIONS ARE HELD	LIMITATIONS ON LENGTH OF REGULAR SESSIONS[b]	LENGTH OF TERM SENATE	HOUSE	BIENNIAL COMPENSATION[g]
Alabama	odd	36L	4	2	$11,000
Alaska	annual	none	4	2	32,300
Arizona	annual	none	4	4	14,800
Arkansas	odd	60C[d]	4	2	3,600
California	annual	none	2	2	48,950
Colorado	annual[a]	160C[c]	4	2	16,250
Connecticut	odd	150C[f]	2	2	4,000
Delaware	annual	173C[f]	4	2	12,050
Florida	annual	60L[d]	4	2	33,600
Georgia	annual	45C[e]	2	2	10,775
Hawaii	annual	60L[d]	4	2	28,860
Idaho	annual	60C[c]	2	2	10,200
Illinois	odd	none	4	2	24,000
Indiana	odd	61C	4	2	11,725
Iowa	annual	none	4	2	13,625
Kansas	annual	180C[c]	4	2	7,050
Kentucky	even	60L	4	2	9,850
Louisiana	annual[a]	60C	4	4	16,500
Maine	odd	none	2	2	4,100
Maryland	annual	70C	4	4	8,300
Massachusetts	annual	none	2	2	26,300
Michigan	annual	none	4	2	36,000
Minnesota	odd	120L	4	2	12,960
Mississippi	annual	125C[e]	4	4	14,500
Missouri	odd	195C[f]	4	2	18,750
Montana	odd	60C	4	2	2,100
Nebraska	odd	none	4	–	9,600
Nevada	odd	60C[c]	4	2	3,900
New Hampshire	odd	177[c,f]	2	2	200
New Jersey	annual	none	4	2	20,000

most important determinant of their voting behavior was their membership in a political party. Although one cannot generalize on the basis of
the Derge study, it does suggest that representative government is not
merely a matter of holding a mirror to the general population.

The base of American state legislatures does not in fact rest upon
theories of functional representation. On the contrary, legislators are
elected periodically from geographically defined constituencies. It is

STATE	YEARS IN WHICH SESSIONS ARE HELD	LIMITATIONS ON LENGTH OF REGULAR SESSIONS[b]	LENGTH OF TERM SENATE	HOUSE	BIENNIAL COMPENSATION[g]
New Mexico	annual[a]	60C	4	2	1,800
New York	annual	none	2	2	36,000
North Carolina	odd	none	2	2	10,000
North Dakota	odd	60L	4	2	3,590
Ohio	odd	none	4	2	25,500
Oklahoma	annual	90L	4	2	16,800
Oregon	odd	none	4	2	10,500
Pennsylvania	annual	none	4	2	24,000
Rhode Island	annual	60L[c]	2	2	600
South Carolina	annual	none	4	2	9,200
South Dakota	annual	45L[e]	2	2	5,000
Tennessee	odd	90L[c]	4	2	8,100
Texas	odd	140C	4	2	11,040
Utah	annual[a]	60C	4	2	3,200
Vermont	odd	none	2	2	6,375
Virginia	even	60C[c,d]	4	2	4,500
Washington	odd	60C	4	2	9,900
West Virginia	annual[a]	60C[d]	4	2	3,000
Wisconsin	odd	none	4	2	21,000
Wyoming	odd	40C	4	2	1,640

KEY: L—legislative days; C—calendar days
[a] Budget session held every other year.
[b] Budget sessions generally more limited.
[c] Salary or per diem allowance stops but session may continue.
[d] Length of session may be extended by extraordinary majority vote.
[e] Alternate sessions more limited.
[f] Approximate length.
[g] Includes salary, per diem, and expenses.
SOURCES: *The Book of States 1970–71*, Vol. XVIII (Chicago: Council of State Governments, 1970), pp. 65–66; compensation figures are from Citizens Conference on State Legislatures, *Compensation Provisions for Legislators in the Fifty States*, Research Memorandum No. 12, June, 1970.

because territorial boundaries can be carved to prefer some groups and to slight others that a linking occurs between territorial base and a type of functional representation. The relationship explodes in the historically contentious issue of reapportionment.

Two analytically distinct processes are commonly involved in reapportioning a state legislature: the carving out of district boundaries (more properly called redistricting); and the apportionment of representatives among the newly created districts (under current Court doctrine, in accordance with population). The importance of the distinction is that redistricting as such is left untouched by the Court's decisions. The gerrymander can exist *if* the Court standard of one-man, one-vote is met.

As a partisan device, the objective of the gerrymander is to carve out legislative districts in such a manner as to enhance a party's majority within the legislature. Thus districts can be created that will concentrate the strength of the minority party and cause it to waste votes in a type of electoral overkill, while spreading the strength of the majority to insure comfortable but not excessive pluralities in the other districts. Alternatively, the districts can be carved out to simply insure majority party victories in as many districts as the distribution of traditional party support permits, without attempting to concentrate minority strength in a limited number of areas. Effective use of the gerrymander would depend upon relatively stable voting patterns in which each political party could depend upon hard-core support. A weak party system in a state known for independent voting and ticket-splitting would make the gerrymander more difficult. A system in which one party was dominant could raise an issue of gerrymandering involving contending factions, but redistricting more likely involves individual complaints that a newly formed constituency affects a member's chance of electoral success.

The extent to which the several techniques of the gerrymander are used has not been systematically investigated because the focus of apportionment studies has concentrated on the degree of urban underrepresentation. An emphasis solely on equality of numbers among legislative districts misconstrues the nature of the problem. The political community is composed, not of abstract individuals, but of individuals in association with one another. What is important in carving out legislative districts is not their equal numbers, but the mix that is contained of groups that are politically significant. It is here that the gerrymander can defy the intent of impartial representation embodied in the one-man, one-vote doctrine. One New York legislator was heard to remark that he could carve out districts equal in number and as compact as a cigar and still improve his party's legislative chances. But to ask the Court to divine how groups should be apportioned within legislative districts would indeed invite them to enter a "political thicket."

The potential of the gerrymander can be illustrated by an interesting assignment Professor Wayne L. Francis gave to his students.[4] For a

4 Wayne L. Francis, *Legislative Issues in the Fifty States: A Comparative Analysis* (Chicago: Rand McNally, 1967), pp. 69–70.

hypothetical state with a fifty-member legislative body, each student was to develop an apportionment plan hewing as nearly as possible to the one-man, one-vote principle. The students were given the population of each county and told that they could employ "multi-member single-county districts, single-member single-county districts, and single-member multi-county districts." The districts had to be drawn along county lines. After the exercise had been completed, the students were then given the normal vote in each county in order to predict the electoral success of the parties. The predictions ranged from one plan that would likely give the Democrats 38 of the 50 seats to one that might provide the Republicans 35 of the 50 seats. Although the experiment does not involve the classical gerrymander, it does bring into sharp focus the fact that "apportionment" as a political issue transcends the problem of merely insuring equal representation of populations.

ORGANIZATION AND
PROCEDURES OF STATE LEGISLATURES

The Role of Party

As in Congress, political parties are assigned a crucial role at the organizational stage of state legislatures. The legislative parties commonly meet in caucus to select their leadership and ratify decisions reached by committees on committees in assigning committee seats. Yet such a partisan role is not universal.

The most obvious exceptions, leaving aside the case of the nonpartisan legislatures of Nebraska and Minnesota,[5] are the one-party and modified one-party states. When a party has little to fear from an organized opposition, conflict is often turned inward among contending factions, cliques, and leaders. Rather than providing a forum for the reconciliation of differing interests and political views within the family, the party is likely to see its power lapse to those who gain control of the formal leadership offices and thus wield the effective power of making committee assignments. Informal caucuses and meetings, sometimes with the governor or his aides in attendance, will replace the party gathering as an organizational device.

On the other hand, where some semblance of two-party competition is maintained, the traditional role of the party caucus is preserved. The interesting question, however, is the degree to which power is centralized

[5] Members of the Minnesota legislature meet in "liberal" and "conservative" caucuses. The relationship of the Democratic-Farmer-Labor party and the liberal caucus is rather close, but the number of conservative caucus members involved in Republican party politics is far less.

in the hands of party leaders or the governor and the extent to which power is dispersed among competing factions and individuals. In some states, party will serve as a label to define the limits of competition for leadership posts and a majority of committee assignments but will signify little else. In two-party Illinois, for example, appeals by candidates for the house speakership have been made to minority party members, exchanging for their support a promise of committee assignments. A bipartisan coalition has even elected a member of the minority as speaker in Illinois. Although the instances cited are rare, they signify that personal or factional feuds that erupt first at the organizational stage, even though settled within the caucus, may reappear later and disrupt the functioning of the legislative party.

The use of the caucus as a partisan device for mobilizing support for issues and programs is no longer attempted by the congressional parties, although the caucus has served that purpose in the past. One may surmise that where squabbles develop in a party caucus over organizational questions, it would be all the more ineffectual as a device for securing agreement on policy stances. However, the caucus is used effectively in a number of state legislatures to put together the numbers necessary for a bill's passage or to block unwanted legislation. The caucus is likely to be most effective where the party has a history of strong leadership, represents interests reasonably dissimilar from its opposite number, and includes legislative members who are ideologically comfortable with their own partisans. In other words, where a measure of party unity is already present, it can be enhanced through periodically called caucuses. As we discussed earlier, the large industrial states of the lower New England, Middle Atlantic and Midwest regions are more likely to, but not necessarily, provide those conditions.

What we are suggesting is that the role of party varies not simply between two-party and one-party states, but among states that have a balance of party strength within the electorate. The effectiveness of party as a device for influencing legislative decisions, which will be treated in detail later in this chapter, does not depend solely or even mainly on a strong caucus. Nevertheless, it does reflect an advanced stage in the organization of the legislative party.

Leadership Posts

It is simpler to designate the formal positions of leadership within a legislature than it is to describe the actual leadership. In some states, principally in the South, the governor is able to secure the selection of his partisans to positions of power and exercise a firm leadership in the legislative process. Yet in South Carolina, legislative leaders are not subservient to the governor and have established an independence uncommon to most states. In other states legislative leadership is not centralized, and bargaining and negotiations among shifting factions and leaders determine the outcome of legislative struggles. In still other states the party leadership is the dominant force in legislative decisions. Whatever the pattern, it must be remembered in the discussion that follows that possession of formal powers is not synonymous with their effective use.

Leadership positions at the state legislative level are superficially similar to those in the Congress. The presiding officer of the lower house is invariably called the speaker. The similarity extends little further. The typical speaker in state legislatures makes all appointments to standing committees and not infrequently chairs the rules committee, powers denied to the national speaker since 1911, when a combination of Democrats and insurgent Republicans rebelled against "Uncle Joe" Cannon. Combined with the authority to make committee assignments, the speaker commonly makes assignments of bills to committees. Because the jurisdictions of committees at the state level, despite their number, are not finely drawn, the speaker is in the formal position of exercising considerable influence over the chances of a bill reaching the floor to be voted up or down. It must be reiterated, however, that the speaker's actions might be bound by a decision in party caucus, commitments made as a price of his selection to the speakership, or by strategies emanating from the governor's office.

In state senates the presiding office is the lieutenant governor in the 38 states that provide for that office. Although he is without the power to participate in floor debate or to vote other than to break a tie, he, surprisingly, is empowered in 13 states to make appointments to standing committees. In the more typical state, the power to make committee assignments rests with a president pro tempore, a committee of the senate, or the senate acting as a body. In states without a lieutenant governor, the senate elects a president whose powers are similar to those of the speaker. Like the speaker, the senate president may not exercise his powers as an independent agent.

At the same time, we do not wish to convey the notion that presiding officers are merely legislative ciphers. They are in a position to exercise considerable influence over the legislative process, especially in states with a weak party structure. They preside over a membership that is generally marked by a high degree of turnover and commonly faced with an arbitrarily determined closing date. Under these conditions, knowledge of the rules of procedures, particularly when based on dimly recalled precedents, can be exchanged for legislative power by a skilled parliamentary tactician. House speakers and senate presidents, as long-term members of their body, are more likely than lieutenant governors to engage in the time-hallowed practice of manipulating the rules. The favors that can be offered by presiding officers in speeding legislation through the legislative labyrinth, in making appointments to interim committees or commissions, in collecting intelligence of who wants what, which they alone acquire because of their central position, are all available to the shrewd leader to squeeze the most effective power from his formal position.

Committees

A popular view of the legislative process among those who have more than a passing understanding of American politics holds that the critical point of lawmaking occurs at the committee stage. Although this may be the case in congressional politics, it is less true of state legislatures. Several factors limit the independent power of state legislative committees. Seniority is not as pervasive a consideration in making committee assignments, and power does not become entrenched over time in the hands of a few; committee staffs are smaller and less professional; and restrictions on sessions do not allow time for careful scrutiny of bills.

A wide variety of committees have been established by state legislatures, although their number has been reduced in recent years. It is not uncommon to find, however, that a few committees described under broad titles receive most of the significant bills introduced. Where this is the case, the task of legislative management is made immeasurably easier since power is distributed in fewer hands. At the same time, any of the key committees, acting as a collegial body or under the direction of a strong chairman, may act independently of the leadership.

The role that committees play in the legislative process is a distinguishing factor between legislatures in which power is centralized and those in which power is dispersed. In states where the governor or the party leadership is in firm control of legislative procedures, the role of committees as independent power centers is marginal. In the absence of strong leadership, power will devolve upon the committees as independent islands of decision-making. Francis asked legislators in each of the fifty states where the most important decisions in their legislatures were made.[6] The responses were grouped into the following categories:

1. a. in the governor's office
   b. in policy committees

2. party caucus

---

[6] Francis, *op. cit.*, p. 73.

3. a. regular committee meetings
   b. on the floor

The most highly centralized, according to Francis, were those in category 1; the moderately centralized were represented by category 2; and the most decentralized are those of category 3. Assigning weights of 1, .50, and .00 to the categories in descending order, a centralization index was computed for each state that is shown in Table 6.2. The column headed "Agreement coefficient of reliability" measures the agreement among the respondents as to their characterization of their state and together with the number of usable responses suggests the reliability of the centralization score.

State legislatures with a high degree of centralization fit no single model. Some are urbanized states (New Jersey, New York, Rhode Island, Connecticut, Pennsylvania) whose strong political parties provide an explanation for the degree of centralization found. On the other hand, a strong governor is more likely the reason for the high centralization scores of the one-party, relatively less urbanized southern states (Alabama, Tennessee, Georgia, Arkansas, Louisiana). States that work through regular committees have neither strong party leadership nor a strong governor and resist attempts by factional leaders to pyramid power. They are more likely to be rural-agricultural states where the demands for leadership are not so pressing.

Rules of Procedure

The procedures followed by state legislatures are partly a consequence of formal prescription and partly the result of informal codes of behavior. The most important formal requirements are those that establish the frequency and duration of legislative sessions, since the amount of time available to lawmakers imposes constraints on the manner of considering legislative proposals. Legislatures that meet in biennial sessions for sixty- or ninety-day periods must find it difficult to weigh carefully the consequences of their legislative actions. They must take care that the procedures they follow allow maximum utilization of the time at their disposal.

Most important bills considered by a state legislature originate with the executive branch, although bills are also drafted by legislative committees, private organizations and, more rarely, individual lawmakers. No matter what its source, a bill must be introduced by a legislative member. It is then referred by the presiding officer to a committee which will study its provisions and decide whether it should be favorably reported. Following committee approval, the bill is scheduled for floor debate,

TABLE 6.2
Classification of States by the Index
of Centralization in Decision-Making

RANK	STATE	CENTRAL- IZATION SCORE	AGREEMENT COEFFICIENT OF RELIABILITY	(50%) PRIMARY CHOICE	NUMBER OF USABLE RESPONSES
1	Alabama	.86	.87	Policy comm.	14
2	New Jersey	.82	.71		11
3	Tennessee	.79	.80	Policy comm.	21
4	Georgia	.75	.79	Policy comm.	10
5	Arkansas	.74	.77	Policy comm.	15
6	Connecticut	.69	.56		16
7	Louisiana	.65	.63	Policy comm.	10
8	Hawaii	.64	.77	Party caucus	15
9.5	Pennsylvania	.60	.84	Party caucus	10
9.5	Wisconsin	.60	.84	Party caucus	20
11	New York	.60	.52		26
12	Arizona	.58	.73	Party caucus	13
13	Kentucky	.56	.35		8
14	Rhode Island	.54	.94	Party caucus	12
17	Delaware	.50	1.00	Party caucus	15
17	Indiana	.50	.67	Party caucus	22
17	California	.50	.63		15
17	West Virginia	.50	.39		13
17	Maine	.50	.00		12
20	Virginia	.47	.63	Regular comm.	15
21	Illinois	.46	.30		11
22	Utah	.45	.76	Party caucus	18
23.5	Michigan	.44	.90	Party caucus	8
23.5	Maryland	.44	.56		16
25	Alaska	.42	.43		19

possible amendment, and the final vote. The successful bill then goes to the second chamber where the process is repeated, although a very few states hold joint committee hearings to avoid duplication of effort. A bill that passes the second chamber unchanged goes to the governor for his signature. Differing versions must be ironed out in conference committee and repassed before being engrossed and sent to the governor. The point to be stressed is that careful deliberations are time-consuming and time is what most state legislatures do not possess in abundance.

To permit a more orderly consideration of the many hundreds of bills introduced in the typical legislative session, all but a handful of states have established timetables for the submission of bills and the reporting of bills from committee. Sixteen states even permit bills to be filed before

RANK	STATE	CENTRAL-IZATION SCORE	AGREEMENT COEFFICIENT OF RELIABILITY	(50%) PRIMARY CHOICE	NUMBER OF USABLE RESPONSES
26	Ohio	.42	.41		18
27	Washington	.40	.61	Party caucus	19
28	Colorado	.38	.69	Party caucus	17
29	Oklahoma	.38	.71		16
30	Kansas	.37	.54		22
31	Montana	.36	.50	Regular comm.	18
32	Massachusetts	.34	.71	Regular comm.	9
33	Missouri	.32	.61		19
34.5	Minnesota	.31	.55		13
34.5	North Dakota	.31	.56	Regular comm.	16
36	Wyoming	.28	.59		20
37	Mississippi	.25	.79	Regular comm.	12
38	South Dakota	.23	.73	Regular comm.	13
39	Texas	.20	.84	Regular comm.	5
40.5	Idaho	.19	.71	Regular comm.	19
40.5	North Carolina	.19	.83	Regular comm.	19
42	New Mexico	.18	.85	Regular comm.	11
43	Iowa	.18	.71		25
44	Vermont	.13	.91	Regular comm.	18
45	Oregon	.11	.87	Regular comm.	19
46	New Hampshire	.09	.93	Regular comm.	11
47	Nebraska	.08	.92	Regular comm.	19
48	South Carolina	.06	.95	Regular comm.	17
49	Nevada	.04	.94	Regular comm.	14
50	Florida	.00	1.00	Regular comm.	13
	Median	.42	.71		15

SOURCE: Wayne L. Francis, *Legislative Issues in the Fifty States* (Chicago: Rand Mc-Nally, 1967), pp. 74–75.

the session has convened. Late submission requires the approval of an extraordinary majority, although a few states allow the governor to request bills at any stage in the legislative process.

To further control legislative time, a majority of legislative chambers provide for rules, steering, or sifting committees to determine priorities in scheduling legislation for floor action. Floor debate commonly can be closed in both houses and senates by moving the previous question or by other parliamentary devices. When confronted with a closing date, legislatures must protect themselves against obstructionist tactics. And when votes are taken, ordinarily time-consuming roll calls are speeded along by electric voting systems presently in use in 35 states.

The formal rules designed to make the best possible use of legislative time are bolstered by more informal codes of conduct expected of individual members. The informal rules establish a working consensus which enables the individual legislators to operate as a unit. Wahlke and his associates classified informal rules that served this purpose into the following categories:[7] (1) Rules that promote group cohesion and solidarity. For example, members are expected to respect the rights of others, to deal impersonally with legislative subjects in floor debate, and to exhibit institutional loyalty. (2) Rules that promote predictability of legislative behavior. The legislator is expected to declare his stand openly and to abide by his commitments. Mutual trust is required because no legislator has the time to study all legislative bills. (3) Rules that channel and restrain conflict. The emphasis of this set of rules is not that conflict is undesirable, but that conflict must be tempered by a willingness to see the other fellow's point of view and to accept reasonable compromises. (4) Rules that expedite legislative business. Many legislators are conscientious in their lawmaking responsibilities and expect a similar attitude of others. The member who speaks too freely on the floor or offers time-consuming amendments of minor consequence is resented.

Although informal, the rules described above are generally recognized in most legislatures and are enforced.[8] The member who violates the group's norms soon finds that his bills do not clear committee, are amended on the floor, or that a majority cannot be mustered to support them. He may also find that he is personally ostracized and his legislative actions distrusted. On occasion, he may be denied favorable committee assignments and special legislative privileges. By whatever means enforced, informal rules of conduct together with more formal prescriptions enable the legislature to function as an institution.

LEGISLATIVE ROLE PLAYING

We have defined the legislative system to include not just the members of the legislative body but groups and leaders external to the formal legislative institution. Although our focus will continue to be on official and informal acts of the legislature, the external influences on legislative behavior must now be stressed.

One way to approach such a complex undertaking is to consider the

[7] Wahlke *et al.*, *op. cit.*, pp. 158–163.
[8] *Ibid.*, p. 154.

various roles played by members of the legislative body.[9] A role, simply stated, is behavior expected of a legislator as appropriate to his position. A legislator may play different roles, depending upon the behavior expected of him by different groups. For our purposes, we shall divide the roles into two categories: Those that arise fundamentally from expectations external to the legislature; and those that arise from the expectations of his fellow legislators.

Roles Derived from External Sources

The legislator must consider a variety of groups in deciding how he will perform his legislative duties. He must consider the commitment he has to his party; he must give thought to how he represents his constituency; he must often evaluate the demands of organized interests within his state; and he must decide how he will support the legislative program of the governor or bills sponsored by other executive agencies. Role orientations derived from external sources are shown below:

1. Party role orientations:
    a. Party man. A person who feels obligated to vote in support of the party program and with his partisan colleagues.
    b. Independent, maverick, or nonpartisan. Roles here are less clearly defined than that for party man, oftentimes stated merely as the opposite of the partisan oriented. A maverick is sometimes distinguished from the independent by voting with the opposite party rather than simply following "principle."

2. Areal role orientations:
    a. District-oriented. The legislator who feels responsible for supporting legislation of benefit to his constituency and who may explicitly place district interests above state interests.
    b. State-oriented. The legislator who in varying degrees places the interests of the state above the parochial interests of his district.
    c. District-state. The legislator who sees his responsibility to both district and state seemingly without consideration of possible conflict.

3. Interest-group role orientations:
    a. Facilitators. The legislator who is friendly toward organized interests, ready to accept their assistance, and knowledgeable about their activities.
    b. Resisters. The legislator who is hostile toward organized interests and does not accept their counsel, yet is knowledgeable about their activities.

[9] The roles presented below are basically those described in Wahlke et al., op. cit., parts 3 and 4, and the bureaucratic role orientations were found in Jewell and Patterson, op. cit., p. 385.

    c. Neutrals. The legislator who has either no knowledge about organized interests regardless of his attitudes toward them, or has no strong views about their activity regardless of what he knows about them.

4. Bureaucratic role orientations:
    a. Executive-oriented. The legislator who acts as a spokesman, defender, and supporter of the executive and his program, or who veiws his role as one in opposition to the executive.
    b. Agency-oriented. The legislator who either speaks for and supports an administrative agency, or one who is an opponent of an agency.

Roles Derived from Internal Sources

The legislator must also have some conception of how he is to work with his fellow legislators in fulfilling the basic purposes or aims of the legislative process. This orientation has been labeled his purposive role. Closely akin but analytically distinct are the norms accepted as appropriate in arriving at individual decisions that will achieve the substantive goals of the legislature, called the representational role. Both of these roles are common to all legislative members. There are some roles, however, that devolve only upon certain members of the legislative chamber as a consequence of their formal position or special status. These orientations are referred to as specialized subroles.

1. Representational role orientations:
    a. Trustee. The legislator who is a free agent in arriving at his legislative decisions, whether because of moral convictions that it is right, because his views are in harmony with those of his constituents, or because constituency views remain unexpressed.
    b. Delegate. The legislator who believes that he must follow the wishes of his constituents rather than rely on his own independent judgment, in the extreme instance, accepting a popular mandate when counter to his own convictions.
    c. Politico. The legislator who combines trustees and delegate role orientations.

2. Purposive role orientations:
    a. Ritualist. The legislator who orients himself toward the tasks of the processes involved rather than the parliamentary goals.
    b. Tribune. The legislator who views his job as the voice of the people, a defender and promoter of popular interests.
    c. Inventor. The legislator who accepts the role of solving the problems confronting government through the initiation and formulation of public policies.
    d. Broker. The legislator who sees his role as reconciling and compromising group conflicts, not merely as a referee, but as a coordinator.

3. Specialized Subroles:
   a. Expert. The legislator who has acquired a subject-matter expertise and is sought out for his counsel for that reason.

   b. Leader. The legislator who exercises influence over others because of a formal leadership position (speaker, majority leader, committee chairman) or simply because of personal leadership traits.

It is important to understand that legislative roles are not the same as legislative behavior. A legislative role is what is expected of a legislator by those with whom he comes into contact. It is, then, normative in character. One assumes that the legislator's behavior often conforms to the roles he is assigned and herein lies their value as descriptive tools. In the sections that follow, we will be more interested in the actual behavior of legislators insofar as one can find patterns in their decision-making.

LEGISLATIVE DECISION-MAKING

Party Influences

Many students of the legislative process believe that effectively organized, competitive parties offer the best hope for a rational link between the voting public and their elected representatives. For the parties to provide this linkage requires that each develop a reasonably consistent attitude toward the major interests and issues within a state, that the policy stances formulated for each party differ from that of the other, and that the program differences be perceived by the electorate in their candidate selections. Party thus serves as a shorthand term to orient the voter in his electoral choices and the legislator in his voting decisions. The voter becomes identified with the party that he believes has best served his interests over time.

Two difficulties arise immediately with regard to the responsible party model described above. The first, which we shall treat in this section, is: Do the parties present reasonable alternatives to the voting public? The second problem, which we have treated elsewhere, concerns whether the voter perceives the general differences in the stands taken by the parties. Both are required if political parties are to serve the theoretical functions described for them.

In attempting to arrive at a determination of whether legislative parties cohere around a legislative program, several factors must be kept in mind. Not the least consideration is the substantial variation found among the states. Partisan conflict in some legislatures conforms to a modified version of the responsible party model that will satisfy all but the purists. Voting in other legislatures, some in which party strength is evenly balanced and some in which a single party dominates, exhibit little party cohesion.

The tests used to determine the existence or nonexistence of party as a reference in legislative voting must be approachd with caution. In most legislatures a majority of bills are passed with unanimous or near unanimous support. One should not expect party battles to develop over all bills introduced in a legislative session. On the contrary, a few bills, because of their transcendent importance to the state, may provide a better test of the nature of conflict within a legislature. And no matter what the signficance of bills, partisan conflict may arise with some issues but be displaced by other types of conflict in different issue areas. Bearing this in mind, we shall now turn to the incidence of partisan conflict.

Roll-call analysis is the most frequently used technique to determine the role of party in legislative votes. To be an accurate measure of legislative partisanship, one must assume that the roll-call vote is an important step in the policy formulation processes of the state. Some critics of roll-call analysis suggest that a more important stage of legislative enactment occurs, not with floor action of a bill, but at the committee stage or informally in the cloakroom. To infer from a legislator's vote his activity in all phases of the legislative process would obviously be incorrect. Nevertheless, it is our judgment that roll-call votes are a significant aspect of legislative decision-making, particularly at the state level, where, as we have indicated, committee work is probably less important than in the Congress.

Among the most commonly used measures of partisan activity are the Rice indexes of cohesion and likeness. The index of cohesion is the absolute difference between the percentage for and the percentage against a particular bill. Thus if a party splits evenly over a measure, its index of cohesion is zero. The party that divides 75 percent on one side of a question and 25 percent on the other has an index of 50. Perfect cohesion is represented by an index score of 100.

The index of likeness is a measure of the difference in voting behavior between parties (or other groups). The index is obtained by subtracting the percentage of yea votes cast by one party on a legislative proposal from the percentage of yea votes cast by the other party, and then subtracting the difference from 100. Thus if the parties each split evenly on a bill, the difference between the percentages of yea votes would be zero and, subtracted from 100, would equal 100 or perfect likeness. If the parties split 25 percent yea votes in one party to 75 percent yea votes in the other party, the difference beween percentages of yea votes would be 50, which, subtracted from 100, would indicate an index of likeness of 50. Complete dissimilarity is represented by an index score of zero.

Table 6.3 presents the results of roll-call analysis in 26 state senates.[10] Based on this table, other studies, and the more impressionistic analyses of American politics, certain generalizations about partisan activity can be made. Partisan behavior appears associated with heavily industrialized and urbanized states of the Midwest, Middle Atlantic, and lower New England regions. These regions are also characterized by a heavy percentage of foreign stock composed in large measure of the second generation of immigrants from southern and eastern Europe. In these states the core of Democratic party strength has come from urban constituencies of industrial workers, principally ethnic and nonwhite groups, who are generally non-Protestant. Republican party support is centered in suburbia, rural areas and small towns, and the more nativist and Protestant groups of the population. By representing their constituencies, the parties have developed policy positions reasonably dissimilar and modeled along the lines of national party politics which serves to reinforce the state divisions.

The two-party states of the mountain and western regions of the country exhibit less legislative partisanship than states such as Ohio, Pennsylvania, and Connecticut. One interesting difference between East and West that may help explain the differing levels of legislative partisanship, apart from the greater number of industrial states east of the Mississippi, is the size and saliency of the ethnic vote. The influx of immigrants into the country at the turn of the century, settling in the big cities of the East and Midwest, produced a distinctive brand of politics marked by policy styles derived from "the immigrant ethos" and political forms based on the urban political machine. On the other hand, the egalitarian influence of the frontier together with the more sparse settlement in the West allowed the newly arrived to be treated as an equal without the necessity of creating defensive political mechanisms to compete with established groups. An individualism was fostered that eschewed partisanship in politics. The effects of these political styles linger on and influences legislative partisanship today.

A comparison of the more partisan minded and the less partisan minded state senates in Table 6.4 reveals that much the same kind of issues were contested along party lines, suggesting that the meaning of the party label is becoming standardized in different sections of the country. The differences lay in the scope and intensity of conflict—that is, more bills provoked party battles in the more partisan senates and party lines were more sharply drawn. It is revealing that issues of immediate self-interest to the parties (election administration and legislative organization) ranked at the top of partisan measures. Nevertheless, bills that likely involved a governor's or a party's program commitments (taxation,

[10] Hugh L. LeBlanc, "Voting in State Senates: Party and Constituency Influences," *Midwest Journal of Political Science*, XIII (February, 1969), 33–57.

TABLE 6.3
Conflict and Cohesion in 26 State Senates,
1959 or 1960

	NUMBER OF SENATORS			NUMBER OF BILLS		MEAN INDEX OF COHESION DEMO-CRATS		REPUB-LICANS		MEAN INDEX OF LIKENESS	
	DEMS.	REPS.	GUB. PARTY	ALL DIV.[a]	PARTY OPP.[b]	ALL DIV.[a]	PARTY OPP.[b]	ALL DIV.[a]	PARTY OPP.[b]	ALL DIV.[a]	PARTY OPP.[b]
California	27	13	D	219	37	58	48	59	57	79	48
Connecticut	29	7	D	6	3	94	90	78	67	42	6
Delaware	11	6	R	188	116	68	84	77	87	37	14
Idaho	27	17	R	161	49	50	58	55	62	70	40
Illinois	24	34	R	274	74	45	75	75	63	56	31
Indiana	23	27	R	243	124	65	65	60	68	56	34
Iowa	18	32	D	241	94	66	69	60	60	66	35
Kansas	8	32	D	82	29	55	49	80	82	63	34
Kentucky	30	8	D	64	25	48	51	51	59	66	45
Massachusetts	23	16	D	158	117	72	78	67	77	37	23
Michigan	12	22	D	142	82	73	81	72	75	46	22
Missouri	26	8	D	57	20	45	49	62	63	67	44
Montana	38	18	R	164	60	66	54	59	56	71	45
Nevada	7	10	D	29	8	55	70	56	43	73	43
New Hampshire	6	18	R	66	41	58	63	35	38	60	49
New Jersey	7	13	D	13	6	79	85	65	90	50	12
New York	24	34	R	64	45	68	76	81	88	35	18
Ohio	20	13	D	305	210	81	83	61	71	39	23
Oregon	19	11	R	219	64	59	55	59	64	69	40
Pennsylvania	22	28	D	260	213	78	82	85	90	25	14
Rhode Island	23	21	R	12	12	99	99	96	96	3	3
South Dakota	20	15	D	162	72	60	67	61	67	59	33
Utah	12	13	R	46	12	50	41	61	53	74	53
Vermont	8	22	R	80	32	63	63	38	41	66	48
Washington	35	14	D	181	90	59	60	71	78	55	31
West Virginia	23	9	R	86	46	73	85	58	73	48	21

[a] Includes all roll calls in which at least 10 percent of those voting dissented from the majority position.
[b] Includes all roll calls with opposing party majorities.
SOURCE: Hugh L. LeBlanc, "Voting in State Senates: Party and Constituency Influences," *Midwest Journal of Political Science*, XIII (February, 1969), p. 36.

TABLE 6.4
*A Comparison of Conflict in Divisive Roll Calls of 26 State Senates
by Issue Categories, 1959 or 1960*

	ALL SENATES	N	MEAN INDEX OF LIKENESS MORE PARTISAN SENATES[a]	N	LESS PARTISAN SENATES[a]	N
Election administration	38	97	20	60	55	37
Legislative organization	38	161	21	88	57	73
Labor	43	212	24	127	58	85
Taxation and revenue	50	400	35	211	64	189
Appropriations	51	280	32	156	68	124
State administration	51	360	40	188	61	172
Transportation and motor vehicles	58	227	42	128	75	99
Local subdivisions	61	393	47	212	74	181
Judicial and legal	62	286	52	139	72	147
Education	63	192	57	94	74	98
Health and welfare	64	116	52	76	79	40
Regulation of business	64	357	57	185	72	172
Natural resources	75	104	68	38	80	66

$r_s = .87$ (comparing the rank order of partisan bills in the more partisan and less partisan senates)

[a] The senates were divided into equal groups by the index of likeness.
SOURCE: Hugh L. LeBlanc, "Voting in State Senates: Party and Constituency Influences," *Midwest Journal of Political Science*, XIII (February, 1969), p. 43.

appropriations, and labor) also aroused partisan loyalties. What was somewhat surprising was the relatively low ranking of health and welfare and business regulations issues as partisan topics. Since our figures are based on all nonunanimous bills under a given issue area, it may be the case that a very few bills that importantly changed existing policy were contested along party lines and thus would represent a better index of partisan conflict.[11]

Constituency Influences

Constituency influences on the vote of a legislator can result from both the areal focus of his representative activities and the style of his decision-making. Although the two roles are frequently confused in interpreting the Bristol speech of Edmund Burke, they are analytically distinct.[12] The

[11] A check of the ten bills in each of the state senates that produced the sharpest party divisions nevertheless found few health and welfare and business regulation issues. *Ibid.*, p. 40.
[12] Wahlke *et al., op. cit.*, pp. 269–270.

first concerns whether the legislator attempts to represent the interests within his district, the interests of his state, or a combination of the two. Regardless of the geographical focus that holds his attention, the legislator may believe that he is a free agent to vote his personal convictions or may feel bound by instructions from his constituency.

In these two sets of role orientations, one finds the principal obstacles confronting legislative parties. Constituency pressures are often viewed as antithetical to party, creating cross-pressures on the legislator who must decide if loyalty to party outweighs possible electoral sanctions. Even if constituency pressures are not evident, many believe that the legislator must balance his independent judgment or conscience against the demands of his party leadership on particular issues. What is often overlooked is the fact that individual attitudes, constituency interests, and party stand frequently reinforce one another and serve as the principal base for responsible party government as we know it. Thus the person with liberal views joins the Democratic party because of his convictions and, as the Democratic party's candidate, is victorious at the polls in a constituency conventionally associated with Democratic party success—perhaps a racially mixed, low-income, urban constituency, heavily populated with industrial workers. When the legislator votes to increase workmen's compensation, he may be said to vote his convictions, his constituency, and his party.

Most legislators would find it difficult to obtain instructions from either their district or their state, depending upon their areal focus, should they desire it. Unable to comprehend the complexity of today's government, the great majority of constituents are either incapable or do not care to express their views. The trustee role orientation, as Wahlke and his associates suggest, may be a "functional necessity."[13] Table 6.5 shows the representational role orientations in four states:

TABLE 6.5
Distribution of Representational Role Orientations

ROLE ORIENTATION	CALIF. $N = 49$	N.J. $N = 54$	OHIO $N = 114$	TENN. $N = 78$
Trustee	55%	61%	56%	81%
Politico	25	22	29	13
Delegate	20	17	15	6
Total	100%	100%	100%	100%

SOURCE: John C. Wahlke, Heinz Eulau, William Buchanan, and LeRoy C. Ferguson, *The Legislative System* (New York: Wiley, 1962), p. 281.

[13] *Ibid.*, p. 281.

A majority of the legislators in the sample surveyed by the Wahlke group did suggest some areal focus for their legislative activities. In other words, although they may not have been *instructed* in any specific way, they nevertheless *perceived* particular district or state interests which they felt called upon to represent. A district orientation was more common in competitive districts than in one-party districts as Table 6.6 indicates.

TABLE 6.6
*Political Character of Electoral Districts
and Areal Role Orientations in Three States*[a]

AREAL ROLE ORIENTATION	POLITICAL CHARACTER OF DISTRICT		
	COMPETITIVE $N = 72$	SEMI- COMPETITIVE $N = 77$	ONE-PARTY $N = 96$
District	53%	48%	33%
District-state	28	34	33
State	19	18	34
Total	100%	100%	100%

[a] California, New Jersey, and Ohio. "Not ascertained" respondents are omitted.
SOURCE: John C. Wahlke, Heinz Eulau, William Buchanan, and LeRoy C. Ferguson, *The Legislative System* (New York: Wiley, 1962), p. 292.

Our own data point to a district role orientation of legislators in states where legislative partisanship is high—that is, we found a significant relationship between constituency characteristics and legislative voting, including districts that were noncompetitive, in state legislatures which contested issues along partisan lines.[14] It is our hunch that the distinction between a district and state orientation is largely a figment of the legislator's imagination. It would be difficult to disentangle a district's interest in a state law from the state's interest, particularly when a district has no unique interest that is not shared by others. What is important in deciding issues in the state legislature is how shared interests can be organized in a vote decision. We feel the political party provides an organizational instrument for this purpose which works effectively when its constituency base is clearly perceived and is differentiated from the opposition party. It is no wonder, then, that a "district" focus is high in states that emphasize legislative partisanship.

[14] LeBlanc, *op. cit.*, pp. 56–57.

Pressure Groups

Pressure group activity has been considered in the literature of the past to be the *bête noir* of representative government. The image of powerful economic interests subverting the popular will by cajoling, intimidating, or buying the votes of legislators to advance or protect their interests remains a commonplace among many segments of the public. Yet this characterization of pressure politics is no longer accepted as valid by students of the legislative process. V. O. Key, Jr., was among the first to argue that, with our legislative representation based on geographical districts, organized interests provide a useful type of functional representation wherein a variety of like-minded people can join together to present their demands more effectively to those in official positions.[15]

The view that powerful business, farm, and labor groups are dominant within a state is given credence by the scale of their activities. The notion of the threat they pose is only partially dispelled by systematic surveys listing the more powerful pressures on state legislators. Thus the AFL–CIO, manufacturing associations, state farm bureaus, truckers, and utilities are frequently cited for their lobbying activities.[16] Yet the fact that groups are organized in American society does not mean that their demands are reckless or unfair, that groups organized within a given area (business, farm, labor) are necessarily united in their legislative endeavors, or that any one group is interested or influential in all policy areas. Further, it does not suggest that organized interests can always work their will even in matters in which they express an interest.

Wahlke and his associates believed that legislators classified as facilitators held the key to pressure group activity within a legislative system.[17] One might presume that facilitators were those who identified with particular interest groups and endeavored to promote their aims in the legislative struggle. Yet this was not the case. Facilitators were more likely economically neutral (neither prolabor nor probusiness) than either of the other two role types (resistors and neutrals). And they were more sophisticated in their perceptions of group activity, fewer of them responding to survey questions in stereotypical terms. Indeed the most significant demographic aspect of the facilitator was his relatively better education.[18] One surmises that the facilitator understands the complexities of today's society and his role in conflict management. It suggests

---

[15] V. O. Key, Jr., *Politics, Parties and Pressure Groups* (3d ed.; New York: Crowell, 1953), p. 152.
[16] Francis, *op. cit.*, p. 42.
[17] Wahlke, *et al.*, *op. cit.*, p. 328.
[18] *Ibid.*, p. 329.

that he may side with an unorganized public as easily as with a prolabor or probusiness stand. Since the pressure tactics of a few organized interests are so visible, the proposition that some legislators are capable of critically evaluating group demands has an important bearing on interest group politics.

The influence wielded by organized interest groups depends to an extent on the character of the political system. Some believe pressure politics will be of less consequence if political parties are strong and effectively organized. This notion assumes that parties are independent organizations of general appeal rather than mechanisms for reconciling differences among the interest organizations that constitute their base. Probably the truth lies somewhere between the two extremes. Political parties cannot afford to be subservient to any single interest and win general election contests. Nevertheless, they must seek support for their candidates and this oftentimes means establishing friendly relations with groups who supply money, skills, and votes to them.[19]

Gubernatorial Influence

The governor of a state has to be interested in the outflow of policy from his legislative assembly. Over the years his power to influence legislative decisions has increased considerably in many states. The more heavily industrialized and urbanized states, in particular, have shown recognition of the desirability of gubernatorial leadership by equipping the governor with formal powers—control over the budget, appointment of subordinate executives—and extending his term of office. But the power of the executive is not measured by possession of formal powers alone. Because he is the most visible state figure, elected statewide in a campaign likely to attract more voters than other state officers, the people look to him for leadership. A skillful governor can translate popular support into political power to guide his program through the legislative process.

Nevertheless, the governor has not emerged triumphantly as legislative leader in all states. In fact, the popular image of the governor as chief legislator needs clarification. The governor's office or the executive branch is undoubtedly the source of most important bills considered by the legislative branch. Most of these bills will pass, probably without much conflict, because they are relatively noncontroversial. In this sense, the "hat" of chief legislator fits the governor's head. Yet the idea of a strong governor conveys also the image of one who fights for his legislative program even should it be resisted by a recalcitrant legislative assembly.

[19] The relationship between political parties and interest groups is discussed more fully in Chapter 3, pp. 61–63.

It is here that one suspects that gubernatorial leadership has been over-sold. Francis found that even on the four issues deemed most important in his state, bills that commonly produced legislative divisions, the gover-nor was seen as pressing hard for legislation in any one of the issues by only 45 percent of the legislative respondents.[20] A governor will obvi-ously select the issues that he fights for, based on the needs of his state and the political circumstances confronting him. Francis found that more governors actively fought for bills involving highways and transportation, administration, civil rights, and finance than, say, election-primaries-conventions, business, labor, or liquor.[21] Yet generalizations tell us very little about the activity of particular governors since some governor was active in every issue category. We are left with the supposition, and it is no more than that, that the governor's willingness to do battle with his legislature has been overstated in the literature.

LEGISLATURES
AND LEGISLATION

The stability of a political system depends in part upon the manner in which political decisions are reached and whether the processes involved are accepted as legitimate. Equally important is whether values are allo-cated in a manner that satisfies the expectations of most segments of the citizen population. Since the legislative system has a key role in authori-tatively allocating values in society, we must examine the ability of state legislatures to pass laws to meet today's problems. Public policies are the ultimate pay-off of legislative activity.

One way to analyze legislative output is to determine what legislators themselves believe to be the most important issues confronting them in a legislative session. They then may be asked whether legislation dealing with the issues was passed. This essentially was the technique used by Francis in his fifty-state survey of legislative issues. On the basis of the responses a crude index of policy success (a passage-defeat ratio) was constructed.[22]

State legislatures acted positively on most of the problems (67 per-cent) they perceived as important.[23] Laws were written despite the fact that partisan, factional, or regional conflicts developed on the legislative floor. Of course, legislative success was higher for some issues which engendered little or no conflict (health, education, and highways-

[20] Francis, *op. cit.*, p. 15.
[21] *Ibid.*, p. 77.
[22] *Ibid.*, p. 18.
[23] *Ibid.*, pp. 53–54.

transportation) than those which were highly contentious (taxation and apportionment). The most troublesome task of the lawmakers, however, was to push a bill through when interest groups battled over its legislative aims. This tells us something about the legislative role in conflict management. One infers that resolving differences among competing interests to clear the way for legislative action must await broad political support or, at least, the forecast that a bill's passage will either crystallize substantial latent support or not draw forth organized opposition. A more positive role in conflict resolution is probably beyond the capability of most state legislatures, given their relative lack of professionalism and part-time character.

Although legislatures with centralized decision-making might be supposed better organized for successful law-making than those in which power is dispersed, the evidence points otherwise.[24] Based on the legislators' own evaluations, the fifty states were placed into equal groups by the degree of centralized decision-making. Those placed in the upper ranks were states in which decision-making was in the hands of the governor or party leaders. Those placed in the lower ranks were those in which major decisions were made in regular committees or on the floor. The policy success of the centralized legislatures was not significantly greater than the decentralized legislatures. One is led again to infer that the general political climate—that is, the attitudes and opinions held by important segments of the population—suggests the directions of state lawmaking.

Legislative policy success did vary with the distribution of party strength within the legislature.[25] States with the highest passage-defeat ratio were those in which one party controlled both the governor's office and the two houses of the state legislature, yet the minority party captured more than a token number of legislative seats. Policy success was lowest in those states in which the party that held the governor's chair lost control of one or both houses of the legislature. Francis' evidence thus tends to support the conventional interpretation of the role of party in marshaling political support.

The policy success of which we are speaking, of course, is simply the passage of legislation. Whether the legislation would be approved by a majority within a state or would satisfy all observers is another question entirely. Mississippi legislators, for example, may respond with alacrity to threats posed by Supreme Court decisions requiring the desegregation of public schools. The response may even meet with widespread approval within the state. Yet others who would have preferred a more positive approach to solving racial inequality may not view the legislative action

---

[24] *Ibid.*, p. 79.
[25] *Ibid.*, pp. 54–58.

as a "policy success." It is our judgment that legislative action over the long run would have to be in accord with the dominant sentiment in a state no matter how viewed by individual segments of the population. In the short run the manner in which political groups are organized and who gains the upper hand will determine the more specific character of legislation.

7. COURTS IN THE POLITICAL PROCESS

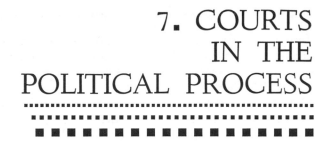

Although the idea is contrary to popular thinking, courts play an important role in the political process of a state. If one accepts David Easton's definition of politics as the authoritative allocation of values in society, the conclusion is inescapable that judges are political actors whose decisions, at times, have important effects on the everyday lives of the members of the political community. Even decisions that have no sweeping impact of general interest to the state—damages awarded the plaintiff in a bodily injury suit or the prison term imposed on the convicted criminal, for example—can have enormous influence on the individual's life. It scarcely is of concern to the unsuccessful defendant that his "misfortune" results from perhaps centuries-old legal practices; the conse-quences remain as bleak. And the numbers touched by the courts suggest that in their sum judicial verdicts constitute an important element in allocating values in society.

Labeling the judges "political actors" would hardly raise eyebrows were it not for the fact that "politics" suggests partisanship, and partisan-ship is more appropriately associated with the executive and legislative branches as they carve out public policies. One does not have to sub-scribe to the carefully fostered myth of legal orthodoxy that judges *find* not *make* the law, however, to recognize the distinctiveness of the judicial process. Although judges may be confronted with issues that also face the executive and legislative branches, may respond in the long run to the social and political forces that influence the thinking of other political actors, may even have contact through litigation with the same interest organizations whose representatives have previously trod legislative halls in seeking their objectives, their role in the political process remains distinctive.

The peculiar judicial role stems in part from the institutional environ-ment in which the judges work and the procedural norms to which they adhere. Thus the courts, despite all the recent emphasis on judicial activism, are ill-equipped to seize the initiative in establishing public policy. They must await the suits that are brought before they may enunciate new policies. And it must be remembered that their discretion-ary power is further circumscribed by the prior policies established in constitutions, statutes, and their own decisions. The same restrictions do not apply to the other branches of government, whose leaders enjoy greater freedom to propose legislative and constitutional changes to meet the exigencies of a changing society.

What is perhaps of equal significance to the more passive role assigned to the courts is the public expectations of judicial behavior. Other politi-cal actors court popular favor, bargain with and compromise differences among competing interest groups, and make the most of their partisan affiliations: such activities are the stock-in-trade of political leaders. Judges, however, are expected to dispense justice impartially, relying on dispassionate and rational analysis, free from the more immediate parti-san and other pressures of politics. Never mind that the ideal is seldom obtained; since it is the public expectation, it defines the overt role judges must play. And it is our judgment that the role expected of a judge does influence his behavior in important respects and differentiates it from the behavior of the more partisan-minded legislator and executive. Thus it would make no more sense to insist that the political process is a seamless web in which the courts do not have a distinctive role than it would be to assume that judges easily shed their past prejudices, biases, convictions, or partisan associations when they don their judicial robes.

In the pages that follow, we hope to make clear just how the courts participate in the politics of a state; but first we must describe the structures, powers, and procedures of state court systems.

STRUCTURE AND JURISDICTION

The Inferior Courts

At the base of the judicial pyramid are found the so-called "inferior" courts, or courts of limited jurisdiction, which try cases involving minor breaches of the peace or civil matters where the claims involved are relatively small. Historically the dispenser of justice at this level has been the justice of the peace in rural settings and the magistrate in urban settings. Paid on a fee basis, often untrained in the law, commonly a hanger-on of the court house or city hall crowd, these justices have been the object of attack by bar associations, automotive organizations, and a variety of civic and good government groups. The public clamor has not been without its impact. Few metropolitan areas now attempt to administer justice with the out-dated justice courts.[1] Although a constitutional office in 35 states, the positions are not always filled and those that are sometimes try only traffic offenses or confine their activities to officiating at weddings and acting as notary publics. This is not to say the stereotypical justice of the peace and magistrate courts have vanished from the scene but to suggest they are likely confined to rural areas and small towns where their continuance is more justified or their abuses have less impact. According to one study, they appear "most active in the mountain and western states of Arizona, New Mexico, Wyoming, South Dakota, Idaho, Montana, Oregon, and Washington, and in the southern states of Mississippi and Alabama."[2]

In place of or together with the justice courts are a bewildering array of courts of limited jurisdiction—county courts, metropolitan courts, municipal courts, traffic courts, small claims courts, juvenile courts, domestic relations courts—which represent a significant step forward in that court personnel are selected from members of the bar who are full-time salaried employees. This presumes a minimal level of professionalism normally associated with courts of law. That it does not meet all criteria of efficient administration of justice will be made clear in the discussion of trial procedures.

By whatever name and by whatever level of professionalism, inferior

[1] Maxine B. Virtue, *Survey of Metropolitan Courts, Final Report* (Ann Arbor: University of Michigan Press, 1962), p. 203.
[2] Kenneth E. Vanlandingham, "The Decline of the Justice of the Peace," *The University of Kansas Law Review,* 12 (March, 1964), 390.

courts have several common characteristics: (1) Their judicial powers are limited to misdemeanors and small claims. The only exception is when they act as committing magistrates in felony cases. Following a pretrial, or preliminary, hearing, the inferior court judge determines whether sufficient evidence exists for the prosecuting attorney to proceed further against the accused. (2) They are not usually courts of record—that is, no public record is kept beyond the names of the parties and their attorneys and the final disposition of the case. The lack of record is an important consideration when appeal is made, particularly when constitutional issues or fine points of law are considered. (3) The proceedings are quite informal and often summary in character. (4) The losing party has the right of appeal to a superior court where the proceedings are more formal.

The importance of the inferior courts stems from the fact that more citizens are acquainted with the administration of justice through them than any other court. That impression is not always one that commands respect for the judiciary, a particularly unfortunate state of affairs because those whose views of justice are formed here (other than traffic offenders) are mainly from that segment of the community already distrustful of social authority. Typical of the cases handled by a municipal court are those brought by police arrest in the Baltimore Municipal Court shown in Table 7.1.

Courts of General Jurisdiction

The second tier of courts are the trial courts of general jurisdiction, known by a variety of names—for example, superior court, district court, and circuit court. These courts have original jurisdiction in all of the more serious criminal cases and civil suits where the amount claimed is substantial; they also hear appeals from the inferior courts, a relatively infrequent proceeding. A state is commonly divided into geographical divisions with a court of general jurisdiction in each. In some states additional courts of general jurisdiction have been established to meet specialized needs, principally the congestion of court dockets in metropolitan areas. County and municipal courts in heavily urbanized communities often exercise jurisdiction which may overlap with both the inferior courts and the general trial courts. In addition, a few states retain a chancery court for all equity proceedings, a carry-over from English jurisprudence.

In the more populous counties and metropolitan areas the court is a multimembered body with the individual judges, formally or informally, specializing in the cases over which they preside—criminal, civil jury, civil nonjury, domestic relations, juvenile, or probate. At this level in the judicial system one can expect that the judges are full-time members of the court and have legal training.

The general trial courts of a state dispense justice in cases whose outcome can have far-reaching consequences to the parties involved. Since only a minority of cases are appealed, the trial court is for many a court of last resort. Even where the issues of law have been settled and no novel interpretation of constitutional and statutory provisions is required, the numbers who are touched by trial court decisions suggest the magnitude of their effect.

Unlike the inferior courts, the general trial courts receive more civil filings than they do criminal filings. The number of filings alone does not indicate necessarily that the civil workload of the courts is greater than its criminal workload, since a greater percentage of criminal cases are likely to be contested. Nevertheless, civil proceedings occupy more of the court's time, largely because of personal injury and property damage cases, the great majority resulting from motor vehicle accidents. For example, personal injury and property damage suits accounted for half of the cases that went to jury trial in the California superior courts in 1968–1969. Whether a proceeding is criminal or civil, of course, important issues of law can emerge that need clarification or possible reinterpretation and, in any case, can be of considerable importance to the individuals involved. Yet in terms of the major judicial issue of court congestion, how the judges spend their time is of no small consequence. Table 7.2 shows the filings in the California superior courts.

Appellate Courts

The final rung in the state judicial ladder are the appellate courts. Every state has a court of last resort commonly but not uniformly called the supreme court. (The New York state general trial court is, confusingly, called "the Supreme Court"). Several of the more populous states also provide intermediary appeals courts, thus including two tiers of courts above the general trial level. Because they sometimes decide major issues of law, the appellate courts share in a type of decision-making that may have profound policy implications for other political actors, privately organized interests, or the general populace of the state.

Appellate courts are multiple-judge courts whose decisions are rendered by majority vote. Although size varies, they almost uniformly sit as three judge courts to meet the workload demands. The exception to this rule is the state with intervening appellate tribunals, where the supreme court commonly sits *en banc*.

TABLE 7.1
Processing of Cases in the Baltimore Municipal Court, 1964

CHARGE	NUMBER OF CHARGES	FINED OR SENTENCED TO JAIL IN MUNICIPAL COURT	PROCESSED IN MUNICIPAL COURT[a]	REFERRED TO CRIMINAL COURT	REFERRED TO JUVENILE COURT	OTHER
Assault, common	3171	1038	1960	93	51	29
Assault, aggravated	3473	1229	1718	365	124	37
Assault on officer	181	93	31	42	13	2
Assault to murder	27	1	4	21	0	1
Assault, threats	956	229	619	81	10	17
Bogus checks	580	147	260	171	1	1
Burglary	1979	6	87	1308	574	4
Carnal knowledge	125	0	11	113	1	0
Deadly weapons	1326	629	453	215	11	11
Disorderly conduct	11490	5834	4819	189	63	585
Disturbing the peace	2837	1020	1087	24	0	706
Drunkenness	9288	5527	3611	23	1	126
False pretenses	270	33	98	135	1	3
Firearms ordinance	299	104	135	53	5	2
Forgery	304	5	20	274	5	0
Gambling	742	59	155	439	17	2

Investigation, held for	3719	0	3659	1	0	59
Larceny	4154	1249	1421	518	893	28
Larceny, auto	374	22	27	107	218	0
Liquor law	709	179	498	32	0	0
Malicious destruction	943	213	476	36	20	16
Manslaughter	88	0	77	9	1	1
Minors possession of alcohol	953	406	530	3	14	0
Murder	134	0	13	111	8	2
Narcotics	368	36	38	287	5	2
Prostitution	215	120	124	37	7	6
Parole violator	383	166	186	6	25	0
Rape, forcible	107	0	20	83	4	0
Receiving stolen goods	171	32	74	62	3	0
Resisting police	170	82	59	26	1	2
Robbery	812	9	43	647	105	8
Rogue and vagabond	58	3	2	53	0	0
Sodomy	81	1	10	54	14	2
Welfare fraud	258	25	231	2	0	0
Vagrancy	275	174	61	5	0	2
Vehicles, unauthorized use	904	381	431	70	12	10

a Includes acquitted and probation without verdict. These figures also include the approximately 1800 persons who received probation after conviction in municipal court as well as all defendants who were convicted but received suspended sentences.

SOURCE: 1964 Baltimore Police Department Annual Report, pp. 33–37. Reproduced in the President's Commission on Law Enforcement and the Administration of Justice, *Task Force Report: The Courts* (Washington: U.S. Government Printing Office, 1967), p. 121.

TABLE 7.2
California Superior Courts: Number of
Filings Per 100,000 Population, by
Type of Proceeding
(fiscal years 1967–1968 and 1958–1959)

POPULATION AND PROCEEDINGS	1967–1968	1958–1959
Total population July 1 (in thousands)[a]	19,478	14,741
Filings per 100,000 population[b]		
All proceedings	2,400	2,103
Probate and guardianship	289	328
Divorce, separate maintenance, and annulment	597	546
Original civil litigation	753	595
Personal injury, death and property damage[c]	243	230
Motor vehicle[d]	172	——
Other[d]	71	——
Eminent domain[e]	59	——
Other civil[c]	451	365
Complaints[d]	213	——
Petitions[d]	238	——
Insanity and other infirmities	107	156
Juvenile	338	270
Delinquency[d]	272	——
Dependency[d]	66	——
Criminal	283	195
Appeals from lower courts	15	10
Habeas corpus	18	3

[a] California Department of Finance, *California Population* (1968).
[b] All figures rounded to nearest whole number. Because of rounding, rates of proceedings may not add to total.
[c] Not a separately reported category prior to 1958–1959.
[d] Not a separately reported category prior to 1967–1968.
[e] Not a separately reported category prior to 1965–1966. In prior years this category was included in "Other civil."
SOURCE: Judicial Council of California, *Annual Report of the Administrative Office of the California Courts,* 1967–1968.

The most striking feature of the appellate system is its small size measured against the tasks set for it. Although the number of cases these courts hear is minuscule compared to the combined totals of superior courts, nonetheless the increasing work load poses major problems for them. What makes the increasing volume of business critical, of course, is that their decisions may have a sweep to which the general trial courts cannot aspire. The solution to their problem, however, is not so straightforward as with the trial courts—by adding to the number of judges. One authority has argued that "increasing the number of judges has the consequence of diffusing responsibility for the performance of the judicial function and so may impair the integrity of the judiciary as an agency of government."[3]

CRIMINAL PROCEEDINGS

Perhaps the greatest single obstacle to efficient and impartial administration of justice in our courts today is the volume of business they undertake. One could argue that other defects of the system (and they relate primarily to the adequacy of justice tendered to the indigent and near indigent and other marginal members of the community who are often found on the nether side of the law) could be solved if the judges could proceed at a more leisurely pace. But such is not the case, and existing injustices can only be exacerbated by overworked and harassed judges, prosecutors who enter the courtroom with only a brief look at less serious cases, and defense attorneys similarly overburdened and ill-prepared.

The administration of state criminal justice is able to work as well as it does, according to one scholar, because of three basic assumptions that underlie the system: "First, only persons as to whom there is relatively high probability of guilt will be brought before the courts. Second, the overwhelming majority . . . of persons brought to the courts will plead guilty and not involve courts, prosecutors, and defenders in the time and expense of contested cases. Third, persons charged with minor offenses will be processed in volume, with a minimum of judicial time spent in disposing of each individual case."[4]

A popular conception of criminal justice has police officers apprehending individuals for alleged criminal activity who then have their innocence or guilt established in a judicial trial. Indeed sometimes this is the case, but the evidence suggests that it is far from common. From one third to one half of all police arrests end with a decision by police, prosecuting attorney, or judge not to press charges.[5] And even should the decision be made to prosecute, the likelihood is that the defendant will

[3] Geoffrey C. Hazard, Jr., "After the Trial Court—The Realties of Appellate Review," in Harry W. Jones (ed.), *The Courts, The Public and the Law Explosion* (Spectrum ed.; Englewood Cliffs: Prentice-Hall, 1965), p. 78.

[4] Edward L. Barrett, Jr., "Criminal Justice: The Problem of Mass Production," *ibid.*, pp. 107–108.

[5] The President's Commission on Law Enforcement and Administration of Justice, *Task Force Report: The Courts* (Washington: U.S. Government Printing Office, 1967), p. 4.

plead guilty. (See Table 7.3.) To clear up popular misconceptions, we wish to describe what we believe are characteristic features of the administration of justice in state courts.

TABLE 7.3
Guilty Pleas as a Percentage of
Total Convictions in Selected States

STATE (1964 STATISTICS UNLESS OTHERWISE INDICATED)	TOTAL CON- VICTIONS	GUILTY PLEAS	
		NUMBER	PERCENT OF TOTAL
California (1965)	30,840	22,817	74.0
Connecticut	1,596	1,494	93.9
District of Columbia (year ending June 30, 1964)	1,115	817	73.3
Hawaii	393	360	91.5
Illinois	5,591	4,768	85.2
Kansas	3,025	2,727	90.2
Massachusetts (1963)	7,790	6,642	85.2
Minnesota (1965)	1,567	1,437	91.7
New York	17,249	16,464	95.5
Pennsylvania (1960)	25,632	17,108	66.8
U.S. District Courts	29,170	26,273	90.2
Average (excluding Pennsylvania)[a]			87.0

[a] The Pennsylvania figures have been excluded from the average because they were from an earlier year, and the types of cases included did not appear fully comparable with the others.

SOURCE: President's Commission on Law Enforcement and Administration of Justice, *Task Force: The Courts* (Washington: U.S. Government Printing Office, 1967), p. 9.

The Decision to Charge

Following his arrest by the police, a not untypical practice is to bring the suspected law violator to the precinct station house where the officer in charge may review the facts and advise if any charges are warranted. The prosecuting attorney's office may be consulted as a matter of routine or only in the more doubtful cases. Any number of circumstances can lead to the suspect's release. He may have been wrongfully accused. Criminal prosecution may create more problems than it will solve—for example, in charges arising from a domestic quarrel. Sufficient evidence to prove the accused guilty beyond a reasonable doubt may be lacking.

Whatever the situation, many lawyers argue that the prosecuting attorney should make the decision to charge inasmuch as he is more likely aware of alternative sentences for the several possible charges, whether the evidence is sufficient for a conviction, or whether the resources of his office would be strained by cases that might be equitably handled otherwise.

The procedures are admittedly informal and are not visible to the public. The possibility of the fabled "third degree" always exists (or police brutality in modern parlance) while the accused is being held in custody and before formal charges are brought. The so-called "Mallory Rule" requires that persons arrested under federal statutes be brought before a commissioner or other committing magistrate within a matter of hours. Twenty-nine states also require that the accused be brought before a judicial officer without unnecessary delay,[6] but the amount of time allowed under the rules varies. Although pre-judicial consultation between police and prosecuting attorney's office need not work against the accused, meaningful investigative work that would justify delay in appearing before a court is unlikely to be undertaken at this stage in the process. Normally, the accused is brought before a judge more quickly in a misdemeanor charge than for a more serious offense. One presumes that the reasons are related to the time involved in preliminary investigations.

Misdemeanors

Following the decision to charge, the defendant is brought before an inferior court judge who will have final disposition of his case. Since the great volume of criminal cases involve misdemeanors, many urban courts process defendants on an assembly-line basis in which the rights of accused persons are, in many cases, systematically ignored. A task force for the President's Commission on Law Enforcement and the Administration of Justice described practices in the Baltimore Municipal Court in the following manner:[7]

> In the cases observed, no defendant was told that he had a right to remain silent or that the court would appoint a lawyer to represent him if he were indigent, notwithstanding the court rule that counsel will be assigned whenever a defendant may be sentenced to more than six months or fined more than $500. We were told that at least one judge takes great care to advise defendants fully, but the three judges we observed did not.

Practices in the Detroit Recorders Court were described in a similar vein:[8]

6 *Ibid.*, footnote 30, p. 84.
7 *Ibid.*, p. 124.
8 *Ibid.*, p. 134.

Most of the defendants whom we observed pleaded guilty and were sentenced immediately, without any opportunity for allocution. When they tried to say something in their own behalf, they were silenced by the judge and led off by the bailiff. A few defendants went to trial, but the great majority of them did so without counsel. In these cases the judges made no effort to explain the proceedings to the defendants or to tell them of their right to cross-examine the prosecution's witnesses or of their right to remain silent. . . .

Felony Cases

The defendant in a felony case is brought before a committing magistrate (usually an inferior court judge) to determine if there is sufficient evidence to hold him for formal charge by grand jury indictment or prosecutor's information. The judge informs the defendant of the charges against him, informs him of his right to counsel which may be assigned to him if he is legally indigent, and sets bail.

Although practice varies, it is unlikely that the indigent receives counsel until after the information or indictment has been filed. The initial appearance before the court, however, can be important to the accused as a discovery device, to learn facts of the prosecution case for later use at his trial. In states that use the information, a preliminary hearing is usually held between the time of the first court appearance and the filing of the information; it is designed for discovery purposes. In the grand jury states the first court appearance may be used in this way. Nevertheless, without counsel, the accused is scarcely capable of judging what is in his best interests. Thus Patricia Wald writes:[9]

> At the preliminary hearing, the defendant has the option of asserting his right to have the government present its case. Appearance of counsel here may be crucial. The defendant may not fully understand that if he waives, he loses one of his best and most effective chances to discover the identity of the government's key witnesses and the nature of the government's evidence. . . .
>
> . . . Without counsel, few felony suspects are adept enough to probe evidentiary weaknesses by cross-examining prosecution witnesses; few are experienced enough to weigh the pro's and con's of taking the witness stand themselves. . . .

The Plea of Guilty

The great majority of felony and nontraffic misdemeanors are processed through guilty pleas. Were it otherwise, the courts would be swamped by the volume of business handed to them. Indeed, the threat

[9] *Ibid.*, p. 143.

of a jury trial is part of defense counsel's strategy in protecting his client's interests. Yet the great majority of misdemeanants appear at their trial without counsel and often are bewildered by the spectacle of justice in urban courts. It is likely that many plead guilty without fully understanding their rights and that some plead guilty to bring the process to a conclusion. Consider the following exchange between judge and defendant in the Syracuse City Court:[10]

> Q: How do you plead to the charge?
> A: I am not guilty of drinking. I don't think. I haven't drunk anything in several months. They might have thought I was drinking because I have epilepsy, but I don't drink.
> Court: Then I am not going to accept your plea of guilty. I will enter a plea of not guilty on your behalf and give you a week to get a lawyer. April 16th for counsel. Do you want any bail here, Mr. N. [the prosecutor]?
> Mr. N: $250.00 bail.
> Court: All right, bail is $250.00 property or cash. Have you got any relatives here in the city?
> A: No.
> Q: Do you have any friends here in the city?
> A: No, not here. They are all in Rochester.
> (Later at the same session of court.)
> Court: Will you listen to me for a moment? We have a procedure here that we have to follow. When you appeared before me earlier this morning, you pleaded not guilty to the charge. Do you now wish to change your plea?
> A: I don't have no choice.
> Q: No, you have a lot of choices. You can continue your plea of not guilty and get a lawyer and have a trial.
> A: But they will take me back upstairs and I want to get out.
> Q: If you plead not guilty to the charge, the only thing I can do is give you a trial. I have no jurisdiction to do anything unless you are convicted after trial or unless you plead guilty.
> A: I told you before I plead guilty.
> Q: You understand that you are entitled to an attorney and that you can plead not guilty to the charge.
> A: I know that, but I don't want to go back upstairs.

Most misdemeanants who plead guilty or who are convicted after the shortest possible trial are sentenced immediately. Unless they are represented by counsel (and perhaps even if so represented), there is unlikely to have been any presentence investigation or probationary report that has inquired into the defendant's background or details of the charge that could assist the judge in imposing sentence. The judge must then make

[10] *Ibid.*, footnote 17, p. 142.

his determination only on the basis of the charge and what information he elicits by questioning the defendant. There is scarcely discretion for individual treatment. A defense attorney may take advantage of the press of court business and obtain, not simply reduced charges, but the minimum sentence for the offense charged. Thus it sometimes happens in misdemeanor cases that "the 'repeater's' knowledge of the arraignment system enables him to obtain a sentence of less severity than the first offender."[11]

For the more serious offenses pretrial negotiations are likely to take place between indictment or information and the scheduled appearance of the defendant before a felony court. Agreements reached between the defense attorney and the prosecutor are not unlike the pretrial settlements of civil cases. At its best, there is much to say for "plea-bargaining." As usually practiced, the defendant pleads guilty to a less serious charge, which lowers the maximum possible sentence. Sometimes, the defendant pleads guilty to a specific charge with an understanding that the prosecutor will recommend leniency or probation, or that the defendant will be sentenced by a particular judge. Whatever the form, plea-bargaining allows some flexibility in treating the individual case or protecting an individual from any harshness in the criminal code.

Nevertheless, plea-bargaining is not without its dangers. By its very nature it is informal and hidden from the public view. The bargaining may take place without adequate investigations. It is quite possible that professional and habitual criminals with expert legal advice are in a better position to take advantage of the procedure than the marginal offender. Above all else, there is the fear that the innocent will plead guilty to escape a possible trial conviction and severe sentence.

CIVIL PROCEEDINGS

The jurisdiction of the court is invoked in a civil proceeding when a plaintiff files a petition with the clerk of court in which he sets out the nature of his complaint against the defendant. The court issues a summons to the defendant accompanied by the complaint or a short statement of the plaintiff's grievances. The summons is a court order requiring the defendant to respond to the allegations. Through an exchange of the "pleadings" of the parties involved, the issues are "joined" and the case is scheduled for trial. Thus, in simplified form, civil cases involve a dispute between private parties in which the state acts as an impartial arbiter. The root causes of problems in civil proceedings are the same as those for

[11] Ralph H. Nutter, "The Quality of Justice in Misdemeanor Arraignment Courts," *Journal of Criminal Law, Criminology and Police Science,* 53 (June, 1962), 217.

the administration of criminal justice—the volume of business the courts are called upon to handle and the suspicion that the poor and near-poor are victims of a less than even handed justice.

The time involved in the disposition of felony cases is short compared with the time involved in disposing of civil suits. In Los Angeles County courts, for example, in 1963, the median time between indictment through information and final disposition for all criminal cases was 50 days. For jury trials alone the median time was 85 days.[12] One does not wish to underestimate the anxiety caused by even a short delay in a criminal prosecution or depreciate any time spent in jail awaiting preliminary hearings or trial. Yet in 1968, the median waiting period between filing a charge and jury trial of a civil case in Los Angeles County was two years.[13] Los Angeles may not be a typical metropolitan area, and practice varies between jurisdictions and from one year to the next. But there is widespread agreement that delay in civil suits is overly long. In some jurisdictions a jury trial may take three or four years, or longer, from initial filing.

The concern over delay in civil proceedings is real enough. The longer the time between filing and trial, the more difficult is it for witnesses to recall events accurately, and the greater the danger that witnesses cannot be located or will be deceased. Moreover, the complainant in a personal injury suit may be forced to settle for a lesser sum than he might obtain through trial procedures because he possesses no other practical alternative. There is evidence that the more serious the injury and thus the larger the size of the claim, the longer the delay of the trial.[14] An even greater motive for an out-of-court settlement is present under such circumstances.

Not all delay is caused by a laggard judicial system. In some instances it is caused by the parties involved or their attorneys. One frequent cause of postponement is the request made by one of the attorneys for additional time to prepare his case. Litigation in personal injury suits is handled in many jurisdictions by a small group of specialists. The backlog of cases built up by an attorney may decide the scheduling of suits. Requests for delay are almost always accepted as a matter of comity and need not result in inefficiency in the system if the court is so organized to move up other cases without a break in schedule. If deadtime is created in the judicial calendar, a postponement further delays court processing of cases.

[12] Judicial Council of California, *Annual Report of the Administrative Office of the California Courts*, 1962–1963, p. 45.
[13] Judicial Council of California, *Annual Report of the Administrative Office of the California Courts*, 1967–1968, p. 141.
[14] Maurice Rosenberg and Michael I. Sovern, "Delay and the Dynamics of Personal Injury Litigation," *Columbia Law Review*, 59 (December, 1959), 1152.

A substantial part of the delay in civil proceedings is caused by the personal injury suit, frequently involving automobile accidents. A large number go to jury trials, the most time-consuming of the court's activities. Thus a not infrequent recommendation is that automobile accident cases be handled by special managers or court appointed masters empowered to make awards, subject, of course, to court review. Other recommendations suggest an auditor to take evidence and make legal rulings while leaving the disposition of the case to the courts. Either practice envisages adding personnel to the judicial system to speed the process along.

A more novel idea that would avoid lengthy litigation is the recommendation of "no-fault" insurance policies. Under such insurance plans the driver of an automobile would be compensated by his own insurance company for medical bills or loss of income occasioned by an accident regardless of who is at fault. A passenger in a car involved in an accident or a pedestrian struck by an automobile would similarly collect from the owner's insurance company. Civil litigation designed to determine blame for the accident could thus be avoided. Proponents of no-fault insurance claim that it can cut premiums in half while fully compensating the severely injured.[15] The reform is opposed by some elements of the insurance industry and by some trial lawyers, in part, at least, because it might adversely affect their livelihood.

Delay is not the only problem area of civil proceedings. Those who are ignorant of legal proceedings and cannot afford to hire a lawyer to protect their interests are at the mercy of unscrupulous landlords, merchants, and operators of loan-shark businesses. Many on the margins of society are unaware of the commitments to which they may be legally held when they fall behind in their rent or installments on a loan or merchandise and are hauled into court no matter what their intentions for honestly meeting their obligations. Frequently they find that they are saddled with court costs and additional interest occasioned by the lapse in payment, and find their wages garnished to meet the demands. They emerge from their court experience embittered with the course of justice and wondering why the complainant has not been similarly compelled to live up to what they think ethically should be his responsibilities.

JUDICIAL DECISION-MAKING

Insofar as the court's role in the political process is concerned, the important issues relate to the character of the decision-making process. What is involved is the quality of justice tendered to all parties, which may be adversely affected by delay in bringing a case to trial or by

[15] See John A. Hamilton, "How to Pay for 15,000,000 Auto Accidents a Year," *The New York Times Magazine*, May 10, 1970, p. 33.

dispensing justice *en masse* without acknowledgment of the individuality of defendants. These matters have been stressed. What is also important is whether characteristics of the litigants or the judge that are or should be external to the case affect the outcome. In other words, are certain classes of litigants found more often on the losing side than not? Do certain types of attorneys win more than their share of cases? Do certain types of judges decide cases differently from other types of judges? An affirmative answer to the questions posed would cause some concern over the impartiality of the courts.

Whether an individual receives fair treatment in criminal prosecutions involves more than the actual trial—in fact, it begins with the initial arrest. There is evidence, as we have noted, that the socially or economically deprived defendant is less likely to be procedurally protected as he moves from arrest to trial. As Table 7.4 indicates, in state felonious

TABLE 7.4
*Disparities in State Felonious
Assault Cases*

	ECONOMIC CLASS		RACE	
	INDIGENT	NONINDIGENT	NEGRO	WHITE
% who received no preliminary hearing	34	21	24	23
% who were not released on bail	73	21	49	36
% who had no lawyer	2	12	13	9
% who had over two months delay from arrest to disposition or trial while in jail	57	43	60	49
% who had no jury trial of those tried	59	54	71	54
% who received a prison sentence rather than a suspended sentence or probation	73	58	67	62
% who received over one year prison terms of those imprisoned	42	35	50	29

SOURCE: The data were taken from Stuart S. Nagel, *The Legal Process from a Behavioral Perspective* (Homewood: Dorsey Press, 1969), Table 8–1, p. 106. They are based on 846 assault cases in 194 counties in all 50 states for 1962. The exact base for each percentage was not given, but sample sizes were generally large enough so that differences are not due to chance. We have extracted only those items in which the difference for one or both of the groupings was 10 percentage points or more. See Nagel's comments in footnote 15, p. 88.

assault cases the indigent is less likely to receive a preliminary hearing, more likely to remain in jail pending trial, and more likely to receive a prison sentence than the nonindigent defender. Excluding the preliminary hearing, the Negro is similarly deprived and, in addition, is somewhat less likely to have legal assistance.

That more indigents had counsel than nonindigents may seem surprising. Stuart Nagel suggests that the relationship may be curvilinear—that is, the poor have counsel appointed, the rich can afford the services of a lawyer, but intervening groups may be unable to afford legal assistance and fail to meet the legal definition of indigency.[16]

Nagel's findings seem to confirm a growing popular impression that the marginal members of the community—the poor, particularly the poor who are members of racial minority groups—do not receive the same quality of justice as others. Of course, indigents may receive a prison sentence rather than probation or Negroes may receive a longer term than others because they are more culpable. But certainly the availability of bail is related to the defendant's resources, and one may wonder whether other procedural rights are fairly applied to them as well.

A second aspect of judicial decision-making is whether the off-the-bench associations of a judge influence the outcome of a trial. For example, to what extent does a judge's political party affiliation affect judicial decision-making? Examining the full court decisions of state and federal supreme courts on a variety of legal issues, Nagel compared the behavior of Democratic and Republican justices in cases in which the Courts were divided. Democratic judges on the same court with Republican judges were more prone to favor:[17]

the defense in criminal cases
the administrative agency in business regulation cases
the claimant in unemployment compensation cases
the finding of a constitutional violation in criminal-constitutional cases
the government in tax cases
the tenant in landlord-tenant cases
the consumer in sales-of-goods cases
the injured party in motor vehicle accident cases
the employee in employee injury cases

The differences in behavior of the two partisan groups were statistically significant.

[16] Stuart S. Nagel, *The Legal Process from a Behavioral Perspective* (Homewood: Dorsey Press, 1969), p. 89.
[17] Stuart S. Nagel, "Political Party Affiliation and Judges' Decisions," *American Political Science Review,* LV (December, 1961), 845. Nagel found other differences between Republican and Democratic judges, which are not reported here because they lacked statistical significance at the .05 level.

This pattern conforms to popular conceptions of party policy views—that is, the Democratic party is widely considered the party of the common man, the protector of the underprivileged and less affluent, and more inclined to use government power to fulfill its objectives; the Republican party is widely considered the party of the middle classes and business interests and more inclined to leave the solution of social and economic problems to the private sector of the economy. One should not conclude, however, that the justice received party tutelage in arriving at his judicial vote.[18] More likely, the judge is conditioned by his prior training and experiences which in their sum effect his philosophical outlook. The same set of principles or convictions or biases that led him into a given political party in the first place also guide his judicial deliberations. Thus the broad congruence found between party affiliation and judicial decision-making should be expected.

Nagel also examined such factors as the judges' age, religion, former occupation, and education. (See Table 7.5.) He found other statistically significant differences in how justices voted in criminal prosecution cases. For example, (1) Catholic judges were more prone to support the defense than Protestant judges; (2) judges who had been former prosecutors were more prone to vote against the defense than judges of different background; (3) members of the American Bar Association were less defense-minded than nonmembers; and (4) liberal judges, as measured by their off-the-bench attitudes, were more defense-minded than conservative judges.[19] The explanation for the differences, with the exception of the former prosecutors, is probably not unrelated to what we said about political party affiliation. A judge's philosophical outlook is conditioned by the life experiences he brings to the bench, which include familial, religious, professional, and fraternal associations. Any one set of relationships may actually convey a particular life style built on a complex of factors. Democratic party affiliation, for example, is often associated with immigrant stock, non-Protestant religions, and lower- or working-class origin. It is also associated with more liberal political and social views. A finding that Catholic judges decide cases differently than Protestant judges probably means that the two groups differ on an even wider set of relationships and values. Now those who are defendants in criminal prosecution cases are more likely than not from socially and economically deprived groups. They are the "underdogs" or unfortunates in society, and the causes of their plight evoke sympathy from those of a liberal frame of mind. From such a characterization of the defendant, then, judges may differ in the central tendencies of

18 *Ibid.*, p. 847.
19 Nagel, *The Legal Process from a Behavioral Perspective, op. cit.*, 235.

TABLE 7.5

How Judges of Differing Backgrounds and Attitudes Differ in Their Criminal Case Decisions

(based on the nonunanimous cases of the state and federal supreme courts of 1955 on which both groups being compared are present)

GROUP 1: HYPOTHESIZED TO BE LESS DEFENSE-MINDED	GROUP 2: HYPOTHESIZED TO BE MORE DEFENSE-MINDED	NUMBER OF JUDGES INVOLVED IN EACH GROUP (1)	(2)	% OF GROUP 1 ABOVE THEIR COURT AVERAGE ON THE DECISION SCORE[a]	% OF GROUP 2 ABOVE THEIR COURT AVERAGE ON THE DECISION SCORE[a]	DIFFERENCE	PROBABILITY OF THE POSITIVE DIFFERENCE BEING DUE TO CHANCE
Party							
Republicans	Democrats	45	40	31%	55%	+24	Less than .05
Pressure groups							
Members of a business group	Did not indicate such membership	15	71	47	52	+ 5	.20 to .50
Members of ABA	Did not indicate such membership	105	88	37	52	+15	Less than .05
Members of a nativist group	Did not indicate such membership	11	33	36	48	+12	.20 to .50
Occupations							
Former businessmen	Did not indicate such occupation	22	71	32	40	+ 8	.05 to .20
Former prosecutors	Did not indicate such occupation	81	105	36	50	+14	Less than .05

Education						
Attended high-tuition law school	Attended low-tuition law school	24	22	54	59	+5	.20 to .50
Age						
Over age 65	Under age 60	67	66	43	42	− 1	Negligible diff.
Geography						
Practiced initially in small town	Practiced initially in large city	31	37	35	35	0	Negligible diff.
Religion and ancestral nationality						
Protestants	Catholics	39	18	31	56	+25	Less than .05
High income Prot. denomination	Low income Prot. denomination	54	54	41	50	+ 9	.05 to .20
Only British ancestry	Part non-British ancestry	96	97	38	47	+ 9	.05 to .20
Attitudes						
Low general liberalism score	High general liberalism score	22	23	27	57	+30	Less than .05
Low criminal liberalism score	High criminal liberalism score	26	17	27	59	+32	Less than .05

[a] Decision Score = proportion of times voting for the defense in criminal cases.
SOURCE: Stuart S. Nagel, *The Legal Process from a Behavioral Perspective* (Homewood: The Dorsey Press, 1969), pp. 230–231.

their decision-making, because of off-the-bench associations which determine philosophical and judicial outlook.

The fact that judges who were formerly prosecuting attorneys were more prone to vote against the defendant than judges with other background is probably unrelated to any liberal-conservative continuum. In other words, their prior profession does not contribute to a general life style or a general set of values but is more directly related to criminal prosecutions. They decide with the prosecution because they carry with them the frame of reference of a previous professional experience.

THE SELECTION OF JUDGES

What we know about judicial decision-making should help us in determining how judges should be selected. If a judge's background and off-the-bench associations influence his legal judgements, or suggest a broad philosophic approach to legal questions, then we change somewhat the nature of the issue. The question is not who is best qualified to judge technical competence in the law but who should determine what the broad approaches to the law should be. It is with these thoughts in mind that we consider the relative merits of appointing and electing judges.

Despite pleas of bar and civic organizations that some form of the Missouri plan be adopted, the most common method of selecting state court judges remains popular election. (See Table 7.6.) Not only is election the first choice of the states, but partisan elections are preferred over nonpartisan contests. The conventional criticism leveled at popularly elected judges is that judicial work, because of its professional character, cannot be easily judged by the voting public. If the election is bipartisan, or if the nonpartisan ballot does not discourage active party involvement, an additional charge is made that the judge is indebted to his party in a way that can only compromise judicial independence and integrity.

The Missouri plan, its proponents claim, will insure that "merit"—that is, professional skill and competence—will prevail in the selection process. Under the plan, a special nonpartisan commission recommends three names to the governor who fills any judicial vacancy by appointing one of the candidates on the list.[20] Thereafter, the judge desiring an

[20] The plan applies to the circuit courts of Jackson County and St. Louis; the three courts of appeal in Kansas City, St. Louis, and Springfield; and the supreme court. Separate commissions (each composed of two lawyers elected by attorneys residing in the court's jurisdiction, two laymen appointed by the governor, and the presiding judge of the appellate court in the area, *ex officio*) make nominations for vacancies in Jackson County and St. Louis. An appellate commission (composed of three lawyers elected by attorneys in each of the three courts of appeals jurisdictions, three laymen appointed by the governor, and the chief justice of the Supreme Court, *ex officio*) make nominations for vacancies in the appellate courts and the supreme court.

TABLE 7.6
Methods of Selection of General Trial and Appellate Court Judges

PARTISAN ELECTION	ELECTION BY LEGISLATURE	NONPARTISAN ELECTION	APPOINTMENT	MISSOURI PLAN[b]
Alabama	Connecticut[a]	Arizona	Connecticut[a]	Alaska
Arkansas	Rhode Island[a]	Idaho	Delaware	California
Colorado	South Carolina	Michigan	Hawaii	Iowa
Florida	Vermont[a]	Minnesota	Maine	Kansas
Georgia	Virginia	Montana	Maryland	Missouri
Illinois		Nevada	Massachusetts	Nebraska
Indiana		North Dakota	New Hampshire	
Kentucky		Ohio	New Jersey	
Louisiana		Oregon	Rhode Island[a]	
Mississippi		South Dakota	Vermont[a]	
New Mexico		Utah		
New York		Washington		
North Carolina		Wisconsin		
Oklahoma		Wyoming		
Pennsylvania				
Tennessee				
Texas				
West Virginia				

[a] Appellate judges selected by legislature; general trial judges appointed by governor.
[b] May not apply to all courts within a state.
SOURCE: The Council of State Governments, *State Court Systems*, July, 1966. Mimeographed.

additional term of office runs in a nonpartisan election in which he has no opposition; the voter is asked simply whether the judge should be retained in office. The mixture of merit, gubernatorial selection, and popular check is said to provide the best of all possible systems.

Whether the Missouri plan offers the panacea claimed for it ultimately depends upon one's evaluation of the quality of judicial decisions handed down. Part of the evaluation will rest upon the technical proficiency with which the judges discharge their responsibilities. Insofar as this matter is concerned, the legal competency of judges apparently has improved in the state of Missouri. At least, the state has not found itself with the embarrassment of a Judge Padberg whose chief occupation prior to his election under the older system had been as a pharmacist and who had previously filed only nine lawsuits—eight for divorce and one for annulment. Yet one must hope that a Judge Padberg is an anomaly of the past, who could not reappear today because of the watchful eye of the bar, newspapers, and civic groups on judicial selections.

The quality of judicial decisions, however, is a more far-reaching issue than that of technical competence. It extends as well to the central tendencies of judicial decision-making. Of what meaning is judicial competence to the defendant who loses an appeal on a criminal prosecution case? The fact of the matter is that the Missouri plan does not take justices "out of politics." It simply means that selection is placed in the hands of other political actors whose motivations, in the broadest sense, are also politically relevant.

Critics of the Missouri plan charge that the organized bar is given disproportionate weight in the judicial selection process. Their objection stems from the belief that bar associations, or their leadership, are conservatively oriented. Thus former Chief Justice Earl Warren is said to have resigned his membership in the American Bar Association for ideological reasons.[21] Yet a recent study of the plan as it operates in Missouri suggests that the criticism is overdrawn.[22] Elections for the lawyer-member places on the commissions in Jackson County and St. Louis are often contested by nominees of rival bar associations. "Plan" judges were not found to be notably more conservative than those selected by popular election. The authors were careful to point out, however, "that the Nonpartisan Court Plan might lead to different results in different states, or even in the same state over different periods of time."[23]

There are alternatives, of course, to the Missouri plan. In California, the governor makes the initial appointment when a vacancy occurs, but the appointment must be approved by a judicial commission consisting of the chief justice of the supreme court, the presiding justice of the appellate court of the district involved, and the attorney general. Thus a commission still checks on a judge's technical competence, but, since this is done after the judicial selection is made, the governor is free to determine the philosophic views he wishes represented in the court system. In other states the governor appoints judges, sometimes with senate confirmation. Yet the underlying issues remain the same regardless of the particular plan in use: the mode of selection can have an effect of the way judges handle and decide cases.

Thus far our discussion has been more speculative than empirical. We must have evidence whether appointed judges act differently from elected judges. Selecting three types of issues in which partisan affiliations have been found to be important (administrative regulations of business, unemployment compensation, and employee injury cases), Nagel compared the judicial behavior of appointed and elected judges. As Table 7.7 in-

[21] Nagel, *The Legal Process from a Behavioral Perspective, op. cit.*, p. 229.
[22] See Richard A. Watson and Rondal G. Downing, *The Politics of the Bench and the Bar* (New York: Wiley, 1964), esp. chap. 9.
[23] *Ibid.*, p. 353.

TABLE 7.7
Judicial Tenure, Methods of Selection, and Conformity to Party Voting Patterns, 1955

GROUP 1	GROUP 2	NUMBER OF JUDGES IN EACH GROUP (1)	(2)	% IN GROUP 1 WHO VOTED CONTRARY TO THEIR PARTY PATTERN	% IN GROUP 2 WHO VOTED CONTRARY TO THEIR PARTY PATTERN	PROBABILITY OF THE POSITIVE DIFFERENCE BEING DUE TO CHANCE
Appointed judges	Elected judges	18	47	39	15	.02% to .05
Judges elected by a nonpartisan ballot	Judges elected by a partisan ballot	29	18	14	17	*a*
Judges with terms longer than 8 years	Judges with terms of 8 or less years	37	28	27	14	.15 to .20
Elected judges with terms longer than 8 years	Elected judges with terms of 8 or less years	20	27	15.0	14.8	*a*
Appointed judges with terms longer than 8 years	Elected judges with terms longer than 8 years	17	20	41	15	.02% to .05

a Negative or negligible difference.
SOURCE: Stuart S. Nagel, *The Legal Process from a Behavioral Perspective* (Homewood: The Dorsey Press, 1969), p. 194.

dicates, statistically significant differences emerge in terms of the way the judges voted in support of the predicted party patterns. No significant differences appeared in comparing only judges elected under a partisan ballot and those elected under a nonpartisan ballot; no important differences separated judges by their length of service; but the divergence between appointed and elected judges was marked.

As we have noted, the fact that political party patterns emerge in decisions of elected judges does not mean that they accept partisan cues in their judgments. It means that a basic viewpoint dictates their choice of party as well as their judicial vote.

We may summarize our discussion in the following way. The courts are involved in the political process and affect the lives of citizens through general pronouncements as well as through individual judgments. Although clearly in politics, judges are nevertheless asigned a role of independence by conventional legal thought. The conflict between the expected role and actual behavior comes to the fore in the judicial selection question. Few can object to the selection of professionally competent judges who mete out impartial justice. Nevertheless, judges of equal legal competence can, and do, disagree, and the disagreement is sometimes based on broad philosophical views. How do we include this dimension of judicial decision-making in our selection process? Partisan elections may be one way to insure that the courts will be sensitive to dominant values in the state—if this is the objective we set for them.

8. GOVERNING COMMUNITIES: FORM, INFLUENCE, AND PUBLIC POLICY

MEANING AND SIGNIFICANCE
OF GOVERNMENTAL FORM

Governmental form is a crucial variable in determining the nature of the governing process and decision-making in a local community. Hence its importance to our understanding of the processes found at this level in the American political system. This and the next two chapters are concerned with governmental form and structure in communities. In this chapter we shall discuss the meaning of local government form and structure and review the traditional types of local government. We begin with an examination of the meaning of this important topic because we believe that more times than not this aspect of the matter has been overlooked and because we are convinced that this is the best way to give substance to the more formal and abstract considerations treated later. Chapters 9 and 10 look into the questions of governmental decentralization in metropolitan areas, reactions to this decentralization, and emerging metropolitan governmental reorganization ideas and strategies.

Governmental form refers to (1) the formal and informal character and internal authority and power assignments of a particular government, and (2) the pattern or type of governmental structure and arrangements in a geographical area (city, county, or metropolitan area, for example) containing more than one local government. For instance, a municipality's governmental character may be based on the mayor-council form; or the governmental system of a particular metropolitan area or a part of a metropolitan area may be classified as a county-unit dominant structure—meaning that the county governments are the most important political units in the area. Further, in a particular government the electorate may directly select the chief executive officer, while in another government the chief executive may be appointed. Local government functions are sometimes lodged in independent commissions or they may be located in departments directly under a mayor or city manager. Additionally, a few metropolitan areas have a metropolitan-wide government for the entire area, while others have a few governments, each serving a large population and land area, and still others possess many local governments, most of which are responsible for only a small population and relatively few square miles in land area. Some areas provide for the assignment of certain functions to one type of government and other areas assign these same functions to another kind of government. All of these examples illustrate different aspects of governmental form, or the nature of governmental structure, character, and arrangements.

In this chapter governmental form is scrutinized in both its legal and extralegal senses. Our objective will be to describe the existing nature of local government, whether consistent or inconsistent with formal definitions, legal prescriptions, or theoretical expectations. Particular emphasis will be placed on the political and economic meaning and implications of various governmental forms and structural patterns. We believe that this analysis expands the scope of what has traditionally been considered part of local government form and structure, and we hope that this broadened scope will add to the reader's insight into the operation of local political systems.

By way of introduction, decisions in local government are not made outside particular environments. We are not ruled by philosopher kings residing in ivory towers. Local determinations in the public policy arena are made by men and women operating within certain channels and constrained by a number of forces and pressures of a legally prescribed or other variety. The types of constraints imposed by the nature of the governmental system and the effects of these constraints on public policy and other matters are the subject matter of this chapter. As one might expect, once the effects of particular governmental arrangements are known (or suspected), specific arrangements will serve as a motivation for certain local groups and interests, which either want to make decisions themselves or want decisions made in a way that will serve their ends or their conception of what the public interest requires. Hence, wherever possible, motivations will also be analyzed.

Before examining in greater detail the meaning of governmental form, we shall advance some definitions. A local government is defined as a public institution created by or in accordance with state law for the purpose of performing one or more public activities or functions designed to serve a public end in a community or communities (institutions crossing state boundaries require, in addition, the consent of the United States Congress). To simplify matters, we accept as falling within the general category of local government the local institutions which the U.S. Bureau of the Census considers local governments.[1] The two broad kinds of local governments are general-purpose governments and special-purpose governments. General-purpose governments refer to units responsible for the normal range of functions (police, fire, water, health, welfare, and so forth) found in local public institutions. The municipal governments of New York, Cleveland, and Detroit are examples of general-purpose governments; so are county and township governments. Special-purpose governments are those given the responsibility for one or a small number of locally performed public functions; school districts and special districts are examples of special-purpose governments.

Although not widely recognized in the past, governmental form has important effects on the content and direction of public policy, the particular pattern of the distribution of power, and the determination of who will rule, who will be given access to the rulers, the specific values to be reflected in the decision-making process and in public policy, the degree and kind of outside influence to be permitted in administrative actions, and whose will and views shall prevail in the execution of policy. The influence of governmental structure at the local level is especially worthy of study because of the tendency until recently to describe local government in terms of legal theory and moralistic abstractions. At the local level as elsewhere in American politics, citizens differ on what they

[1]   U.S. Bureau of the Census, *1967 Census of Governments,* Vol. 1, *Governmental Organization* (Washington, D.C.: U.S. Government Printing Office, 1968).

consider important, what they believe their government should do, how government should perform its responsibilities, and whose interests should be represented and to what degree by government in general or by certain agencies or processes in government. These differences can be traced to a number of factors, but they often are related to economic and social class considerations. Organizations will normally be formed to reflect and promote the interests of particular segments of the community, and these organizations will couch membership interests in terms of philosophical goals which will appear to coincide with the objectives of nearly everyone in the community. The organizations will take positions on local public policy proposals and on the nature of governmental structure within which public policy decisions are made. Different groups will often take different positions on both public policy and governmental structure, partly because of the contrasting premises, interests, expectations, and values represented by the various organizations. Government at the local level does not "resolve" the conflict between these groups and interests, as is commonly held, except in the short run; like other institutions of certain kinds, it provides a peaceful means by which conflict can continue. And more than this, the very government that serves these groups in this respect is an object of group manipulation and is structured in certain ways by the groups it is serving.

Concerning the significance of governmental structure, the most valued stakes and therefore the most sharply contested matters are public policy, and patterns of access to the decision-making process. Since the nature of governmental structure affects both, it is a key factor in the objective sense in local politics and it is important to local groups. Probably the more sophisticated and politically rational of local groups spend the greater portion of their energies on shaping governmental structure rather than on immediate issues because of the institutionalizing and causal nature of the former.

Another point to be considered in the analysis of governmental form is that public officials and employees in local government are to one degree or another "interests," often organized, which can influence the character of governmental structure and determine to some extent the nature of decisions, particularly of an administrative variety, made within that structure. Also, local government administrators are normally differentially affected by the various patterns of governmental arrangements, and far from being detached observers waiting for the public will to be registered on governmental structure questions, are often active partisans of one kind or another when such a question becomes an issue.

Economic and other determinists would contend that certain basic factors account for all social behavior, and that government structure and form, especially within one culture such as that found within the

United States, have little independent effect and meaning. To the economic determinist, variations in form are likely to be explained in terms of underlying economic forces, and differences not reflective of these forces are not considered real differences or are not considered important. The authors of this text do not adhere to any pure determinist point of view. We wish only to review the various forms of government (here at the local level) and to see if they are associated in any special way with certain variables such as class interest, the nature of political and economic factionalism, specific public policies, and the like.

Empirical fact demonstrates that certain kinds of governmental structure and organizational form and practices are directly related to specific types of public policy and political group views and interests. In its broadest sense the reform movement in American local politics is testimony to this. Reformers in local government almost invariably have been drawn from the ranks of the middle and upper-midle classes and have espoused the characteristic values of that segment of society in their efforts to bring about governmental change at the local level. The reformers' preference for the council-manager form of municipal government and the protection of key local functions such as planning and parks from the general political process tends to reflect these values. By campaigning for this point of view, reformers probably assumed that their structural preferences, if adopted, would effect public policy changes and influence access patterns. Regardless of what reformers assumed, however, as a result of community acceptance of such structural modifications (council-manager government and the isolation of key local functions), the ethnically and lower-middle-class-dominated political machine stood to lose considerably.

The council-manager form of government, in fact, is often if not normally the choice of communities in which the upper-middle class comprises a substantial proportion of the residents. Such a local political system is far more prevalent among middle- and upper-middle-income suburban jurisdictions than it is among large lower-middle-class central cities. The council-manager form is also associated with homogeneity in class structure, degree of ethnicity, and type of economic base. If a community has at least—that is, no lower than—a middle-class social structure, a strong possibility exists that it will have a council-manager government. Parenthetically, lower- and working-class jurisdictions, even if they are more or less homogeneous in class composition, will be slow to adopt the manager plan, if in reality they ever do. Ethnicity also seems to affect government structure: the greater the ethnic diversity, or more accurately, the larger the proportion of community residents with an ethnic background, the greater the likelihood that the community will have a mayor-council form of government. Furthermore, localities with a personal service, professional, retail, and finance economic base are more likely to have council-manager governments than are communities with a manufacturing or diversified industrial base.[2]

Support for and opposition to changes in municipal government form is not random and normally can be more or less predicted. Labor and low-income groups, for example, have normally been at best lukewarm toward council-manager government and will often oppose a change from a mayor-council to a council-manager plan. Upper- and middle-income groups and the business community (particularly the larger business interests) can usually be expected to support such a change. As Edward Banfield and James Wilson point out, a more businesslike approach in government and the "elimination of politics" aspects of the manager form has meant in practical terms reducing the power and representation of low-income workers and minorities.[3]

Reform of municipal government in Philadelphia is a good illustration of the significance of governmental form. Reform interests in that city rode to power through the mayorality, electing first Joseph Clark and later Richardson Dilworth to that position. Because of the city-wide electoral base to the office of chief executive, middle- and upper-middle-class reformers found their resources, especially blue-ribbon candidates, to be most effective. Through important changes in city government, including the elevation of the position (and image) of the mayor, the implementation of a civil service system, the establishment of a city development corporation, and the promotion of powerful city planning and urban renewal agencies, reform elements were able to institutionalize their values and virtually assure a diminished role in city policy-making for the more ethnically and lower-middle-class-oriented city council and Democratic party organization (reformers Clark and Dilworth were Democrats but not of the ward variety, which type dominated the party organization). The public policy consequences of the rise of the reformers to positions of influence are reflected in Philadelphia's ambitious urban renewal and downtown redevelopment measures insititued and extended under reform-mayor auspices and sometimes over the opposition of the more "parochial" interests in the city.[4]

---

[2] For a discussion of the various forces that may impact upon a community's choice of one or another form of government, see John H. Kessel, "Governmental Structure and Political Environment," *American Political Science Review*, 56 (September, 1962), 615–620; also see Thomas R. Dye, *Politics in States and Communities* (Englewood Cliffs: Prentice-Hall, 1969), pp. 218–223.

[3] Edward C. Banfield and James Q. Wilson, *City Politics* (New York: Random House, 1963), p. 171.

[4] Edward C. Banfield, *Big City Politics* (New York: Random House, 1965), p. 116. That different groups are represented in different offices in another city is discussed by Robert H. Salisbury in "St. Louis Politics: Relationships Among Interests, Parties, and Government Structure," *Western Political Quarterly*, XIII (June, 1960), 498–507.

In the Maryland suburbs of Washington, D.C., middle- and upper-middle-class citizens associations and some other groups heavily influenced by middle- and upper-middle-class residential interests have long opposed independent agencies responsible for planning and providing water and sewer services, urging the transfer of powers from these independent units to a general-purpose government. Business and real estate interests, with the implicit support of the lower and lower-middle class, have vigorously and successfully opposed such a transfer. The reason for the position of both sets of interests is basically the relative influence each expects it would have under one as opposed to another location of these powers—with business believing its interests are best protected under present arrangements (independent operation of the agencies) and the citizens groups convinced that their purposes would be best served with a change. Both groups, however, discuss their respective views on this organizational question in philosophical terms, with the business community favoring a process "independent of politics," and the citizens arguing for a process more "politically responsible" (to elected officials, whom the citizens groups assume they can control). As is often the case in local politics, philosophical concepts here are used to mask power drives (this says nothing, of course, about the sincerity of the philosophical conviction of either group); also found in this conflict are differing ideas as to what constitutes the public interest in a particular situation.

In the vanguard of those promoting metropolitan government in this country have been the larger business interests in the center core of the central city and the upper-middle-class residents both inside and outside the city. Opposing metropolitan government have been the smaller businesses, suburban commercial interests, Negroes, and the lower income groups in general. The existence of these patterns of support and opposition is likely to lead one to assume that a restructuring of governmental organizations within the metropolitan area may have some influence on public policy and access to government. Larger businesses feel that they will benefit from an expansion in the electorate which would come from the establishment of a metropolitan-wide government, since this would mean in most areas of the country bringing into the local decision-making process more middle- and upper-middle-class participants. However, suburban businesses, especially those in real estate, are not prepared to jeopardize their power position on matters such as zoning and sewer extensions through a basic change in the metropolitan decision-making structure, which could decrease their influence.

In general, the movement for metropolitan reorganization short of the creation of a metropolitan-wide government but involving some modification of government structure may also have some meaning for public policy and in terms of the distribution of power over policy. In urging a reassignment of governmental authority in one or more functional areas from local governments (each serving a small part of the metropolitan area) to a metropolitan-wide governmental institution, groups often expect a more broadly based—that is, *different*—public policy to emerge and implicitly assume that the metropolitan institution will effectively reduce the relative influence of interests and organizations considered undesirable (for example, interests that oppose public expenditures in certain new program areas). The full impact of various kinds of metro-politan reorganization will not be known for some years because most metropolitan-wide institutions are political infants, but available evidence leads us to the conclusion that some interests will have greater control over metropolitan institutions than they did previously over decentral-ized local governments and that others will have reduced influence as a result of the transfer of activities to metropolitan organizations.

The way in which a specific area other than a metropolitan area (say a portion of a metropolitan area) is divided for political or governmental purposes further will likely affect public policy and patterns of influence. And, as indicated, this is just another example of a local government structure question. For example, if a 100-square-mile area is characterized by a number of small general-purpose governments (for instance, town-ships), the public policies of this area, considered generally, will prob-ably differ from what could be expected if that same area had, say, one government (a county government perhaps) responsible for public policy. Governments with larger jurisdictions, holding other factors con-stant, are likely to be associated with interest-group influences different from those linked with governments with smaller jurisdictions or popula-tions. Normally, more variety in patterns of interest-group representation is permitted in larger units, in which the "citizens" (or the majority) are more likely to be merely one input into the political system. In smaller units a single dominant interest (in fact, often a majority element) may dictate policy. Differences in suburban land-use policies can sometimes be traced to this source. In small suburban governments a powerful ma-jority interest may zone most or all land in such a way to exclude un-wanted classes of people; such a policy may be harder to enforce in a larger government in which other interests are effectively represented. Fear of oppressive majorities controlling small areas (states) led the founders of this nation to propose a restructuring of the American poli-tical system through the establishment of an independent national govern-ment which would cover a larger area than the state governments and would therefore be less subject to the schemes of a single majority fac-tion. This suggests that the structure of government and control over that government are not unrelated phenomena.

Metropolitan areas have been growing rapidly in the last several decades. Population movement and growth patterns have most assuredly affected the distribution of power in communities, and changes in the power positions of certain interests are often related to a transformation in the government structure stemming from population composition shifts. Sometimes, in growing suburban rings, especially in the early stages of population in-migration, the existing form and structure of government may become, or, in fact, be used, as a means to perpetuate the rule of the kinds of forces that have controlled in the past. Often, under such circumstances, the new residents (especially if they are in the middle- or upper-middle-income class) will press for changes in governmental structure, generally to give themselves a greater or controlling voice in the community, or at least to better enable them to have a significant influence over the functions (such as education and planning) of greatest interest to them. Governmental structure then may become a major consideration in motivating political actors and will in reality be viewed by many concerned forces as a strategic factor in the struggle for political dominance. A change from a "rural" to an "urban" type of government, or from some traditional form (such as a commission) to a council-manager government may very well be reflective of a change (if not the immediate cause of a change) in the relative power position of the various interests in the community, and will likely have important public policy and access pattern implications. In an upper- or middle-class suburban jurisdiction such a change in governmental structure will probably mean shifts in public policy as follows: from a policy that recognizes the private marketplace as the determinant of land-use to one that provides for rigid government control of land use; from a policy that encourages commercial and high-density development to one that requires single-family residential and low-density development; from a volunteer to a professional-municipal fire department policy. There is nothing inherently superior about these new policies (or for that matter the structure or forces behind the structure that produced them): the newly arrived residents are just convinced that they are superior and consistent with the community's welfare in the same sense that the older controlling groups believed (and probably still do, after the change) that the previous policies were best. In the final analysis the question boils down to which interests are afforded the greatest opportunity to influence public policy, and to the access patterns to be permitted or encouraged under one as opposed to another governmental arrangement. And, with the change in governmental structure, those favoring the new policies should on the average prevail—that is, if the government has been "properly" reorganized. Nearly every metropolitan area in the United States is to some extent affected by population movements and shifts and by the resulting restructuring of political influence patterns, conflict over and some change in government form, and the emergence of new public policy. Population movement in and of itself, however, does not cause change in government structure and public policy: only pressure and group influence can do this. In an organized and mature society change does not occur any easier in local government than it does anyplace else. Governmental restructuring is not solely (if, indeed, it is at all) an intellectual experience, and like other comparable change, must be seen in terms of its *political* dimension. To view such action in the light of the "needs" of the population or the increasingly urbanized nature of the jurisdiction (both common interpretations) alone is to overlook a basic element of the situation.

In several areas of the country it has been demonstrated that special district governments encourage access patterns not necessarily found in general-purpose governments. For a variety of reasons, states and localities have created limited-function governments to handle one or a few local or area-wide activities. In special districts with authority over land-development-related matters (utilities and public improvements), developers and real estate interests may dominate the policy- and decision-making processes.[5] Along this same line, the use of special boards as a means of separating the educational from other functions of local government probably has had some effect on policy outcomes in the schools area. Most local public education systems in this country are independent of general-purpose governments. This independence has often assured those most deeply involved in education—that is, the professional educators and interested lay groups such as the PTA—control over the education function. The remainder of the chapter will be devoted to a description and explanation of the varieties of governmental forms and structures found in American local government.

TYPES OF LOCAL GOVERNMENTS

The major governmental unit categories at the local level are (1) city government, (2) county government, (3) New England town government, (4) township government, (5) special district government, and (6) school government. The first four types are general-purpose governments; the last two are special-purpose or limited-function units.

Somewhat surprising to foreign visitors to the United States, and indeed not fully appreciated by Americans, is the large number of local government units in this country. Of the over 80,000 governments in the nation, all but 51 are considered local governments. Included in this number are approximately 18,000 municipalities, 3,000 counties, 17,000 townships (covers some towns), 21,000 special districts, and nearly 22,000 school district governments (Table 8.1). Overall, the trend in recent years has been toward a reduction in the number of governmental units; but this decline is accounted for almost entirely by school district consolidation, merger, and reorganization—the number of school governments dropped from over 50,000 in 1957 to under 22,000 in 1967. The only category of local government registering any significant increase in numbers was the special district. The number of municipalities rose slightly, while the number of counties and townships remained relatively constant during the decade 1957–1967. The internal character and functional responsibilities of many counties and townships in urban areas, however, have changed in response to various pressures.

The average number of governmental units per state is over 1,600, although there is a wide range between the state with the largest and the state with the smallest number of local governments (Table 8.2). Illinois, with nearly 6,500 local government units, including 2,300 special districts and 1,350 school districts, provides quite a contrast with Hawaii which has less than 20 local governments. Together, California, Illinois, Kansas, Minnesota, Nebraska, New York, Ohio, Pennsylvania, South Dakota, and Texas contain more than one half of all the nation's governmental units. The dominant unit of local government in large parts of the New England states of Connecticut, Maine, Massachusetts, New Hampshire, Rhode Island, and Vermont is the town, referred to here as the New England town (included in the township class in Tables 8.1 and 8.2). A number of states use the township form of local government for a variety of purposes: Illinois, Indiana, Kansas, Michigan, Minnesota, North Dakota, Ohio, Pennsylvania, South Dakota, and Wisconsin each have at least 1,000 townships within their borders. Illinois and Pennsylvania have

TABLE 8.1
Governmental Units in the United States

	1967	1962	1957
U.S. government	1	1	1
State governments	50	50	50
Local governments	81,248	91,186	102,341
Counties	3,049	3,043	3,050
Municipalities	18,048	18,000	17,215
Townships	17,105	17,142	17,198
School districts	21,782	34,678	50,454
Special districts	21,264	18,323	14,424

SOURCE: *1967 Census of Governments.*

TABLE 8.2
Local Government Units by State, 1967

STATE	ALL LOCAL GOVERNMENTS	COUNTIES	MUNICIPALITIES	TOWNSHIPS	SPECIAL DISTRICTS	SCHOOL DISTRICTS
Alabama	796	67	359	—	251	119
Alaska	61	9	51	—	—	1
Arizona	394	14	62	—	76	242
Arkansas	1252	75	423	—	352	402
California	3864	57	400	—	2168	1239
Colorado	1252	62	251	—	748	191
Connecticut	413	—	34	149	221	9
Delaware	170	3	52	—	65	50
District of Columbia	2	—	1	—	1	—
Florida	827	67	383	—	310	67
Georgia	1203	159	512	—	338	194
Hawaii	19	3	1	—	15	—
Idaho	871	44	194	—	513	120
Illinois	6453	102	1256	1432	2313	1350
Indiana	2669	92	550	1009	619	399
Iowa	1802	99	945	—	280	478
Kansas	3668	105	623	1543	1037	360
Kentucky	952	120	359	—	273	200
Louisiana	733	62	270	—	334	67
Maine	698	16	21	469	127	65
Maryland	361	23	151	—	187	—
Massachusetts	654	12	39	312	247	44
Michigan	2903	83	522	1253	110	935

State					
Minnesota	4184	87	850	1817	148	1282
Mississippi	783	82	268	–	272	161
Missouri	2917	114	856	343	734	870
Montana	1103	56	125	–	209	713
Nebraska	4391	93	538	486	952	2322
Nevada	146	17	17	–	95	17
New Hampshire	515	10	13	222	89	181
New Jersey	1421	21	335	232	311	522
New Mexico	307	32	88	–	97	90
New York	3485	57	616	931	965	916
North Carolina	752	100	437	–	215	–
North Dakota	2757	53	357	1378	431	538
Ohio	3283	88	933	1324	228	710
Oklahoma	1773	77	522	–	214	960
Oregon	1456	36	222	–	800	398
Pennsylvania	4998	66	1005	1554	1624	749
Rhode Island	109	–	8	31	67	3
South Carolina	561	46	259	–	148	108
South Dakota	3510	64	306	1050	106	1984
Tennessee	791	94	297	–	386	14
Texas	3446	254	883	–	1001	1308
Utah	445	29	213	–	163	40
Vermont	656	14	65	238	72	267
Virginia	373	96	229	–	48	–
Washington	1652	39	267	63	937	346
West Virginia	455	55	225	–	120	55
Wisconsin	2490	72	568	1269	62	519
Wyoming	472	23	87	–	185	177

SOURCE: *1967 Census of Governments.*

the greatest number of municipalities, while California plus these two states lead all others in the special district class. Independent school districts are found in large numbers again in California and Illinois as well as Minnesota, Nebraska, South Dakota, and Texas; in four states—Hawaii, Maryland, North Carolina, and Virginia—all school systems are operated as part of general-purpose governments.

In general, the states have highly complex and diversified systems of local government. This pattern has emerged partly for historical reasons (the county and township in particular) and partly because of recent pressures (special districts and often municipalities).

The significance of local governments is in no way diminished, nevertheless, either because of their large numbers or because of the complexity of the structure of community political systems. Local governments are responsible for the activities of a governmental character that affect the daily lives of the vast majority of all Americans. In most urban areas local governments are the primary determinants of, in the basic sense, where populations will live, many of the kinds of services and amenities available and accessible to the residents, and the way in which land will be used or allocated. And there is hardly a more fundamental governmental consideration in this country than the nature of land-use in communities. Many other examples of key local functions could be cited to illustrate the importance of community governments—education, water supply, urban renewal, rail rapid transit, and local highways and streets are but a few.

The role that local governments plays in the American political system can perhaps be understood better by an examination of local public expenditures and revenues (local government finances, however, do not give one a good picture of the impact of such regulatory activities as zoning). Local governments spent nearly $70 billion in fiscal year 1967.[6] Of this amount, city governments accounted for $24.4 billion; school districts were next, spending $23.5 billion. County government public outlays were $12.9 billion; townships (including New England towns) spent $2.3 billion; while special district governments had expenditures of $4.5 billion. Furthermore, local governments collect about the same proportion of all governmental tax revenues in the country as do the states, and about one fourth of the amount raised by the national government.

GOVERNING THE MUNICIPALITY

City governments are to be distinguished from other local governments in that they are general-purpose governmental corporations, or municipal corporations. City governments operate with charters provided

6 This figure reflects aid from the national and state governments.

by the state government; and states now commonly give cities home-rule authority, under which municipalities exercise considerable discretion and independence (of state control) in developing and carrying out local powers. Technically, the term "city government" applies not only to the larger municipalities' governing institution but also to smaller communities which may not be called "city" but village, borough, or town (not of the New England variety though)—that is, when such communities have regular general-purpose governments. It is important not to confuse a city or municipal government, such as the government of Atlanta, with an area that has the city "name"—such as Silver Spring, Maryland. Atlanta is both a specific geographical area and the name we often give to its municipal government; Silver Spring happens to be simply an area near Washington, D.C. with no municipal government.

The forms of government used in municipalities are mayor-council, council-manager, and commission. The three forms are not equally distributed across all population classes in the country (Table 8.3). The mayor-council plan, for instance, is the prevalent form in the largest and smallest of American municipalities. More specifically, all cities with a population of over 1,000,000, over four fifths of the cities in the above-500,000 population category, and over three fifths of the municipalities in the 5,000-to-10,000 class operate under mayor-council governments. Council-manager government is most popular among middle-sized cities —that is, communities ranging in population from 25,000 to 500,000. The commission form is used in less than 10 percent of American cities, and is least commonly found in the largest and smallest of these cities. The mayor-council form is still the most widely used of the three plans, although the manger concept has been gaining new municipal adherents with the passing of each year.

Mayor-Council Form

Under this plan a chief executive is elected at-large by the city voters directly to the office of mayor and normally serves as the city's top administrator, while the city council or governing body is independent of the executive branch in the administrative sense and has general policy-making responsibility for the municipality. The mayor, however, shares this policy authority with the council in some respects and sets policy for the administration. As this suggests, an elective chief executive and separation of powers are clearly distinguishing features of this form of government.

The mayor-council plan contains two variations: the strong-mayor and weak-mayor systems. The dominant traits of the strong-mayor system are (1) the concentration of executive and administrative authority in the office of the mayor; (2) the appointment of the key executive officers and

TABLE 8.3
Form of Government in Cities, 1967

POPULATION GROUP	TOTAL NO. OF CITIES	TOTAL NO. OF CITIES IN SURVEY	MAYOR-COUNCIL		COUNCIL-MANAGER		COMMISSION	
			NO.	%	NO.	%	NO.	%
Over 500,000	27	27	22	81.5	5	18.5	–	–
250,000–500,000	27	27	11	40.7	13	48.2	3	11.1
100,000–250,000	96	93	33	35.5	50	53.8	10	10.7
50,000–100,000	232	215	83	38.6	116	54.0	16	7.4
25,000–50,000	476	439	166	38.2	233	53.6	40	9.2
10,000–25,000	1166	1072	511	47.7	488	45.5	73	6.8
5,000–10,000	1168	1112	686	61.7	378	34.0	48	4.3
All cities over 5,000	3192	2985	1513	50.6	1283	43.0	190	6.4

SOURCE: International City Managers' Association, *The Municipal Year Book 1968* (Washington, D.C., 1968), pp. 54, 134.

department heads by the mayor; (3) preparation of the executive budget (for the administrative agencies) by the mayor or by an officer responsible and directly accountable to the mayor; (4) generally, the restriction of the governing body to broad policy-making responsibilities (as opposed to the direct exercise of administrative authority or detailed supervision of the executive branch); and (5) legislative veto power on the part of the mayor. Often, especially in the largest cities, a mayor operating under this system will appoint a chief administrative officer or managing director (Philadelphia) who supervises the administrative activities of the major departments of the municipal government.

The strong-mayor plan is based on the Hamiltonian premise that visible and powerful leadership by a single individual heading up the administrative operations of government and independent in the immediate sense of the authority of the legislative body is a healthy ingredient if not a necessary prerequisite to the successful operation of a democratic political system. Democratic politics often tend to cause an impressive degree of decentralization of formal authority and actual power, and the strong-mayor concept is designed in part to counter such a tendency, at the same time attempting to guarantee the democratic exercise of this centralized power.

Basically, the weak-mayor system differs from the strong-mayor version in terms of the location of the responsibility for the administration of the executive branch of government. Under the weak-mayor plan the mayor's executive authority is restricted and shared with the council, giving the city many times, for all intents and purposes, a plural executive. This system grows out of the American fear of the concentration of power in the hands of a single person, a key part of the American political tradition since the early colonists' experience under the British Crown.

The governing of this nation's cities has become one of the most difficult tasks of modern society. Some hold, in fact, that governing a city the size of New York, especially given the nature of municipal functions, is virtually an impossible job, and recent evidence appears to bear out this theory to some extent. It has been suggested that the greatest hope for containing conflict, easing tensions, and making social and economic advances in cities rests with a strengthening of the position of the mayor. Modern-day reformers in municipal politics have called for a manipulation of the governmental structure, including concentrating more authority in the office of the mayor and consolidating various decentralized but related agencies and functions into larger and more logical administrative groupings, to this end. Probably the greatest obstacle to enhancing the position (in power terms) of the mayor, however, is the civil service system, which has removed most appointments in city government from the political sphere (including the mayor's political influence), which extends in some instances to officials immediately below the mayor (department heads) as well as to most division heads (immediately under departments), and which is often administered by an independent commission separated from the mayor. With this and other evidence, it would seem that the formal structure of municipal government has effectively hemmed in most mayors, and that the average mayor's options in seeking out power sources instead fall in the political category. In view of the fact that political party machines have declined as forces in city politics, mayors are now commonly encouraged to make alliances with various nonparty groups in the city, such as businessmen (in urban renewal) or municipal employees (in budget and pay raise matters), as a means of compensating for the constraints imposed upon them by the city government structure. Furthermore, the absence of what might be considered sufficient formal authority and power appears to have caused mayors to look increasingly to Washington for political and economic support, which has tended to make the nation's city governments heavily dependent on federal policy. In their search for power bases, mayors are destined to become, directly or indirectly, major drains on the country's and numerous communities' tax resources: the typical program that must be supported by the mayor to bolster his political position is economically costly.

In general, mayor-council forms of government are most common in localities with significant concentrations of working-class, nonwhite, and ethnic minority groups, and in cities with a manufacturing, industrial, or diversified economic base.

Council-Manager Plan

The council-manager form of government is an outgrowth of the municipal reform movement and as such it stresses the principles of economy, efficiency, and professional administration. It further emphasizes the importance of keeping politics and political influences out of the administrative branch of local government. Often, the manager plan is part of a general reform package which also includes at-large elections, nonpartisanship, and a merit system. The middle class fear of corruption, waste, and favortism in municipal government as well as a respect for expertise and professionalism led to the introduction of council-manager government at the local level in America.

The council-manager plan is based on the same concepts that have guided the structuring of the operations of the modern private business corporation and in fact is an adaptation of the characteristic practices and styles of corporations, the dominant units in our economic system, to local government. A business corporation has stockholders who elect a board of directors, which in turn selects a president or chief executive officer. The board of directors makes policy for the firm based more or less on stockholder wishes, and the management carries out the policy to achieve the company's objectives. In municipal government the voters are the equivalent of the stockholders, the city council or governing body the equivalent of the board of directors, and a city manager the equivalent of a corporate president. The whole idea in city-manager government is based on the premise that policy and administration can be logically separated and that the council should make policy and the professional manager execute this policy—a principle known in public administration circles as the policy-administration dichotomy. Recent organizational theory and simple observation have cast considerable doubt on the operational validity of this principle, and, as a result, council-manager government partisans no longer necessarily believe that this principle must be an important or major factor in a community's consideration of the council-manager plan.

Manager government was first adopted in this country in Staunton, Virginia, in 1908. By 1967, 43 percent of all American municipalities with a population of 5,000 and over were using the plan. Cities in the 25,000 and over population category are more likely to have the manager form than any other type of government (Table 8.3). In the year for which the most recent count was made, 76 communities were added to the council-manager rolls, swelling the total number of such governments to 2,218.[7]

The council-manager plan is found in only a few of the nation's very largest cities. Only five of the 27 cities with a 1965 population of over 500,000 have manager governments: Dallas, San Antonio, San Diego, Kansas City, and Phoenix. And all of these cities adopted the plan before reaching the 500,000 population mark. Possibly one reason why the major cities do not normally use the manager form is the concern that some have that a professional manager may not provide the kind of dynamic and aggressive policy and political leadership expected of a chief executive; in any event, some political scientists have not been particularly impressed with the potential of such a government except, perhaps, for small, single-class suburban enclaves. Evidence, however, is available that suggests that the absence of policy leadership on the part of city managers is not an intrinsic element of this plan of government. In recent years, in particular, an increasing number of city managers have openly

[7]   This total is greater than that found in Table 8.3 because it includes all cities, towns, and other urban places using this form, and not just cities in the 5,000-and-over population range. The figures cited here also cover some Canadian communities (less than 100 of the total of 2,218). International City Managers Association, *The Municipal Year Book 1968* (Washington, D.C., 1968), pp. 132–134.

and actively participated in policy-making and political (interpreted in the broadest of senses) processes.[8]

In addition to the socioeconomic and city-size characteristics already discussed, localities experiencing relatively rapid growth rates are more likely to use the manager plan than cities with more stable (or declining) populations.

Commission Form

Originally highly regarded by reformers, the commission form of government soon fell into disfavor and was displaced by the manager concept. This plan was adopted first by Galveston, Texas, in the wake of a hurricane which virtually destroyed the community (a commission of five businessmen was established to run the city). Other municipalities, impressed by Galveston's rebuilding program and the fact that business-men had managed affairs so effectively, soon adopted the plan. Indeed commission government was early considered a "businessman's" govern-ment. In time, however, the manager plan began to be seen as more consistent with the principles of business efficiency, and numerous cities abandoned their commission governments. Today, only a small number of American municipalities operate under the commission plan (Table 8.3). Jacksonville, Florida, is one of the major cities that recently discarded the commission form; consolidated now with Duval County, Jacksonville has a mayor-council system.

Theoretically, there is no separation of powers under the commission form. In fact, commission-plan governments are the only example of a general-purpose municipal public institution with a single branch of government. This is so since technically there is no independent local judiciary in communities (the local judiciary is legally part of the state system) and because legislative and executive powers in commission governments are combined. The commissioners who serve on the govern-ing body are also the chief executive officers; thus, such governments have in effect a plural, or collegial, executive, which also is the policy-making

---

[8]   Recent developments in Dayton, Ohio (the first large city to switch to the coun-cil-manager form, incidentally) under City Manager Graham Watt are instructive. Manager Watt has become a leading figure in the city's political power structure. Watt has established an array of new programs and operations in city hall, particu-larly to cope with the demanding and explosive problems of slum and ghetto areas. He has launched an aggressive Model Cities effort to upgrade the most depressed of Dayton's low-income neighborhoods and has continually lobbied in Washington for more funds and assistance in several program fields. At one point, Watt even offered to lead a march of Negroes to demonstrate his sincerity in searching for solu-tions to black grievances. Watt does not fit the traditional image of what a good manager is supposed to do. But then again, times have changed—and so apparently have some managers.

board. Each commissioner is normally given administrative authority over specific major departments or functions. This organizational pattern tends to lead the creation and perpetuation of a number of more or less independent feudalistic-type agencies, operating within the general framework of municipal government but not subject to much overall central governing board guidance and direction. In actuality, municipal departments often enjoy considerable autonomy from centralized forces, regardless of the plan of government; but the commission form appears to reinforce and extend the somewhat natural bureaucratic movement toward general municipal decentralization (internal agency decentralization, however, is not necessarily characteristic of the otherwise decentralized department).

GOVERNING THE COUNTY

About 3,000 counties cover virtually every section and state of the United States. Only Connecticut, Rhode Island, and limited portions of other states (such as the independent cities of Virginia) are not served by county governments. In Louisiana, counties are called parishes and in Alaska, boroughs. From 1962 to 1967, there was a net increase of six counties, resulting from the formation of nine boroughs in Alaska, the consolidation of Davidson County and Nashville, Tennessee (the new government is considered a municipality), and the elimination of two Virginia counties—Princess Anne and Norfolk, both of which became parts of independent cities.

County governments are, technically, unincorporated political subdivisions of states. Their powers vary somewhat by state and by areas within specific states. Traditionally, the county has been an important unit in rural areas in many parts of the nation, and in this light the county seat has often served (as it still does) as a social, economic, and political center for the residents and farmers of the surrounding countryside. County governments have key responsibilities in the Midwest, West, and South, although they are relatively weak (if, indeed, they exist at all) in the New England states. Where a uniformly strong system of lower-level grass-roots government—such as townships, towns, or cities—is found within the boundaries of counties, the county government may perform only a few functions.

In the South the county is often the dominant unit of local government, particularly outside of major cities. This has meant, in effect, that the local political system in the South has been somewhat less complex and less fragmented than that found in other regions. Lodging local authority in counties, which normally cover a relatively large land area (the average county in the country contains over 1000 square miles), has deterred the creation of smaller units of government to serve developing urban population concentrations, which in turn has undoubtedly facilitated major metropolitan government reorganization. The few general-purpose metropolitan-wide governments are all located in the South. Counties in this region commonly perform a wide range of public functions, including in many instances education. The centralized organizational structure of the Anglican church, a basic institution in the southern coastal colonies at the time of the founding of this nation, along with the area's large-plantation agricultural economy, contributed importantly to the rise of a county-centered local government system in many parts of the South.[9]

Today the average county government has essentially a commission form of government, with the governing body members being elected by districts (or political subdivisions of the county) or at-large by the voters. In a minority of counties the governing body is composed of township supervisors who sit *ex officio* on the county board. This is called the "supervisor form"; under the "commission form" county legislators are selected for county positions directly by the electorate.[10] The county governing body—board of commissioners, board of supervisors, commissioners court, county court, and the like—normally has both policy-making and administrative powers, although it shares such powers with other elected county officials (for example, sheriff, treasurer, county clerk, and coroner).

On the average, counties have not been viewed by political scientists as particularly flexible and modern instruments of grass-roots democracy. The two most common criticisms are that county governments have archaic organizational structures and that these units have only limited, if any, capacity to perform nonroutine and nonrural functions, being ill-equipped in most instances to handle the pressing demands of a rapidly growing urban society.

Although it is true that counties were originally developed to serve rural America, a number of counties in urban areas have not stood still in the light of expanding populations and changing political patterns. These counties have reorganized substantial portions of their governmental and administrative structures and added urban-type activi-

9   Alan P. Grimes, *American Political Thought* (New York: Holt, Rinehart and Winston, 1960), p. 24.
10 George S. Blair, *American Local Government* (New York: Harper & Row, 1964), pp. 180–181. For further useful information on county governments, see U.S. Bureau of the Census, *Governing Boards of County Governments: 1965* (Washington, D.C.: U.S. Government Printing Office, 1965), and Herbert Sydney Duncombe, *County Government in America* (Washington, D.C.: National Association of Counties, 1966).

ties. Some counties have adopted home-rule charters and some metro-politan units have switched to county-manager and county-executive governmental systems. Home-rule charters permit counties to function more independently of the state government, making it somewhat difficult to distinguish a county from a municipal corporation; while the manager and executive forms encourage a concentration of authority and responsibility in a single office in the administrative sphere of govern-ment, the development of a more streamlined organizational structure, and a more precise division of powers between the legislative and executive branches. In the county-manager plan the governing body selects a professional manager to administer the county's general execu-tive affairs; and this plan represents a substantial change from past prac-tices (for example, under the commission system). Under the county executive form, a chief executive (known as county executive or super-visor) is elected by county voters and has some degree of administrative authority, including possibly the power to prepare and coordinate execu-tive branch budget, set general administration policy, veto legislation, and appoint key executive officers (which may include a single chief ad-ministrative officer). The county-manager plan is similar to the council-manager plan used in cities; and the country-executive form is similar to the mayor-council system (although not all county executives have as much power as the chief executive under the strong-mayor plan). County-manager governments exist, for example, in metropolitan Dade County, Florida, and Arlington County, Virginia. Probably the "purist" illustration of the county-executive system is the government of Baltimore County, Maryland, where the county executive serves as the top official in the ad-ministration, makes broad administrative policy, and appoints a chief ad-ministrative officer who supervises department heads and is responsible for daily administrative operations. Other counties using some version of county-executive government include Nassau, Westchester, and Erie in New York, Hudson and Essex in New Jersey, Milwaukee County, Wis-consin, and Jefferson Parish, Louisiana.

Furthermore, in recent years, counties have shown an increasing willingness to broaden their scope of services, and counties in urban areas now have urban renewal, public housing, planning, economic develop-ment, urban law enforcement, air pollution, model cities, and other comparable programs. Not all urban counties perform all of these func-tions; yet a large number perform some of them. Undoubtedly, most county governments have limited responsibilities for local public activ-ities, concentrating largely on poor relief, road and bridge construction and maintenance, supervision of county institutions, and the like. Never-theless, the large territory encompassed within the borders of most of these units of government make counties ideal candidates for the assumption of new local public responsibilities.

NEW ENGLAND TOWN GOVERNMENT

The dominant unit of the local political system throughout much of New England is the town. In 1967, there was over 1,400 towns (including "plantations" in Maine and "locations" in New Hampshire) in the six New England states. The New England town corresponds generally to the township and county governments in certain other parts of the United States, in that it serves rural and urban areas alike and virtually blankets the states where it is used. Additionally, like the county and township, the New England town is unincorporated. New England towns possess the normal functions of local general-purpose units of government, including highways and welfare; and urbanized towns often have the functions commonly associated with municipalities.

The roots of the town-dominated local government pattern in New England can be traced in part to the congregational nature of the internal structure of the early Puritan church; thus, each government, like each church, covered only a small area.[11] Further, the small-farm economy and defense (from Indians) considerations seemingly had the effect of keeping governmental units in New England small and close to the people.

The New England town is the home of the town meeting, the most celebrated example of pure or direct democracy in America. Whatever may have been the case in the past, however, the town meeting has declined in significance in the grass-roots governing process in New England; in some instances, especially in Massachusetts, the concept of the "representative" town meeting has been adopted, under which individual citizens may attend legislative sessions, be heard, and elect officers, but not (as in the pure form of town meeting) vote on policy matters.[12] In theory the town meeting is still considered the legislative body of the New England town, with a board of selectmen chosen by the qualified citizens serving as the executive agency. A typical town will have other elected officials, such as a town clerk. New England towns do not have mayors, although there will be a president of the board of selectmen, and increasingly towns are hiring managers to supervise the administrative activities of government.

[11] Grimes, op. cit., p. 24.
[12] Representatives of the voters, numbering perhaps a 100 or so, serve as the delegates of the voters in such town meetings. Charles R. Adrian, State and Local Governments (2nd ed.; New York: McGraw-Hill, 1967), p. 215.

TOWNSHIP GOVERNMENT

This country has over 15,000 organized township governments, including towns in New York and Wisconsin. The terminology here can be confusing, but townships are unincorporated subdivisions of the county, usually covering most or all of the area within a particular county containing such a government. Towns in New York and Wisconsin resemble townships elsewhere and are therefore included in the township category. Also, as noted, the New England town is similar in many ways to a township; and although we do not discuss townships and New England towns under the same heading, the Census Bureau combines the two in its count of local government units. (See Tables 8.1 and 8.2.) Furthermore, incorporated towns, found in various parts of the country are considered municipalities and should be distinguished from the New York and Wisconsin and New England towns. Finally, townships as treated here are sometimes called civil townships, or townships with governmental organization and functions, to be differentiated from "congressional," or "survey" townships, which are six miles square and used for land description and location but not governing purposes.

Townships will not normally be found in all areas of the states with this kind of grass-roots government. Usually, townships contain a small population—only 5 percent had 10,000 or more inhabitants as of 1967. This suggests the rural character typical of most townships; and the degree and type of governmental activity in townships have been consistent with that character. Quite often, township functions amount to little more than overseeing a minor road system, although townships may have welfare, health, education, law enforcement, and other responsibilities as well.

Normally, general clerical and administrative duties are within the province of a township clerk, while the policy-making authority in townships rests with a board of trustees, supervisors, or commissioners. In reality, township government executive power is divided among several officers (treasurer, assessor, highway commissioner, and the like); further, no clear policy-administration dichotomy can be observed or serves even as a theoretical guide in most townships. In this respect, townships operate much like counties.

In some areas of the country township governments are strikingly similar to smaller incorporated municipalities, administering urban functions such as planning, zoning, and subdivision regulation, and operating as the principal grass-roots-level general-purpose public institution. For example, townships in Pennsylvania and New Jersey may exercise a broad range of municipal powers, serve densely populated urban areas (often middle- and upper-middle-class suburbs), and have modern governmental organization structures, not uncommonly based on the council-manager plan used in cities. These urban townships have secured the services of professionally trained managers (who may begin their careers in such a unit), professional planners, and other highly educated administrative officials.

At the same time, most students of local government have not been overly optimistic about the future of townships as viable and active units of local government, capable of absorbing the pressures and accommodating the demands of growing population centers. Townships do exist, however, and many of these institutions have acted as though they were anxious and eager to survive; consequently, as conditions have required, many townships have changed to the extent possible under the circumstances. Whether the inherent limitations of the size of township jurisdiction (in terms of both population and land area) plus the traditional conservatism of township governments (including the urban variety) will serve as fundamental barriers to the future adjustment and adaptation of these grass-roots units cannot be known at this time. In the meantime, it is abundantly clear that at least a number of urban townships are not prepared to become historical statistics.

SPECIAL DISTRICTS

Dotting the metropolitan landscape are a growing number of special district governments. In fact, special districts appear to be on the rise in many areas outside of urban and metropolitan regions. Special district partisans argue that these governments are flexible and efficient instruments and are easily formed to serve local public needs of various kinds. Clearly, in any event, districts are popular.

As indicated previously, a special district is an example of a special-purpose unit of government. A special district is defined as a government created by action of local government(s) or a local electorate under state enabling legislation or other state authority, (directly) by the state government, or by legislative action of the governing bodies of two or more states with the consent of Congress, for the purpose of performing one or more public functions in a designated geographical area, and operating independently or substantially independently of general-purpose or other governments. In practice, special districts are typically established by governing bodies of general-purpose local governments under state enabling legislation or directly by special act of the state legislature. The formation of interstate districts by interstate compact requires both state legislative action and the consent of Congress. Special districts may also be established by state administrative agencies or state courts, and the basic authority for their creation is sometimes found in the state constitution.[13]

Special districts are not insignificant units of local government. Somewhat over one half of the nation's special districts have their own taxing power; many have the authority to incur debt and issue bonds (in fact, special districts accounted for one fifth of all local government indebtedness in 1967), levy special-benefit assessments, and charge for services; and districts may have jurisdiction over an area that extends beyond the boundaries of any one general-purpose local government or even beyond the boundaries of a single state. Special districts include governments called "authorities," although not all authorities are special districts (some authorities are an integral part of general-purpose governments). The governing board members of special districts are commonly selected by popular election or by officials (often the governing bodies) of the general-purpose local governments in the area served by the district.

Virtually all special districts are responsible for only a single function—fewer than 500 of the country's 21,264 district governments carry on more than one activity. The functions most frequently performed by special districts are natural resources, fire protection, urban water supply, and housing and urban renewal (Table 8.4). The greatest numerical increase in special districts in recent years has been found in the urban water supply and housing and urban renewal categories.

Among the most frequently cited reasons for the development of special districts are their isolation from politics, their businesslike features, their flexibility in crossing political subdivision boundaries, and their effects on relieving already heavily burdened general-purpose governments (which may be legally or politically extended to the limits of their financial capacity) of additional pressures. Opponents contend that districts are often obscured from public visibility, influenced unduly by a single interest in a community, and politically irresponsible. Further, many are disturbed by the fact that special districts add to the complexity of local government structure. In the final analysis, special districts must be seen as another example of the adaptability of the American system of local government.

[13] The major works on special districts are Advisory Commission on Intergovernmental Relations, *The Problem of Special Districts in American Government* (Washington, D.C.: U.S. Government Printing Office, May, 1964); John C. Bollens, *Special District Governments in the United States* (Berkeley: University of California Press, 1957); and Robert G. Smith, *Public Authorities, Special Districts and Local Government* (Washington, D.C.: National Association of Counties, 1964).

TABLE 8.4
Special District Governments, 1967

	NUMBER	PERCENT
Single function	*20,811*	*97.9*
Natural resources	6,539	30.7
Soil conservation	2,571	12.1
Drainage	2,193	10.3
Irrigation, water	904	4.2
Flood control	662	3.1
Other	209	1.0
Fire protection	3,665	17.2
Urban water supply	2,140	9.9
Housing and urban renewal	1,565	7.4
Cemeteries	1,397	6.6
Sewerage	1,233	5.7
School buildings	956	4.5
Highways	774	3.6
Parks and recreation	613	2.9
Hospitals	537	2.5
Libraries	410	1.9
Other	982	4.9
Multiple function	*453*	*2.1*
Total	21,264	100.0

SOURCE: *1967 Census of Governments.*

GOVERNING PUBLIC EDUCATION

Public education at the elementary and secondary levels is a task of local governments, normally of special school districts. In 1967, there were 23,390 school systems in the nation, of which nearly 22,000 were independent school governments. In reality, school systems operate somewhat autonomously even when they are technically part of general-purpose governments.

School government has been largely private government—that is, school districts have successfully isolated themselves from the pressures and concerns of other more broadly based local governments, the result of which has been some specialized patterns of control over the education function. Schools, nevertheless, are quite important to local government, as education expenditures constitute a major portion of all local public spending, especially in the suburbs of our metropolitan areas. The role of state and local government in education is examined in detail later in the book.

CONCLUSION

In this chapter we have emphasized the significance of governmental form and structure in shaping public policy and access patterns at the local level; we also have reviewed the key categories of local government in America. This discussion demonstrates the importance of understanding the political—and the legal and the informal—as well as the formal aspects of government structure. Different political interests and socioeconomic levels were found to be associated with certain governmental forms and policy preferences. The chapter also shows that urban and rural communities are served by a wide variety of governmental types and structures, ranging from the most modern adaptations to a rapidly urbanizing society to the more traditional forms designed for a predominantly agrarian economy. We shall now turn to a more intensive analysis of governments in the metropolitan areas.

9. GOVERNMENTAL DECENTRALIZATION IN METROPOLITAN AREAS

CENTRALIZATION AND DECENTRALIZATION OF POPULATION

Population centralization in urban areas continues unabated. In 1790, only 5 percent of the country's inhabitants resided in urban areas; by 1920, urban residents constituted over 50 percent of the population. Census takers in 1960 discovered that in excess of 70 percent of Americans were living in urban areas, and by the 1970s, probably 80 percent or more of the population will be considered urban.

Most of the urban population is concentrated in the metropolitan areas of the United States. By 1960, the metropolitan areas had attracted nearly 63 percent of the nation's residents, and by the time the 1970 statistics are tallied, this figure should surpass the 70 percent mark. In 1969, the country had 228 metropolitan areas—technically termed standard metropolitan statistical areas (SMSAs). Each metropolitan area has a core known as a central city, and usually includes a county which contains the central city, and sometimes contiguous counties.[1]

A distinct trait of metropolitan areas has been an outward movement of population—that is, population decentralization within the metropolitan context. As of 1960, a slim majority of metropolitan Americans still lived in central cities—in 1950, by contrast, nearly 60 percent of the metropolitan population were residents of central cities. Now over one half of the people in metropolitan areas are located in central city suburbs—that is, that part of the metropolitan area outside of the central city.[2] Metropolitan suburbanization has been greatest, furthermore, in the Northeast and West. In some metropolitan areas—such as the Boston, Wilmington (Delaware), and Pittsburgh SMSAs—approximately 75 percent of the population resides in the suburbs (and this was in 1960!). Projections suggest a continuation of this decentralization trend.[3]

METROPOLITAN AREA
GOVERNMENTAL STRUCTURE

The governmental implications of the population movement to urban and metropolitan areas and within metropolitan areas to the suburbs are reasonably clear. Initially, cities expanded their boundaries to accommodate and serve the growing urban population concentrations outside their borders. In some parts of the United States (such as the Southwest) municipalities are still adjusting in this respect to encompass newly urbanized areas. Elsewhere, however, city governments have long ceased

[1] Defined, a standard metropolitan statistical area is an urban population concentration marked by political subdivision boundaries and which has as its center a central city (or twin cities) of at least 50,000 population. In most parts of the United States a county (or counties) which contains the central city is part of the metropolitan area. This county may be called the central county. Contiguous counties are also in the metropolitan area if they are socially and economically integrated with the central city or central county, and are generally nonagricultural in character. In New England the SMSA includes a city of 50,000 or over and surrounding cities and *towns* which meet certain criteria.

[2] U.S. Bureau of the Census, *Current Population Reports*, Series p-23, Special Studies, No. 27, "Trends in Social and Economic Conditions in Metropolitan Areas" (Washington, D.C.: U.S. Government Printing Office, 1969), p. 2.

[3] Patricia Leavey Hodge and Philip M. Hauser, *The Challenge of America's Metropolitan Population Outlook—1960 to 1985* (Washington, D.C.: U.S. Government Printing Office, 1968) chap. 2.

to change their boundaries as the metropolitan population has increased and moved outward. In recent years the effect of population movement patterns in metropolitan areas has been the establishment of new and the strengthening of existing suburban governmental units. The post–World War II surge in suburban municipal government incorporations, the annual addition of large numbers of suburban special district govern-ments, and the bolstering of the position of present suburban general-purpose governments (such as counties and townships) with the arrival of new residents has served to downgrade the relative importance of the central city government in the metropolitan area government scheme of things. Now the vast majority of metropolitan government units, like most of the metropolitan area population, are found in the suburbs.

The central issue in this chapter is the nature of the division of govern-mental authority in metropolitan areas. Specific figures concerning this issue are particularly revealing. As of 1967, nearly 21,000 local units of government were located in the country's over 200 metropolitan areas—an average of 91 governments per metropolitan area. More precisely, metropolitan areas contain 16,000 general-purpose and special-purpose nonschool governments and 5,000 school districts. (See Table 9.1.) These

TABLE 9.1
Governments in Metropolitan Areas, 1967

	NUMBER
Counties	404
Municipalities	4,977
Townships	3,255
Special districts	7,049
School districts	5,018
Total	20,703

SOURCE: *1967 Census of Governments.*

areas include 9,000 general-purpose counties, municipalities, and town-ships, and 7,000 special districts (excluding school districts). Most of these local governments serve small geographical areas and small popula-tions outside of the central city. For instance, the majority of municipal-ities and townships of SMSAs have populations of less than 5000, one fourth of the metropolitan area school systems contain no more than 300 students, and most special districts are engaged in limited operations covering only portions of the suburban or metropolitan area. Further, municipalities and townships often have jurisdiction over a land area of less than five square miles. Demonstrating considerable overlap in governmental authority, less than one fourth of the school systems in SMSAs have boundaries that correspond to those of general-purpose governments, and most metropolitan area residents are served by a number of governmental units (including perhaps a city, county, township, metropolitan-wide special district, and school district along with several local special districts and authorities).

The metropolitan area political and governmental structure is made even more complex as a result of the fact that over 100 of the 228 metropolitan areas cross county boundaries (over 50 SMSAs cover at least three counties), and that each of 30 metropolitan regions has its land area located in more than one state. Additionally, metropolitan area residents have at their call over 133,000 elected representatives, 87,000 of whom are on governing bodies. Municipalities alone elect over 45,000 public officials.

These figures mean that nearly all functions of local government within the metropolitan area are performed by agencies, units, and officials operating on a local and not a metropolitan-wide basis. These functions include fire protection, law enforcement, planning, zoning, subdivision control, building and housing codes, local streets, public works, sewer, water, air pollution, education, health, welfare, libraries, parks, recreation, public housing, urban renewal, transportation, and so on.[4] At the same time, it is true that certain activities (such as planning) are conducted on a metropolitan area-wide basis through a metropolitan organization (which may or may not be a government); but, even in these cases, the enforcement power and implementation authority is almost always found at the local (or perhaps state) and not metropolitan level. In terms of both planning and execution of governmental matters broadly affecting significant portions of the metropolitan area, the local government activities most likely to be administered on a metropolitan-wide scale are probably transportation and parks.[5]

---

[4] The staff of the Advisory Commission on Intergovernmental Relations reviewed some of the governmental functions performed within the metropolitan area and ranked these activities according to its conception of which functions were most and which least local. This ranking, with the "most local" first and the "least local" last, follows: fire protection, public education, refuse collection and disposal, libraries, police, health, urban renewal, housing, parks and recreation, public welfare, hospitals and medical care facilities, transportation, planning, water supply and sewage disposal, and air pollution. It should be stressed that this listing does not necessarily coincide with actual current local and metropolitan-wide performance patterns. Advisory Commission on Intergovernmental Relations, *Performance of Urban Functions: Local and Areawide* (Washington, D.C.: U.S. Government Printing Office, September, 1963), pp. 8–23.

[5] Other functions of a more limited nature sometimes administered on more than a single jurisdictional and possibly on a metropolitan-wide basis include airports, bridges, tunnels, navigational ports, water supply, sewage disposal, and housing.

The picture that emerges from the present metropolitan governmental arrangements is not a happy one to the rational mind: a general fragmentation and "balkanization" of local government authority characterizes metropolitan political systems. The nature of these systems often leads to duplication in effort, confusion in the assignment of authority, a number of taxing governments within a single general-purpose local government's boundaries, and the absence of the coincidence of governmental and natural population boundaries. The following section examines the typical reactions to the governmental conditions of the metropolitan areas.

RESPONSE TO METROPOLITAN
GOVERNMENT DECENTRALIZATION

Generally, two kinds of reactions have characterized the responses to metropolitan governmental decentralization. These reactions can be discussed, at least for analytical purposes, in terms of the following groups: (1) the metropolitanists (or regionalists); and (2) the decentralizationists. In the broadest of senses, the metropolitanists favor change—normally of some basic variety—in governmental patterns and structure in metropolitan areas. Appalled by division and fearful of disunity, the metropolitanist sallies forth with the banner of municipal reform writ large. Decentralizationists, on the other hand, are reasonably satisfied with the existing state of things, may support limited and voluntary governmental restructuring, and believe on the average that more harm than good may result from basic government change.

The philosophical differences between these two groups tend to be reflective of the contrasting positions taken on governmental centralization-decentralization by two great American theorist-statesmen: James Madison and Thomas Jefferson. In the Federalist *Papers* Madison extolled the virtues of a large representative republic, one which covered a large land area (see Chapter 2). Such a system, Madison argued, permits the expression of numerous and often conflicting points of view and allows for enlightened and mature deliberation in the process of considering alternative public policies and actions. Madison's contention was that the enlargement of the democratic society through the establishment of an independent central unit would likely assure the effective regulation and control of local majoritarian factions or parties, thus resulting in the promotion of a broader public interest, the preservation of the liberties of the people, and the protection of minority rights.

Jefferson had little if any faith in Madisonian political logic, and instead warned his fellow citizens of the dangers of the concentration of power in government institutions removed from the direct control of the people. Jefferson did not oppose centralized authority outright, but he did fear making excessive power assignments to governments remote from the people. The most certain means to protect liberty was not, as Madison would have it, the development of a strong central regime (indeed, this was the road to tyranny!), but the location of key functions of government in small units close to the people. Jefferson's favorite unit was the ward, which would cover no more than 25 to 40 square miles. Even the county seemed a bit distant to this partisan of grass-roots democracy.[6]

The basic philosophical question then which separates the metropolitanists from the decentralizationists today has deep roots in the American intellectual political tradition. This question is a special matter in the annals of political theory; it has something to do with what Arthur Maass calls the "areal division of powers."[7] The conflict here is essentially a disagreement over the proper "areal division of powers"—or, put in other words, over the division of powers among areas or regions within a political community (such as a metropolitan area). The "areal" dimension of the division of political powers has attracted the attention of political philosophers in past centuries, is helpful in interpreting the nature and degree of applicability of contributions made by some philosophers, and has concerned a number of modern theorists and political scientists. Rousseau, for instance, believed that his ideal political system had the best chance of being accepted and successfully used in relatively limited geographical settings. Therefore, to this philosopher, the area over which government was to rule became an important factor in determining the possibility of implementing an ideal polity. The classical ancient philosophers Plato and Aristotle implicitly based their theories on the political universe known to them—the Greek city-state—and not on a larger order of political things, suggesting to the modern observer that these theories are most valid for smaller geographical areas corresponding to the ancient city-state. More recently, British theorists and scholars John Stuart Mill and H. G. Wells have addressed themselves at some length to the consideration of the distribution of authority over different-sized areas. Contemporary American political scientists, such as Roscoe Martin and Robert Wood, have examined governmental institutions in the light of the "area and power" aspect of political theory. These examinations include the study of governmental power as its exists in the metropolitan area.

[6] Samuel P. Huntington, "The Founding Fathers and the Division of Powers," in Maass (ed.), *Area and Power, A Theory of Local Government* (New York: Free Press, 1959), pp. 175–179.

[7] Arthur Maass, "Division of Powers: An Areal Analysis," in Maass (ed.), *Area and Power, A Theory of Local Government* (New York: Free Press, 1959), p. 10.

As we saw in the case of Jefferson and Madison, not all political observers have come to the same conclusion concerning the appropriate area over which governmental units should exercise control or the degree of power to be assigned to these units. If the test of the soundness of a political philosophy is its acceptance by societies for the purpose of governing, then the Madisonians proved themselves superior to the Jeffersonians as they toppled the forces of local autonomy when the Articles of Confederation were scrapped and the Constitution of the United States adopted. The modern counterparts of the Madisonians— that is, the metropolitanists—have been considerably less successful, however. That is to say, metropolitan governmental institutions are still decentralized, notwithstanding the efforts of the metropolitanists to effect change. But, the metropolitanists might gently remind us that the powerful Roman Empire was not created out of the small-unit-dominated city-state-based political system that preceded it, without careful preparation, building, and philosophizing; nor did the modern nation-state grow from the rubbles of the tiny feudalistic governments that served as key political forces in an earlier age, without grinding through a similar process. There is no reason to assume that over the long run the metropolitanists will not be victorious, but the immediate outlook is not at all bright. What are the metropolitanists' arguments? What is their program and how do they expect to achieve their goals? We shall attempt to answer these questions in the next section, after which we shall look at the decentralizationists.

THE METROPOLITANISTS

The metropolitanists contend that an organic and functionally and socially interdependent community exists within the metropolitan area, and that to some extent the metropolitan region is a rationally defined area, reflecting similar geographical and geological factors as well as economic unity. With such an integrated foundation, or substructure, it seems only to make sense to have a governmental system, or superstructure, consistent with the foundation. A single area-wide government, or perhaps a federated two-level governmental structure extending throughout the metropolitan area, would allow the appropriate framework for the consideration of public policy to emerge, and would likely guarantee the elevation of the "whole" and the "public interest," and the subordination and submergence of the "part" and "private interests," to their proper places. A metropolitan-wide government would eliminate the likelihood of decisions being made on the basis of narrow, petty, and "false" local loyalties, and would encourage the development of broader points of view. Smaller units of government in the metropolitan area are unresponsive, uneconomical, inefficient, and wasteful. By the same token, a unified larger polity would be responsive, economical, efficient, and effective on a grand scale. Furthermore, the metropolitanists argue, the traditional values which have supported the present distribution of power must give way to more "significant" and "meaningful" values, and current orderings of philosophical priorities must be reconsidered. The values of access, personalized government, direct control and influence, population homogeneity, and internal small-unit jurisdictional philosophical agreement should be subordinated to impersonal issue-directed identification with right-thinking (usually moderate to liberal) leaders, professional, expert, and bureaucratic government, indirect control (voting, hearings), population heterogeneity, diversity, and debate.[8]

Unlike the Madisonians (that is, the Founding Fathers), the modern metropolitanists are not organized to achieve their objectives—that is, to effect metropolitan government. It is true that some organizations such as the National Municipal League (not to be confused with the National League of Cities, which represents municipal governments) have served as a sort of clearinghouse for ideas on the subject and to some degree as a platform for the metropolitanists, but the political clout of these organizations is quite limited. Further, the metropolitanists have not advanced a political strategy by which metropolitan government can be promoted; nor do they appear to be particularly sensitive to the matter of political feasibility or practicality. Concerning the organizational question, the absence of any nationwide organization that could effectively lobby for metropolitan change is understandable—that is, metropolitan governmental structural revisions cannot be brought about on a nationwide basis because of the large number of metropolitan areas, and because political allegiances (even of the metropolitanists) are likely to be at the community level. On the average, metropolitan government advocates have permitted their arguments to rest on their merits. Valuable in setting directions and awakening decision-makers to broadly stated possibilities, the typical action program of the intellectually oriented metropolitanists is not an action program at all. The metropolitanist commonly urges us in our various political capacities—that is, as the rulers of localities, states, or the nation—to shift functional responsibilities and to rearrange governmental systems in the metropolitan area in accordance with a certain

---

[8] The philosophy of the metropolitanists can be found in the following works: Luther Gulick, *The Metropolitan Problem and American Ideas* (New York: Knopf, 1962); articles by Paul Ylvisaker and Robert C. Wood in Maass (ed.), *op. cit.;* Roscoe C. Martin, *Grass Roots* (University, Ala.: University of Alabama Press, 1957); Lewis Mumford, *The Culture of Cities* (New York: Harcourt, Brace and World, 1938). For an analysis of the metropolitanist position, see Anwar Syed, *The Political Theory of American Local Government* (New York: Random House, 1966).

list of criteria, usually quite general. Missing from this agenda, however, is a political strategy that contains a workable means by which we might put together the basic elements of a coalition within metropolitan areas to produce metropolitan government.

Still, the more politically concerned of the metropolitan reformers, such as Professor Robert Wood, have spent time on the general matter of the "means" of securing metropolitan government. And Wood's logic is convincing. He contends, for instance, that metropolitan government must be based on the existence of some foundation of political consciousness.[9] In other words, there must be among the residents of the metropolitan area a specific, natural, and politically interrelating activity on which some region-wide institution might be developed, and to which institution functions might be assigned. Wood believes that the only identifiable metropolitan community is probably that of the delocalized commuter. Therefore, following Wood's reasoning, metropolitan governmental reorganization must begin with the commuter, or, to put it in governmental function terms, the transportation activity. Transportation, like no other functional area except perhaps schools (which, incidentally, localities will simply not give up), will bring out the "political animal" in the metropolitan resident. Although any organization stressing the single function of transportation will have limited jurisdiction and authority, the structure will have to be founded on a community or political constituency. In view of the fact that this forms the base of the activity (and not engineering considerations, for example), transportation can serve as the initial step, or "transitional device," in the creation of a more powerful regional institution with comprehensive governmental authority.

Along these same lines, Paul Ylvisaker suggests that a combination of planning and zoning might be an appropriate interim measure to serve as a vehicle for developing broader political change in the metropolitan area (Ylvisaker is therefore interested in the *means* of attaining metropolitan government).[10] He describes the planning-zoning function as an alternative candidate to Wood's transportation, noting that it "evokes equal interest"; by implication, at least, Ylvisaker sees his function as superior to Wood's because it "strikes at an earlier phase" of community growth and "permits more . . . control." In the light of recent experience (especially since Wood and Ylvisaker wrote on the subject), it would appear that Wood, the academic, relied more on the criterion of political feasibility than Ylvisaker, the practitioner. It is true that most if not all metro-

[9] Robert C. Wood, "A Division of Powers in Metropolitan Areas," in Maass (ed.), *op. cit.*, pp. 66–69.
[10] Paul Ylvisaker, "Some Criteria for a 'Proper' Areal Division of Governmental Powers," in Maass (ed.), *op. cit.*, pp. 42–43.

politan areas have metropolitan-wide planning agencies of some kind, and that transportation (excluding transportation planning) is still largely a local and not metropolitan-wide affair. However, seen in terms of the relative power possessed by the existing metropolitan planning and transportation units, the latter clearly comes out on top. Metropolitan-wide planning commissions have little if any independent plan- or program-implementation power, including the zoning authority (which Ylvisaker linked with planning), a cherished local prerogative in nearly every metropolitan area. Even in the few metropolitan areas with metro-politan-wide general-purpose governments, these governments do not always have complete zoning control over the entire metropolitan area (zoning may be shared with lower-level governments). Furthermore, meaningful planning (or planning with a chance of being carried out) is almost exclusively a local responsibility in metropolitan areas. Any basic restructuring of the planning-zoning function in metropolitan regions would be a major undertaking not likely to succeed, particularly in the light of the economic and political resources of those dependent on the current decentralized assignment of this activity. There are considerably fewer metropolitan-wide transportation agencies than metropolitan planning boards; but a number of the former have both planning and implementation or operational authority. For example, the Southeastern Pennsylvania Transportation Authority not only plans the mass transit system for the Philadelphia metropolitan area but also operates the transit system (which includes buses, streetcars, trackless trolleys, and subway-elevated cars). The Massachusetts Bay Transportation Authority has similar responsibilities for the Boston metropolitan area; the San Francisco Bay Area Rapid Transit District, for the San Francisco area; and the Washington Metropolitan Area Transit Authority, for the National Capital region.

Although Wood was the closer of the two to being right in the short run, we have said nothing about which of the functions is most likely to lead to a more general metropolitan government. In the sense that both scholars considered their suggestions only as temporary instruments to serve broader ends, only time will tell which (if either) has advanced the more realistic concept.

DECENTRALIZATIONISTS

The opponents of metropolitan government would in some respects include large segments of the metropolitan area population. We make this statement because the absence of action to change the present system as well as the absence of change reflects to some extent satisfaction with governmental arrangements in the metropolitan area and because most attempts to effect significant change in these arrangements have been voted down by metropolitan area residents. Further, the metropolitan-wide institutions we have today have not on the average stemmed from voter approval or grass-roots citizen demands, but from action taken by politi-cal, governmental, and private business leaders, at least partly in re-sponse to federal government incentives or requirements. The most common type of metropolitan organizations—planning agencies, volun-tary councils of governments, and transportation planning bodies—are nurtured by federal grants and/or required by federal law. Without federal leadership it would be safe to say that metropolitan-wide institu-tions would be both fewer in number and somewhat weaker than is the case. As it is, existing metropolitan organizations are not what one would consider powerful, and, at the moment, these units have little impact on regional development and metropolitan public policy. This is all sugges-tive of the underlying strength of metropolitan government opponents.

Decentralizationists are divided roughly into two camps: (1) those opposed to virtually all if not all change in metropolitan political systems; and (2) those opposed primarily to the more far-reaching of the pro-posals for metropolitan government change. The first group is antago-nistic to both metropolitan-wide general-purpose government and other metropolitan organizations which, although not general metropolitan governments, might lead in that direction. The second group is also not favorable to general-purpose metropolitan-wide government and to special-purpose or limited-function metropolitan-wide government in the more sensitive functional areas (such as schools), particularly if such a limited unit would have enforcement powers and operating programs; but this group is not necessarily found among the opponents of certain metropolitan-wide organizations, including governments, that are volun-tary, advisory, or clearly restricted in authority or jurisdiction.

A point of clarification is in order here. The key trait of a metropolitan-wide organization is that it covers (or has jurisdiction over) all or sig-nificant portions of the metropolitan area; thus, such an organization is to be distinguished from existing local governments which normally cover only a part (usually a small part) of the metropolitan area. Further, a metropolitan-wide organization may have a governmental or private legal base; and metropolitan-wide governmental organizations may be of a general-purpose or special-purpose (limited-function) variety. Metropoli-tan-wide private organizations (which include at least some of each type of the most common kind of metropolitan organizations mentioned previously) and special-purpose or limited-function governments are less distasteful to decentralizationists of all persuasions than the govern-mental and general-purpose forms respectively. The two groups of decentralizationists are entirely united only in their collective opposition to metropolitan-wide general-purpose government.

The first group of metropolitan government opponents is composed in part of highly conservative, perhaps right-wing, organizations and individuals who tend to equate metropolitan government with socialism and (sometimes) communism or the first stages in the development of a worldwide government.[11] Such forces generally view any metropolitan-wide governmental or institutional proposal, almost regardless of its character and scope, as offensive to their values and un-American. These persons are heavily ideologically motivated, it would appear, and their local political agitation is normally not limited to campaigns against any form of metropolitan government and may include opposition to fluoridation in the local water supply, sex education in the schools, open-housing legislation, and the like. The nationally circulated *American Mercury* and *Dan Smoot Report* have at times promoted the far-right ideological position on metropolitan government. Although the more or less permanent cadre in this group of decentralizationists may be small in number, at any given time, say when a specific metropolitan government proposal is about to be acted upon, this small element can expect support from organizations and interests who for other than ideological (or at least broadly based ideological) reasons may look with disfavor on metropolitan government. Not an insignificant factor and often just below the surface in metropolitan government campaigns and in many discussions on metropolitanism is race. Interestingly, the racial issue works two ways, in each respect though causing metropolitan constituent interests to line up with the first group of decentralizationists. First, white suburbanites may fear that a change in the balance of power at the local level will take place as a result of metropolitan government, with Negroes gaining at the expense of whites. At the same time, central city Negroes are not always particularly fond of metropolitan government, seeing it as a threat to their growing political base in the city, and reasoning that in the metropolitan context they would constitute a distinct minority submerged in a

[11] Incidentally, metropolitan government represents a political and not an economic change (as implied by the term socialism). The charge that the establishment of a metropolitan-wide general-purpose government is socialistic in and of itself cannot be substantiated. This is so because such a restructuring of the metropolitan governmental system would not directly or basically affect the nature of the economic system. This restructuring would not necessarily result in any more government ownership of business (such as transit systems) than would be the case prior to the change. Also, a new metropolitan government does not necessarily mean the addition of any new governmental regulatory powers. However, it is true that a shift in government authority from the local to the metropolitan level might affect the nature of the decision-making process in a particular functional area which has some control over the private sector, perhaps making it easier for a new government to impose restrictions on land-use, to extend such restrictions to new geographical areas, or to regulate a certain category of business.

sea of white suburban votes. In addition to these two forces, others likely to lend *ad hoc* support to the conservative position are suburban, fringe area, and county government employees and officials, suburban newspapers, business and farm interests outside the central city, and rural areas within the metropolitan region.[12]

The second group of decentralizationists includes the majority of the more active local government officials within the typical metropolitan area. Although this group's position is one of opposition to general-purpose metropolitan government, its members often warmly endorse some forms of metropolitan reorganization, including voluntary councils of government and limited-function authorities or agencies in functional areas such as transit and parks. This group nearly always supports strongly metropolitan planning commissions or councils. To this group the values of local self-government, grass-roots control of local public institutions, some degree of social and economic homogeneity, and citizen access are important, but the existence and preservation of these values are not considered threatened by metropolitan-wide cooperation and the introduction of a broader point of view into the local decision-making process, at least insofar as certain activities are concerned. In addition to the more active of the local officials, local citizens associations, community-wide federations of citizens associations, the larger of the suburban businesses, various professional organizations, and some labor unions can be expected to adhere to the principal tenets of this group. Community metropolitanists—such as metropolitan (downtown) newspapers, central-city chambers of commerce, various specialized types of central-city business interests, the League of Women Voters, and municipal research organizations—will often ally themselves with this group of decentralizationists in the latter's support of restricted metropolitan change.[13] Usually, metropolitanists view such change as only an initial step, and this normally sets them apart from the decentralizationists.

Recently, a substantial degree of academic legitimacy has been extended to the decentralizationists, as a number of political scientists and others have pointed out in scholarly fashion that the current system of local government in metropolitan areas is not altogether without merit and may in fact serve useful purposes, that metropolitan reform efforts often fail to take political reality into account, and that arguments for metropolitan change may be considerably more romantic than logical, particularly in the political sense. These academic decentralizationists

[12] Advisory Commission on Intergovernmental Relations, *Factors Affecting Voter Reactions to Governmental Reorganization in Metropolitan Areas* (Washington, D.C.: U.S. Government Printing Office, May, 1962), p. 13. See also Scott Greer, *Metropolitics* (New York: Wiley, 1963), p. 30.

[13] *Factors Affecting Voter Reactions to Governmental Reorganization in Metropolitan Areas, op. cit.,* p. 13.

should be treated more or less as a third group independent of the other two classes of decentralizationists.

In recent years, the political science discipline has been split into traditional and behavioral wings. The traditionalists concerned with local government have been in the vanguard of the metropolitan government reorganization movement, at least at the academic level. To many traditionalists it made good common sense to seek a restructuring of local government in the metropolitan area as a means of bringing order and sense of symmetry to a seemingly chaotic situation. In recent years some political scientists with an interest in local government have in effect challenged the positions of the earlier scholars, suggesting to the current observer that an undoubtedly healthy spirit of idealism may have clouded the approach and conclusions of the earlier students of metropolitan governments.

Duane Lockard, for instance, criticizes what he considers overrationalization on the part of some metropolitan government reformers, emphasizing that regional or metropolitan areas are not clearly definable and that even if they were the "drastic recarving of the political universe [proposed by the metropolitanists] . . . would be exceedingly difficult to produce."[14] Furthermore, Edward Banfield and Morton Grodzins deny the existence of any "natural" environment or region within the metropolitan area, and go on to raise significant questions about some of the assumptions underlying the metropolitanist position.[15] For instance, metropolitanists believe that efficiency and economy are virtues of metropolitan government—that is, because of economies associated with large-scale governmental operations and the elimination of overlap and duplication, the argument goes, it will be possible to secure more or better quality services for each local public dollar spent or the same service for fewer dollars (that is, compared to the present system). Banfield and Grodzins demonstrate that through the addition of a nonmonetary dimension to efficiency—such as the value placed on local autonomy or suburban independence of the central city—many residents may be prepared to pay more for services rather than make the change in government structure, and to do so generally within the framework of "efficiency." They also state that available evidence shows that expenditures increase on a per capita basis as the size of the community increases (which would argue against metropolitan government, if anything) and that although cost per unit of service does decrease as the size of the locality increases (pro metropolitan government), it does so only up to a

[14] Duane Lockard, *The Politics of State and Local Government* (New York: Macmillan, 1963), p. 505.
[15] Edward C. Banfield and Morton Grodzins, *Government and Housing in Metropolitan Areas* (New York: McGraw-Hill, 1958), pp. 32–36.

certain point—to about 50,000 in population—at which time what economists call diseconomies of scale apparently set in and costs do not decrease much beyond that.

Others have revealed that upon close examination there is already a metropolitan framework which through a variety of means permits area-wide problems and matters to be considered, and which is characterized by a negotiation and decision-making process accommodating diverse interests.[16] Some hold, in fact, that metropolitan "solutions" and a metropolitan point of view are as likely to be brought about by bargaining among the various governmental units composing the metropolitan area political system as through (the insistence on the use of) some model of cooperation for the metropolitan area as a whole. An analogy can be cited in the world at large, in which the international objective of peaceful cooperation is as likely to result from a balance of power among nation states—in reality, more so—as from the efforts of the international organizations or the advocates of world government. The existing governmental system in the metropolitan area further encourages certain political expressions and activity on the part of numerous subgroups and subcultures, including minorities, and therefore seems to add to the stability of the metropolitan area social system in general and the psychological well-being of its residents in particular. In this light, tampering with the metropolitan area governmental structure in any basic way, even if it were possible, may not be as wise as would initially appear to be the case.

A few final considerations which bear heavily on the matter of metropolitan government reorganization are the following:

1. To what extent are metropolitan problems caused by the structure of government in the metropolitan area? Put another way, are metropolitan problems simply *problems*, unrelated to government structure, not caused by inadequacies in government structure, and therefore not subject to remedy through a change in the governmental system? For example, most metropolitan area residents would probably agree that the provision of sound housing for the disadvantaged is a *problem* in the metropolitan area and one that is not currently being *solved*. The provision of government housing is a function of local government. Will a metropolitan government build more housing for the poor than is currently being built by existing local governments? What evidence do we have that it will?

[16] See Vincent Ostrom, Charles M. Tiebout, and Robert Warren, "The Organization of Government in Metropolitan Areas: A Theoretical Inquiry," *American Political Science Review,* 55 (December, 1961), 831–842. See also Thomas R. Dye, "Metropolitan Integration by Bargaining Among Sub-areas," *American Behavioral Scientist,* V (May, 1962), 11.

2. Will the manipulation of the metropolitan area governmental system result in a change in the relative strength of the various interest groups and other political forces which determine in the main the way *any* government operates, local or metropolitan? If certain groups and interests now dominate the political and public policy processes in decentralized local governments all throughout the metropolitan area, can we be certain that these same groups and interests will not dominate the political and public policy processes in the metropolitan area-wide government? Back to our example, in what respects and by what means will the "right" forces be given greater influence—say those that want more low-income government-supported housing, are willing to tax the people to get this housing, and locate such housing where required—and the "wrong" interests (that is, those opposed to such action, those who currently block such action) lose influence?

3. Is there truly a sense of community in the metropolitan area broad enough to support any significant change in government structure? Although the answer to this question must be relative and inexact, weighty evidence abounds that suggests the absence of a metropolitan-wide community. Important racial,[17] political party,[18] fiscal,[19] and social status[20] divisions characterize the internal fabric of metropolitan America. Often these disparities distinguish the central city from the suburb (race for example), but they also differentiate suburb from suburb within the same metropolitan area.

4. Under a new metropolitan-wide government, would it not be likely that a newly created metropolitan government administrative bureaucracy would have such concentrated power that it could virtually rule the metropolitan area in matters of concern to it? For instance, could the metropolitan citizenry withstand the united strength of the organized employees of a new metropolitan government when it came to issues like budget expansion and tax and civil service pay increases? The relative power of local government bureaucracies in the quest for the resources of the metropolitan area may well escalate with the development of a single metropolitan-wide government. It is not clear that countervailing power forces would be generated to compensate for this possibility.

[17] Advisory Commission on Intergovernmental Relations, *Metropolitan Social and Economic Disparities: Implications for Intergovernmental Relations in Central Cities and Suburbs* (Washington, D.C.: U.S. Government Printing Office, January, 1965), p. 17.
[18] Edward C. Banfield, "The Politics of Metropolitan Area Organization," *Midwest Journal of Political Science*, I (May, 1957), 77–91.
[19] Robert C. Wood, *Suburbia, Its People and Their Politics* (Boston: Houghton Mifflin, 1958), pp. 214–217.
[20] Thomas R. Dye, Charles S. Liebman, Oliver P. Williams, and Harold Herman, "Differentiation and Cooperation in a Metropolitan Area," in Michael N. Danielson (ed.), *Metropolitan Politics* (Boston: Little, Brown, 1966), pp. 261–271.

5. How consistent is metropolitanism with the interests of certain especially submerged minorities, such as Negroes and Puerto Ricans? These groups are just now beginning to gain more adequate representation under the existing decentralized metropolitan governmental structure and furthermore are, in a number of instances, calling for an even greater decentralization of the current system. A centralization of local power in a metropolitan-wide government would hardly seem consistent with the political aspirations of such minority interests.

In short, these are all matters that cannot be taken lightly by those who consider metropolitan areas, their governments, and their problems to be issues of great significance, meriting serious examination and the most careful of analysis.

THE POLITICAL ENVIRONMENT
OF THE METROPOLITAN AREA

So far in this chapter we have concentrated primarily on the governments of the metropolitan area. An important related consideration not yet systematically discussed is the interest-group structure of the metropolitan area. Metropolitan area interests concerned with the operations and public policies of metropolitan area local governments include business (general and specialized), civic, citizen association, political party, municipal employee, labor, and many other organizations. Since at least one of the objectives of all of these groups is to influence the actions of local government, they are often organized along the lines of governmental jurisdictions. As is true generally in the American federal system, governmental access points in the metropolitan area will tend to shape the organizational base of the private interests that seek to gain a voice in or control over particular public policy decision-making processes. Specific examples of interest groups operating in the various parts of the metropolitan area are cited in other parts of the book.

10. METROPOLITAN
REORGANIZATION
STRATEGIES

Political decentralization is undoubtedly the dominant governmental theme in the metropolitan area. Yet, any number of metropolitan reorganization proposals have been advanced to reverse or at least moderate some of the effects of the current decentralization pattern. Some of these proposals have been accepted widely, while others are infrequently if ever adopted. Some would have an effect on governments throughout the metropolitan area; others affect only a portion of the metropolitan area. We shall examine all major metropolitan reorganization proposals in this chapter, with the only criterion for the inclusion of the proposed change being its potential for adding some dimension of centralization to the metropolitan area political system. It must be noted that we are not limiting our discussion to metropolitan government per se or even to metropolitan *government* reorganization; in fact, many of the reorganization concepts call for no metropolitan-wide government of any kind—that is, of either a general- or special-purpose variety—or for no reduction in the number of governments in the metropolitan area. This is to say that "reorganization" may have a somewhat restricted meaning and need not necessarily involve a change in government structure; a reorganization may only affect the way a government operates (including some of the functions it will perform perhaps or the framework within which its officers consider and make decisions). Finally, we are concerned with strategies of metropolitan reorganization, which is another way of stating that we wish the student to be familiar with the possibilities of metropolitan change as well as with action that has taken place on the metropolitan front.

Broadly, three types of metropolitan reorganization are possible: (1) that involving no change in government structure or organization; (2) that requiring some but limited change; and (3) that necessitating major change. The preponderance of political weight in the metropolitan area governmental systems is solidly on the side of the status quo; proposed metropolitan change is then initially placed in a disadvantaged position. In a technical sense this is so in part because of the large number of existing independent access and potential veto points found in the metropolitan area political system. However, the degree of political feasibility associated with a metropolitan reorganization proposal will be significantly related to the extent and nature of change to be brought about by the proposal. Reorganizations that will result in major change will be less acceptable politically on the average than those requiring only minor change. The greater the effect on governmental structure (up to and including the creation of a metropolitan-wide government), the more difficult it is to gain approval for the proposal. Further, change that is more or less of a permanent nature will be much harder to achieve than that of a temporary kind which can be terminated easily. These are laws of metropolitan political dynamics which have nearly as much validity as the laws of physical science. We shall review each of the three forms of metropolitan reorganization in order.

METROPOLITAN CHANGE: I

Probably most consistent with the spirit of the American political tradition and most compatible with deeply held American values is the kind of change that is really not much of one and which is voluntarily agreed to by all parties and interests concerned. This is essentially the character of the first approach to metropolitan reorganization. In this category is found the sort of organization, program, or activity based on the assumption that certain advantages can be realized through joint, more broadly based, or more centrally oriented actions or discussions. Normally, although not always, voluntary cooperation is a distinctive element of this reorganization strategy. Specifically, this class of metropolitan change includes informal cooperation, the contract plan, councils of governments, and extraterritorial jurisdiction.

Informal Cooperation

Various forms of informal cooperation among independent units of government have existed at the local level for decades. What is involved here then is the adaptation of a device facilitating unification of action used in rural and smaller urban areas to the metropolitan area. This approach is typified by joint or cooperative action by two or more governments in such matters as firefighting, police teletype, the use of maintenance equipment, and planning; informally established organizations of public officials representing one or more functional areas in their local jurisdictions meeting periodically within a metropolitan area to discuss mutual problems and interests would be encompassed as well. As the term "informal" suggests, the type of activity conceived here does not necessarily require the use of a written contract or the backing of specific legislative sanction. In many instances informal cooperation will take place among local governments or governmental officials on a submetropolitan (broader than a single jurisdiction, but not covering the entire metropolitan area) rather than on a metropolitan-wide basis. The exchange of police information is an illustration of an activity that may extend to all major local governments in the metropolitan area, and the police teletype is a means to this end.

Contract Plan

Under the contract concept, interjurisdictional or intergovernmental agreements are formulated and entered into by two or more governments. Such agreements are legally considered contracts and will normally be quite specific in terms of their performance and time dimensions. Intergovernmental contracts may stipulate the performance of some function(s) or the provision of service(s) by one of the parties at agreed upon rates, or may call for individual or joint/cooperative action by one or more of the governmental parties to the agreement. Parties to such contracts are not necessarily limited to local governments, and may include the state or national government.

Two general classes of contracts used by local governments in metropolitan areas are service contracts and land development and regulation contracts. Service contracts require the provision of services or equipment or the performance of functions in one or more areas of governmental responsibility such as libraries, personnel, public health, welfare, purchasing, tax assessment, flood control, police, airports, and so on. These contracts are divided into the limited and multifunctional varieties, distinguished from each other on the basis of the number of functions or services involved. The service contract has been long associated with the Los Angeles metropolitan area, as Los Angeles County has been a leader in the development of this plan. Through several different means including contract, Los Angeles County has made many county services available to municipalities.[1] Municipal-county contracts in the Los Angeles area may cover one, a few, or numerous services and functions, up to over 40 in all; and Los Angeles County has innovated in the area of making service "package" contracts with municipalities—the service package idea is commonly called the "Lakewood Plan," so-named after the initiation of such a contract between the county and the municipality of Lakewood in 1954. From the locality's standpoint the Lakewood Plan is attractive since a community can retain basic policy-making authority in its municipal government and at the same time contract for many local services with a larger and more efficient unit of government, thus not saddling itself with a number of bureaucratic responsibilities and expensive administrative undertakings.

From the philosophical angle of the metropolitanist, service contracts, and especially the package kind, can be considered a favorable development. In other words, through this plan it is theoretically possible for a single government to perform area-wide as well as "local" functions, notwithstanding the existence and legal independence of municipal or other lower-level units, and thereby promote the metropolitan point of view. However, in practice the service contract concept is apparently not without its effects on the growing balkanization of the governmental structure of metropolitan areas. In Los Angeles County, from 1939 to 1954, no new municipalities were created; but between the institution of the Lakewood Plan and 1964, 31 new municipalities were established in the county and nearly each one of these cities used the package contract.[2] Such a consequence (undoubtedly unexpected and unplanned) is seen by the metropolitanists as undesirable and by anybody's count may

[1] County-municipal cooperation in Los Angeles County may take the form of transfer of functions from the city to the county, a single-function contract, general service agreements (that is, multifunction service contract), special district, and joint action. Roscoe C. Martin, *Metropolis in Transition* (Washington, D.C.: U.S. Housing and Home Finance Agency, September, 1963), pp. 14–15.

[2] John C. Bollens and Henry J. Schmandt, *The Metropolis, Its People, Politics, and Economic Life* (New York: Harper and Row, 1965), p. 390.

negatively affect the ultimate prospects of bringing about a truly metro-politan-wide approach.

Service contracts are not limited to the Los Angeles area and are part of metropolitan area intergovernmental arrangements in other sections of the country as well. Also, service contracts are not restricted to a situation in which municipalities contract with a county; suburban areas, for example, often contract with central cities for the provision of certain services like water to outlying jurisdictions. Variations of the service con-tract plan further include agreements between metropolitan area local governments calling for the joint performance of a function, contracts covering the construction and operation of facilities, and agreements involving the supplying of mutual aid in emergencies.

Land development and regulation contracts represent an emerging form of intergovernmental activity in the metropolitan area. Perhaps the best example of this type of agreement are watershed development project contracts, used in urban as well as rural areas. Watershed projects are carried out by several governmental units, including perhaps local, state, and national government agencies. Parties to local watershed agreements will be the U.S. Department of Agriculture (Soil Conserva-tion Service) and key relevant nonnational governments, such as the local soil conservation district, the governing board of the local general-purpose government whose jurisdiction covers the project area, and possibly other agencies. In watershed projects the sponsoring govern-ments are responsible for building flood control structures (dams), developing other physical watershed improvements, and promoting water-shed area conservation practices, including if necessary the appropriate regulation of land-use to assure land development in accordance with standards incorporated in the watershed plan. This latter provision may in effect require a signatory party government with zoning power to restrict land-use to certain (low) population densities and specific kinds of development (such as large-lot residential use). One might speculate that land development contracts will become more popular in the future in the outlying portions of metropolitan areas as the potential and effects of land-use controls become better understood and more widely ap-preciated.

Councils of Governments

The council of governments is a prime illustration of a voluntary metropolitan-wide approach to governmental unity in the metropolitan area, and as such does not directly affect or pose any immediate threat to current governmental structure patterns. Councils of governments are sometimes referred to as metropolitan or regional councils and are associations of local general-purpose governments in the metropolitan area, representing primarily elected officials in these governments. Metropolitan councils are established to provide a forum for the discussion, examination, and proposal of courses of action concerning problems and issues having a metropolitan dimension or impact. Theoretically, councils of governments can be private agencies, existing perhaps as a private nonprofit corporation or by general agreement of local governments in the area, or governmental organizations operating pursuant to state enabling legislation or other laws or authority. Each metropolitan area with a regional council will have only one such body.

These associations of local governments are somewhat restricted in the exercise of power. They may discuss and advise; they do not have the authority to enforce or implement. Nor can they at present operate programs that extend beyond data collection, planning, studies, research, and the like. It is nevertheless true that regional councils may be so effectively linked formally or informally with organizations that do have execution powers or that they have so successfully developed such a private bank of political capital that they may be influential in the metropolitan area decision-making processes. Furthermore, recent national government legislative and administrative actions have served to strengthen the political position of regional councils.

Although councils of governments are composed essentially of elected officials of member local governments, one should not underestimate the role of local government administrative officers or regional council professional staffs in the operations of these councils. Local government and council staff administrators and professionals appear to dominate the internal policy process found in regional councils, while the more active of metropolitan area elected officials seem to have considerable influence over the general policy pronouncements. It should be noted that most local elected officials in the metropolitan area do not serve their local governments on a full-time basis, normally have regular private jobs or practices, and therefore have only limited time to contribute to their local governments and even less to an association of governments.

Partisans of councils of governments often suggest that the chief advantage of these organizations is their voluntary nature. Yet, this is precisely where the councils are weakest, as it is this characteristic that forms the primary obstacle to their both considering and taking significant action. The freedom of metropolitan area local governments to join or not to join or to withdraw has proved to be an effective deterrent to discussion and action by regional councils, particularly in obviously controversial functional areas such as public housing. In some metropolitan areas with councils of governments, important local governments have remained outside of regional councils, choosing not to belong or to withdraw after having been a member.

With rare exceptions, special-purpose governments do not participate in metropolitan councils of governments. The virtually systematic exclusion of school governments from membership in regional councils tends to create a rather large gap between the stated objectives of these councils (that is, that they represent an attempt by the local governments in the metropolitan area to seek solutions to common problems) and the reality of the situation, in view of the huge chunk of local public expenditures accounted for by metropolitan area school systems and in the light of the significant impact of such governments on the general metropolitan area political and social environment.

Some political scientists have studied recent developments in councils of governments in various parts of the United States. Roscoe Martin believes that these regional councils can serve useful purposes, and that the chances of success are greatest when councils consider noncontroversial matters, when the proposed solution will not adversely affect any member government, when any proposed decision is self-executing (that is, the decision does not require action by member local governments), and when the proposal costs member governments little or nothing.[3] On the whole, the verdict on councils reached by Professor Martin was mixed. It was a similar conclusion that led Royce Hanson, after an exhaustive case study of the Metropolitan Washington Council of Governments, to speculate whether the role of the organization was "transitional rather than perpetual."[4]

A generally favorable commentary came from a survey of eight regional councils conducted under the auspices of the Advisory Commission on Intergovernmental Relations. This study reported that councils of governments may have the political capability to become action organizations in some areas, with the ability to perform operating programs, and further that regional councils, contrary to earlier assumptions, can function without consensus.[5] This seems to suggest that metropolitan councils may be developing in a way inconsistent in some respects with what many conceived to be their original purpose. Nevertheless, the fears of some that councils of governments are not effective institutions for the advancement of metropolitan-wide leadership, policy innovation, and more or less independent action programs should be allayed, at least for the time being.

Two important pieces of national legislation have had a considerable effect on some councils of governments and seem to have promoted the council-of-governments cause throughout the United States. The first was

[3] Martin, op. cit., p. 49.
[4] Royce Hanson, The Politics of Metropolitan Cooperation: Metropolitan Washington Council of Governments (Washington, D.C.: Washington Center for Metropolitan Studies, 1964), p. 70.
[5] Royce Hanson, Metropolitan Councils of Governments (Washington, D.C.: Advisory Commission on Intergovernmental Relations, August, 1966), pp. 30–33.

the Housing and Urban Development Act of 1965 (section 701g) which authorized federal grants to "organizations composed of public officials . . . representative of the political jurisdictions" in metropolitan areas to undertake "studies, collect data, develop regional plans and programs" and to perform other activities that the national government finds necessary or desirable for the solution of metropolitan problems. The authority in this legislation is quite broad; the legislation's one limiting feature is that "to the maximum extent feasible" grants are to be used for matters relating to the "developmental aspects" of the total metropolitan area, including research and planning in land use, transportation, housing, economic development, natural resources, community facilities, and the general improvement of the environment. Numerous additional councils of governments were created in various metropolitan areas following the 1965 congressional enactment.

The Demonstration Cities and Metropolitan Development Act of 1966 (especially section 204) further enhanced the position of councils of governments. This legislation requires local governments in metropolitan areas to submit certain federal grant and loan applications to the agency responsible for metropolitan planning, which is "to the greatest extent practicable, composed of and responsible to local elected officials." Neither the 1966 nor the earlier act mentions specifically councils of governments, but the implication is clear enough. According to the 1966 law, applications for national government assistance in open space, hospitals, airports, libraries, water facilities, sewerage, highways, transportation, water development, and land conservation within the metropolitan area must be submitted "for review" to the appropriate regional organization.

One is led to wonder: Why this flurry of council of governments legislative activity? There are several answers to this question. First, councils of governments are composed of elected officials who head up general-purpose local governments which are ultimately responsible for plan and program implementation within the metropolitan area. Second, the regional council approach is politically feasible (for reasons already stated) and is favored by many local-government elected officials, especially the more active, liberal, and metropolitan-oriented of these officials (the latter probably have a disproportionate degree of influence in councils of governments). Third, it has become abundantly apparent that more drastic metropolitan surgery will not work in most metropolitan areas. Fourth, many are convinced that metropolitan area local governments will not provide the necessary financial or political support for metropolitan councils. The first point is particularly important. In the past—that is, prior to the advent of councils of governments—virtually the only kind of metropolitan organization in existence was the metropolitan planning commission. Metropolitan planning commissions have been cautious and conservative, probably reflecting their boards' composition (mainly private citizens, including businessmen).[6] Those wanting positive government action on a metropolitan area-wide basis have believed that metropolitan organizations representative of public elected officials would be more likely to take the initiative in the metropolitan area and set region-wide priorities. In some areas regional councils are more apt to be aligned with the more liberal forces in the metropolitan area than has been the case with metropolitan planning commissions.

Today councils of governments are certainly in a state of transition, moving from metropolitan discussion groups to institutions grasping for an independent power base within the metropolitan area political system. Specific councils such as the Association of Bay Area Governments of San Francisco, the Mid-Willamette Valley Council of Governments (Salem, Oregon), and the Metropolitan Washington Council of Governments have come a long way since their creation within the last ten or fifteen years (the first council of governments was the Supervisors Inter-County Committee in Detroit, established in 1954). Although councils of governments have not to date built the sort of political foundation necessary for them to be considered a major force in metropolitan communities, all signs point to their continued growth. Metropolitan councils are now represented in Washington by the National Service to Regional Councils, a public interest group initially funded by the U.S. Department of Housing and Urban Development and sponsored by the National League of Cities and the National Association of Counties.

Extraterritorial Jurisdiction

Three kinds of activities are covered in this category: (a) the location of public facilities such as city dumps, sewage treatment plants, and detention centers outside the boundaries of the city; (b) the provision of various services such as water and sewer to residents or areas outside the city limits; and (c) the regulation of certain matters like land use in areas near or bordering on but outside the city.

Most states authorize municipalities to locate certain facilities in areas not within their corporate boundaries, and probably the majority of American cities take advantage of this authority. However, this is by no means a key extraterritorial jurisdiction power. The second type of extraterritorial jurisdiction should not be dismissed lightly by those wanting

6 Private citizens have been the most numerous group on metropolitan planning commissions. The remaining positions have been divided somewhat evenly among elected and appointed officials. U.S. Housing and Home Finance Agency, *National Survey of Metropolitan Planning* (Washington, D.C.: U.S. Government Printing Office, 1963), p. 24.

the development of a metropolitan perspective; extraterritorial provision of services can be used as an important means of effecting a more centrally directed land-use and population-movement pattern in the metropolitan area. For example, some cities charge residents of the metropolitan area receiving city water higher rates if such residents live outside the city, a practice that has a tendency to encourage suburbanites to look more favorably on annexation. Other stipulations that may accompany city services, including those affecting land development, may well add a metropolitan dimension to suburban decision-making. Generally, this kind of extraterritorial authority is to be distinguished from the service contract in that it covers services for unincorporated areas while the contract plan applies to incorporated jurisdictions (some overlap may exist between the two however).

By far the most significant extraterritorial power is land-use regulation by the city of areas near the city but outside the municipal corporation limits. Over half of the states permit cities to exercise subdivision control outside their boundaries; considerably fewer states authorize similar zoning regulation.[7] Most commonly, land-use control of this sort extends to three miles beyond the municipal limits, although both zoning and subdivision regulation may cover contiguous areas up to five miles (or more) from the city. Within metropolitan areas, both central cities and suburban municipalities may have certain extraterritorial jurisdiction power, although central cities are more likely to have such power than suburban municipalities.[8] Extraterritorial regulatory authority is most meaningful and useful in many areas in the Southwest and in some portions of other sections where central cities are not surrounded by incorporated suburban governments.

METROPOLITAN CHANGE: II

The following reorganization approaches have some although limited effect on the structure of local government in the metropolitan area: annexation, special district, metropolitan planning commission, metropolitan transportation planning board, urban county, and city-county separation. The structural implications of these strategies of metropolitan reorganization vary somewhat with the concept but may include changes in the structure of any particular government (for example, annexation,

[7] Advisory Commission on Intergovernmental Relations, *Alternative Approaches to Governmental Reorganization in Metropolitan Areas* (Washington, D.C.: U.S. Government Printing Office, June, 1962), p. 21.

[8] International City Management Association, *The Municipal Year Book 1969* (Washington, D.C., 1969), p. 238.

urban county) or a change in the general structure of government in the metropolitan area or portion thereof (for example, special district, metropolitan planning commission).

Annexation

The great cities of many American metropolitan areas initially grew through the annexation of urbanized and urbanizing areas adjacent to their boundaries, a technique of municipal adjustment to population movements used extensively up to the latter part of the nineteenth century. With few exceptions, there was little annexation activity from about 1900 until after World War II,[9] since the war, annexation has again been on the upswing, taking place especially in such southwestern and far western cities as Houston, Oklahoma City, Phoenix, Dallas, and San Diego.

Defined, annexation is a means by which the geographical boundaries of certain local governments are expanded to include contiguous or nearby land areas not previously part of the jurisdiction of the local government. Annexation is relevant to our discussion of metropolitan reorganization because it is theoretically one method by which government jurisdiction boundaries and natural population settlement patterns can be made consistent with one another, municipal services are provided adjacent urbanized areas, and more orderly development can take place. In reality, annexation is often a political question, commonly involving the interests of various organizations including affected local governments, with tax considerations, something akin to imperialistic-type aggression, and more favorable regulatory treatment at stake. The practical and political aspects of annexation are important, as is the theory of the topic.

Several techniques are used to effect annexation: state legislative determination, popular decision in the annexor (doing the annexing) and/or annexee (being annexed) city or area, action of the municipal legislative body, judicial determination, and consideration by an independent body.[10]

States in which the legislature has exclusive final authority over some or all municipal boundary changes or in which the state legislature has made local boundary changes include Pennsylvania, Georgia, Delaware, and Rhode Island. Popular determination in the annexor city is sometimes required after or in conjunction with a vote of or petition submitted

[9] Bollens and Schmandt, *op. cit.*, p. 404.
[10] Information on the specific methods of annexation is based on National League of Cities, *Adjusting Municipal Boundaries, Law and Practice* (Washington, D.C., 1966), an outstanding summary work on the legal aspects of annexation. The appendix of this report contains a state by state review of annexation.

by the adult residents or property owners of the area being considered for annexation. When an annexee area votes or petitions for annexation, the municipality to which the area is to be annexed must normally approve before the action takes effect.

A third type of annexation is achieved through unilateral action of the municipal legislative body, a means used, for example, by some cities in Texas, Missouri, and Nebraska. In some cases rather strict criteria must be met (such as the existence of a certain population density in the area proposed for annexation) before municipalities may add to their jurisdiction. The fourth method, found in Virginia and Indiana, is accomplished through judicial decision. In Virginia, the circuit court makes the final determination on annexation on the request of a municipality proposing annexation, a county, a majority of the voters or landowners of an area wanting to be annexed, or a town that wishes to be annexed to a city. A specially constituted court composed of one judge from the area involved and two judges "remote" from the area sits to hear arguments and render a judgment.

A final method—consideration by an independent body—is used by Minnesota. An organization known as the Minnesota Municipal Commission makes annexation determinations. This commission has as its members three gubernatorial appointees and, in certain annexation proceedings, specified county officials in the affected area.

Like extraterritorial jurisdiction, annexation is of limited value in large sections of the United States—and for the same reason. Annexation is well suited to a growing urban or metropolitan area in its initial decentralization stages. Once population decentralization has been a long-time characteristic of the area, the chances are slim that annexation can be called upon to promote metropolitanism.

Some legal authorizations and provisions encourage the use of annexation (unilateral municipal governing body action); others discourage it or make it next to impossible. In addition, socioeconomic factors appear to play a significant role in the relative success of annexation as a municipal expansion instrument. Integration through annexation is more likely to take place where there is similarity of the populations to be merged.[11] In the areas of the nation where annexation has been most widely used (Southwest and West), central cities and suburbs commonly share similar socioeconomic characteristics (in reality, southern and western cities enjoy a higher social status than their suburbs).[12]

[11] See Thomas R. Dye, "Urban Political Integration: Conditions Associated with Annexation in American Cities," *Midwest Journal of Political Science*, 8 (November, 1964), 430–446.
[12] Advisory Commission on Intergovernmental Relations, *Metropolitan Social and Economic Disparities: Implications for Intergovernmental Relations in Central Cities and Suburbs* (Washington, D.C.: U.S. Government Printing Office, January, 1965), p. 12.

Special District

In the literature of political science and public administration, the special district has not been accorded the highest honors. Often, in fact, special district governments are viewed as obstacles and impediments to the solution of metropolitan problems—in part because of their tendency to fragment further the local government structure of the metropolitan area—and not as helpful vehicles by which to overcome these problems. However, special districts can be and are in many instances organized and operated in a way acceptable to leading students and practitioners of local government.

The basic nature of special districts is discussed in Chapter 8. Not all special districts will be treated in this chapter; we are concerned here only with those that do or could exist in metropolitan areas. Special district units in the metropolitan area can be classified according to the following dimensions: the area served, the number or range of functions performed, and the means by which board members are selected. Taking these points in order, special district governments can serve a geographical area within a locality (that is, within or coincident with a general-purpose government boundary), a portion of the metropolitan area extending beyond the boundaries of a single general-purpose government but not covering the entire metropolitan area, the total or entire (or substantially so) metropolitan area, or a region encompassing more than one metropolitan area. We can consider the first of our examples a local special district, the second a submetropolitan district, the next a metropolitan unit, and the last a regional special district government. Further, special districts may have responsibility for one or a few functions—that is, they may be categorized as single-function or multifunction (two or more) governments. Finally, governing boards of special districts may be selected by a variety of methods, including appointment by and/or from the chief elected executives and governing bodies of general-purpose governments whose residents are served by the special district, appointment by or from other public officials, or direct popular election. The first means of selection is based on the constituent-unit principle (appointments come from constituent government units) and has received wide support among political scientists and general-purpose government officials.

Within metropolitan areas most special districts serve a relatively small geographical area—that is, they are either local or submetropolitan governments. The typical public housing authority would be an illustration of a local district; the Maryland–National Capital Park and Planning Commission in the suburbs of Washington, D.C., is a submetropolitan unit. A relatively small number of districts—about 100 in all—cover an entire metropolitan area. Metropolitan districts include the Port of New York Authority, the Cleveland Metropolitan Park District, the Metropolitan Sanitary District of Greater Chicago, and the Municipality of Metropolitan Seattle. Some districts—the regional variety—extend across metropolitan area lines and may in fact have jurisdiction in two or more metropolitan areas. The Metropolitan Water District of Southern California, for instance, covers large portions of six counties (and several metropolitan areas) in southern California: Los Angeles, San Bernadino, Riverside, Orange, Ventura, and San Diego.[13]

The vast majority of the special districts in metropolitan areas perform only one basic function—and this fact limits their attractiveness as devices of metropolitan reorganization, particularly when it is coupled with the point that most districts operate on a local or submetropolitan scale. The Municipality of Metropolitan Seattle is one of the few examples of a metropolitan district with more than one function—and it only technically qualifies in the latter instance, as it has sewer and water pollution powers (however, the potential is here since the state law under which the Seattle district was established allows it to add water supply, public transportation, parks and parkways, planning, and garbage disposal functions). The New York Port Authority is responsible for such a broad range of transportation activities, including airports, port facilities, bridges, tunnels, bus transit, and so forth, that it might reasonably be classed as a multifunction metropolitan district. Probably the closest this nation has come to the creation of a truly multifunction metropolitan-wide special district was a 1959 attempt to add such a unit in the St. Louis metropolitan area. The St. Louis proposal provided for a new metropolitan special-district government with control over metropolitan highways, mass transit, economic development, master planning, police training and communication, civil defense, and sewerage.[14] The plan was rejected by the voters of the St. Louis metropolitan area.

The often obscure and politically invisible methods by which the governing boards of special districts are selected has caused many experts considerable heartache.[15] Yet, the constituent-unit selection concept is appealing and presumably adds an element of political responsibility to the governing process in special district organizations. A number of dis-

[13] Winston W. Crouch and Beatrice Dinerman, *Southern California Metropolis* (Berkeley: University of California Press, 1963), p. 6.
[14] See Advisory Commission on Intergovernmental Relations, *Factors Affecting Voter Reactions to Governmental Reorganization in Metropolitan Areas* (Washington, D.C.: U.S. Government Printing Office, May, 1962), p. 13, and Scott Greer, *Metropolitics* (New York: Wiley, 1963), p. 30.
[15] See Advisory Commission on Intergovernmental Relations, *The Problem of Special Districts in American Government* (Washington, D.C.: U.S. Government Printing Office, May, 1964), esp. pp. 67–70.

tricts in metropolitan areas are structured on the basis of this principle, including the Metropolitan Capital Improvement District of Denver, the Bay Area Air Pollution Control District, the San Francisco Bay Area Rapid Transit District, the Washington (D.C.) Suburban Sanitary Commission, the Metropolitan Water District of Southern California, and the Municipality of Metropolitan Seattle.

In our opinion, the special district operating in the entire metropolitan area and responsible for a single but basic function (such as transportation) is just about the most realistic means of attaining any degree of metropolitan integration. Of all of the possibilities, it is most consistent with the fundamental nature of the American political system, and the philosophy behind it coincides with the values and practical interests of large numbers of residents in the metropolitan area. The interstate (compact) district found in metropolitan areas is perhaps the most promising of the recent developments in this area.[16]

Metropolitan Planning Commission

The metropolitan planning commission was the first major instance of a practical response to the decentralized character of governmental rule in the metropolitan area. The typical metropolitan planning body was created in the mid- or late-1950s under state enabling legislation and is a governmental (as opposed to a private) organization. Presently there are several hundred metropolitan (including submetropolitan) planning agencies, and probably every metropolitan area in the nation has a planning board with authority over a substantial portion, if not all, of the metropolitan area. For the most recent year for which comprehensive figures are available (1964), 150 metropolitan areas (139 agencies) had some form of metropolitan planning.[17]

In general, metropolitan planning commissions have limited authority—in the main, they may adopt plans and review certain proposed projects of metropolitan area local governments. They do not have the power of plan implementation or land-use regulation. Nor do they administer regular operating programs. Thus, their role is essentially advisory.

A minority of metropolitan planning boards have been established directly by special act of the state legislature, and as such may operate as

16 Examples of metropolitan special districts created by interstate compact are the Port of New York Authority and the Washington Metropolitan Area Transit Authority (in the National Capital region).
17 See U.S. Housing and Home Finance Agency, *1964 National Survey of Metropolitan Planning* (Washington, D.C.: U.S. Government Printing Office, 1965); and U.S. Housing and Home Finance Agency, *National Survey of Metropolitan Planning, 1963, op. cit.*

an arm of the state government. It would appear that this means of creating metropolitan organizations enhances the prospects of bringing about metropolitan-wide coordination. An example of this approach—a state agency responsible for planning in one metropolitan area—is the Regional Planning Council which serves the Baltimore metropolitan area. This organization was created in 1963 by the Maryland state legislature to prepare, adopt, and revise a comprehensive plan for the development of a region to include the city of Baltimore and Baltimore, Anne Arundel, Carroll, Harford, and Howard counties (Baltimore City and Baltimore County are independent governmental entities). Local governments in the area served by the council control most of the seats on the council's governing board, and local elected official representation was expanded in 1967 (consistent with the provisions of the national Demonstration Cities and Metropolitan Development Act of 1966). Local governments are required by state law to contribute to the council, and the state government also advances funds to the agency. Additionally, the Regional Planning Council has certain review power over local proposals under both state and national legislation. In effect, the Baltimore council represents a combination of some of the features of the conventional metropolitan planning commission and a council of governments, is backed by the legislative and financial power of the state government, and is dominated by local governments, an uncommon mixture indeed.[18] This experiment bears watching.

Metropolitan Transportation Planning Board

The Federal-Aid Highway Act of 1962 essentially made it mandatory that a "continuing comprehensive transportation planning process" be developed in each of the nation's metropolitan areas by July 1, 1965. The objective of this enactment was to promote the coordination of highway and other transportation planning in metropolitan areas and to assure that the effects of highways on urban development were considered.

While it is true that metropolitan transportation planning did not originate with the passage of the 1962 Highway Act, a number of metropolitan transportation planning groups trace their roots (including their present composition) to the requirements of this legislation.[19] The transportation planning process may be carried on in or through any one of several administrative structures in the metropolitan area, but a particular board or committee will be given primary responsibility for this plan-

[18] There is evidence that suggests that this may not be peculiar to Baltimore. See Graduate School of Public Affairs, State University of New York at Albany, *1968 Survey of Metropolitan Planning* (Albany, 1968), p. 11.

[19] *1964 National Survey of Metropolitan Planning*, pp. 14 ff.

ning. The key transportation activity of state and local governments in most metropolitan areas is highways. And highway planning has been dominated by the state governments, specifically by independent highway departments or commissions. Whether states and their highway departments will set the tone in the metropolitan transportation planning processes—they are represented in these processes—is uncertain. In any event, local government and metropolitan area-wide viewpoints should be more easily aired with this new development.

The National Capital Region Transportation Planning Board is an illustration of a transportation planning agency created pursuant to the 1962 legislation. This board operates under the authority of a memorandum of agreement and does not have governmental status. Its voting membership is composed of three representatives of the local legislative bodies of governments in Washington's Maryland suburbs, three from such bodies in the Virginia suburbs, three from the governing board of the District of Columbia, and one representative each from the Maryland (state), Virginia, and District of Columbia highway departments.[20] No basic conflict over the desirability, location, or effect of highways exists between the dominant force in most local governments and state highway departments in the Washington metropolitan area; thus, metropolitan transportation planning in the National Capital region has been a relatively quiet matter.[21]

Urban County

Counties with general government authority are found within 205 of the 228 metropolitan areas of the nation. Altogether, there are over 400 counties in these metropolitan areas, and each of these units contains significant concentrations of urban residents. Because counties have a large land area within their borders and since many county governments encompass an entire metropolitan area, counties have been seen by some as the natural custodians of local government area-wide powers in metropolitan regions.

The urban-county concept means essentially the transformation of a rurally oriented county government structure and functional pattern to an urban system, giving the government the capability of performing a wide range of municipal-type functions throughout the entire county. The adoption of the urban-county plan may involve the elimination or downgrading of certain elective or other offices traditionally found in

[20] Metropolitan Washington Council of Governments, *Governments of the Washington Metropolitan Area* (Washington, D.C., January, 1968), pp. 87–88.
[21] This does not mean that there are no disagreements in the community over transportation planning. There are—and some private interests as well as some local legislators strongly oppose certain key highways planned for the region.

county governments, the addition or expansion of urban-related activities, the transfer of some governmental responsibilities from lower-level local governments to the county, and the streamlining of the executive and legislative branches, including the replacement of boards and commissions with single directors and a more precise assignment of powers in a central executive or office. A government may attempt to switch to the urban-county plan at one time—and such attempts have often failed to gain approval—or slowly change its governmental structure and gradually expand its functions. Probably, most urban counties fall in the latter category, although some important initial change (such as home rule) usually will have facilitated the move toward an urban county form.

The development of a full-fledged urban county plan will normally require the approval of affected voters and must, of course, be permitted under state law or the state constitution. Urban counties are found in some of the major metropolitan areas and around a number of the larger cities. Only one such urban county, however, qualifies as a metropolitan government or a "metropolitan county"—Dade County, Florida, which is responsible for a broad variety of metropolitan-wide functions in the Miami metropolitan area. Dade County is discussed under federation.

City-County Separation

In view of the fact that counties commonly serve populations residing within as well as outside municipal and other lower-level governments in the county, and since this arrangement may cause some confusion if not overlapping and duplication, some urban areas have moved to separate their city and county governments. Under this concept a city will have responsibility for providing services for residents living within its corporate limits, while the county will continue to have authority for areas outside municipal corporation boundaries. Most major city-county separations, however, took place over a half century ago—that is, before the emergence of the modern metropolitan area.

Cities that have separated from their counties include St. Louis, Baltimore, San Francisco, Denver, and the numerous independent municipalities in Virginia. Cities in Virginia may become independent of counties upon reaching a certain population; Virginia separations, in fact, are about the only recent experiences with this sort of metropolitan change. Political scientists do not consider this mechanism a particularly useful one for promoting metropolitan centralization; in reality, it seems to work in the opposite direction, especially with the emergence of the urban county and the movement of urban residents to the suburbs (that is, the county area) of the central cities.

METROPOLITAN CHANGE: III

Governmental reorganization requiring important structural changes in the metropolitan area political system has taken place in a few metropolitan areas. The two kinds of metropolitan change found in this class are city-county consolidation and metropolitan federation. Students of American local government can point to three major recent examples of metropolitan-wide consolidation and one instance of metropolitan-wide federation, all of which are found in the South, a section of the country characterized by a somewhat unique local political and social structure. These four units can be considered and termed "metropolitan governments"—that is, metropolitan-wide general-purpose governments. They are the only such governments in the United States.

City-County Consolidation

City-county consolidation represents the merger of the chief municipal government and the county government within a particular area. Other types of consolidation in the metropolitan area include mergers of municipalities and school district mergers; the consolidation of two or more counties or of two or more cities and a county are also possibilities. For city-county consolidation to be complete, one government must be the consequence—that is, where two governments previously existed. It should be noted, nevertheless, that even if consolidation is accomplished, the resulting government will not necessarily "explain" the entire governmental structure of the metropolitan area which the consolidated unit covers; other municipalities and local governments exclusive of the central city and county may continue on as independent units within the boundaries of the new government.

City-county consolidation partisans argue that by eliminating one unit of government and lodging all functions in a single area-wide government it is possible to reap the advantages of economies of scale, greater efficiency, and unified leadership. The city-county consolidation concept of metropolitan government has been criticized on the grounds that it allows for only one metropolitan unit, leaving or providing for no grass-roots or local level (as would be the case under federation), and therefore constituting too sharp of a departure from current practice.[22] Theory

[22] A proposal combining the consolidation and federation approaches was made in Sacramento; in this case, the consolidation of the five cities and the county in the area was recommended, as was the subsequent creation of a subordinate borough structure in the consolidated unit. Public Administration Service, *The Government of Metropolitan Sacramento* (Chicago, 1957).

notwithstanding, consolidation has proved to be slightly more popular than federation, although neither is widely embraced.

The three major recent city-county consolidations are Jacksonville and Duval County, Florida; Nashville and Davidson County, Tennessee; and Baton Rouge and East Baton Rouge Parish, Louisiana. These are not all of the instances of city-county consolidation (either recent or distant past), but they are the most significant and far-reaching of the contemporary examples.[23]

JACKSONVILLE   The new consolidated City of Jacksonville became a reality in 1968 after receiving the overwhelming approval of the metropolitan area voters in 1967. Prior to the merger, the Jacksonville area had two major general-purpose governments, one for the city and one for Duval County, with each governed by a separate commission. The new government has responsibility for the area covered previously by the county and operates under a strong-mayor plan. Some remnants of fragmentation remain: not all municipalities in the county are part of the consolidated unit; and education is the responsibility of an independent elective school board.

In a case study of the Jacksonville action, the United States Chamber of Commerce concluded that several factors contributed to the victory: the existence of significant problems under the previous government arrangements, including high taxes, school disaccreditation, and grand-jury indictments; leadership by prominent citizens; broad representation on the commission which proposed the consolidation; support of an active mass media; and political compromise.[24] In any event, in the light of the final vote, whatever was done was apparently done right.

NASHVILLE   In 1962, following an unsuccessful consolidation effort in 1958, the citizens of the Nashville area voted to merge Nashville and Davidson County and to form a new government—the Metropolitan Government of Nashville and Davidson County.[25] As in Jacksonville, the metropolitan government of Nashville is a municipality and uses the

[23] Several important city-county consolidations occurred over 50 years ago (New York, Boston, and elsewhere). Within the past two decades there have been other consolidations of cities and counties and consolidations involving only cities in metropolitan areas. Not included in this discussion is the Indianapolis-Marion County, Indiana consolidation, which took effect in 1970. Called UNIGOV, the new unit came into being through an act of the Indiana state legislature.

[24] Chamber of Commerce of the United States, *Jacksonville, Florida, Merges City and County Governments* (Washington, D.C., 1968), p. 4. For information on certain powers of the new government, see National Commission on Urban Problems, *Building the American City* (Washington, D.C.: U.S. Government Printing Office, 1968), pp. 209, 337–338.

[25] The major works on Nashville are Brett W. Hawkins, *Nashville Metro: The Politics of City-County Consolidation* (Nashville: Vanderbilt University Press, 1966), and David A. Booth, *Metropolitics: The Nashville Consolidation* (East Lansing: Michigan State University, Institute for Community Development, 1963).

strong-mayor-council form. A few independent municipalities are still found in the Nashville area.

It is instructive to note that in 1958 the political and economic power structures of the city and county were virtually unanimous in their collective support of metropolitan government; opposition was limited to several city councilmen, suburban fire and police companies, small suburban businesses, and a few other groups. Yet the proposal lost. In 1962, on the other hand, the political power structure was divided—the city political organization campaigned against it—and the economic forces were unable to maintain a united front as in 1958. Yet metro won. It appears that the "city machine's" opposition made the proposed new government more palatable to the suburbs, which had voted against consolidation in 1958 (while city voters were favoring it). Also, two actions of the city between 1958 and 1962—a municipal tax on commuters who used city streets and Nashville's annexation of some 50 square miles of suburban land area—seemingly encouraged many suburbanites to look kindly on consolidation in 1962. Finally, the numerical expansion and localizing of the proposed new government's council (compared to 1958) made merger more attractive the second time around.

A key feature of the Nashville consolidation is the new government's use of a flexible two-service/tax-district concept, under which an urban services district is used for the densely populated portions of the jurisdiction (initially the area covered by Nashville) and a general services district for all areas in the government. Each major portion of the population served by the new government has a tax level consistent with the (number and intensity of) services it receives, meaning, in effect, lower taxes for the less densely settled suburban and rural sections. The urban services district can be expanded as required.

BATON ROUGE   In the late 1940s, the Louisiana political climate was favorable to metropolitan change: first, it was easy to amend the state constitution (and this was required for consolidation); and second, consolidation needed only a single, parish-wide majority (separate city and suburban majorities are required in some areas).

In the strictest sense, Baton Rouge was not a complete consolidation: the city and parish retain their separate legal identities, and an overarching area-wide metropolitan structure links the city to the parish. Specifically, the governments of the city and parish are interlocked through a parish council composed of the seven members of the city's council and two members elected from the rural area of the parish outside the city, and through a mayor-president, elected at-large throughout the entire parish, who presides over both councils, appoints certain officials in both jurisdictions, and prepares the budget for the city and the parish.

Among the various functional areas the integration was the most thoroughgoing in planning and public works (including roads). Comprehensive planning was new to the area with the adoption of the new metropolitan government and was delegated to a planning commission which serves the whole parish. Public works was made the responsibility of a new department, again with metropolitan area-wide authority.

As in Nashville, a tax and service plan is used that allows different areas with varying service requirements to be taxed accordingly; however, instead of two districts, Baton Rouge operates with three—urban, industrial, and rural. Furthermore, as in Nashville as well as Jacksonville, some municipalities were basically unaffected by the restructuring of the area political system.

Following an extensive study of Baton Rouge's experience with consolidation, William Havard and Floyd Corty reported significant evidence of lingering fragmentation but nevertheless concluded that the record of the new metropolitan government was "impressive."[26]

Metropolitan Federation

Two concepts distinguish federation from other metropolitan reorganization strategies: (1) the existence of two levels of government, with one government extending throughout the metropolitan area and with legally prescribed interrelationships and a specified division of functions between the levels; and (2) the representation of the "lower" (covering the smaller area) in the "higher" level of government. One metropolitan federation is found in the United States: Miami-Dade County, Florida; and two others exist on the North American continent: Toronto and Winnipeg in Canada.

MIAMI   The Greater Miami Dade County political system meets the two standards: it is a two-level arrangement, one government covers the metropolitan area, and the two levels are legally interrelated; and, as initially established, the lower level was represented in the metropolitan-wide government.[27]

Under the Miami area governmental reorganization approved in 1957, the new metropolitan government was empowered to perform functions of an area-wide nature, including planning, parks, expressways, urban renewal, housing, police and fire protection, water supply, and so on,

---

[26] William C. Havard, Jr., and Floyd L. Corty, *Rural-Urban Consolidation: The Merger of Governments in the Baton Rouge Area* (Baton Rouge: Louisiana University Press, 1964), pp. 140–143.

[27] A proposal for a metropolitan government in Miami was made by the Public Adminisrtation Service in 1954: *The Government of Metropolitan Miami* (Chicago: Public Administration Service, 1954). The proposed government was based on the federal principle.

while municipalities retained control over local activities such as zoning. As a demonstration of the legal interrelationship between the two tiers of government, the metropolitan-wide government sets minimum service standards which must be met by the municipalities. According to the terms of the original charter, the larger of the municipalities were to elect delegates to the area-wide governing body. Under this provision, initially only the city of Miami qualified, but later other localities became eligible. A recent amendment to the charter under which the government operates changed the method of selecting members of the legislative body.

The new government in the Miami area was narrowly voted after an extensive campaign waged by proponents and opponents of metro. Technically, the voters did not create an entirely new government or political system. What they did was to approve a charter which provided for a broadening of the powers and a restructuring of the government of the existing county unit (Dade County). Under the new system the county was given a county-manager government, the status of some county offices was changed, and the county governing body was reorganized.

Factors facilitating the adoption of the new metropolitan government in Miami include the following: first, the absence of an entrenched political machine or important traditional political organizations in the area (such forces are not active supporters of metropolitan government even though they do not always openly oppose it,[28] as did the city machine in Nashville); second, the relatively newcomer and transient nature of Miami's population—thus, attachments to existing governmental institutions and arrangements were not as great as is the case elsewhere; third, the vigorous backing of the business community, including the Miami-Dade County Chamber of Commerce and the major newspapers; and finally, the use of an impartial expert in the development of the metropolitan government concept.[29]

Although the government of the Greater Miami area has weathered some serious legal and political storms, it cannot be considered to this day safely established. The Dade County League of Municipalities (representing the municipal governments in the area) was a principal foe of metro in 1957 and has continued to plague the new government.

TORONTO   The Municipality of Metropolitan Toronto was created by the Ontario provincial government and began operations in 1954.[30] The government is run by a metropolitan council, which includes repre-

---

28 Scott Greer, *Metropolitics* (New York: Wiley, 1963), p. 63.
29 See Edward Sofen, *The Miami Metropolitan Experiment* (Bloomington: Indiana University Press, 1963), pp. 213–214.
30 For information on the Toronto federation, see Frank Smallwood, *Metro Toronto: A Decade Later* (Toronto: Bureau of Municipal Research, 1963).

sentatives of the city of Toronto and six suburban municipalities (no metropolitan board members are directly elected to the metropolitan government). Functions are divided between the metropolitan government and the lower-level municipalities, with the former possessing authority over water supply, sewage disposal, housing, arterial highways, metropolitan parks, regional planning, and certain health and welfare programs among other matters, while the municipalities have responsibility for such activities as police, fire, local streets, local parks, local planning and zoning, and libraries.

Although many have hailed the Toronto system and its accomplishments, especially in mass transit, there has been considerable conflict in the new government—specifically, for instance, between the wealthier suburbs and the city over education and to some extent transit, and between the poorer suburbs and the city over public housing. This conflict has been reflected in sharp divisions in the metropolitan board, often bordering on stalemate or majority coercion.

It would be a mistake to attempt to use the Toronto experience as a guide (for good or bad) for metropolitan areas in the United States. There are important differences between the political systems and traditions of Canada and the United States. The Canadian provincial government has and exercises virtually unilateral control over metropolitan areas and their local governments. The Ontario government simply created the Toronto metropolitan government, assigned it certain functions, and gave the municipalities a voice in determining metropolitan policy. In 1966, the Ontario legislature "restructured" the suburban municipalities, reducing their numbers from twelve to six and changing their boundaries. Such action is unheard of in the United States. It is true that American state governments theoretically have authority over metropolitan areas and local governments within their borders, but state governments are notably reluctant or perhaps politically unable to change local government structure and powers. Furthermore, it is unlikely that any American state would permit a major metropolitan structural change without local voter approval. In other words, American state governments may have the legal authority but they do not have the power or the desire to establish metropolitan government. State governments, in reality, are more reflections than manipulators of local power structures. Apparently this is not the case among provincial governments in Canada.

WINNIPEG   The Metropolitan Corporation of Greater Winnipeg was brought into existence by an act of the Manitoba provincial legislature in 1960. Area-wide functions were assigned to the metropolitan government, while local activities remained in the hands of municipalities. The metropolitan government's legislative body is composed of ten members, about equally divided between city and suburban representatives.

The Future of Metropolitan Government

The prospects for metropolitan government or significant metropolitan change (annexation) appear greatest in the South and Southwest. This is partly because of the structural simplicity (relatively speaking) of local political systems in the South and because of the socioeconomic similarity of the city and suburban populations in the South and Southwest. The absence of these features in other sections of the country—especially the Northeast and Mid-Atlantic metropolitan areas—substantially dims the possibilities of metropolitan reorganization in such sections. Further, probably the most likely practical way for metropolitan government to be achieved will be through the leadership of big downtown businesses who believe that the present pattern of governmental arrangements significantly disadvantages them. Even then, however, they will need an "issue."

A final point is in order. As can be seen through an analysis of the operations of the new government in Toronto, metropolitan government should not be confused with metropolitan cooperation. To an extent, this principle is also reflected in the Miami area's new government. It is entirely reasonable to argue, in fact, that conflict is a natural and should have been a predictable result of metropolitan government, particularly in view of the fact that such a system introduces broader considerations into the metropolitan decision-making process. The creation of a new area-wide government may cause certain questions previously noncontroversial or invisible to many metropolitan area residents to be elevated to a level of conflict. Whether the generation of this conflict will serve as a healthy and stabilizing input into the metropolitan political system should become clearer as the metropolitan story unfolds.

11. POLITICS AND POWER STRUCTURES IN THE CITY

■ ■ ■ ■ ■ ■ ■ ■ ■ ■

The politics of the city is more visible and undoubtedly more widely discussed than the politics of any other segment of state and local affairs. This is probably a result of the emphasis placed on city elections and issues by the mass media and of the magnitude of the social and political strife, disorganization, and factionalism broadly characteristic of American central cities.

The purpose of this chapter is to examine in some detail city political life and to outline the various influences that affect city government and therefore constitute city politics. After the introductory comments on the current impressions of the position and status of the city in American

politics, we shall review the degree of centralization found in city political systems, the effect of certain population characteristics on the actions,
organization, functions, and public policy of city government, the nature
of interest groupings, issues, and patterns of conflict in city politics, and
finally city or community power structure studies.

THE CITY IN AMERICAN POLITICS

In its Forty-fifth Annual Congress of Cities in 1968, the National
League of Cities officially proclaimed that city government was the "only"
unit of government in the American federal system able to "respond
directly" to citizen needs, "flexible enough" to adapt to local conditions,
and capable of providing "immediate" service for the people.[1] That
statement was made by the representatives of the nation's cities after the
many riots and near-revolutionary acts of violence which plagued large
numbers of cities in the middle 1960s. In *Big City Politics*, a book published prior to the mid-1960s riots, Harvard Professor Edward C. Banfield
reported that all of the cities studied were "honestly and ably run," that
"today" no big city "is . . . notorious for its bad government," and that
one feature shared by big city governments was their "remarkable ability
to manage and contain . . . conflicts. . . ."[2] In the light of this analysis
and its substantial documentation, one can only wonder: What went
wrong? Or alternatively: Why were the sores of discontent so invisible?

In 1968, the National Advisory Commission on Civil Disorders—the
Kerner Commission—dramatically revealed that municipal political systems had failed in precisely those respects that the National League of
Cities claimed that only cities are qualified to act.[3] From the standpoint
of the slum resident, the commission observed, "city government appears
distant and unconcerned, the possibility of effective change remote."[4]
The Civil Disorders unit specifically pointed to merit systems that exclude Negroes from many city government jobs, certain representational
concepts such as at-large elections that work against the Negro minority,
city manager government that has proved less responsive to the needs of
the ghetto poor than the city machines it replaced, a bureaucracy that has
not effectively linked city hall to the Negro, and a generally white, mid-

[1] National League of Cities, *National Municipal Policy* (Washington, D.C., 1969),
p. 33.
[2] Edward C. Banfield, *Big City Politics: A Comparative Guide to the Political Systems of Atlanta, Boston, Detroit, El Paso, Los Angeles, Miami, Philadelphia, St. Louis,
Seattle* (New York: Random House, 1965), pp. 11, 13.
[3] Named for Otto Kerner, the then Governor of Illinois, and chairman of the Commission.
[4] *Report of the National Advisory Commission on Civil Disorders* (New York:
Bantam, 1968), p. 288.

dle-class-dominated welfare system. Detecting an apparent relationship between the violence and municipal government, the Kerner group explained that every major disruptive incident was preceded by a series of "unresolved grievances" and a "high level of dissatisfaction" with local authorities.[5] The commission's recommendations contained a familiar ring: the development of better communications between the city government and the ghetto, an improvement in the capacity of cities to respond, and the involvement of slum residents in municipal government policy-making processes.

The reaction of individual mayors and other city officials to Negro discontent was varied. Conservative Mayor Sam Yorty of Los Angeles (scene of the early Watts riot) flatly stated that his city's government was doing all it could to serve its citizens, although he did note that Los Angeles could never have gotten a Human Relations Commission before Watts. Liberal Mayor Jerome Cavanagh of Detroit placed the primary blame for the condition of cities on Congress—for not advancing the needed programs and funds. The prevailing viewpoint of municipal councilmen and administrators attending the immediate postriot 1967 Congress of Cities in Boston was in sharp contrast to the conclusions of the Civil Disorders Commission; by far the majority of the officials believed the root of the problem was either a conspiracy with origins outside of their cities or the presence of a few ill-willed local radicals, possibly associated with the Community Action Agency (the poverty program organization), and not the faulty or imperfect operation of city government. This pretty well summarized the feelings of white Americans interviewed in a 1967 Harris poll. When asked by *Congressional Quarterly* in 1967, most mayors were reported to consider the lack of jobs among blacks to be the fundamental cause of the disruption.

The events of the mid-1960s and mounting urban problems are beginning to take their toll among municipal executives, and it now appears that city mayors are becoming even more politically vulnerable than the much-troubled state governors who, on occasion, are retired by voters rebelling against tax hikes. The office of mayor is increasingly a political graveyard—at least this was the trend in the late 1960s. Among the prominent mayors leaving city politics in 1969 were

—Arthur Naftalin of Minneapolis who returned to the University of Minnesota and who was succeeded in office by a "law-and-order" chief executive, Charles S. Stenvig, former policeman;

—Ivan Allen, a national municipal spokesman and a political/racial moderate;

—Richard Lee of New Haven, known for his city's aggressive urban renewal policy;

[5] *Report of the National Advisory Commission on Civil Disorders, op. cit.,* p. 284.

—Joseph Barr of Pittsburgh, inheritor of the steel city's Lawrence-Mellon Democratic machine-big business dynasty;

—A. W. Sorenson of Omaha, a respected National League of Cities official and a Republican liberal;

—Milton Graham of Phoenix, popular and well-known southwestern leader;

—William Walsh of Syracuse, administrator of a city afflicted with intense poverty politicking and factionalism; and

—Cavanagh of Detroit.

The outgoing head of the United States Conference of Mayors, Mayor Terry D. Schrunk of Portland, Oregon, told conference members in 1969 that the association of elected city executives had suffered many political casualties over the past year, indicating that nearly half of the 39 mayors in conference leadership posts were either no longer in office or about to leave office. Mayors John Lindsay of New York and Samuel Yorty of Los Angeles both sustained stunning (but temporary) defeats in their respective primaries in the same year. Furthermore, nearly all of the parting executives had distinguished records in office, favorable national images, and worked for progressive change in their cities. The continuation of racial polarization in large cities will likely shorten the political careers of white moderate mayors, although it is entirely possible that the preservation instinct will shove such officials sharply to the left in many instances, giving them a strong political base in the black community.

CITY POLITICAL SYSTEMS

City political systems can be readily classified according to the nature of the distribution of influence in the community. That is, the patterns of influence in a locality may range from a high degree of centralization to extreme dispersion throughout the city's population and interest groups. A city's political system includes, but is not limited to, the general-purpose municipal government. Also part of a city political system are (1) other local governments operating within the city government's boundaries, including perhaps a county government, townships, a school district, and any number of limited-function units such as a public housing authority or a transit authority; and (2) private forces and institutions such as political parties, nonpartisan organizations, civic and citizens associations, business interests, labor unions, organized and unorganized public employees and officials, nationalities, social welfare and health groups, certain families and individuals, and racial organizations which exert directly or indirectly some influence over city government policy. National and state governments as well as private interests outside of the city may also play a role in shaping decisions in the city government and would therefore constitute inputs into city political systems.

In general, influence in the larger city political systems is highly decentralized. In fact, today there is probably not a city of 50,000 or over, if indeed there is a city of any size, ruled entirely by a single power elite; although it is true that some cities have a more centralized power distribution pattern than others. The mere existence of large quantities of public units other than the city government and of numerous private interests militates against any significant power concentration in one central location. The growing influence of federal agencies in internal matters of city government and the commonly conflicting policy positions of the many private and public forces impacting upon city policy-makers further have an unmistakably centrifugal effect on community power. Within the city government itself, four factors are important causes of decentralization: a formal dispersal of authority, agency-clientele links, a protective civil service system, and intergovernmental and professional ties.

Policy and administrative authority may be assigned formally to many more or less independent bodies, agencies, commissions, and offices, making centralization of power difficult at best. Major departments and boards in city government are often linked with private interests, not infrequently organized, which have a stake in particular city agencies and which may be economically or otherwise dependent upon or affected by decisions of such agencies. City department clientele groups include, for example, a local chapter of the National Association of Social Workers, a board of realtors, a citizens committee on child care, a local education association (affiliated with the National Education Association), and a citizens planning organization. These groups are closely related to and aligned with specific municipal agencies, and may serve as political supporters of, as well as sources of pressure for, these agencies.

After an exhaustive survey of municipal personnel practices in all parts of the United States, the Municipal Manpower Commission concluded that city civil service systems had cut deeply into the power base of the central political/governmental leadership in city government, fostering a protective and independent attitude on the part of subordinate administrative units, officials, and personnel.[6] (See also Chapter 2.) Additionally, professional and administrative employees of city government are increasingly faithful to and guided by norms, standards, and values emanating from public and private organizations outside the city government,

[6] Municipal Manpower Commission, *Governmental Manpower for Tomorrow's Cities* (New York: McGraw-Hill, 1962).

particularly from higher level governments in the federal system. Planning, health, welfare, recreation, park, public housing, urban renewal, and other municipal officials are often as likely, if not more likely, to identify with their counterpart government agencies and officials at other levels and with their private professional associations as they are with their own mayor or city council. Much of this external influence is no doubt subconsciously translated into municipal actions and policy; but it nevertheless reduces the effective power of local leadership (unless, of course, the local leadership is in full agreement with these outside forces), tending at the same time to encourage a "nationalization" of local policy, to curtail generally the role of peculiarly local forces and locally perceived needs in city decisions, and to mold power distribution patterns in accordance with the aspirations of individual municipal bureaucracies. Municipal officials now spend as much as a quarter or more of their working time away from their city offices in national and regional conferences, professional meetings, research organization and foundation-sponsored seminars, and simulated action and decision sessions.

Los Angeles and Minneapolis are examples of cities with highly decentralized governments.[7] In Los Angeles, the presence of a score of independent boards responsible for a number of functions in the city government and in Minneapolis the absence of any significant formal centralized administrative authority have severely restricted the influence of city leaders. Both of these cities' governments normally operate in near-feudalistic fashion, with control resting in decentralized baronies free from all but the most extreme of central pressures.

New York City's political system is somewhat decentralized—and this is so even though New York's mayor has more formal authority than executives in many other large cities (including Chicago). The nation's largest city has a multicentered decision-making sytsem which at a minimum inhibits the concentration of broad powers in the office of the mayor or in any other central administrative unit. Decisions in New York are in reality the responsibility of a variety of offices, agencies, and groups (in addition to the mayor and other leadership forces) such as party leaders, public officials divided by functional area, branches of government, and differences in tenure, organized bureaucracies separated by levels, function, trade, or profession, administrators of various closed personnel systems, agencies of the state and federal governments, any number of nongovernment interest groups, and the electorate.[8] The diffused nature

[7]   See Edward C. Banfield and James Q. Wilson, *City Politics* (New York: Random House, 1963), pp. 81, 110–111, and Alan A. Altshuler, *The City Planning Process, A Political Analysis* (Ithaca: Cornell University Press, 1965), pp. 190–192.
[8]   Wallace S. Sayre and Herbert Kaufman, *Governing New York City* (New York: Russell Sage Foundation, 1960), chap. III.

of New York's political system constitutes impressive evidence on which to challenge the elitist and iron law of oligarchy theories which hold that the larger the organization the more centralized the rule.[9]

New Haven and Chicago are illustrative of the moderate centralization of influence pattern. Although New Haven's political system is best characterized as "competitive" and not "monolithic," that city's political order under Mayor Lee was transformed from a "pattern of petty sovereignties" into an "executive-centered coalition."[10] And it was this power source that gave the mayor much influence over key public policies in urban redevelopment, public education, and political nominations.

It may surprise some to learn that Chicago has a weak-mayor plan of government.[11] Banfield points out, in fact, that the Chicago area "from a purely formal standpoint, can hardly be said to have a government at all."[12] Nevertheless, the extragovernmental institution known variously as the Democratic party, the party organization, or the machine has been strategically used by Chicago's municipal leaders to counteract the high degree of formal decentralization. The consequence has been an unusual if not unique centralization of power in the hands of the mayor. A recent behavioral study of Chicago's municipal government found that the widespread assumptions about the location of influence in a central position were justified; and that this particular pattern of influence had important policy effects in the area of poverty.[13]

POPULATION CHARACTERISTICS
AND CITY GOVERNMENT

Among the more important forces shaping city government are the *size* and the *social* and *economic* composition of the community's population. Although other factors are undoubtedly significant inputs into the city's processes, size and social and economic considerations explain much in city government.

City governments perform both "political" and "service" functions[14]— that is, cities manage conflict and serve as arbiters of community differ-

[9] Robert V. Presthus, *The Organizational Society* (New York: Random House, 1962), chap. 2.
[10] Robert A. Dahl, *Who Governs?* (New Haven: Yale University Press, 1961), pp. 200–201.
[11] Martin Meyerson and Edward C. Banfield, *Politics, Planning and the Public Interest* (New York: Free Press, 1955), p. 287.
[12] Edward C. Banfield, *Political Influence* (New York: Free Press, 1961), p. 235
[13] J. David Greenstone and Paul E. Peterson, "Reformers, Machines and the War on Poverty," in James Q. Wilson (ed.), *City Politics and Public Policy* (New York: Wiley, 1968), pp. 280–282.
[14] Banfield and Wilson, *City Politics, op. cit.*, chap. 2.

ences,[15] while also providing a typical range of local government services (water, sewer, and the like) for their residents. Service functions are performed by city governments of all sizes, although the kind of service may vary by size of the city's population. However, political and arbiter activity is more likely to be characteristic of the larger cities. This is not to suggest that the political function is limited to the largest cities (it may be found to some extent in certain smaller cities as well), but it is clearly more pronounced in such communities. Large city political systems provide a means by which varied factions may peacefully compete, and often the city government will accommodate different interests and serve as a mechanism promoting compromise between a number of forces, "allowing" each important group or interest some control over particular public policies and some degree of representation in the government itself. These are also the cities that have traditionally been most likely to meet the employment demands and satisfy the business aspirations (licenses, contracts) of the more disadvantaged segments of the community, a function carried out, of course, for the price of the votes of the disadvantaged.

Size is further related to form of government and the nature of electoral systems used in cities. As pointed out in Chapter 8, the largest of the nation's cities (including all over 1,000,000) are governed under the mayor-council plan, while council-manager government is most popular in middle-sized communities. In addition, ward or district elections as a means of selecting members of the municipal governing body and partisan (Republican-Democrat) electoral systems are more frequently larger rather than smaller city phenomena. There appear to be logical reasons for these patterns. The mayor-council system is probably more consistent with the immediate interests of the ethnically and racially diverse populations of the major cities, for mayors are more "political" than city managers and therefore seek out the support of and in turn assist minority and nationality groups. The ward-based electoral system similarly encourages the separate representation in city government of different community subcultures, as the various groups tend to segregate themselves (or at least to be segregated) by neighborhood; and neighborhoods are well-represented under the ward plan. The use of the partisan ballot means essentially rule by the local Democratic organization in large cities (nonpartisanship may mean *de facto* Republican or at least conservative control); this provides a necessary base for the liberal national Democratic party whose dominance of or substantial influence in the national government is usually a prerequisite to the funneling of federal money and resources to big cities.

[15] Oliver P. Williams, "A Typology for Comparative Local Government," *Midwest Journal of Political Science*, 5 (May, 1961), 150–164.

The Municipal Manpower Commission reported that cities with over 250,000 people will more often have civil service systems—and systems covering more administrators—than cities below that population figure; and furthermore administrators in the larger cities are likely to be promoted from within than are their counterparts in smaller communities.[16] Larger cities also perform more services, regulate more, and have more activities within city government. For example, the incidence of urban renewal programs is greater in larger than smaller cities: well over 80 percent of the cities in the above 250,000 class have at least one urban redevelopment project compared, for instance, to less than 50 percent of the cities in the 50,000 to 100,000 category.[17] Additionally, the very smallest of metropolitan area cities (under 5,000) are less likely than cities in higher population groups to have a planning board and the related land-use and building regulations of zoning, subdivision regulations, building codes, and housing codes; in these functional fields metropolitan area municipalities above 50,000 are significantly distinguished from those below 50,000 only in the use of housing codes, as 85 percent of the former cities and only 50 percent of the cities in the latter category have housing codes.[18]

Commonly, community political conflict can be analyzed in terms of underlying economic and social class differences—that is, government and politics are among other things a means by which different economic groups advance and protect their economic interests. In fact, city government and municipal public policy are, to important community forces, vehicles for the institutionalization and promotion of certain economic interests; and although government and policy are not usually viewed this way consciously by the groups and individuals involved, both municipalities and their public policy are used in this way.[19] One technique of gaining insight into the meaning of the impact of economic forces on city government is to compare cities with one another. Through this method, one study detected correlations between social and economic characteristics of communities—specifically, social class, ethnicity, and home ownership—and particular kinds of public policy.[20] The results of this study will be presented.

Social class appears to be negatively related to city expenditure and

[16] *Governmental Manpower for Tomorrow's Cities, op. cit.,* pp. 152–154.
[17] Raymond E. Wolfinger and John Osgood Field, "Political Ethos and the Structure of City Government," *American Political Science Review,* 60 (1966), 321–323. This, incidentally, was one of Wolfinger and Field's less controversial findings.
[18] Allen D. Manvel, *Local Land and Building Regulation* (Washington, D.C.: National Commission on Urban Problems, 1968), p. 24 (Table 2).
[19] See Chapter 8 for a discussion and illustrations of this principle.
[20] Robert L. Lineberry and Edmund P. Fowler, "Reformism and Public Policies in American Cities," in James Q. Wilson (ed.), *City Politics and Public Policy* (New York: Wiley, 1968), pp. 97–123.

tax policy—that is, the higher the class structure or "the more middle class the city," the lower the taxes and spending (relative to the personal income of the city). And this correlation holds no matter how social class is measured—by income, education, or occupation. Second, the existence of significant ethnic and religious minorities in a city is likely to exert an upward pressure on taxes and spending. The two public policy variables correlate positively with the degree of ethnicity (nationality groups) and religious heterogeneity; and this is true generally, regardless of the community's form of government or the nature of its electoral system. The strongest predictor of tax and spending policy, however, seems to be the proportion of owner-occupancy dwelling units in cities (incidentally, this measure is not the same as social class, as the two are only weakly related at best). As can be seen in Table 11.1, owner-occupancy and taxation-expenditures policy are inversely related in each of the city government form and electoral system categories, which means that the greater the incidence of owner-occupancy, the lower the taxes and expenditures (again relative to the income of the city's residents) under each government plan and electoral system type. The correlations in Table 11.1 are particularly strong for the mayor-council, partisan, and ward-based systems (all nonreform characteristics) and commission governments.

INTERESTS AND CONFLICT
IN CITY POLITICS

Not all political life in the city is based on conflict, but much of it is. We shall examine in this section the various interests in city politics, the forces that make city political systems what they are. We are not limiting our attention to organizations traditionally considered interest groups, although interest groups are among the more influential elements in city political systems. We shall also review areas of conflict in municipal politics and discuss group strategies and coalitions.

The following interests are well represented and well organized in many American municipalities: business; civic groups; labor, including municipal employees; neighborhoods; the press; social welfare, housing, and health groups; minorities; political parties; and professional organizations.

BUSINESS   The private sector of the American economy is a powerful force in all political systems in this country, and the city is no exception. At the community level private businesses may influence the actions of government in any one of three ways: first, through the use of the resources or prestige of a particular business firm or corporation; second, through a general association of businesses, such as a chamber of com-

TABLE 11.1
Correlations Between Owner-Occupancy Housing
and Taxes/Expenditures in Municipal Government

CORRELATIONS OF OWNER-OCCUPANCY WITH:	GOVERNMENT FORM			ELECTORAL SYSTEM			
				ELECTION TYPE		CONSTITUENCY TYPE	
	MAYOR	MANAGER	COMMISSION	PARTISAN	NONPARTISAN	WARD	AT-LARGE
Taxes	−.57	−.31	−.73	−.64	−.45	−.56	−.48
Expenditures	−.51	−.23	−.62	−.62	−.40	−.50	−.40

SOURCE: Robert L. Lineberry and Edmund P. Fowler, "Reformism and Public Policies in American Cities," in James Q. Wilson (ed.), *City Politics and Public Policy* (New York: Wiley, 1968), p. 116.

merce; or third, through a more specialized association of business interests, such as a retailers or realtors group. Of course, individual businessmen may be members of boards or commissions in city government or may belong to any number of community organizations which take stands on city matters, and in these ways also affect municipal policy-making processes.

The post–World War II economic decline in the central city caused big downtown business interests in a number of municipalities considerable alarm. Their reaction to the decay of the center core and the outward movement of population (and therefore economic resources) was to establish special organizations whose primary mission was to rally support for the revitalization and upgrading of city downtown areas. These organizations have operated largely outside the local chamber of commerce and their backers were not unimportant interests taken into account in the passage of the national urban renewal program, initially enacted in 1949 and expanded in 1954. Examples include the Greater Philadelphia Movement, composed of the big business elite of the Philadelphia area, and the Allegheny Conference in Pittsburgh.

Several observations can be made about the role of business in city political life:

1. National corporations are not usually significantly involved in city politics and local decision-making.

2. Business—especially big business (by community standards)—has become greatly concerned about its image. Thus, organized business is not always anxious to make its views publicly known and is often reluctant to get "involved" even when its interests are at stake, especially if such involvement "looks bad" for business. The rise of the professional manager and his replacement of the independent entrepreneur is somewhat responsible for this tendency.

3. Business is not a monolithic force in city politics. The business community is sometimes divided on municipal public policy, partly because of the large numbers and varying kinds and sizes of businesses in the locality and partly because of the wide range of (alternative) city policies and the differential effects of these policies on business.

CIVIC GROUPS   Every major city has one or more civic groups. Civic associations have broad community interests, are usually selective in membership, and are organized on a city- or metropolitan-wide basis. They will often have a small paid professional staff, and are sometimes indistinguishable from certain types of business organizations. Included in this category are municipal research bureaus. Commonly, these units are dominated by businessmen and professionals, frequently drawn from the liberal/progressive segments of the local community. *Civic* groups are not to be confused with *citizens* associations, which are treated later.

LABOR   Labor is organized primarily through the AFL-CIO, and at the community level an AFL-CIO council will serve as an organizational base for local labor units. In the larger metropolitan areas the AFL-CIO council will have a Committee on Political Education (COPE), which concerns itself with local (and other) political matters, including the election of prolabor officials in city government. The AFL-CIO has made significant inroads among municipal employees through the American Federation of State, County, and Municipal Employees and through other affiliates of the national union (firefighters, transit workers, teachers, and the like). Municipal employees are also often organized outside of the AFL-CIO, for example, by groups such as the National Education Association. Needless to say, the bargaining power of city employees has been enhanced considerably through these organizations.

Except in specialized areas (codes), the role of organized labor, exclusive of municipal unions, in the formulation of city policy has been limited. This is due to some extent to labor's concentration of its economic and political resources at decision-making points at the state and national government levels. In subnational governments, state legislation is more likely than municipal action to broadly affect the working man.

NEIGHBORHOODS   Neighborhood citizens associations exist in cities to protect particular areas within the community from unwanted city policy (that which disturbs the character of the neighborhood) and generally to advance the interests of these areas. These organizations are most likely to be found in the city's middle- and upper-middle-class residential sections, and they may be affiliated with a city-wide federation and thereby become involved in broader community-wide matters. On the average, citizens associations are somewhat conservative in policy stance, and unlike civic associations will not have a paid staff.

PRESS   In cities the press is often an influential force in certain types of municipal elections (city-wide, nonpartisan) and can affect the course of action on some major issues. Of course, simply by determining what will be covered in the newspapers, the press may mold opinion and attitudes on a variety of municipal matters. Furthermore, the press will usually be prominent among the supporters or opponents of important municipal government change. The existence of a small number (only one in some cases) of newspapers in most cities additionally contributes to the potential power of the press.

SOCIAL WELFARE, HOUSING, AND HEALTH GROUPS   Partisan liberals are now organized through certain welfare, housing, and health associations. One of the primary objectives of such groups is to promote favorable city government action in the various social fields. Therefore, these organizations—the most visible of which in some areas is the health and welfare council—will frequently push for higher municipal expenditures and more liberal benefits in the city's welfare-related programs.

MINORITIES   Many minority groups have been active in municipal politics for decades; nationalities found that special organizations were effective vehicles to promote their ends. At present, the most visible of these groups are Negro organizations—for example, local branches or chapters of the National Association for the Advancement of Colored People (NAACP), the Congress on Racial Equality (CORE), and the Student Nonviolent Coordinating Committee (SNCC). Currently growing in importance in some communities are organizations of Latin-Americans (in El Paso and San Antonio, for examples).

POLITICAL PARTIES   Political parties are perhaps best described as coalitions of interests, although they are interests in and of themselves as well. The Democratic party is the dominant party organization in most of the largest cities. Republicans control numerous smaller cities; their major city stronghold was Philadelphia, where the ruling Republican machine was routed in the early 1950s by an alliance of reformers and the Democratic organization. Political parties are organized on a jurisdiction-wide (usually county) basis and are divided into wards or districts and (at the lowest level) precincts within the city. The city may have its own *de facto* or official "independent" party (that is, independent of the county party). It should be noted that neither the Democratic nor Republican party is organized metropolitan-wide, except to the extent that the county party or congressional district party organization happens to serve in this capacity. Some cities have nonpartisan organizations which advance candidates and policies in city government—examples are the Charter Party in Cincinnati and the Citizens for a Better City in Falls Church, Virginia.

PROFESSIONAL ORGANIZATIONS   The final group includes organizations of professionals such as doctors, dentists, architects, and planners—for example, local affiliates of the American Medical Association (AMA), the American Dental Association (ADA), the American Institute of Architects (AIA), and the American Institute of Planners (AIP). Although such groups do not exist chiefly to influence the actions of local government, they do so both directly through making their positions on specific policies known and indirectly by spreading particular professional values throughout the city bureaucracy and elsewhere.

We have omitted some participants in municipal policy-making processes (church and taxpayers groups, for example); in addition, we have not covered, broadly speaking, school policy or educational interests. But, in general, the forces described are the most important local influences on city government (we have not included national, state, or regional officials, agencies, or organizations in this analysis; they also may affect the behavior of city political systems as discussed earlier in the chapter). Of course, municipal government administrators and policy-makers who respond to the pressures of these forces play a crucial and perhaps independent role as well.

At present there is substantial disagreement among the many community groups over municipal policy. Current city government concerns include poverty, crime, treatment of minorities, schools, taxes, land-use, and transportation. In the larger cities, especially, most if not all of these issues are related to race. This leads us to suggest that at the moment the most critical political issue in American cities is race, a matter brought forcefully to our attention through the national war on poverty, specifically the community action program. Racial and other city issues are discussed at length elsewhere in the book and will not be covered here.

A typical pattern of political mixing in cities has been the development of coalitions of the "disadvantaged" to oust the present power structure (disadvantaged should not be seen only in economic terms). Nationality and ethnic groups have often joined forces in the past to do battle with the Protestant middle class and business community. In the larger cities the former groups normally succeeded in removing the latter from most public offices, later experienced considerable internal factionalism, and most recently appear to be reuniting in common cause against the Negro. However, following the theory of the "coalition of the disadvantaged," the Negro is gaining support in a number of instances from the downtown businessmen and the white upper-middle class. In some instances the new coalition is being formed within the structure of the minority Republican party—for example, in New York City, Paterson (New Jersey), and Springfield (Massachusetts), where Republican mayors were, for the first time in recent years, brought to power in the mid-1960s through an alliance of low-income blacks and prominent downtown businessmen. In other areas, such as Cleveland, a similar coalition has been responsible for the election of a new-style Democratic mayor (Carl Stokes, a Negro).

COMMUNITY POWER STRUCTURE
ANALYSIS

Earlier in the chapter, we talked about the location of power and influence in city political systems. A somewhat more general study of community power structures has been made by a number of political scientists and sociologists. Nevertheless, community power structure analysis is restricted to the study of cities (although not necessarily defined in the legal sense of the term) and therefore should be reviewed along with city politics.

The consequences of community power analysis can be seen in three areas: first, power structure studies have added substantially to the information available about local politics—that is, about the prizes and stakes in community politics, the alternative strategies and tactics used by community influentials, and the degree of power wielded by various types of community interests in the allocation of local resources. More broadly, these studies have advanced our knowledge of the local decision-making processes. Second, community power analysis has contributed to the continuing stream of power structure literature and particularly to elitist thought. Now grouped with the sophisticated and universalistic theory of the behavior of elites in the political and social systems of the past (Mosca, Pareto, Michels, Sorel, Machiavelli) are the apparently more mundane studies of the American communities of Middletown, Atlanta, and Kenosha.[21] Third, students of community power have assisted in clarifying our understanding of data collection and research methods.

Community power structure studies generally can be classed in one of two schools: elitist and pluralist.[22] Examples for each category are given in Table 11.2. The two schools are distinguished from one another in terms of both study findings and research method. Furthermore, elitist studies have been done by sociologists and pluralist studies by political scientists, additionally separating the two schools.

The sociologists' examinations of community influence have come to the conclusion that by and large there exists in American localities a social and economic elite, that political and civic leaders are subordinate to this elite, that power is exercised by this elite over all major issue areas (inside or outside government), and that the community can be defined and described by its social class structure, with the upper class ruling and the lower class being ruled. By way of contrast, political scientists have detected several power centers in the communities they studied and have found that political leaders are key community decision-makers, that no single elite or social class dominates all major issue areas, that resources are not easily transferred from one issue area to another, and that localities' power structures are characterized by the interplay among a multiplicity of local groups and actors, tied together only in part and then through a political institution.

[21] See, for instance, W. G. Runciman, *Social Science and Political Theory* (Cambridge: Cambridge University Press, 1965).
[22] This discussion is limited to the major community power structure studies.

TABLE 11.2
Community Power Structure Studies

ELITIST	PLURALIST
Muncie, Indiana Robert S. Lynd and Helen M. Lynd, *Middletown* (New York: Harcourt Brace Jovanovich, 1929).	New Haven, Connecticut Robert A. Dahl, *Who Governs? Democracy and Power in an American City* (New Haven: Yale University Press, 1961).
Muncie, Indiana Robert S. Lynd and Helen M. Lynd, *Middletown in Transition* (New York: Harcourt Brace Jovanovich, 1937).	Syracuse, New York Roscoe C. Martin *et al.*, *Decisions in Syracuse* (Bloomington: Indiana University Press, 1961).
Newburyport, Massachusetts W. Lloyd Warner (ed.), *Yankee City* (New Haven: Yale University Press, 1963).	Chicago, Illinois Edward C. Banfield, *Political Influence* (New York: Free Press, 1961).
Morris, Illinois W. Lloyd Warner, *et al.*, *Democracy in Jonesville: A Study in Quality and Inequality* (New York: Harper & Row, 1949).	New York, New York Wallace S. Sayre and Herbert Kaufman, *Governing New York City* (New York: Russell Sage, 1960).
Philadelphia, Pennsylvania E. Digby Baltzell, *Philadelphia Gentlemen* (New York: Free Press, 1958).	
Atlanta, Georgia Floyd Hunter, *Community Power Structure* (Chapel Hill: University of North Carolina Press, 1953).	

Community power analysts, however, have agreed on a number of points:

1. Formal government institutions are only part of any community power structure. An overconcentration on government *per se* may prove misleading in pinpointing power.

2. Small groups govern American local communities. Sociologists and political scientists have found that a small number of community activists control policy; the two scholarly disciplines differ over the number of groups involved in community decision-making and what the groups represent.

3. There are close links between the economic and political sectors in the community.

4. Community values (not necessarily directly or formally expressed) constrain local decision-makers.

5. Business is an important element in all city power structures.

6. Organized labor has limited influence in communities.

7. Few groups are involved in community decision-making processes.

8. The public has little direct influence over community decision-makers.

9. The public has limited interest in and knowledge of community political and economic activity.

In addition, community power studies show generally that the degree of pluralism in the locality is related to the size of the community and its socioeconomic level. Specifically, larger communities have been found to have less monolithic (or more pluralistic) power structures—that is, power structures in which power is not concentrated in a single office or elite.[23] To an extent, the size factor differentiates the elitist from the pluralist cities; all of the communities studied by political scientists are large while the cities examined by the sociologists tend to be smaller (and further were studied earlier, in the 1930s and 1940s when the cities were even less highly populated). It also appears that wealthier cities are more likely to have pluralist power structures than poor ones, a finding consistent with the results of cross-cultural analyses of the relationship between economic forces and the nature of political arrangements in nation-states.[24]

[23] Cf. Robert E. Agger, Daniel Goldrich, and Bert E. Swanson, *The Rulers and the Ruled* (New York: Wiley, 1964), pp. 682–683.
[24] See James S. Coleman, "The Political Systems of Developing Areas," in Gabriel Almond and James S. Coleman (eds.), *The Politics of Developing Areas* (Princeton: Princeton University Press, 1960), pp. 538–544, and Seymour Martin Lipset, *Political Man* (Garden City: Doubleday, 1960), pp. 31–40.

Robert Presthus, in probably the most systematic power structure study done to date, has advanced a single framework which has served to draw together the political science and sociological studies of community power.[25] Presthus holds that the gap between the two schools is not as wide as it may appear to be, that political scientists and sociologists may have been viewing the same phenomenon but labeling it differently, and that the methods used by each school are valuable but at the same time deficient in certain respects. The study of community power will not end with *Men at the Top;* in the future, analytical techniques will no doubt be refined and new conclusions reached in this important field.

POLITICAL LEADERSHIP IN LARGE CITIES

We have pointed out in this and other chapters the many constraints that shape the nature of and the possibilities for the development of central governmental leadership in cities. One factor that contributes to the emergence of political leadership in larger cities has not been discussed; it can be seen from a review of the community power-structure studies. As indicated, one conclusion that linked the political scientists and sociologists was that small groups dominated city political life—and this can be interpreted to mean that leadership is found in all cities of all sizes. However, the nature of this leadership varies along city-size lines, with economic groups or leaders playing the dominant role in smaller (the sociologists') cities and with political groups exercising considerable power if not constituting the most influential force in larger (or the political scientists') cities. Another way of putting it is that in smaller cities (Muncie, Newburyport, Morris) or larger cities in earlier stages of development (Atlanta, Philadelphia), power is likely to be concentrated in an economic elite, while power in larger cities is at least in part located in the hands of political and governmental leaders. What this means is that larger and therefore more fully developed and more complicated social systems are associated with political systems that have important power assignments and significant community responsibilities. In smaller and less complex social systems on the other hand, there is a tendency for community influence to be the property of the economic sector. In short, government and politics count for more in larger cities than in their smaller counterparts. Thus, the probability of finding (and developing) powerful political leaders is (sociologically speaking) greater in larger

[25] Robert Presthus, *Men at the Top, A Study in Community Power* (New York: Oxford University Press, 1964).

cities. We must conclude then that size is a significant factor in determining the possibilities for the creation of strong political leadership. By the same token, it is reasonably clear that leadership is found in all cities, although it may simply not be as visible—that is, *political*—in smaller cities.

12. SUBURBAN POLITICS

"Suburbia" is not a neutral word: Americans have distinct impressions of their suburbs, or the outlying metropolitan fringes. For some, the suburbs mean the areas inhabited by the rich and the well educated; for others, suburbia is a haven for whites or for a particular kind of whites; and for still others, the word "suburb" has certain normative connotations—it is where the "better" people live, or the morally depraved, and so on. In fact, there are so many different conceptions of the suburbs that it is not a simple task to present the typical understanding of this, the newest sociological form in urban America.

Perhaps to begin with it would be helpful to advance two definitions (or theories) we can use to examine suburbs: the "upward class mobility" theory and the "suburban circle" theory. The first of these concepts holds that suburbia is that portion of the metropolitan area characterized by aspiring middle-class and stable upper-middle-class families. The suburbs are then the "nice" part of the urban area, are defined primarily in the social class sense, and are invariably located outside the central city. Suburbs are seen in terms of open space, big lots supporting large single-family homes, tree-lined streets, and personal and efficient governments operating in small geographical settings. The central city, on the other hand, is the home of the lower-class Negroes and the lower-middle-class ethnic groups, negatively contrasted with suburbia by its industrial activity, traffic congestion, slums, small lots, tenement houses, and large, inefficient, and corrupt government.

The second concept—the suburban circle theory—is a more technical one. It states simply that suburbia is that part of the metropolitan area that is not within the central city—in other words, the noncentral-city portion of the metropolitan area. This means that the suburbs are the geographical and population segments of the metropolitan area that encircle in part or entirely the central city and are economically and in other ways integrated with the city.

Depending to a large extent on whether one adheres to the upward class mobility or suburban circle theory, particular facts and images come to mind when the suburban issue is raised. This chapter will start with a review of general suburban population trends, discuss suburbs from the somewhat unusual vantage point of the suburban circle theory, and then return to the more commonly recognized suburban polity, with its middle-class features and philosophical underpinnings.

THE SUBURBAN POPULATION MOVEMENT

Americans are a mobile people. And one of the most significant of the nation's population movement trends in recent years has been reflected in soaring suburban population figures. Between 1950 and 1960, 85 percent of the population increase took place within metropolitan areas; and at least three fourths of the metropolitan increase occurred within suburban rings. In the final analysis the proportion of the total metropolitan population rise found outside cities and in the suburbs could have been as high as 97 percent during the 1950–1960 decade—that is, if population boosts resulting from annexation are excluded from central-city population figures.[1]

[1] Leo F. Schnore, "Municipal Annexations and the Growth of Metropolitan Suburbs, 1959–1960," *American Journal of Sociology*, 57 (1962), 406, 409. This section of the chapter covers population trends from 1950 on. It should be noted, however, that

In 1960, a slim majority of metropolitan Americans still lived in central cities, and, as pointed out in Chapter 9, this represented a substantial decline from the 60 percent recorded in 1950. Put another way, the suburbs had slightly over 40 percent of the metropolitan population in 1950 and about half of the metropolitan residents by 1960. In two regions, by 1960, the majority in metropolitan areas already lived in the suburbs—55 percent in the Northeast and 51 percent in the West.[2] Between 1960 and 1968, metropolitan areas again accounted for most of the nation's population increase, with the suburbs capturing nearly all of the new metropolitan residents (Table 12.1). Furthermore, for the first

TABLE 12.1
Metropolitan Area Population Changes, 1960–1968

	1960 (MILLIONS)	1968 (MILLIONS)	CHANGE 1960–1968 (PERCENT)
United States	178.7	198.1	11
Metropolitan areas	112.4	128.0	14
Central cities	57.8	58.2	1
Suburbs	54.6	69.9	28
Suburban population (proportion of metropolitan population)	49 %	55 %	

SOURCE: U.S. Bureau of the Census, *Current Population Reports,* Series p-23, Special Studies, No. 27, "Trends in Social and Economic Conditions in Metropolitan Areas" (Washington, D.C.: U.S. Government Printing Office, 1969), p. 2.

time in the history of the United States, suburbanites outnumbered central city inhabitants in 1968—by a 55 to 45 percent margin.

Projections from past trends show that 90 percent of the future

recent metropolitan population trends have deep roots. Metropolitan areas have been gaining a disproportionate share of the population at least since the decade beginning in 1900, while suburban rings have grown at greater rates than central cities since the decade 1920–1930. See Leo F. Schnore, "Metropolitan Growth and Decentralization," in William M. Dobriner (ed.), *The Suburban Community* (New York: Putnam's, 1958), pp. 3–20.

[2] Suburbanites constituted 43 percent of the metropolitan area population in the other two regions—the North Central and South. Advisory Commission on Intergovernmental Relations, *Metropolitan Social and Economic Disparities: Implications for Intergovernmental Relations in the Central City and Suburbs* (Washington, D.C.: U.S. Government Printing Office, 1965), pp. 234–249. The figures in this survey are based on an analysis of 1960 Standard Metropolitan Statistical Areas.

metropolitan area population growth will be suburban in nature and that by 1985 nearly two-thirds of all the people in metropolitan areas will reside in the suburbs.[3]

THE SUBURBAN CIRCLE THEORY

Viewed in terms of the suburban circle theory, suburbs do not differ significantly in the socioeconomic sense from central cities. A 1965 study of metropolitan area cities and suburbs came to the following conclusions:[4]

1. Few generalizations dividing central cities from suburbs along socioeconomic lines were possible.

2. Only race consistently separates metropolitan central cities from their suburbs.

3. Selected nonrace socioeconomic variables distinguished central cities from suburbs in the expected manner only in the largest and the northeastern metropolitan areas.

4. In the South and West, general expectations were reversed, with the higher socioeconomic groups in the cities (not the suburbs).

The aggregate income, education, and housing differences between central cities and suburbs are slight, as can be seen in Table 12.2. For instance, the proportions of families in the lower and higher income categories are identical or about the same for central cities and suburbs; and between 55 and 60 percent of both central-city and suburban residents had less than four years of high-school education in 1960, with slightly less than 10 percent of both populations completing four years or more of college (in fact, the statistics reveal that central-city residents are more likely to be college graduates than suburbanites). Surprisingly, there is proportionately more substandard housing in the suburbs than in central cities. This suggests that there are wide socioeconomic differences found throughout the suburbs (suburbs apparently have both the best and the least desirable housing in the metropolitan area). Suburbs are, however, higher on the socioeconomic scale than cities in the largest metropolitan areas as well as in the northeastern metropolitan areas—and this generalization holds for education, income, employment, and housing. It seems that the expected socioeconomic differences are greatest in the metropolitan areas experiencing the highest degree of population

[3] Patricia Leavey Hodge and Philip M. Hauser, *The Challenge of America's Metropolitan Population Outlook—1960 to 1985* (Washington, D.C.: U.S. Government Printing Office, 1968), chap. 2.

[4] Advisory Commission on Intergovernmental Relations, *op. cit.*, pp. 11–12.

TABLE 12.2
*Selected Socioeconomic Characteristics
of Metropolitan Central Cities and Suburbs, 1960*

| | PERCENTAGE FOUND IN | |
	CENTRAL CITIES	SUBURBS
Nonwhite	15	7
Northeast	9	2
North Central	10	2
South	25	15
Income under $4,000	29	26
Income $15,000 and over	4	4
Less than 4 years H.S.	57	56
Four years or more college	9	8
Unsound housing	11	16

SOURCE: Advisory Commission on Intergovernmental Relations, *Metropolitan
Social and Economic Disparities: Implications for Intergovernmental Relations in the Central City and Suburbs* (Washington, D.C.: U.S. Government Printing Office, 1965), pp. 13–19, 166, 183.

decentralization or suburbanization. In the South and West, the suburbs
have lower status levels on the average than cities.

Race, nevertheless, does distinguish cities from suburbs—and in the
expected manner, as shown in the following figures:[5]

METROPOLITAN NONWHITE POPULATION

	1960	1950	1940
Central city	15%	12%	11%
Suburban	7%	7%	8%

The percentage of nonwhites (essentially Negroes) living in the central
city in 1960 was about twice the figure for the suburbs. And metropolitan
racial segregation has been on the upswing, as the distribution of Negroes
in the metropolitan area was considerably less even between central cities
and suburbs in 1960 than it was in 1940 and 1950.

The concentration of the Negro in the city will probably be an important population trait of metropolitan areas in the future. Patricia Hodge
and Philip Hauser project in Figure 12.1 that between 1960 and 1985,
cities will lose 2.5 million whites while simultaneously doubling their
Negro population from 10 to 20 million. At the same time, the proportion

[5] Advisory Commission on Intergovernmental Relations, *op. cit.*, p. 17.

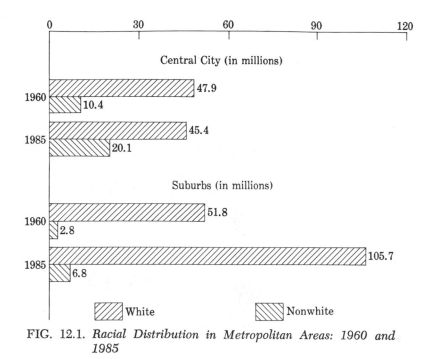

FIG. 12.1. *Racial Distribution in Metropolitan Areas: 1960 and 1985*

SOURCE: Patricia Leavy Hodge and Phillip M. Hauser, *The Challenge of America's Metropolitan Population Outlook, 1960–1985* (Washington, D.C.: National Commission on Urban Problems, 1968).

of Negroes in suburbs will likely remain relatively static. The Census Bureau reports that from 1960 to 1968, the white suburban population leaped by 16 million; during the same years the nonwhite suburban population rose by less than one million.[6]

The assumed central-city suburban split is not valid then for most metropolitan areas except in the one respect noted. In some metropolitan areas a geographical rather than a governmental boundary standard can be helpful in metropolitan sociological and political analysis. For example, the National Capital region is best divided into east and west sections. As can be seen in Figures 12.2, 12.3, and 12.4, both the central city (Washington, D.C.) and the suburbs are divided into their eastern and western segments, with the lower educational and income levels and home values located on the east side (lighter shades) of the metropolitan

6 U.S. Bureau of the Census, *Current Population Reports*, Series p-23, Special Studies, No. 27, "Trends in Social and Economic Conditions in Metropolitan Areas" (Washington, D.C.: U.S. Government Printing Office, 1969), p. 2.

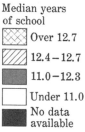

Median years
of school

Over 12.7

12.4 – 12.7

11.0 – 12.3

Under 11.0

No data
available

FIG. 12.2. *Education Level by Census Tracts, National Capital Region*

SOURCE: National Capital Regional Council, *1960 Census Facts by Tracts, Metropolitan Washington* (Washington, D.C.: Metropolitan Washington Council of Governments, 1963), pp. 24–25.

Median income
($ thousand)

Over 8.0

6.5–8.0

4.8–6.4

Under 4.8

No data
available

FIG. 12.3. *Income Level by Census Tracts, National Capital Region*

SOURCE: National Capital Regional Council, *1960 Census Facts by Tracts, Metropolitan Washington* (Washington, D.C.: Metropolitan Washington Council of Governments, 1963), pp. 28–29.

Median home values
($ thousand)

	Over 19.6
	16.1 – 19.6
	13.3 – 16.0
	Under 13.3
	No data available

FIG. 12.4. *Home Values by Census Tract, National Capital Region*

SOURCE: National Capital Regional Council, *1960 Census Facts by Tracts, Metropolitan Washington* (Washington, D.C.: Metropolitan Washington Council of Governments, 1963), pp. 88–89.

area and the highest on the west side (darker shades). Washington, D.C. proper is largely separated sociologically into two parts by Rock Creek park, and the higher socioeconomic status groups are found to the west and the lower levels to the east of Rock Creek; white-Negro living patterns also follow the creek, with whites residing to the west and Negroes to the east.

The Washington metropolitan area suburban population is also usefully classified into east and west; and in this case, the twofold categorization transcends state and local political subdivision boundaries. The major western suburban counties of Montgomery (Maryland), Arlington, and Fairfax (both Virginia) are the wealthiest units in the region, no matter what measure of wealth is used (education, income, home value), and share the higher-level socioeconomic characteristics of the portion of the District of Columbia west of Rock Creek. Meanwhile, Prince Georges County, Maryland, which constitutes essentially the eastern suburban part of the metropolitan area, generally has the lowest socioeconomic status features among the region's suburbs, possessing a social and economic character similar to that found in the eastern half of the city with the major exception of race—Prince Georges, the suburb, is nearly completely white and the eastern portion of Washington, D.C., the city, is nearly completely black.

The political implications of the use of the suburban circle concept are clear: no single-class, conservative, Republican suburban stereotype emerges.[7] By studying all suburbs and not just middle- and upper-class suburbs, we find different party allegiances and varied political outlooks in metropolitan fringes. Basically, sociologists and political scientists adhering broadly to this theory have concluded that socioeconomic factors and not suburban residents are the crucial determinants of political behavior in the suburbs, and that these forces will have a similar effect on metropolitan residents living on either side of the city line. Since the suburbs are composed of many social classes, the resulting political posture will vary largely by social class. In this light, upper-middle-class suburbs act politically like upper-middle-class neighborhoods in central cities (conservative and Republican); by the same token, lower-middle-class suburbs have political characteristics similar to those of lower-middle classes in the central city (economically liberal and Democratic). Only if race were to become a metropolitan issue would the suburbs likely coalesce (in the Republican party or a local conservative Democratic party), and this would be just a temporary development in all probability (there is already evidence that this is happening, and the coalition so-formed will last as long as race is a major issue).

---

[7] For a critical treatment of this matter, see William M. Dobriner, *Class in Suburbia* (Englewood Cliffs: Prentice-Hall, 1963).

In the Washington metropolitan area, political behavior parallels social class lines (outlined above): all of the western suburban counties are either controlled locally by the Republican party or in recent state lower house elections have registered pluralities for the GOP (state and local elections are good tests of party loyalty), while the eastern suburban area—Prince Georges County—has an entirely Democratic state delegation and county governing body.

In a study of a West Coast lower-income suburban community, Bennett Berger found that the suburban resident's way of life was a function of a number of variables, including age, income, education, occupation, and so forth, and that "this is as true for suburbs as it is for any other kind of modern community."[8] Specifically, Berger's suburbanites thought on the average that they were done rising occupationally, were overwhelmingly Democratic in party affiliation, and saw themselves and their suburban neighbors as members of the working class.[9] Domination of Delaware County, Philadelphia's lowest income Pennsylvania suburb, by the powerful McClure machine and the ruling war board also paints a picture inconsistent with what might be expected in suburbia.[10]

Frederick M. Wirt examined 150 suburbs and further discovered that the Republican vote was by no means uniformly high, that although one half of the suburbs studied were Republican, the other half were Democratic or competitive two-party jurisdictions, and that high-income and high-rent suburbs tended to be Republican and manufacturing suburbs to be Democratic.[11]

THE MIDDLE-CLASS
SUBURBAN POLITY

The remainder of the chapter is limited to a discussion of middle-class residential suburbs, or suburbs in the middle or higher socioeconomic categories.[12] What we present here does not normally or necessarily apply to lower- or lower-middle-class residential suburbs or to nonresidential suburban areas. In this light, we shall look at suburbia from the upward class mobility point of view. We begin with a review of the

[8] Bennett M. Berger, Working-Class Suburb: A Study of Auto Workers in Suburbia (Berkeley: University of California Press, 1960), p. 13.

[9] Ibid., pp. 16–81.

[10] Charles E. Gilbert, "Politics in a Suburban County," in Duane Lockard (ed.), Governing the States and Localities (London: Macmillan, 1969), pp. 76–89.

high-rent suburbs tended to be Republican and manufacturing suburbs

[11] Frederick M. Wirt, "The Political Sociology of American Suburbia: A Reinterpretation," The Journal of Politics, XXVII (August, 1965), 647–666.

[12] The best work to date on the political ethic of middle-class suburbs is Robert C. Wood, Suburbia, Its People and Their Politics (Boston: Houghton-Mifflin, 1958).

typical suburban political values and then dissect the suburban political processes.

Suburban Political Values

Various factors account for the attractiveness of the suburbs to Americans. In general, many are convinced that this part of the metropolitan area contains a social system and physical surroundings most compatible with their existing and anticipated life styles. Furthermore, an unwanted and private-regarding social and political structure in the central city has served as a distinct suburbanizing force.

Probably the most appealing aspect of the suburban political system is its small unit, grass-roots governmental character. The prospects of having a responsive local democratic government operating close to the people and within a small geographical area has undoubtedly lured many to the suburbs. And this grass-roots government image forms the foundation for the more important of the suburban political values. At the same time, this grass-roots democracy ideology is by no means a purely political matter; it commonly has economic, religious, and racial overtones. In the last analysis, the democratic philosophy of the suburbs appears to be as much an instrument for the achievement of social and economic homogeneity as a means of facilitating citizen participation in local public decision-making. Much of suburbia in reality is found in small jurisdictions with small populations; the majority of suburban municipalities have no more than four square miles of land within their borders and serve populations of less than 5,000 (see Chapter 9). Thus, the ideology is to an extent borne out in practice. Further, suburbanites have vigorously protected their governments from external intrusions and consolidation by successfully opposing metropolitan reorganization efforts, thereby blocking any major move toward economic or social integration throughout the metropolitan area.[13]

The suburban grass-roots-based political theory is not new to American political thought or to the American political tradition. The small republic as an essential feature of an ideal political order is deeply embedded in this nation's political mores and intellectual history. The architects of the first independent governments in this country—that is, the early states—strongly believed that true democracy could take place

---

[13] A review of the votes on 18 metropolitan reorganization proposals in various parts of the United States shows that suburban residents were almost always less likely to favor or more likely to oppose the reorganization than city voters. In six of the 18 instances, the measure won in the city and lost in the suburbs. Advisory Commission on Intergovernmental Relations, *Factors Affecting Voter Reactions to Governmental Reorganization in Metropolitan Areas* (Washington, D.C.: U.S. Government Printing Office, 1962), pp. 26, 35–68.

only in smaller units of government.[14] Thomas Jefferson also contributed to this tradition by proposing the location of key governmental powers in tiny ward democracies, each covering a small land area within the confines of a single county. The municipal home-rule movement of more recent vintage is reflective of similar philosophical convictions.

Another part of the suburban political value structure is the suburbanites' distaste for political conflict and factionalism. Suburban inhabitants want their political order to be firmly grounded in honesty, nonpartisanship (in spirit if not in fact), rationality, and expertise; and they contend that governmental and administrative issues should be decided on their merits and not as a result of the interplay, bargaining, and trading among various groups and interests. Competing political organizations and parties have no legitimate place in suburban governments, and the suburban political system is theoretically structured so as to operate in the most efficient and economical of fashions, thus eliminating the need for and rationale behind the traditional political organization. A professional manager with competent and properly trained civil servants selected impartially and through objective examination should guarantee boss-free and nonpolitical government. As might be expected, this ideal is in no sense universally realized in practice. As a matter of fact, conflict and amateur government are typically important elements in suburban political systems.

Finally, suburban values seem to breed political conservatism in general and Republicanism in particular. Throughout the country the middle- and upper-middle-class suburban jurisdictions are more likely to vote Republican at all levels of government than are the neighboring central cities, not uncommonly found in the Democratic column. In northeastern, mid-Atlantic, and north central metropolitan areas especially, middle-class suburbs are normally distinguished from cities in political affiliation and voting patterns, with the suburbs supporting the Republican and the cities the Democratic party.

Issues and Actors in Suburban Politics

The major issues in the suburbs are education and land-use. And neither of these issues can be separated from taxes, another issue of great interest in the suburban jurisdiction. Taxes, however, are really integrally part of the education picture and to a lesser degree land-use; the bulk of local suburban taxes go for schools and the way land is used more than any other factor affects the amount of local revenue produced and required in the average suburb. The school issue is an important considera-

[14] Merrill Jensen, *The Articles of Confederation* (Madison: University of Wisconsin Press, 1940), p. 244.

tion in many suburbs because of the emphasis middle-class families place on education broadly and on preparing youth for first-rate colleges more specifically.[15] And land-use is a crucial matter to suburbanites because policy in this area determines the nature of physical (and in reality social) development that will be found in the community. Both major issues are reflected in functional activities of suburban government that are rooted in the suburban political fabric and in which the decisions made are almost purely localized, not subject to any basic extent to the criteria or review of metropolitcan, state, or national officials and agencies. The key powers in each of these two functional areas strongly influence the character of the entire metropolitan area, and these powers can be expected to remain in the hands of suburban governments for the indefinite future. This is true even in the light of mounting demands of national experts and authorities that suburban governments be stripped of at least some of their control in education and, especially, land-use. Efforts to transfer any important powers in either function to a metropolitan government will likely meet with stiff opposition from suburbanites.

Other governmental concerns of middle-class suburban populations are commonly delegated to administrative bureaucracies and cast in a politically invisible mold.[16] Functions such as police, building codes, and water supply are handled by suburban government agencies according to the rules of expertise and efficiency and are theoretically free of any citizen interest group pressure. Although the average middle-class suburban government department has probably been thoroughly "urbanized" and "professionalized," some functions are still affected if not controlled by the rules of an earlier political order. For example, fire units (often volunteer) and some law enforcement activities continue to be carried out in the more traditional "political" manner and furthermore have a conventional "social" meaning (that is, the functions serve as social headquarters for certain groups) in some suburban areas.

We must hasten to point out that schools and land-use are not the only political considerations in the suburbs. There is considerable politics in virtually all suburban government functions and decisions, which is to say that there are important power and public policy implications of decisions of any magnitude in any number of suburban functional areas. However, most suburban functions and public actions are simply not prominently considered or significantly contested in the public arena. Yet, in all major suburban functional areas some community interests stand to gain and others to lose from one or another decision or policy; therefore, these interests will attempt to influence actions that will affect them. This

[15] See James Bryant Conant, *Slums and Suburbs* (New York: McGraw-Hill, 1961), chap. IV.
[16] Wood, *op. cit.*, pp. 162–163.

is no less true of suburban areas than of central cities. In the broadest of senses then, the full range of top-level functions and decisions in suburbs must be viewed as political in nature.

Suburban Schools

Suburban public education is nearly always the responsibility of an independent governmental unit or school district and not of a general-purpose government.[17] In most suburban areas the school system accounts for a large portion of local public spending, commonly comprising two thirds and frequently as much as three quarters of the local budget. By contrast, in a typical larger central city, educational outlays constitute only about one third of the local expenditures, and the school function is probably more likely to be fiscally integrated with the general-purpose government than is true for suburbs.[18] To the extent that the independence of the suburban school has contributed to low visibility in the educational arena, the autonomous mode of operation has apparently meant high economic pay-offs for educational bureaucracies in the suburbs.[19]

Although consensus and shared values characterize the suburban educational ideology, this goal is not always achieved in the schools issue area. This holds even though professional educators and interested lay citizens have forcefully attempted to isolate the educational decision-making process from influences and opinions that might tend to immerse this vital function in the baths of controversy and to subject it to critical public scrutiny and extrabureaucratic examination.

The primary participants in the suburban educational decision-making process include the following groups:

1. The educational hierarchy, including the school board and school system administrators.

2. School teachers.

3. Parent-Teachers Association (PTA).

4. Nonpartisan organizations with a special interest in education.

---

[17] Roscoe C. Martin, *Government and the Suburban School* (Syracuse: Syracuse University Press, 1962), p. 39.
[18] See National League of Cities, *Education and Manpower Strategies and Programs for Deprived Urban Neighborhoods* (Washington, D.C.: U.S. Office of Education, May, 1968), p. 7.
[19] One study of 1,054 school districts found that low voter turnout on school bond issues correlated positively with favorable voter action on these issues. Richard F. Carter and John Sutthaff, *Voters and Their Schools* (Stanford: Stanford University Press, 1960).

5. Public officials outside of education.

6. Political parties.

Undoubtedly the most influential of these forces are the first three and particularly the first two—that is, the elected and appointed officials who actually run and teach in the suburban schools. The vast majority of suburban school boards are elected by the public, and in this respect the interests of the public at large serves as an input in the educational hierarchy. The average suburban school board appears to be generally representative of the middle-class suburban population; it is dominated by the professional, managerial-business owner, and white-collar occupational classes.[20] In all probability, high-level school administrators have as much or more control over educational policy in the suburbs as the elective school board, although the two groups are likely to be in broad agreement, making their relative influence hard to detect and analyze.

Teachers are likely the most rapidly growing power force in suburban schools. Suburban teachers are typically organized through a local affiliate of the National Education Association; the major competing organization—the AFL-CIO American Federation of Teachers—has made few inroads in suburban educational establishments. The local teachers education association may formally or informally represent the teachers in intraschool system bargaining, and in any event has proved to be an effective organizational vehicle by which teachers have been mobilized for political action and public opinion shaped along desired lines. Organized teachers are increasingly becoming more involved in suburban educational politics, not infrequently working for the more liberal school board candidates and urging approval of school tax and salary hikes and bond issues. Teachers can also normally be expected to campaign for curriculum experimentation and the principles of progressive education. In their new political role, suburban teachers are now often indistinguishable from their big-city counterparts and have clearly been moving away from the "small-town" apolitical teacher model.[21] While political activism by teachers may be inconsistent with the suburban ideology, the resulting expanded power exercised by teachers over education policy is quite compatible with the suburban middle-class "rule by experts" government philosophy.

The Parent-Teachers Association (PTA) is perhaps more of an informal force in the suburban school than some of the other educational groups and interests, and in reality may be more influenced by the professional schoolmen than vice versa. It is not too much of an oversimplifi-

[20] Martin, *op. cit.*, p. 43.
[21] See Harmon Zeigler, *The Political Life of American Teachers* (Englewood Cliffs: Prentice-Hall, 1967), p. 80.

cation to observe in fact that the PTA is essentially an instrument of the school bureaucracy in many suburbs, serving as a strategic means by which administrator and teacher political interests may be conveniently advanced and legitimated. The PTA is organizationally based around a particular school, although local PTAs will likely be linked together in a community-wide group as well.

Nonpartisan organizations are those formed on an *ad hoc* or permanent basis to bring pressure to bear on school decision-makers, and may include taxpayers associations, neighborhood citizens associations, and specially constituted education civic groups.[22] The organizations vary widely in attitude, ranging from the highly conservative groups stressing traditional education and the three R's, opposing progressive education, and fighting school tax increases to those on the opposite or liberal side of the political spectrum (favoring higher teachers' salaries, expanded facilities, new approaches, and the like); or the organization may have no particular philosophy or ideology in education and instead have immediate, limited, or specific objectives. Sometimes, nonpartisan groups with similar and general titles but different positions are formed for political action in education, substantially adding to the confusion and complexity of suburban education politics.

Where a general-purpose government must vote school taxes or budgets or when the school system seeks state legislation or funds, other public officials such as governing board members or state legislators may become important actors in the suburban educational process. Normally, however, the greatest and most meaningful pressure on these officials will come from school partisans, and this serves to curtail if not eliminate the independent influence of noneducation officials in suburban schools. Finally, political parties, including the solely local variety, may also take positions on suburban educational policy and in school board elections. Republican and Democratic party stands, nevertheless, will often be somewhat publicly camouflaged, largely because of suburban resident resistance to partisan interference in the school system.

Land-Use Politics

Suburban land-use policy-making authority will rest with the governing body of the general-purpose governmental unit and the suburban government planning commission and department. The most important land-use policy in the suburbs is made through zoning, although land-use

---

[22] Norman D. Kerr (pseudonym), "The School Board as an Agency of Legitimation," in Alan Rosenthal (ed.), *Governing Education: A Reader on Politics, Power, and Public School Policy* (New York: Doubleday, 1969), pp. 144–145. The Kerr article presents the results of an analysis of politics in two suburban school districts outside a large northern city.

activities cover more broadly comprehensive physical planning, subdivision regulation, and frequently public facilities programming as well. All of the local land-use powers are explained in detail in Chapter 17.

Suburban zoning controls population density and lot size and therefore forms the base of suburban land-use politics. Other land-use authority in the suburbs essentially works to reinforce, builds upon, or has to be consistent with the fundamental development patterns set by zoning, and is, under these circumstances, less significant than zoning. Comprehensive planning is purely advisory and can be implemented by government only through zoning; subdivision regulation must build upon existing zoning, and public facilities programming has to be generally consistent with zoning policy.

Making land-use an issue in suburbia are the large amounts of undeveloped land in the outlying portions of the metropolitan area and the differing views within the community over the proper use of land.[23]

The constellation of interests actively concerned with land-use politics includes neighborhood citizens associations, real estate interests, general business organizations, and public officials. Neighborhood citizens associations exist primarily to protect limited geographical areas from undesirable land uses and policies, and their public policy stance is therefore largely negative. Citizens associations will attempt to incorporate low-density and residential neighborhood preservation principles in suburban general plans and zoning ordinances; once such principles are adopted by the suburban governing body, the citizens groups will guard against land-use changes—normally meaning that they will oppose rezonings (or a change in the zoning map for their neighborhood). Some communities have citizens planning organizations which promote what they consider to be sound planning and development policy for the jurisdiction as a whole rather than a single neighborhood (neighborhood associations may also belong to a community-wide federation). Citizens associations of whatever kind represent the "newcomer" segments of suburbia and as a result tend to be dominated by middle- and upper-range salaried administrators and executives, professionals, and well-educated middle-class housewives—and not local business and entrepreneurial interests.[24] Often, citizens associations pressure public officials into enacting a zoning policy requiring large-lot (one-acre minimum or higher) development for much or all of the suburban land area, thus effectively limiting residential development to the upper-middle class.[25]

---

[23] In 1960, fewer than 26,000 of the 310,000 square miles of land area in SMSAs were urbanized.
[24] See Scott Greer, *Governing the Metropolis* (New York: Wiley, 1962), p. 98.
[25] See James G. Coke and Charles S. Liebman, "Political Values and Population Density Control," *Land Economics,* 37 (1961), 354.

A second force in suburban land-use politics is the real estate segment of the business community, including landowners, land developers, land speculators, builders, and zoning attorneys. Landowners are those who hold land in fee simple; land developers will acquire land from owners for the purpose of preparing it for use; land speculators acquire temporary ownership or control of land and hope to sell for a high profit; and zoning attorneys represent any or all of the above before suburban governing bodies and other agencies with land-use control authority. The real estate community is commonly aligned against citizens associations, and will favor high density and nonresidential land-use policies for large sections of the locality. Sometimes part of the local real estate alliance are realtors, engineers, architects, and subcontractors. The general business organizations (chamber of commerce or board of trade) will typically side with its real estate constituents, although its stands and interests will be more general than those of the real estate forces.

The final group of actors are public officials—and this includes the governing body, the planning commission and department, state highway officials, other key administrative agencies, and the judiciary. The sub-urban general-purpose government legislative body is often subject to citizen discipline, and this frequently leads that body to adopt low-density, status quo, and preservation land-use policies.[26] At the same time local elected legislators are sensitive to the growth and expansion demands of the economic marketplace and to the pressures and resources of the real estate community, and this tends to serve as a countervailing power to the citizens associations.

The suburban planning commission and staff are normally advisory to the local governing body, and will have plan adoption and revision authority, prepare the zoning ordinance and textual amendments, render advisory opinions on proposed zoning changes, and administer subdivision regulations. The planning staff will commonly be composed of professionals well versed in planning theory and liberal values, while the commission will frequently represent either the citizens or real estate point of view (or be split between the two), which may lead to an undercurrent of conflict and distrust between the lay and professional portions of the planning bureaucracy. State highway officials determine the location of major roads in the suburban jurisdiction, and consequently strongly influence land-use patterns. Suburban communities appear to have little control over the policies of state highway departments.

Other administrative units that are part of the suburban land-use processes include water, sewer, and codes agencies. All three of these functional areas and others may significantly affect land-use and develop-

26 Raymond and May Associates, *Zoning Controversies in the Suburbs* (Washington, D.C.: National Commission on Urban Problems, 1968), p. 78.

ment policy and are therefore seen by community interests as access points and instruments by which to influence such policy. Last, the judiciary can and does render decisions on suburban zoning and subdivision control matters. In the main, the state courts of this nation are less constrained by majoritarian pressures in the land-use field and are more concerned with the protection of private property rights than are local governing boards. In view of the laws of economics, this in effect makes the state judiciary on the average a high-density and commercially oriented force in suburban land-use decision-making processes, meaning that the judiciary is about the last realistic glimmer of light for those who would tear away at the social class walls of suburbia.

13. THE POLITICS OF FINANCES

Expenditures by government at all levels totaled $259 billions in 1967, a sum equaling 38 percent of the gross national income. State and local governments alone spent $137 billions on current expenditures and capital outlay. Staggering as these figures are, their explanation is simple enough. They were the result of public policies forged in the heat of political competition. In short, they were demands perceived by those who gained control of governmental offices. Nevertheless, given their sheer magnitude, is there any wonder that politicians are peculiarly sensitive to issues that touch the pocketbook?

The problems confronting state and local authorities in deciding how and from whom money is to be raised is no simple task. Few are cheerful about the size of their tax bill. The problem would be less irritating if there were general agreement as to how the tax burden should be distributed. Since there is no unanimity on who should pay how much taxes, the matter is resolved only through oftentimes intense political struggles.

Each of the governmental levels has specialized in the sources from which it draws its tax revenue. The federal government relies heavily on individual and corporate income taxes. State governments emphasize some form of sales tax. Local jurisdictions depend mainly on the property tax. The fact of specialization inhibits one governmental level from invading too far the tax preserves of the other, in part from fear, probably more apparent than real, of overburdening a given tax source.

The extent to which tax bases have become segregated among the several governmental levels results in an unevenness among them in their ability to raise revenue and the fairness with which they distribute burdens. The federal government can expect its revenue to increase automatically with rises in income without increasing the rate of taxation. In fact, it can even consider that reductions in corporate or individual income tax rates may so stimulate the economy that additional revenue can be raised through the lowered rates. State and local governments are not similarly advantaged. Although increases in the volume of retail sales produce greater revenue from sales taxes, it does not produce proportionally as much additional revenue as the income tax does from a growth in personal income. Increases in property values have no impact upon revenue from the property tax unless the property is reassessed, an act often viewed by the taxpayer in the same light as a tax increase.

Since their tax systems do not automatically produce revenue proportionate to rises in income, state and local governments are confronted by the necessity of periodically revising their tax rates upwards in order to provide the services demanded of them. The process is inefficient and cumbersome. State legislatures and city councils often move slowly in authorizing tax increases and the consequences are seen in revenue yields that lag behind public service needs.

A second serious problem encountered by state and local governments is that their tax systems are regressive not progressive in character. A regressive tax is one in which the burdens of taxation decrease with ability to pay. A progressive tax is one in which the burdens of taxation increase with ability to pay. That state and local taxes are indeed regressive in character is shown in Table 13.1. Since it also is the case that the tax rate of the national government is progressive, despite the fact that few in the highest tax brackets actually pay the proportionate amount appearing in tax schedules, the level of government-assigned responsibility for a given public service has important tax implications.

TABLE 13.1
Federal, State, and Local Taxes as a Percentage of Total Income for All Families by Income Class, 1965[a]

TAX	UNDER $2,000	$2,000 TO 2,999	$3,000 TO 3,999	$4,000 TO 4,999	$5,000 TO 5,999	$6,000 TO 7,499	$7,500 TO 9,999	$10,000 TO 14,999	$15,000 AND OVER
					INCOME CLASS[b]				
Federal:									
Individual income	1.9	3.1	4.5	6.4	6.9	7.7	8.8	10.0	16.1
Corporate income[c]	4.5	4.3	5.5	3.6	3.9	3.4	3.4	5.3	10.9
Excises and customs	3.3	3.1	3.3	3.1	3.0	2.8	2.6	2.4	1.5
Estate and gift	–	–	–	–	–	–	–	–	4.6
Social insurance	3.2	3.4	3.8	4.1	4.0	3.8	3.5	3.3	1.7
Total	13.0	14.0	17.1	17.3	17.9	17.8	18.4	21.1	34.9
Total excluding social insurance	9.8	10.6	13.3	13.2	13.9	14.0	14.9	17.8	33.2
State and Local:									
Individual & corporate	.6	.6	.8	.9	.9	.9	1.1	1.2	2.2
Sales, excise, etc.	6.1	5.5	5.6	5.3	5.1	4.8	4.4	4.0	2.6
Property	6.9	5.2	4.7	4.2	4.2	3.8	3.5	3.3	2.4
Death and gift	–	–	–	–	–	–	–	–	1.3
Social insurance	1.5	1.4	1.4	1.4	1.3	1.3	1.2	1.1	.7
Total	15.1	12.7	12.6	11.8	11.5	10.8	10.1	9.6	9.1
Total excluding social insurance	13.6	11.3	11.2	10.4	10.2	9.5	8.9	8.5	8.4

[a] The 1965 estimates are based on total taxes and income shown in the national income accounts for 1965. However, they take no account of the shift in the distribution of income from 1961 to 1965.

[b] The income class limits are expressed in money income after personal taxes. "Personal taxes" consist mainly of Federal, state and local income taxes. The total income on which the percentages in the body of the table are based is a broad income concept equivalent in the aggregate to net national product.

[c] Half of the burden of the corporate tax is assumed to be shifted forward to consumers and half is assumed to fall on shareholders.

SOURCE: Tax Foundation, *Tax Burdens and Benefits of Government Expenditures by Income Class, 1961 and 1965* (New York: Tax Foundation, 1967), p. 20.

A governmental responsibility undertaken solely from state and local tax revenue will place a greater burden on the lower income groups, while a governmental program undertaken by the national government or supported largely by national funds will place a greater burden on the upper income groups.

Even if state and local tax systems were elastic (would automatically provide additional revenue at least proportionate to rises in income) and were progressive in character, a problem would remain in achieving a balance between taxable wealth and needed public services. As we discuss below, some states are wealthier than others and are in a better position to provide the programs required of them. The same disparity holds true among local jurisdictions. For example, a lack of taxable resources to meet the problems confronting them is probably most severe in the beleaguered central cities. Their fiscal plight is unlikely to improve substantially unless higher governmental levels assume a greater share of their educational, welfare, or other major costs. Indeed, the conclusion is inescapable that the resource-public services disparity can be met only if the national government assumes a greater fiscal responsibility for programs now administered at state and local levels.

STATE TAX POLICIES

General and special sales levies are the most important source of taxable revenue of state governments (see Table 13.2) and have been since the late thirties. The precarious fiscal position of the states in the thirties, stemming from the prolonged depression, required tax officials to supplement revenue derived from the historically important property tax. Beginning with Mississippi in 1932, the general sales tax spread rapidly and had been levied in 24 states by the close of the decade. Although viewed at the time as a temporary expedient, it proved an effective revenue producer. Not only was it continued in most of the states where it had been adopted, but other states later followed suit so that today all but a dozen states tax general sales.

Selective sales and gross receipts taxes had been enacted prior to the thirties. The most important of these was the gasoline tax. With the spread of the automobile and the rise in gasoline consumption, the states were quick to tap this revenue source and, by 1929, it had been overlooked in no state. The money derived from this tax is often earmarked for use in road construction. Special levies on alcoholic beverages followed the repeal of Prohibition, while tobacco taxes, first introduced in the twenties, became more widespread during the thirties. One might guess that levies on these commodities are related to the view that vices should be discouraged by tax burdens.

TABLE 13.2
State Government Tax Revenue in 1967–1968

TYPE OF TAX	AMOUNT (MILLIONS OF DOLLARS)	PERCENT OF TOTAL
Property	912	2.5
Individual income	6,231	17.1
Corporation income	2,518	6.9
General sales and gross receipts	10,441	28.7
Motor fuel	5,178	14.2
Alcoholic beverages	1,138	3.1
Tobacco products	1,886	5.2
Motor vehicles and operators licenses	2,485	6.8
Death and gift	872	2.4
All other	4,738	13.0
Total	36,399	100.0

The problems encountered by the states in their heavy reliance on sales taxes relate to the lack of fiscal balance in their tax programs. A sales tax places a heavy burden on low-income groups. Moreover, when levied on food and drugs, which accounts for a substantial proportion of necessary expenditures in low-income budgets, the tax is viewed by some as particularly objectionable. (For this reason, both of these items are excluded from taxation in 14 states, while eight others exclude taxes on prescription medicines.) Although relatively easy to administer and good revenue producers, the regressive features of sales taxes suggest that they should be offset by more progressive taxes.

One alternative for states to lessen their dependence on sales levies is to tax personal and corporate income. Actually the use of the state income tax in its modern sense is not new, dating from the Wisconsin enactment of 1911. In fact, of the 40 states that have some form of income taxation, all but eight were enacted prior to 1940. Yet only in comparatively recent years has the income tax produced substantial revenue for state governments.

The levies on corporate income are commonly a flat rate (although sometimes applying only to earnings exceeding a certain figure). Nor are the rates levied on personal income sharply progressive. The steepest charge is the 12 percent placed on taxable income in excess of $20,000 in Wisconsin. Nevertheless, the Commission on Intergovernmental Relations believes that even a flat rate on personal income can be a good revenue producer and equitable in its impact if accompanied by appropriate deductible items and personal and dependent exemptions. To be effective, according to the Commission, the income tax should produce an amount equal to 20 percent of the federal income tax collections in that state. In 1968, only 11 states met that criteria:[1]

	PERCENT
Alaska	25.3
Delaware	21.7
Hawaii	26.5
Idaho	25.4
Minnesota	29.0
New York	20.6
North Carolina	21.1
Oregon	31.5
Utah	21.4
Vermont	30.4
Wisconsin	32.8

One of the more significant developments in the administration of the state income tax is the use of the federal tax base for state tax purposes, now a practice in 14 states. Not only is this a convenience for the taxpayer, but it improves enforcement by facilitating a check by state officials of federal income tax returns (for states with cooperative arrangements with the Internal Revenue Service). At least two states (West Virginia and Alaska) have so integrated their income tax with the federal tax that the taxpayer's bill is computed as a percentage of federal tax liability. Even the states that do not make use of federally defined taxable income model their tax laws after federal provisions dealing with capital gains, dividends, itemized deductions, and the like.

Although state revenue problems, we feel, revolve about the question of maintaining a balanced system—questions basically concerning how and where to levy a sales tax and ways to tap corporate and individual income—the states also collect money from other sources. Motor vehicle registration, although primarily a regulatory device when first introduced, soon became a revenue producer and remains an important source of money in all states. With the exception of Nevada, all states have enacted inheritance taxes, and a dozen others have enacted gift taxes (property transfer during life). The combined inheritance and gift taxes have provided approximately 3 percent of total tax collections in recent years. Other miscellaneous taxes provide no single additional important source of revenue for the states.

[1] Commission on Intergovernmental Relations, *State and Local Taxes, Significant Features* (Washington, D.C.: U.S. Government Printing Office, 1968), p. 6.

LOCAL TAX SYSTEMS

Tax revenue from local governments has been and remains almost synonymous with property taxation. Next to the yield from personal and corporate income taxes, the property tax provides more revenue, considering all governmental levels, than any other tax source. The property that is commonly taxed includes real property (land, buildings, and other improvements) and personal possessions. Personal property is divided into two classes: tangible (furniture, jewelry, automobiles, and similar objects) and intangible (stocks, bonds, and other evidences of wealth). Taxes on real property account for most of the property tax revenue.

Administration of the property tax includes three steps. First, there must be a determination of the assessed value of a property. Typically, state laws require that real property be valued at fair market value. However, few local assessors are inclined to follow the state directive. If the property is assessed at a known percentage of market value the implications to the taxpayer are slight. Where such uniformity is unknown, the taxpayer has no basis for judging the fairness of his assessment and is handicapped in proving overassessment on appeal. The second step is the determination of the rate to be charged. Taxing officials estimate the revenue from other sources, determine generally the costs of services required, and fix the property tax accordingly. Obviously the decision between cutting a budget and raising the tax rate is an agonizing one and does not proceed in the cut-and-dried manner described; but with a given assessed valuation and tax rate, one can predict, on the basis of past delinquency, the amount of revenue anticipated. The third step is the actual tax collection which involves few important policy questions.

Despite the secure position that property taxes occupy in the local government revenue system, it has undergone persistent criticism. Much of the objection centers about the unfair burden placed on individual taxpayers and groups of taxpayers, exacerbated by the regressive features already noted. The individual taxpayer may be the victim of inept valuation practices and cumbersome appeal procedures to which only the sophisticated find access. Groups of taxpayers may be victimized by the balkanization of local government and find themselves in a taxing jurisdiction with heavy demands but a weak property tax base. Of course the splintering of political jurisdictions constitutes a problem no matter what tax is utilized. Yet the limited tax flexibility of local governments often prevents them from taxing the principal source of wealth within their community which may be income, not property. The problem may be even more complex since most young "homeowners" have precious little equity in their homes yet do not share their tax bills with the mortgage company. And the elderly couple whose income is sharply reduced upon retirement nevertheless continues the same payment on the home they own.

Outcries against the unfairness of the property tax have produced a variety of responses—underassessment, exemptions—which have not solved the problem. Too often the time-honored practice of underassessing real property proceeds on no systematic basis, and the property taxpayer, knowing that his home is assessed under market value, is uncertain of how to compare his valuation to others. The practice of providing homestead exemptions, a development of the thirties, offers some relief to the taxpayer but provides alike for rich and poor and offers no advantage to the apartment dweller who pays his property tax masked in rental charges. Church, educational, and governmental property are also commonly exempt, although revenue-producing property owned by religious groups has recently been called into question.

Granted the difficulties inherent in fair assessment and the regressive features of the tax, some positive steps can and have been taken in some states to improve property tax administration. An important step forward is the professionalization of the assessors office. Echoing the plea of good government groups, we see no logical reason why the tax assessor should be an elected official. The position should be filled by appointment based on professional qualifications. And state laws requiring valuation at fair market price could be rendered more flexible if at the same time local officials were called upon to establish a uniform rate at which property is to be assessed. With adequate appeal procedures, the taxpayer then could point to a fixed rate to determine the fairness of his assessment.

The most imaginative scheme designed to aid the low income homeowner has been the Wisconsin tax credit plan enacted in 1964.[2] Under provisions of the act, the homeowner receives a rebate on his property tax that exceeds 5 percent of his family's income. The tax rebate is paid from state funds, however, and thus does not weaken the local tax structure. The plan also has the effect of aiding low income jurisdictions. Because of the tax relief granted, the political decision to raise local taxes is not so vexing.

Local governments have the same incentive as state governments to diversify their tax systems—that is, to provide equitable and fiscally sound sources of revenue. But local governments encounter difficulties other than that prime tax sources have been preempted by either the federal or state governments. The imposition of local nonproperty taxes will normally require specific constitutional or statutory authorization, since the powers of local governments still are controlled by the so-called Dillon rule. Under this court doctrine, powers flowing from the charter

2 Commission on Intergovernmental Relations, *op. cit.*, p. 9.

of a local government are to be narrowly rather than broadly construed, ruling out the possibility of implying powers from a charter in a manner similar to constitutional interpretation at the national level. The mere fact that a state constitution or enabling statute contains no mention of nonproperty taxes in itself would prohibit most local jurisdictions from diversifying their tax base. Since states that have authorized nonproperty taxes have restricted the authority to specific local governments and to specific taxes, the use of taxes other than on property is far from uniform. Urban jurisdictions have been the most active in expanding their tax bases, with the nation's 51 largest cities collecting over half of all local nonproperty taxes in 1961. Table 13.3 shows the use of local nonproperty taxes by states.

The principal nonproperty taxes enacted by local jurisdictions are levies on sales, income, and utility services. The chief revenue producer has been the general sales tax, followed by special levies on public utility gross receipts. The income tax yield is third in importance despite the fact that its use is more restricted than that of sales levies. Other special levies on cigarettes, gasoline, and amusements produce relatively smaller amounts in the aggregate.

The diversification of the local tax system is not an unmixed blessing unless part of a coordinated state-local system of taxation. What one jurisdiction does can affect what others may do. (Thus the fact that Pennsylvania has permitted the use of the local income tax was said to have discouraged the enactment of a state income tax.[3]) A need for coordination may also arise to insure that local governments are not at a disadvantage in attracting new business ventures. The Commission on Intergovernmental Relations believes that while tax policies may be discounted as an influence on plant location among distant states, or even neighboring states since the competitive situation usually produces tax policies that are not out of line, significant variations in tax policies within a state, particularly within a metropolitan area, does have an impact on management decisions of where to locate. General and special levies on sales and taxes on salaries and wages added to property taxes may affect the competitive relationship between business within and those outside the taxing jurisdiction.[4]

State cooperation with local governments in tax administration, by formal arrangements and informal consultation, is common. We shall mention two examples. The most frequently used device is that of tax sharing. A tax is imposed and collected by the state but its proceeds are

[3] Commission on Intergovernmental Relations, *Tax Overlapping in the United States 1964* (Washington, D.C.: U.S. Government Printing Office, 1964), p. 225.
[4] Commission on Intergovernmental Relations, *State-Local Taxation and Industrial Location* (Washington, D.C.: U.S. Government Printing Office, 1967), p. 70.

TABLE 13.3
Local Nonproperty Taxes as a Percent of Total Local Taxes, 1962

UNDER 5 PERCENT		5 TO 10 PERCENT		10 TO 15 PERCENT		15 TO 20 PERCENT		20 PERCENT OR MORE	
Indiana	0.5	Wyoming	5.6	Georgia	11.2	Washington	16.0	Kentucky	20.5
Maine	0.8	Montana	5.7	Illinois	11.2	Florida	16.5	Virginia	20.7
Connecticut	0.8	Delaware	6.0	Tennessee	11.2	Missouri	18.7	Louisiana	22.1
New Hampshire	0.9	South Dakota	6.3	West Virginia	11.3	Mississippi	19.4	New York	23.0
Michigan	1.1	Texas	7.0	California	11.9			Pennsylvania	23.8
Iowa	1.3	South Carolina	7.3	Utah	11.9			New Mexico	24.9
Massachusetts	1.3	Arkansas	7.5					Nevada	25.4
Wisconsin	1.7	Nebraska	7.5					Alaska	26.0
Rhode Island	1.8	Arizona	8.0					Hawaii	33.0
Idaho	2.3	Colorado	8.6					Alabama	44.2
Vermont	2.3	Maryland	8.6					Dist. Columbia	63.0
Minnesota	2.8	New Jersey	9.0						
Kansas	2.9	Ohio	9.4						
North Dakota	3.4								
Oregon	3.4								
North Carolina	3.5								
Oklahoma	4.7								
Number of states	17		13		6		4		11

SOURCE: Commission on Intergovernmental Relations, *Tax Overlapping in the United States* (Washington, D.C.: U.S. Government Printing Office, 1964), p. 47.

shared with local governments, ordinarily on the basis of collections within a jurisdiction. The advantages of such a system are evident. Only one tax collection agency is required and it is the superior one in terms of compliance. Interjurisdiction competition is alleviated by the common rate levied. Since it is state imposed, there is greater likelihood or at least potentiality for a coordinated state-local system. Yet tax sharing has its drawbacks. It places limits on fiscal independence at the local level and prescribes a tax that may be unneeded.

A somewhat similar technique but with important exceptions is the tax supplement, sometimes referred to as the "piggyback" tax. Under this device, the local government simply adds its rate to that of the state levy. The state collects the tax and returns the appropriate share to the local jurisdiction. Thus the advantages inherent in state collection machinery are utilized without destroying local initiative. However, there is some evidence to indicate that when a state does authorize a tax supplement, the local jurisdictions are likely to exercise their option to do so, at least if a local referendum is not required.[5] To the extent that local variations are possible, the tax supplement does little to overcome problems of inter-jurisdictional rivalry in attracting commerce and industry.

INTERSTATE VARIATIONS
IN TAX SYSTEMS

Considerable variations exist among the states in the tax systems they and their local governments have enacted. One could not hope to explain all of the factors that influence the types and levels of taxation employed in given states. Nevertheless, because a state's political leaders are continuously confronted with the problem of balancing tax policy against expenditure demands, it is important to know something about a state's *fiscal capacity*—that is, the tax resources potentially available as revenue producers. A state's fiscal capacity constitutes the single most important variable in explaining variations among the states in tax revenue. But it is not the only factor. Some states may use their capacity to raise tax revenue more fully than others—that is, some states put forth a greater *tax effort* than others. Fiscal capacity and tax effort are two analytically distinct ways of explaining differences among the states in their tax policies, and information about each is important in evaluating a state's tax system.

There is no one method of computing a state's fiscal capacity (and

[5] Commission on Intergovernmental Relations, *Tax Overlapping in the United States 1964, op. cit.*, p. 229.

from it, a state's tax effort) that is without limitations.[6] The most common economic indicator of fiscal capacity is the personal income estimates prepared by the Department of Commerce. Personal income figures show the amount of income received within a state and thus available for taxation regardless of where it was produced. It does not reflect all of the income produced within a state that might be taxed through a variety of corporate income and business taxes. Income produced within a state, however, may go elsewhere in the form of profits and dividends and thus escape certain forms of taxation (sales, personal income) in the originating state.

Any measure of income, of course, has limitations in suggesting a state's fiscal capacity for the simple reason that many state and local taxes are based on other forms of wealth. The obvious example is the property tax, the most important single source of revenue for state and local governments. An alternative way of comparing the capacity of states to raise revenue would be to apply a uniform system to each of the states to determine their potential tax yield. The problem occurs in determining the elements of such a uniform system. What taxes should be included? What rates should be charged? One possibility is to devise a uniform tax system that is a cross section of the patterns currently in existence.[7] The aggregate yield of such a "representative" tax system would be the same as that under the present tax systems of the states, but for any single state the revenue might be higher or lower for any given tax or for all taxes.

Table 13.4 suggests the differences among the states in their fiscal capacity. No matter what measure of capacity is used, southeastern states have far less ability to raise tax revenue than other areas. On the other hand, far western states show a greater fiscal capacity than other regions no matter what index is used. One can notice that a state's fiscal capacity does vary with the measure of capacity used. Although the two different income measures show relatively little variation, one sees that the income from dividends and interest received by New England and mideastern residents places their regions higher in personal income than in income produced. The reverse is true for the Southwest because of absentee ownership particularly in mineral production.

The differences between yield from a representative tax system and capacity measured by personal income are more marked. The Plains, Rocky Mountain, and southwestern states show a much higher relative ranking on the representative tax yield measure. Conversely, the New England and mideastern states have a relatively higher ranking when

6 See Advisory Commission on Intergovernmental Relations, *Measures of State and Local Fiscal Capacity* (Washington, D.C.: U.S. Government Printing Office, 1962), chap. 1.
7 *Ibid.*, p. 9.

TABLE 13.4
*Measures of Fiscal Capacity
Among the States, 1960*[a]

STATE AND REGION	PERSONAL INCOME	INCOME PRODUCED	YIELD OF REPRE- SENTATIVE SYSTEM
United States	100	100	100
New England	111	101	97
Maine	83	72	78
New Hampshire	92	83	98
Vermont	83	78	85
Massachusetts	113	105	96
Rhode Island	100	89	87
Connecticut	129	115	112
Mideast	116	114	100
New York	125	128	105
New Jersey	120	111	105
Pennsylvania	102	97	91
Delaware	136	97	112
Maryland	108	94	93
District of Columbia	133	159	126
Great Lakes	107	109	105
Michigan	104	101	99
Ohio	106	106	103
Indiana	97	102	101
Illinois	119	126	116
Wisconsin	98	96	97
Plains	92	96	107
Minnesota	91	97	103
Iowa	91	96	114
Missouri	100	103	99
North Dakota	72	80	108
South Dakota	70	81	107
Nebraska	91	100	119
Kansas	92	87	113
Southeast	72	73	76
Virginia	83	85	81
West Virginia	76	81	74
Kentucky	70	74	74
Tennessee	70	69	71
North Carolina	69	76	72
South Carolina	62	60	60

TABLE 13.4 (*Continued*)

STATE AND REGION	PERSONAL INCOME	INCOME PRODUCED	YIELD OF REPRE-SENTATIVE SYSTEM
Georgia	72	74	69
Florida	91	83	101
Alabama	66	65	66
Mississippi	53	48	57
Louisiana	74	81	88
Arkansas	61	56	69
Southwest	87	95	113
Oklahoma	83	89	94
Texas	88	96	120
New Mexico	84	92	102
Arizona	89	96	99
Rocky Mountain	94	97	116
Montana	92	96	129
Idaho	83	84	108
Wyoming	104	108	161
Colorado	101	101	114
Utah	86	96	101
Far West	118	116	119
Washington	104	102	102
Oregon	102	94	103
Nevada	126	142	146
California	124	121	126
Alaska	117	117	69
Hawaii	96	96	76

a Figures are per capital amounts as a percentage of U.S. average.
SOURCE: Data are taken from Advisory Commission on Intergovernmental Relations, *Measures of State and Local Fiscal Capacity* (Washington, D.C.: U.S. Government Printing Office, 1962), Table 16, pp. 54–55.

personal income is the measure of capacity. The explanation is simple enough. Because of its widespread use, the property tax contributes a significant portion (44 percent) of the yield of a representative tax system. Since high per capita property values are not synonymous with high personal income, the two measures produce different results of fiscal capacity.

TABLE 13.5
Measures of Tax Effort
Among the States, 1960[a]

STATE AND REGION	PERSONAL INCOME	INCOME PRODUCED	YIELD UNDER REPRE- SENTATIVE TAX SYSTEM
United States	100	100	100
New England	98	108	112
Maine	119	139	126
New Hampshire	101	112	95
Vermont	132	141	130
Massachusetts	103	111	121
Rhode Island	96	109	112
Connecticut	82	93	94
Mideast	99	101	115
New York	113	112	136
New Jersey	85	93	97
Pennsylvania	85	89	96
Delaware	73	103	87
Maryland	92	105	106
District of Columbia	79	67	85
Great Lakes	93	92	95
Michigan	104	108	110
Ohio	88	88	91
Indiana	92	88	87
Illinois	85	81	88
Wisconsin	108	112	110
Plains	103	99	89
Minnesota	119	112	105
Iowa	113	108	91
Missouri	75	73	76
North Dakota	136	124	91
South Dakota	140	121	92
Nebraska	94	87	72
Kansas	116	124	96

A state's fiscal capacity does not tell the whole story of why some states have more tax money to spend than others. The remaining ingredient is the tax effort each state makes which may be determined by comparing actual tax collections to a state's fiscal capacity. Table 13.5 shows the relationships. The Far West, which ranked consistently high in

TABLE 13.5 (*Continued*)

STATE AND REGION	PERSONAL INCOME	INCOME PRODUCED	YIELD UNDER REPRESENTATIVE TAX SYSTEM
Southeast	99	99	95
Virginia	82	81	84
West Virginia	97	91	101
Kentucky	83	80	80
Tennessee	95	96	93
North Carolina	99	91	96
South Carolina	103	107	106
Georgia	97	95	102
Florida	103	113	90
Alabama	91	92	91
Mississippi	120	133	113
Louisiana	126	116	106
Arkansas	100	112	90
Southwest	97	89	74
Oklahoma	105	99	94
Texas	92	84	67
New Mexico	104	96	84
Arizona	121	112	104
Rocky Mountain	116	112	93
Montana	121	116	86
Idaho	116	115	89
Wyoming	115	111	73
Colorado	114	115	100
Utah	117	104	98
Far West	113	116	111
Washington	113	116	114
Oregon	113	123	113
Nevada	109	97	93
California	114	116	109
Alaska	71	71	116
Hawaii	124	125	155

[a] Figures are stated as a percentage of U.S. average.

SOURCE: Data are taken from Advisory Commission on Intergovernmental Relations, *Measures of State and Local Fiscal Capacity* (Washington, D.C.: U.S. Government Printing Office, 1962), Table 24, pp. 75–76.

measures of fiscal capacity, also ranks consistently high in measures of tax effort. But other regions do not show the same relationship between capacity and effort. In fact, the striking revelations in comparing the two tables is the lack of any consistency. The seven states that were 10 percent or more above the national average on all measures of tax effort included Hawaii, Mississippi, Maine, New York, Oregon, Vermont, and Washington—states ranging from urbanized to rural, wealthy to poor, and with all levels of public service. In similar fashion, the five that ranked at least 10 percent below the national average on all of the effort indicators also show marked variations—Illinois, Kentucky, Missouri, Virginia, and the District of Columbia.

The importance of the tax effort scale is to suggest to states that are below the national average that they may raise additional tax revenue without overloading their fiscal resources. Such a move may not be practical in all instances because of fixed patterns of taxation that have applied in the past and that place obstacles in front of taxing available forms of wealth. Or it may be the case that particular forms of wealth (farmlands) have been inflated. Yet it should cause state and local leaders to look more closely at their ability to raise revenue when expenditure demands are strong.

SOURCES OF NONTAX REVENUE

The principal source of revenue for state and local governments comes from taxation. However, these governments also derive revenue from sources other than taxes. Fees and charges (for a variety of services provided on a semicommercial basis such as recreation, hospitalization, or highway and bridge travel) have always accounted for a substantial amount of revenue. Several states have a monopoly on the sale of packaged liquor of a particular alcoholic content. Many municipalities operate their own public utility and transportation systems. Yet the most significant source of nontax revenue involves intergovernmental transfers of money or grants-in-aid.

National grants to states are not of recent derivation, but date from our early history when Congress transferred public lands to the states for the development of public schools. Yet it has only been since the thirties that the grants have accounted for a substantial portion of state and local expenditures and have engendered a public controversy over their use. Under terms of the more recent grants, state and local agencies commonly are required to match the national payment according to some formula, which may be on a dollar-for-dollar basis or may require only a minor contribution by the states. The funds are allotted according to several criteria, such as area, population, or need, which vary among the grant programs. The states must spend the money only for the purpose authorized by Congress and must meet certain minimal standards and policy guidelines in the administration of the grant program.

The basic rationale of the modern grant-in-aid is that the national government must assume responsibility for solving pressing national problems that the states are unwilling or unable to solve themselves. Such a position raised grave constitutional issues in the past which now have been resolved in favor of national authority to act. The constitutional objections stemmed from the Tenth Amendment: it was argued that the national government lacked power to undertake responsibility for activities assigned to the states under our federal system. But support for the grant-in-aid program was found in the taxing and spending powers of the Congress. The taxing and spending clause of the Constitution, said the Court, is an independent grant of power—that is, the federal government need not limit its spending authorizations to support activities specifically delegated or enumerated in the Constitution.[8] Under its spending powers, Congress has authority to appropriate tax money for any truly national need. Today the grant-in-aid is no longer a legal but a political issue. How wise is it for the national government to financially support activities administered by state and local agencies?

The fact that the states may not be able to solve particular governmental problems (for example, relief functions during the Depression of the thirties) is related to their fiscal capacity. If an issue looms large in the public's mind (an education lag between the United States and the Soviet Union following Sputnik; crime in the streets following civil disorders and the growth in the rate of serious crime), then pressure exists on the national government to use its superior financial resources to provide a solution. The citizen does not neatly separate government into compartmentalized levels in his own mind. He wants an effective response to what he considers to be national problems and often turns to the national government.

Many argue that grants are necessary to equalize the financial strength of states to insure at least minimal levels of service. Whether they achieve this purpose today is far from clear. Few of the grant programs actually make their grants on the basis of need (aid to primary and secondary education under the Education Act of 1965 is a conspicuous exception). And while it is true that the poorer states do depend upon the national grant for a larger share of their operating budgets than the more wealthy states, it is also the case that, in terms of per capita amounts of federal aid, the poor states have no advantage over the rich states.

[8]   *U.S.* v. *Butler,* 297 U.S. 1 (1936).

Critics have challenged the grant-in-aid movement since its modern development. They complain that the national government should not use its financial strength to induce or coerce the states into action. These critics see in the grant the growth of centralized government and the loss of independence for state and local units. Sometimes implicit in their views is the belief that, if national aid is not forthcoming, the particular function will not be funded adequately at the state or local level. In fact, we suspect that much of the centralization issue is not based on abstract values of appropriate responsibilities for each governmental level but rather is based on whether a given function is viewed as an appropriate responsibility for any government to undertake. For example, we doubt that critics who object to the use of national aid to secure compliance to school integration decrees are the same as those who object to national funds to aid local police departments in combating crime in the streets.

A second criticism of federal grants is that they limit the flexibility of state and local budgetary authorities. The reasoning is somewhat as follows. The state will get more for its tax dollar if it is put into federal grant programs. State officials are thus under a certain compulsion to contribute to nationally aided programs. Yet this may not be where the state's greatest need lies. For this reason, many state leaders argue that the national government should make unrestricted or block grants to the states which would then determine how the money would be spent. Although a reasonable request from the view of providing flexibility in state and local finances, the unrestricted grant is not without its problems. How does one insure that a state will use its national funds in the most constructive fashion? More specifically, if one believes our major domestic issues can be subsumed under the rubric of "urban crisis," can one depend on state governments to react any more positively to urban problems than they have in the past, particularly with the growing suburban strength in state legislatures? And would not the problem be exacerbated if, as of this writing, Republicans controlled more statehouses and Democrats occupied more city halls? It seems to us that the block grant idea would make sense only if there existed some national control over "pass-through" requirements, for example, in the proportion of funds which would be channeled to central city governments.

Critics of the federal grant also point to the fact that if the national government would free certain tax bases (gasoline, cigarette, amusement taxes), the states could then provide from tax money what now comes in federal grants. Rather than accepting a large national contribution for the interstate highway program, for example, the states could increase their gasoline taxes up to the amount of the relinquished national tax without any additional burden on the taxpayer. The problem occurs because not all states would be similarly advantaged. Although the size of per capita grants to rich and poor states are similar, the amounts of money paid to the national government which are used in part to support federal grants vary. In this sense, an equalization principle is built into grants-in-aid and renders impractical the tax relinquishment plan.

Federal grants to state and local governments are only one phase of intergovernmental revenue transfer. Increasingly, the states are spending more of their operating budget on grants to their local subdivisions. Some of the same criticisms that apply to federal grants to states apply as well to state grants to localities, although probably not with the same degree of intensity that can be engendered over the centralization issue with Washington involved. And the states have been more flexible, in certain respects, than the federal government. Some have adopted the shared and supplemental tax plans, both of which accomplish the objectives of unrestricted grants. Yet the inability or unwillingness of most states to devise a plan of either grants or shared taxes that equates program need with fiscal resources remains a complaint of the financially weak jurisdictions.

HOW THE MONEY IS SPENT

An examination of state and local expenditure budgets tells us much about the assignment of governmental responsibilities under the federal system. The amount of money spent on a given function, of course, cannot be equated with its significance to the well-being of a polity. The size of the budget supporting a state's judicial system is comparatively small, for example, but few would question its essentiality to the state's political system. Nevertheless, because revenues are a scarce resource and competition is keen for the budget dollar, the priorities established in the distribution of funds are one measure of the importance of state and local governmental undertakings.

The remarkable fact is that state and local governments, in the aggregate, show considerable consistency in the manner in which they allocate budget dollars. As Table 13.6 shows, the five most costly activities of state and local governments in 1942 continued to occupy their same relative position in 1967. More money is being spent today than in former years, of course, and it is not due simply to rises in the cost of living or the growth in population. It is due as well to decisions to offer improved governmental services. And changes have undoubtedly occurred in the types of governmental programs offered to state and local residents in such policy areas as urban renewal or welfare activities that extend beyond the traditional categorical assistance plans. But in spite of

TABLE 13.6
Direct General Expenditures of State and Local Governments,
1942 to 1967

ITEM	1942	1950	1955	1960	1964	1965	1966	1967
Total (millions of dollars)	9,190	22,787	33,724	51,876	69,302	74,546	82,843	93,350
Percent of total								
Education	28.1	31.5	35.3	36.1	38.3	38.3	40.2	40.6
Highways	16.2	16.7	19.1	18.2	16.8	16.4	15.4	14.9
Public welfare	13.3	13.0	9.4	8.5	8.3	8.5	8.2	8.8
Health and hospitals	6.4	7.7	7.5	7.5	7.1	7.2	7.1	7.1
Police protection and correction	4.3	3.4	3.6	3.6	4.7	4.7	4.6	4.5
Sanitation and sewerage	2.5	3.7	3.4	3.3	3.3	3.2	3.1	2.7
Interest on general debt	6.1	2.0	2.5	3.2	3.4	3.3	3.2	3.2
All other	23.0	22.2	19.2	19.8	18.1	18.4	18.2	18.1
Per capita (dollars)								
Total	68	150	204	288	362	385	423	472
Education	19	47	72	104	139	147	170	192
Highways	11	25	39	52	61	63	65	70
Public welfare	9	19	19	24	30	33	35	42
Health and hospitals	4	12	15	21	26	28	30	34
Police protection and correction	3	5	7	10	17	18	19	21
Sanitation and sewerage	2	6	7	10	12	12	13	13
Interest on general debt	4	3	5	9	12	13	14	15
All other	16	33	39	57	66	71	77	85

SOURCE: U.S. Bureau of the Census, *Statistical Abstract* (Washington, D.C.: U.S. Government Printing Office, 1969), p. 414.

changes in the quantity and quality of services, the same basic patterns emerge today that were true 25 years ago.

State governments allocate over four fifths of their current expenditures to four major functions: education, highways, welfare, and health and hospitals. Not all of the current operating budgets for these functions are spent by state agencies. Somewhat over one third of current expenditures actually go to local governments in the form of grants. Expenditures for education dwarf all others, accounting for two fifths of total current operating costs. Of this amount, better than half goes to local units of school administration. The state spends the remaining school funds largely on public higher education. One sees mirrored in educational costs the beliefs of middle-class society in the importance of education for social and economic well-being.

Highway expenditures account for the next largest portion of the budget, with state agencies spending most of the money directly on the network of state roadways and interstate highways. The benefits accruing to economic development from an efficient transportation system, plus a need to move the 90 million motor vehicles in use today, dictate sizable highway outlays. Approximately 30 percent of state highway expenditures come from federal sources for the national interstate highway program. The remaining funds are derived from various highway users revenue—the gasoline tax, motor vehicle registration fees, and toll charges.

Welfare and health and hospitals constitute the largest remaining items of state expenditures. Outlays for these activities have been encouraged by federal grants and contribute to the governmental policy that has been described as welfare-statism. The Depression drove home to many that there were classes of unfortunates in American society who could not provide for their own needs. The plight of the economically deprived gave credence to the view that government must accept responsibility for providing assistance to those whose wants could not be met through private resources. The debate over governmental responsibility today is no longer so keen, although specific policies suggesting a radical departure from existing laws or having racial overtones remain contentious.

The expenditure pattern at the local governmental level is not unlike that at the state level in terms of the major costs of government. Expenditures for education account for almost one half of the operating budgets of local governments. No other activity approaches the dollar volume committed to teaching children. Money spent on welfare and hospitals accounted for 12.5 percent of current expenditures in 1967, while the construction and maintenance of streets and roads amounted to 7.7 percent of budget funds. Housing and urban renewal were allocated only 2.4 percent of all local government expenditures in 1967.

It should be obvious, of course, that the full range of activities at either the state or local level cannot be comprehended by emphasizing major costs. Yet sometimes it is important to stand back and see how the aggregate amount of money is allocated within the public sector. The emphasis on education, highways, and health and welfare at state and local levels of government is plain to see. The distribution of funds must be related to the dominant values within our society. On the basis of budgetary allocations, one could argue that middle-class emphasis on education and concern for the convenience and economic advantages of efficient transportation are tempered by a commitment to aid the underprivileged. Some see in such a policy a neglect of the economically and socially deprived and point to the fact that the public share of the gross national product has remained remarkably constant over the past forty years.[9] Indeed, much of the protest activity of today's college youth may be seen as a challenge to the traditional allocation of available resources.

INTERSTATE VARIATIONS
IN EXPENDITURES

If political science is to be more than a descriptive discipline, it must also be able to explain. Insofar as the expenditure programs of state and local governments are concerned, the challenge to political scientists is to explain why some states spend more money than others in providing the traditional public services described above.

Although the literature on the subject is heavily technical in nature, the general approach used can be simply described.[10] The expenditure variations to be explained are stated in terms of per capita figures, since total amounts spent would predictably vary with the population of a state. The expenditure figures used are commonly combined state and local expenditures, since the extent to which services have been either centralized at the state level or supported by state grants is not uniform. Most of the variables that have been used successfully to predict per

[9] G. Theodore Mitau, *State and Local Government: Politics and Processes* (New York: Scribner's 1966), p. 579.

[10] See, for example, Solomon Fabricant, *The Trend of Government Activity in the United States Since 1900* (New York: National Bureau of Economic Research, 1952); Seymour Sachs and Robert Harris, "The Determinants of State and Local Government Expenditures and Intergovernmental Flow of Funds," *National Tax Journal*, XVII (March, 1964), 75–85; Glenn W. Fisher, "Interstate Variation in State and Local Expenditures," *National Tax Journal*, XVII (March, 1964), 57–73; Ernest Kurnow, "Determinants of State and Local Expenditures Reexamined," *National Tax Journal*, XVI (September, 1963), 252–255; and Ira Sharkansky, *Spending in the American States* (Chicago: Rand McNally, 1968).

capita expenditure variations relate to the taxable wealth within a state. Thus high per capita expenditures have been found associated with states of high personal income, advanced industrialization, and extensive urbanization.

A finding that a state's per capita expenditures are closely linked to its wealth may not sound too startling. Yet it carries with it important implications. It means that such political considerations as voter participation, the degree of party competition, or the quality of political leadership do not affect greatly the amount of money that a state spends. In fact, Thomas R. Dye has argued that the level of economic development, not matters we normally call political, have the greatest influence on the public policies adopted in a state.[11] We are prepared to accept Dye's conclusions, with reservations, if public policy is measured in a way that is related to per capita expenditures. We believe that over the long run state spending will be closely related to state wealth. But, we are inclined to believe that in the short run, political factors do affect decisions on public policy.

Sharkansky provides support for the view that certain political variables have an effect upon state spending policies.[12] Although using different predictors than Dye, he found, for example, that gubernatorial tenure was related to the percentage of change made in per capita expenditures. Since the per capita expenditures of a state are actually a product of its historical spending patterns, the increments of change made in any one year have relatively little effect on the overall per capita amounts. The increments of change are thus always lost in the total in interstate comparisons. But it is precisely in the increments of change that political variables are most likely influential. Because he measured the change that occurred in spending among the states, Sharkansky could conclude that "immediate and transient phenomena, including the motivations and strengths of specific individuals and organizations, may exercise considerable influence on the increments of change which occur at any one time."[13]

THE POLITICS OF BUDGET-MAKING

The general public often views budget-making as the special preserve of the accountant and the financial wizard. Credence is given such a view by the recruitment practices (preference shown those with accounting

[11] Thomas R. Dye, *Politics, Economics, and the Public* (Chicago: Rand McNally, 1966).
[12] Ira Sharkansky, *Spending in the American States* Chicago: Rand McNally, 1968), pp. 73–76.
[13] *Ibid.*, p. 75.

and management training) of agency offices involved in the budgetary process. What is obscured by such a notion is that the budget document is a statement of a government's program in financial terms. The columns of figures portrayed in the document can be translated into the probable quality of education offered school children, the adequacy of a family welfare budget, the number of weekly garbage collections by sanitary workers, the efficiency with which a road network moves traffic, or any of a number of governmental activities of general or special interest to the citizens of a state. To determine the amount of money to be allocated to a given activity is to make a decision on the substantive policies of government and goes to the heart of the process of politics.

Because budgetary allocations are so crucial to what a government can do, the role played by the governor or mayor in the process is an important determinant of his mastery of his job. The older literature would in part classify chief executives as "strong" or "weak" on the basis of their authority over budget preparation. The strong governor or mayor would have responsibility for preparing budgetary estimates to submit to his legislature or city council. The weak executive would share his authority with a budgetary commission composed of elected subordinates, members of the legislative body, or both. Such neat characterizations of "weak" and "strong" models of executive leadership overlook many aspects of the leadership role, but they nevertheless convey the significance of controlling the allocation of financial resources.

Governors in all but seven states and most mayors of large cities have formal authority over budget preparation. Whether they use their authority to provide effective leadership for their city or state depends upon a complex of factors we have discussed elsewhere. The immediate concern of this section is the character of the budget-making process itself and the way it affects budgetary decisions.

The typical budgetary procedure begins with the request by the budget-making authority for estimates of expenditures from each department or agency. It usually will be accompanied by broad policy directives to be followed in the preparation of estimates, sometimes specifically pointed at the expansion or contraction of given programs, sometimes a general request to hold the line on expenditures or to forego all but the most essential construction projects. The agencies prepare their estimates and submit them to the budget office where they are reviewed and compared for conformity with the chief executive's program. Examiners from the budget office may work with particular departments when questions arise over the sums submitted. The budget office next compiles the budget requests, prepares revenue estimates, and confers with the governor or mayor over the final figures which will be sent to the legislature.

What appears as a straightforward process in which the governor or mayor guides the development of a budget that suits his program needs is far from the case. The constraints upon the chief executive's decision-making are such as to limit severely the flexibility with which he deals with budgetary matters. In the first place, the most important consideration in developing or reviewing an agency's request is the amount of money spent in the previous budgetary year. Prior expenditures represent to budget-makers the funds already considered necessary for the maintenance of established programs and acquire a certain legitimacy as a consequence.[14] Budget officials thus focus their attention on the amounts of additional funds requested and seldom give the entire program a searching review. The result is the remarkable stability found among state and local expenditure patterns already commented on.

Budgetary flexibility is restricted as well by the widespread use of earmarked or dedicated revenues at both the state and local level. This is the case, of course, with national grants-in-aid, which can be spent only for the purposes authorized. But many types of taxes, special assessments, and fees levied by state and local governments are also restricted in their uses. It is common to find, for example, some or all of the gasoline tax restricted to highway construction, fees from hunting and fishing licenses dedicated to conservation or recreation projects, or revenue from state-operated package liquor stores reserved for such socially "good" purposes as education. Since, on the average, more than 50 percent of state revenue is tied up by earmarking devices, limitations on the governor's budgetary discretion is substantial. However, when the earmarked revenue must be supplemented by revenue from the general fund, the governor can control the incremental changes in a program and this may be his major interest.

A further factor that may limit a chief executive in making basic decisions concerning the allocation of the budget is the character of accounting information that is available in his city or state. Most governors and mayors would probably like to isolate the costs of particular programs so they could be compared in terms of his own program goals (for example, a mayor might wish to know the costs of drug control programs, or programs aiding underprivileged youth). He would be even happier if he had some measure of performance in the program (for example, what it costs to rehabilitate an addict or to provide particular services for a child). Yet the accounting information he is given, more likely than not, shows the objects (personal services, supplies, equipment, travel) for which particular agencies spend their money. Insofar as the accounting information shows only who spends the money for what objects of expenditures, it obscures the central question of why the money is being

14 *Ibid.*, p. 35.

spent. The effect is to focus attention on particularistic decisions and discourages an attempt to focus on broad policy alternatives.

Finally, the chief executive and his budget advisers must negotiate with the agency heads in readying the estimates for legislative consideration. The agency heads will want what they consider their fair share of the budget pie and will likely request more funds than the preceding year if, for no other reason, to demonstrate a satisfactory rate of growth in their programs. There is a belief on the part of many involved in budget-making that an agency request should be somewhat greater than the amount anticipated to allow an opportunity for others to display their economy-mindedness by cutting the funds requested. Aside from the informal rules on how to play the game, however, piecing the budget together involves a calculus of the effect of particular programs on the general public, the clientele served by an agency, and the political actors, both within and outside of government, who have evinced an interest in the distribution of funds.

The submission of the budget to the legislature or city council gives the budgetary allocations more public visibility and intensifies the struggles over its final shape. The budget is commonly submitted to the lower house of the state legislature and then follows the normal path of bills—that is, referral to committee, hearings, reporting to the full house, debate, and final passage. The process is then repeated in the upper house and, after differences have been ironed out, goes to the governor for his signature or possible veto, including item vetoes. City councils often hold public hearings on the mayor's budget and representatives of interest organizations as well as agency heads are invited to appear as witnesses.

Three points must be emphasized in the appropriation stage. First, although the variations are not widespread, differences do exist among states and cities in the formal relations between the executive and legislative branches in handling the budgetary requests. Some states and cities require the budget agency to submit the original agency request along with its own recommendations and thus encourage agency heads to press for the restoration of funds that have been cut. Other state legislatures and city councils may only cut out or decrease items in the executive budget but may not increase the funds allocated to any activity. The more standard practice, however, is one in which the legislature receives only the chief executive's estimates and may revise such figures upwards or downwards at their discretion.

Second, neither the legislature nor the city council is likely to undertake a thorough reshaping of the budget presented them. They have neither the time nor the expertise. State legislatures commonly work within a controlled time frame and have only limited staff assistance. City councilmen usually have other employment and discharge their public responsibilities in their after-hours time. Still, the executive's budget does not usually escape unscathed. Individual budget items will attract the attention of some who feel the sums allotted are either too great or too small. If in a budget-cutting mood, the legislature may round figures or reduce all or some types of expenditures by a specified percentage. The attack on the budget, however, will usually be piecemeal. Indeed, in most states and larger cities the budget will be "marked up" in subcommittees which work independently of each other. What emerges will not always meet with the mayor's or the governor's approval, but usually his budget is the point of departure for any changes made.

Third, the ability of the governor or mayor to retain the items he considers essential for his program goals depends upon the skill with which he employs the political resources available to him. In this regard, the tactics of the chief executive differ little from those employed in other struggles with the legislature. He trades on his party affiliation, the strength of his support among the general and special publics, and his relations with key legislative figures, and he calculates carefully which programs are worth the conflict entailed. One will naturally find much variation among chief executives in the efforts and skills that are employed.

If there is a common thread running through our discussion of state and local finances, it is that general constraints exist on the amount of money a state or city spends and the purposes for which the expenditures are made. The revenue resources available in a state are probably the single most important factors determining the amount of money a state and its cities spend. The pattern of expenditures in the past is probably the greatest influence on how expenditures will be spent in the future. Even the mechanics of the budgetary process are likely to inhibit a thoroughgoing review of budgetary allocations. It is these constraints, together with the political interests identified with the existing pattern of state finances, that must be confronted by political actors who would change the direction of public policies.

It would be a mistake, of course, to dismiss the incremental changes that do occur in the funding of particular programs. They are the real stuff of political battles and over the long run might be quite significant in determining the path governments are to take. And it is in the incremental rather than sweeping changes of public policy that political actors such as governors and mayors can leave their mark by the skillful use of their resources.

14. THE POLITICS
OF PUBLIC
EDUCATION

Educating the American student population is a costly undertaking. For the school year ending in 1968, $54.6 billion, almost 7 percent of the gross national product, was spent on education by public and private school, college, and university systems. The lion's share of educational expenditures, more than three fourths of total costs, was borne by publicly controlled systems. State and local governments contributed slightly less than 65 percent of total educational costs, making them the largest educational entrepreneurs.

Any realistic consideration of educational expenditures must lead to the conclusion that so costly a governmental activity cannot be divorced from politics. No political leader can be unmindful of the educational system when he knows that its support substantially affects the taxes paid by his constituents. The attitude of some educators that the educational function somehow should be above politics is unrealistic for two reasons. In the first place, the plea of the educator does not mean that he wishes education to be free of politics; it simply means that he wishes the educational function to be controlled by a different set of political leaders, either the professional educators themselves or a lay board which acts publicly for their interests. In this endeavor they have been successful in many communities.

But the conventional educators are unrealistic from a second point of view. They cannot escape the fact that they must compete in the political market place for the allocation of the tax dollar. Isolation of the educational function from the more normal political and administrative controls may protect the decisional authority of the professional educator in internal school matters, but it cannot protect him from decisions compelled by an inadequate budget. Indeed, the superintendent who does not have a grasp of political processes may be a feeble competitor for scarce tax dollars. As one perceptive educator has written:[1]

> The irony of the attitude that power-wielders should not be involved [in education] is that these people are already involved in the deciding of educational projects. Everytime they get together at a downtown office and "lop off" the school budget, they kill the hopes the teachers had for making the school curriculum more comprehensive. Consequently, it is not, realistically speaking, a matter of involvement; it is a matter of appropriate involvement.

At the same time, one must understand that education occupies a somewhat privileged position in American society. As far back as the seventeenth century in some colonial legislatures and generally by the middle of the nineteenth century, education was recognized as a public responsibility. Its contribution to economic development has been particularly valued by a nation aspiring to economic preeminence. Perhaps the assertion by the Educational Policies Commission of the National Education Association (NEA) that "schools, more than natural resources, are the basis of prosperity" is a bit strong, but it suggests the peculiar emphasis placed on education by a middle-class society. Any wonder, then, why educators feel that isolating education from other governmental programs is a wise course to follow? It is a necessary governmental function which, they believe, must be supported adequately. Yet

[1] Ralph B. Kimbrough, *Political Power and Educational Decision-Making* (Chicago: Rand McNally, 1964), pp. 288–289.

what is an adequate educational budget when there are mounting demands upon government to solve other problems brought on by a burgeoning population in an urban, industrial society is a matter of no little disagreement. This is the crux of the matter. Educational groups can no longer rely simply on the symbolic and practical value of education as a means for obtaining funds. They must actively compete for their share of the tax dollar with a realistic understanding of the play of politics.

THE POLITICAL STRUCTURE
OF PUBLIC SCHOOLS

The basic unit of public elementary and secondary school systems almost from their inception has been and remains today the local school district. Although the term "school district" encompasses a variety of types, it conventionally describes an administrative unit in which control is vested in a locally elected lay board that is empowered to levy and appropriate tax money and appoint a superintendent to act as its chief executive officer. Such a school district is a separate administrative unit and legally a limited purpose local government and is to be distinguished from the "school district" that is nothing more than an attendance unit— that is, a geographic area serviced by a given school for the purposes of distributing the school population. In some cases, the school district is coterminous with other governmental units but remains largely independent of them. Thus, in the South, the county is the primary unit of administration but schools are usually not a part of the general county government.

The pattern of school administration exemplifies two values strongly held by broad segments of the lay public: local control of educational policies and program and independence from other political units. The underlying philosophy of the school's organizational arrangement has become so ingrained in the American political and social tradition that administrative reform faces formidable obstacles. The one activity of school boards most likely to be circumscribed is that of school finances. In many urban jurisdictions an agency independent of the school system holds authority over the rate of the school levy or the size of the school budget.

In some states an intermediate unit of school administration exists between the local school board and the state agencies. Begun as an adjunct of the state agencies, the principal responsibility of the unit (commonly located at the county level, its head referred to as the "county superintendency") was to supervise and assist weaker school districts within its jurisdiction. With the strengthening of school districts through consolidation, the traditional role of the intermediate district has withered.

The most formidable challenge to local control of educational policy comes not from intermediate school units but from state educational agencies. Prompted by revenue from land grants and other state monies for public education, the states began to set up boards to supervise the disbursement of funds to local districts in the second quarter of the nineteenth century. From this outgrowth there have developed state boards or departments of education in all but three states—Michigan, Illinois, and Wisconsin. Initially the state board served chiefly as a gatherer and clearing house of information and remained so until about 1900. Gradually, the state agency began to exercise more positive powers, inspecting and supervising local systems for comformity with state laws—compulsory attendance, curriculum, and teacher requirements. At some time around 1930, the state departments began to exercise leadership to upgrade state educational systems. From that date the size and professional character of state departments have improved spectacularly. Today state agencies have the power to formulate policies and issue regulations that implement the constitutional and statutory provisions covering public education. Commonly these include:

Type and rate of local tax levies

Minimum qualifications of teachers

Minimum salaries to be paid teachers

Number of grades and types of schools

General content of curricula

Number of school days

Size and design of school buildings

Size of equalization grants to local systems

The growth in state influence does not mean that the school systems of a state are of a uniform quality. Most state policies (salaries, curricula, teacher qualifications) set only minimum standards and leave much flexibility to the school districts with a strong tax base to go well beyond state requirements. Yet the evidence of an enlarged state role is dramatically seen in the assumption by the state of an increasingly greater share (almost 41 percent in 1968–1969) of educational costs in the public schools. With the leverage of the equalization grants, state school officials have also succeeded in eliminating many uneconomical and educationally unsound school districts through consolidation. The number of school districts abandoned since 1940 is a spectacular 80 percent, although there remains a scattering of one-teacher elementary schools. The extent to which state officials have succeeded in centralizing educational adminis-tration, of course, varies among the states. The evidence suggests that the school systems of the less economically advanced states depend more heavily on state aid and, as a partial consequence, are more susceptible to state influences. The more well-to-do states and school districts have less need for state aid and fewer incentives to compromise local autonomy.

If one leaves aside for the moment the question of finances, it might be argued that the central administrative issue should not be framed in terms of whether control is local, but whether there is lay control over the professional educators. The professional has been identified by Thomas H. Eliot as (1) the school teachers, organized into the National Educa-tional Association and, more recently, into teacher unions; (2) the in-structional staff at state teachers' colleges and university departments of education; and (3) the school administrators, with the superintendent the kingpin of the district school organization.[2] Eliot suggests that the professionalization of the several elements of the school system may signify the existence of national standards adhered to by each. If this is the case, then, there may be more in common between state and local educators than between educators at any level and lay groups, including other political actors in the system.

The thrust of the thinking of those with specialized training in teach-ing and educational administration is that the lay public should not "interfere" with the educational system. But where should the line be drawn? Even so able an educator as James B. Conant became entrapped in the policy-administration dichotomy when he suggested that lay school boards should concern themselves with policy not administration and, further, should keep hands off of curricular affairs.[3] Students of public administration long ago realized that policy-making and administration were inextricably intertwined and that no administrator can suggest at what point in the discharge of his responsibilities policies emerge. And what could be closer to the heart of educational policy-making than questions of curriculum? Most professional educators held to the view, at least privately, that "the school board's primary functions, aside from directing the district's business affairs, are to hire and support a com-petent professional as superintendent, defend the school against public criticism, and persuade the people to open their pocketbook."[4]

The fact of the matter is that professional educators have generally

2 Thomas H. Eliot, "Understanding of Public School Politics," *American Political Science Review,* LIII (December, 1959), 1033–1034.
3 *Ibid.,* p. 1032.
4 *Ibid.,* p. 1033.

resisted what in effect constitutes the most serious threat to their control—the subordination of the educational system to a general (county or city) government. Independence has been achieved under the guise of freeing education from "political" control. Of course we are dealing here with semantical matters. What politics signifies to most is partisan politics, or more precisely, political favoritism. Defined in its most sterile way as the authoritative allocation of values in society, it is quite obvious that the debate is not over freeing education from politics but, as we suggested earlier, of locating the agency responsible for making political decisions affecting the educational function. The semantic distortion of the controversy leaves the professionals in an excellent vantage point to pursue their interests as they see them.

The professional educators, of course, do not have unlimited discretion in shaping the educational system to their tastes. They must still work within acceptable bounds of the political system. This was shown clearly in a study of educational decision-making in three midwestern states "to determine how and by whom power was exercised."[5] Seldom did educational issues arising in the state legislature come there as a consequence of demands of a general public. On the contrary, concern among important segments of the public were important only insofar as educational groups were able to utilize it in laying out their claims. Yet although the demands were articulated by professional educational groups, there was no certainty they would be acceded to by governor, legislature, or other agency of general control. The authors concluded that[6]

> there is in each state a subtle pyramiding of power *in terms of who articulates the demands.* This power lies predominantly in the hands of the official spokesmen for the organized interests, the professionals who are limited only by what the political system will allow or (just as importantly) by what they think it will allow. Exclusively lay interests have little to say about what is needed, although they may have a great deal to say about what is finally gotten.

ISSUES IN THE PUBLIC SCHOOLS

There exist no organized antischool groups. Such an endeavor would be preposterous on the face of it. But this is not to say that issues do not arise from time to time that unleash strong counterpressures to those of the professional educational groups. These may be classified broadly as

[5] Nicholas A. Masters, Robert H. Salisbury, and Thomas H. Eliot, *State Politics and the Public Schools* (New York: Knopf, 1964), p. 261. The states studied were Illinois, Michigan, and Missouri.
[6] *Ibid.*, p. 270.

either perennial or episodic.[7] Those that are episodic relate to questions of curriculum, district organization plans, professional leadership of the schools, or like subjects. Under a special set of circumstances any one of these matters could become an explosive issue but typically are dormant. The one issue that continually recurs is that of school finances.

Traditional questions of curriculum concern its adequacy measured against the needs of contemporary society. Following the Sputnik triumph of the Soviets in the late fifties, school boards found support for increased emphasis on science and mathematics. When *Why Johnny Can't Read* received a wide audience, professional educators were placed on the defensive in justifying the use of the sight method in teaching beginning readers. From time to time the choice of required reading by an English teacher causes shock among those who do not perceive a distinction between smut and literature. More recently, urban schools have been under citizen pressure to correct the sad neglect of Negro history and culture in their curricula. Other than the minimum requirements set by state agencies, these questions are decided at the local level and not infrequently involve a struggle between lay groups and professional educators who jealously guard what they feel are their special areas of competence.

Questions of district organization, apart from their fiscal implications to capital construction and the economies of size, are related to the convenience or safety of school children in getting to the school facility. Actually, the two sets of issues are necessarily related. Questions over the size of a district organization arise because professional educators believe, for example, that a truly good small high school is prohibitively costly. School district consolidation, they believe, is the more efficient policy to pursue. Yet this inevitably means that children in some neighborhoods will have farther to travel to and from school and that the consolidated high school will have to be located in one community rather than the other, with all that this means to local pride.

The professional leadership of the schools may be at stake in school board elections inasmuch as the board has the power of appointment and removal of the school superintendent. The retention of the superintendent or, in unusual circumstances, the retention of controversial members of the teaching staff may hinge on the outcome of the election contests. Indeed, election politics can cut across most basic issues of educational policy. Has the superintendent been backward in educational reform? Has an aggressive building policy raised the tax levy to an uncomfortable level? Has the designation of attendance units caused racial reverberations? Are the students performing satisfactorily in nationally standard-

[7] Jesse Burkhead, *Public School Finance* (Syracuse: Syracuse University Press, 1964), pp. 143–144.

ized achievement tests? These are the questions that emerge from time to time in school board races.

The one issue that has traditionally cut across all others is that of school finances. Good schools—those with acceptable pupil-teacher ratios, adequate specialized training and counseling, satisfactory athletic and other extracurricular facilities, and competitive if not generous salaries—cost money. Other factors affecting the quality of a school might involve questions of educational policy over which professionals disagree; but the issue normally obtains a level of public significance when it reaches the citizen through his pocketbook. Indeed, there is some evidence that the populace is stiffening its resolve to resist increased educational costs. The saga of Youngstown, Ohio, may not be typical, but it does suggest the extremes to which the taxpayer's revolt may be taken. Following the defeat of six school levies by the voters between December, 1966, and the fall of 1968, the superintendent closed the public schools after the Thanksgiving recess because he had run out of money.

The willingness of school districts to spend money in educating school children is not alone a question of school district politics. If this were the case, one would expect that educational expenditures would follow no predictable pattern, since the outcome of fiscal struggles would depend upon the skill and resources of the contestants in each of the districts. Yet expenditures for education do fall into a pattern, which suggests that district politics are to an extent circumscribed by external conditions.

If one starts with the assumption that a good education is highly valued in American society, the patterns found among the states in school expenditures are more understandable. Because education is looked upon as a resource of economic development generally, and personal fortunes individually, most states are willing to accord educational expenditures some priority. This means that the more prosperous states will spend more on education simply because they have greater resources (compare columns 1 and 2 of Table 14.1).

At the same time, even the relatively economically disadvantaged states will show a strong effort to provide an acceptable educational program for its children. Thus the percentage of personal income within the state they devote to educational costs frequently is greater than that of more prosperous states (compare columns 1 and 3 of Table 14.1). Only nine states that ranked below the national average in per capita income were also below the national average in terms of educational "effort"—that is, the percentage of personal income devoted to education.

The linkage of personal income and school expenditures raises an issue of the basic significance of education to American society. Can equality of opportunity be a realistic goal of our society if the quality of education offered a citizen depends upon the affluence of the school district in

TABLE 14.1

A Comparison of State Rankings in Per Capita Personal Income and per Pupil Expenditures

PER CAPITA PERSONAL INCOME, 1967		
1.	Connecticut	$3969
2.	New York	3759
3.	Illinois	3750
4.	Alaska (29;$2,804)	3738a
5.	New Jersey	3668
6.	California	3665
7.	Delaware	3642
8.	Nevada	3583
9.	Massachusetts	3541
10.	Washington	3521
11.	Maryland	3421
12.	Michigan	3396
13.	Hawaii	3331
14.	Rhode Island	3328
15.	Ohio	3213
16.	Indiana	3196
17.	Pennsylvania	3187
	United States	3159
18.	Wisconsin	3156
19.	Colorado	3135
20.	Minnesota	3116
21.	Iowa	3109

PER PUPIL EXPENDITURES, 1968–69		
1.	New York	$1140
2.	Alaska (11;$740)	987a
3.	New Jersey	913
4.	Connecticut	826
5.	Oregon	793
6.	Wisconsin	787
7.	Maryland	775
8.	Rhode Island	756
9.	Delaware	745
10.	Pennsylvania	743
11.	Illinois	742
12.	Wyoming	715
13.	Iowa	707
14.	Arizona	698
15.	California	697
16.	Montana	696
17.	Nevada	685
18.	Minnesota	684
	United States	680
19.	Hawaii	677
20.	Massachusetts	673
	Washington	673
22.	Michigan	665

CURRENT EXPENDITURES AS PERCENT OF PERSONAL INCOME		
1.	Alaska	8.0%
2.	New Mexico	7.4
3.	Wyoming	7.0
4.	Utah	6.9
5.	Montana	6.6
6.	Arizona	6.2
	Minnesota	6.2
	North Dakota	6.2
	Oregon	6.2
10.	Louisiana	6.1
11.	Nevada	6.0
12.	Delaware	5.9
13.	Arkansas	5.7
	Maryland	5.7
	Washington	5.7
16.	Idaho	5.6
	Mississippi	5.6
	South Carolina	5.6
19.	California	5.5
	Colorado	5.5
	Iowa	5.5
	South Dakota	5.5
	Vermont	5.5
	Wisconsin	5.5

22.	Nebraska	$3081				
23.	Oregon	3063	23.	Colorado	661	
24.	Kansas	3060	24.	Vermont	660	
25.	New Hampshire	3053	25.	Florida	647	
26.	Wyoming	3002		Kansas	647	
27.	Missouri	2993	27.	Indiana	640	
28.	Florida	2853	28.	Ohio	634	
29.	Vermont	2825	29.	Louisiana	632	
30.	Virginia	2804	30.	New Hampshire	624	
31.	Montana	2765	31.	Missouri	619	
32.	Texas	2744	32.	New Mexico	611	
33.	Arizona	2720	33.	Virginia	600	
34.	Maine	2657	34.	North Dakota	585	
35.	Oklahoma	2643	35.	South Dakota	552	
36.	Utah	2604	36.	Maine	547	
37.	South Dakota	2590	37.	Idaho	545	
38.	Idaho	2575	38.	Kentucky	535	
39.	Georgia	2541	39.	Georgia	530	
40.	North Dakota	2487	40.	Utah	527	
41.	New Mexico	2477	41.	West Virginia	521	
42.	Louisiana	2456	42.	Nebraska	510	
43.	North Carolina	2439	43.	North Carolina	506	
44.	Kentucky	2426	44.	Oklahoma	496	
45.	Tennessee	2394	45.	Arkansas	486	
46.	West Virginia	2334	46.	Tennessee	485	
47.	South Carolina	2213	47.	Texas	480	
48.	Alabama	2163	48.	South Carolina	478	
49.	Arkansas	2099	49.	Mississippi	465	
50.	Mississippi	1896	50.	Alabama	380	

25.	Hawaii	5.4
	New York	5.4
	West Virginia	5.4
28.	Florida	5.2
	Michigan	5.2
	North Carolina	5.2
	Virginia	5.2
32.	Kansas	5.1
	Maine	5.1
	United States	5.1
34.	Indiana	5.0
	New Jersey	5.0
	Tennessee	5.0
37.	Georgia	4.9
38.	Texas	4.8
39.	Missouri	4.7
	Pennsylvania	4.7
41.	Ohio	4.6
	Oklahoma	4.6
43.	Nebraska	4.5
44.	Alabama	4.4
	New Hampshire	4.4
46.	Kentucky	4.3
47.	Connecticut	4.2
	Illinois	4.2
49.	Rhode Island	4.1
50.	Massachusetts	3.9

a All dollar amounts for Alaska should be reduced by one fourth to make the purchasing power of Alaska figures comparable to figures reported for other areas of the United States. The adjusted figure and rank for Alaska are given in parentheses.
SOURCE: National Education Association, *Rankings of the States*, 1969, pp. 32 and 60.

which he resides? Some of the disparities that exist among school systems—for example, between well-to-do suburbs and central cities—can be partially overcome by more realistic state aid formulas. But given the variations in taxable wealth among the states, a satisfactory solution to educational inequality will probably require a greater national effort. Local revenue sources still provide for slightly over half of educational expenditures and much of the balance is provided by state funds. The federal contribution, doubled after passage of the Elementary and Secondary Education Act of 1965, has risen to only 8 percent of public school costs.

The 1965 act nevertheless represents a major breakthrough for proponents of national assistance. Three obstacles were surmounted: (1) the fear that national aid would mean national control; (2) the belief that grant money would be used to speed school integration; (3) the dispute over whether national aid should go to school children enrolled in parochial schools. Taking advantage of his impressive plurality in 1964 and pursuing his "war on poverty," President Johnson obtained congressional approval for direct aid to school districts serving economically deprived school children. Although the Act's funds have bolstered school systems in depressed areas (the federal share of school costs in Mississippi was 23 percent in 1968), marked disparities remain among the states. The door has been opened, but yet only slightly.

THE SPECIAL CASE OF RACIAL INTEGRATION

If any issue has wracked the public educational system in recent years, it has been over providing equal educational opportunities for Negroes. Beginning with the historic decision in *Brown* v. *Board of Education of Topeka*[8] in 1954, progress toward integration of public schools has been painfully slow in the South and has presented vexing problems elsewhere.

At the time the Brown decision was handed down, segregated public schools were maintained in 17 southern and border states and the District of Columbia and was a matter of local option in four additional states. No firm date for compliance with the Court's mandate was set, although "all deliberate speed" was required. The District of Columbia, urged by President Eisenhower to make practices there a model for the nation, led the way and quickly abandoned its dual system. Progress followed next in the border states, through a variety of schemes that would ease the transition to an integrated system. But in the deep South states of the Confederacy, resistance not compliance became the order of the day.

8   347 U.S. 483 (1954).

Taking advantage of the absence of a specific timetable to desegregate the public schools, most southern school districts awaited court orders before undertaking first steps. Because of the number of districts in the South, and the time consumed in litigation, inaction served well southern objectives of delay. The leadership in some southern states was more aggressive. Governor Faubus of Arkansas called out the national guard to prevent the enrollment of Negro students in a Little Rock high school. Elsewhere members of White Citizens Councils and Klansmen joined with others in sometimes violent demonstrations as a handful of Negro school children entered a white school for the first time. In more genteel Virginia, the state provided tuition grants for students attending private schools, a device thinly disguised to continue segregated conditions through "private" education.

That the South would resist the court order was entirely predictable. A region does not shrug off easily its cultural and social traditions. Yet we seemingly have come to an end of the first phase of the school integration controversy. As of this writing (early 1970), the Court has invalidated one by one the state laws that have sought a legally acceptable plan to avoid the court mandate. In its October term of 1969, the Court bluntly told Mississippi officials that the time had come to integrate the public schools immediately.[9] Table 14.2 shows the progress made eleven years after the Court ordered all deliberate speed in ending separate educational facilities for Negro and white school children.

Phase two of the segregation controversy concerns the extent to which both social and economic conditions have provided a means to evade the court doctrine. School attendance units in American education have long been based on the neighborhood concept. At the same time, segregated housing patterns place Negroes together in their own neighborhoods, and whites together in different neighborhoods. As a consequence, a majority of Negroes find themselves still attending schools with a predominantly Negro enrollment even in northern cities, as Table 14.3 shows.

Although a Negro's educational achievement, as indeed any student's educational achievement, is influenced by his home and neighborhood environment (which affects his motivations and aspirations and his exposure to verbal and other experiences which improve conceptual facilities), some evidence suggests that Negroes of similar background attending predominantly white schools achieve better than Negroes attending predominantly black schools.[10] Herein lie the reasons why civil rights advocates stress the necessity of overcoming *de facto* segregation. Yet plans devised to achieve racial balance by merging attendance units

[9] *Alexander* v. *Holmes County*, 24 L. Ed. 2d 19.
[10] Office of Education, *Survey on Equality of Educational Opportunity* (Washington, D.C.: U.S. Government Printing Office, 1966), vol. 1, p. 22.

TABLE 14.2
Public School Desegregation (Negro Pupils Attending School with White Pupils as of December 9, 1966)

	NEGRO PUPILS ATTENDING SCHOOLS LESS THAN 95% NEGRO		NEGRO PUPILS ATTENDING SCHOOLS 95 TO 99.9% NEGRO		NEGRO PUPILS ATTENDING SCHOOLS 100% NEGRO	
	PERCENTAGE	NUMBER	PERCENTAGE	NUMBER	PERCENTAGE	NUMBER
Total 17 states	17.3%	589,620	7.1%	239,770	75.6%	2,571,540
Southern states	12.5	363,290	4.4	126,160	83.1	2,410,000
Alabama	2.4	6,570	2.3	6,300	95.3	260,900
Arkansas	14.5	17,140	2.1	2,480	83.4	98,650
Florida	14.7	41,120	6.1	17,060	79.2	221,550
Georgia	6.6	22,610	3.3	11,300	90.1	308,450
Louisiana	2.6	6,850	.9	2,370	96.5	254,050
Mississippi	2.6	6,840	.6	1,580	96.8	254,700
North Carolina	12.8	44,850	2.8	9,810	84.4	295,650
South Carolina	4.9	12,120	1.1	2,720	94.0	232,550
Tennessee	21.9	40,600	9.8	18,170	68.3	126,550
Texas	34.6	117,050	12.7	42,960	52.7	178,250
Virginia	20.0	47,540	4.8	11,410	75.2	178,700
Border states	45.1	226,330	22.7	113,610	32.2	161,540
Delaware	84.8	20,440	15.2	3,660	0	0
Kentucky	88.5	38,230	0	0	11.5	4,980
Maryland	40.5	88,980	23.5	51,630	36.0	79,150
Missouri	26.7	34,710	37.5	48,750	35.8	46,540
Oklahoma	40.5	24,950	15.2	9,360	44.3	27,290
West Virginia	83.4	19,020	.9	210	15.7	3,580

SOURCE: *Congressional Quarterly Almanac, Eighty-ninth Congress, 2nd Session, Vol. XXII, 1966, p. 478.*

TABLE 14.3
*Extent of Elementary School Segregation
in Selected Nonsouthern School Systems*

CITY	PERCENTAGE OF NEGROES IN 90 TO 100% NEGRO SCHOOLS	PERCENTAGE OF NEGROES IN MAJORITY NEGRO SCHOOLS	PERCENTAGE OF WHITES IN 90 TO 100% WHITE SCHOOLS
Los Angeles, Calif.	39.5	87.5	94.7
San Diego, Calif.	13.9	73.3	88.7
San Francisco, Calif.	21.1	72.3	65.1
Denver, Colo.	29.4	75.2	95.5
Chicago, Ill.	89.2	96.9	88.8
Gary, Ind.	89.9	94.8	75.9
Baltimore, Md.	84.2	92.3	67.0
Boston, Mass.	35.4	79.5	76.5
Detroit, Mich.	72.3	91.5	65.0
Minneapolis, Minn.	None	39.2	84.9
St. Louis, Mo.	90.9	93.7	66.0
Omaha, Nebr.	47.7	81.1	89.0
Buffalo, N.Y.	77.0	88.7	81.1
New York City, N.Y.	20.7	55.5	56.8
Cincinnati, Ohio	49.4	88.0	63.3
Cleveland, Ohio	82.3	94.6	80.2
Columbus, Ohio	34.3	80.8	77.0
Portland, Oreg.	46.5	59.2	92.0
Philadelphia, Pa.	72.0	90.2	57.7
Pittsburgh, Pa.	49.5	82.8	62.3
Providence, R.I.	14.6	55.5	63.3
Seattle, Wash.	9.9	60.4	89.8
Milwaukee, Wis.	72.4	86.8	86.3
Washington, D.C.	90.4	99.3	34.3

SOURCE: U.S. Commission on Civil Rights, *Racial Isolation in the Public Schools* (Washington, D.C.: U.S. Government Printing Office, 1967), pp. 4–5.

or busing school children meet the opposition both of educators who revere the traditional school organization and white groups that resent further social change that is not court ordered.

The value of integrating the public schools is not accepted by all segments of the black community nor all advocates of black rights. Indeed, Negro leaders in some cities, notably New York, have attempted to gain control of their neighborhood schools under school decentralization plans. Their objective is to transform the educational curriculum to better serve the needs of ghetto dwellers. At the same time, the blacks want the schools staffed by those sympathetic to their aims. These objectives bring them squarely into confrontation with teachers who traditionally have resisted control from lay groups. In the case of New York City, the problem was exacerbated by the threat of firing or transferring unionized teachers and the racial overtones that emerged when black leaders were opposed by the predominantly Jewish teaching staffs.

There are no pat solutions to the problem of equalizing the Negro's educational opportunities. Indeed, the public school population of some cities has become so overwhelmingly black that racial balance cannot be achieved short of busing school children to suburban schools. Whether mixing school children of diverse backgrounds is pedagogically sound remains a contentious issue. It is our own belief that educational inequalities cannot be solved by simply focusing on the adequacy of public school systems in teaching black children the traditional school subjects. The causes of black underachievement must be attacked at its core, and that is found in the squalid conditions in which the Negro has lived in a society that has never been able to accept him as an equal.

THE PUBLIC ROLE
IN HIGHER EDUCATION

Although public colleges were established in the first few decades of the nineteenth century, legislative support was inadequate to establish them as distinctive institutions whose costs were more reasonable or curricula different from privately controlled colleges.[11] Following the Civil War, the press for reform in the traditional college system was symbolized by the passage of the 1862 Morrill Act. Public provisions for higher education no longer had as their purpose the support of colleges for the education of the gentleman in philosophy, languages, and the classics, but was directed increasingly at training in the mechanical and agricultural arts and other practical fields that would equip the young for a place in the country's economic life. Even those public institutions not benefited by the Morrill Act were subject to the same forces at work. Thus the distinction grew between the public and the private colleges, culminating by World War II in the following characterization by Christopher Jencks and David Riesman:[12]

• • •

The public sector had subordinated the old liberal arts rhetoric to a new vocabulary which stressed job training and social progress. It was devoting

[11] Christopher Jencks and David Riesman, *The Academic Revolution* (Garden City: Doubleday, 1968), p. 258.
[12] *Ibid.*, p. 267.

the bulk of its resources to terminal undergraduate curricula geared to the real and imagined needs of employers. Its graduate programs were, with a few important exceptions, upward extensions of those undergraduate curricula. The private sector, on the other hand, had clung somewhat more tenaciously to the old liberal arts, reorganizing them in such a way as to make them mainly pregraduate subjects.

• • •

A distinctively public role in higher education, insofar as curricular objectives are concerned, has diminished in the years since World War II. Just as the pre-World War II differences were attributable in part to the different sources of support for public and private institutions (the public college or university depending upon tax monies, the private schools relying on private gifts and tuition), the tendencies toward similarity also have been due to financial reasons. The influential factor has been the substantial role played by the national government in funding higher education. (See Table 14.4.) The federal largesse has been directed mainly at graduate education and research activities. Thus the better state universities have been able to keep pace with the better private institutions despite the traditional emphasis of state schools on undergraduate training. Indeed, the federal grants perhaps have caused the state legislator of today to view with greater charity the graduate professionalism and scholarship of his state university.

The universities which have benefited most from federal grants are a minority of the total number of colleges and universities. Nevertheless, they are the better institutions of the country whose faculty play an elite role in the professional associations of academic disciplines and tend to produce uniformities within teaching areas of all schools, public and private.

Indeed, if the public institutions of higher learning serve a distinctive purpose today, it is found in an educational philosophy of extending upward the policy of free public schooling. College enrollment has tripled since the early 1950s, and over two thirds of the students attend publicly controlled institutions. The growth has not been due simply to an increase in college age youth but reflects as well a broadened awareness of the advantages of college training. In 1951, only 24 percent of persons aged 18 to 21 were in college; in 1967, that percentage had swelled to 47.

To provide space for those seeking admission, existing institutions have expanded their staff and facilities; the state university has created additional branches; teacher training institutions have been transformed into full-fledged colleges or universities; and two-year colleges have been established to offer both preparatory and terminal curricula. With over 500 established in the past ten years, the development of two-year institu-

TABLE 14.4
Current-Fund Income of Institutions of Higher Education, 1963–1964
(amounts in thousands of dollars)

| | CURRENT-FUND INCOME, BY CONTROL OF INSTITUTION | | | | | |
| | PUBLIC AND PRIVATE | | PUBLIC | | PRIVATE | |
SOURCE	AMOUNT	PERCENT	AMOUNT	PERCENT	AMOUNT	PERCENT
Total current-fund income[a]	$9,591,330	100.0	$5,368,679	100.0	$4,222,651	100.0
Educational and general income	7,830,033	81.6	4,396,869	81.9	3,433,164	81.3
Tuition and fees from students	1,899,455	19.8	582,865	10.9	1,316,589	31.2
Federal Government	2,170,749	22.6	1,053,794	19.6	1,116,955	26.5
Research	1,797,095	18.7	754,450	14.1	1,042,645	24.7
Other Federal income	373,654	3.9	299,344	5.6	74,310	1.8
State governments	2,133,665	22.2	2,077,724	38.7	55,941	1.3
Local governments	240,355	2.5	230,404	4.3	9,950	.2
Endowment earnings	266,214	2.8	27,443	.5	238,770	5.7
Private gifts and grants	551,507	5.8	113,857	2.1	437,650	10.4
Other educational and general income	568,088	5.9	310,780	5.8	257,309	6.1
Auxiliary enterprise income	1,610,426	16.8	906,358	16.9	704,068	16.7
Student-aid income	150,871	1.6	65,453	1.2	85,419	2.0

[a] Because of rounding, detail may not add to totals.

SOURCE: U.S. Office of Education, *Digest of Educational Statistics, 1968* (Washington, D.C.: U.S. Government Printing Office, 1968), p. 90.

tions has been the most striking trend in the move to expand college facilities. The quality of education they offer is suspect in the eyes of some in the academic profession.[13] Yet the preparatory curriculum they offer is modeled along the lines of four-year institutions where many of their graduates go.

The fact of relatively cheap education offered at public institutions is one of the more important characteristics, other than the religious affiliations of some private schools, that tend to distinguish the student bodies of public from private institutions. Tuition costs at private schools, except those with generous scholarship allowances, restrict enrollment to students from financially secure families. Schooling at public institutions is less expensive and this contributes to their democratic image. Quite apart from the costs involved, children of working- and lower-class families apparently believe that they will be socially and intellectually more comfortable in a public institution. At the same time, public institutions attract a variegated student body if, for no other reasons, than that in many regions of the country they offer the most distinguished instruction.

THE POLITICAL STRUCTURE
OF PUBLIC HIGHER EDUCATION

Control of public higher education in America has struck a balance between European models of either vesting control in a state ministry of education (France) or vesting administrative control in the faculty (England).[14] A lay board commonly has legal power over university administration which insures a certain autonomy of operations without escaping entirely public accountability to the governor and legislature. The university or college and its regents are thus a part of state government but not under the same supervisory relationship as other operating departments.

The structure of formal control has undergone change in recent years. At one time it was typical to place each public institution of higher learning under its own board of control. More recently there has been an attempt to achieve some structural coordination within a state's higher educational system. As early as 1909, all state supported institutions in Iowa were placed under a single nine-member board of education. At least a dozen states have adopted a comparable plan. Some states have placed the university system under a president with chancellors serving at each of its campus centers, while the control of other state institutions

---

13 *Ibid.*, p. 482.
14 Theodore Mitau, *State and Local Government: Politics and Process* (New York: Scribner's, 1966), p. 440.

are separately directed. Still other states have adopted coordinating councils and interuniversity committees to avoid duplication of educational services and provide a clearer perspective of over-all educational resources.

Although control of the public university or college is vested in lay boards whose legal powers are rather sweeping, many familiar with the administration of contemporary higher education believe their powers to be exaggerated. In the first place, faculty groups commonly have effective control over academic appointments, tenure, curricula, and admission policies. Student groups have attacked with increasing success an older institutional practice of acting in *loco parentis* and now govern their codes of social behavior. The university president has, of necessity, assumed responsibility for keeping the peace among the contending and sometimes contentious interests of the university while at the same time devoting considerable energies to securing federal and foundation grants and insuring legislative support. Although the trustees are active in selecting a new president, their most important administrative task, and although student unrest and legislative threats at retaliation are occupying their time, their role in governing institutional affairs remains marginal.

Yet to describe the political structure of higher education today by focusing on its formal governance or even the informal sources of influence within the university structure is inadequate. If the sole or primary mission of the university were to teach students, then we might profitably focus on the interrelationships of students, faculty, administration, regents, and agencies of general governmental control. But today's universities, both public and private, have an inescapable, additional role thrust upon them in providing and interpreting the theoretical knowledge essential for an urban, technological society. Scholars are called upon to testify, consult, and advise both government and business on a wide range of topics within their professional competence. Some shuttle back and forth between university positions and government and business employment. The most distinguished universities, public and private, have almost inexorably been sucked into a troika involving their scholars, defense-related governmental agencies, and corporate business. It is no accident that government contracts are often awarded business enterprises that cluster about the most prestigious educational institutions.

The university has been caught in the web of forces, technological, economic, and social, that have caused a strain in the network of societal relations generally. Less a conscious decision on the part of governing boards, administrative staffs, and faculties than an unconscious drift which some believe has compromised the university's intellectual independence, university resources have been called upon to help solve problems facing government and business without a critical appraisal of where such a policy leads. The radical left's charge of a conspiracy among universities, the defense establishment, and corporate business at least has caused a self-examination among some within the university community. Such an examination must uncover the interests, external and semiexternal, that have a stake in university affairs and constitute a part of its political structure.

ISSUES IN PUBLIC HIGHER EDUCATION

Much of what we might say about the political issues in higher education has already been covered in our discussion of the public schools. Insofar as the general governmental control over the regents and the university are concerned, the perennial issue is that of finances. The administrative and teaching staffs would prefer to deal with a generous legislature that would accede to their budgetary demands without questioning their instructional and research activities. But the realities of state finances dictate otherwise. Expressed in terms of 1967–1968 dollars, total expenditures by public higher educational institutions increased from $3.9 billion in 1957–1958 to $11.2 billion in 1967–1968. So costly a program must receive careful scrutiny by budgetary officials and state legislators who are confronted by equally insistent claimants for other state needs.

From time to time, a state legislature may delve into internal university affairs by inquiring into curriculum or personnel matters amid cries from the teaching faculties of meddling, witch hunt, or invasion of academic freedom. But such occasions are more episodic than not. There are, however, two contemporary problems confronting today's universities that deserve special treatment and they are discussed in the following paragraphs.

Federal Grants and Federal Influence

American public higher education has been enormously influenced by federal action taken in response to national needs. The first was the Morrill Act which gave the state university the distinctive role discussed previously. The second emerged with the scientific grants made to universities during World War II and which have continued since.[15] With-

15 Clark Kerr, *The Uses of the University* (Cambridge: Harvard University Press, 1963), p. 48. Many of the ideas in this section are taken from Kerr's perceptive analysis.

out conscious planning, the federal government, through its grants, has shaped the character of the leading universities of the country, both public and private.

Grants to colleges and universities have been made principally in the physical and biomedical sciences and almost negligible contributions have been made to the humanities. Grant policy has had the effect of creating a preferred class at the university—the professor who has more time and better facilities for research than his less fortunate colleagues in the humanities. There is some evidence that the funding is attracting the more able graduate students, which can have a long-range effect on comparative faculty talent between the "hard" sciences and the humanities.[16] The end result could be an unbalance in the quality and distribution of a university's arts and sciences offerings.

Federal funding has been used principally for research and for graduate rather than undergraduate instruction. The graduate student is not neglected by research grants because his instruction is tied so closely to research activities that it likely is improved. The same is not true of undergraduate teaching. The scholar with the research grant wants his time protected and oftentimes desires little exposure to the classroom, particularly that of undergraduates. Turning the classroom over to junior faculty members has little appeal to the undergraduate who feels his interests are being neglected.

All universities have not benefited equally from federal largesse. On the contrary, much of the money has been concentrated in a relatively few institutions. These institutions already are the ones turning out the largest number of PhDs. The impact of such a grant policy is that the good get better and, quite possibly, the weak get weaker, as they see their better scholars siphoned off by the stronger universities.

What is involved further in the matter of federal grants is the extent to which the university has lost its traditional academic independence and has entered into a partnership with the federal government. Academic research is often a costly undertaking which can be supported only by sizable grants from, among others, the very institutions about which the intellectual is supposed to be objectively critical. Higher educational resources are particularly significant in an advanced technological society and must play a major role in its continuance. Yet what is partly behind student protests on college campuses is the way in which the university has become involved in what the radical rhetoric suggests is support of the "military-industrial complex." Grants are simply the most visible way such alleged ties are expressed. If indeed the university has allowed itself to be shaped unthinkingly by external forces, it is a time for an agonizing reappraisal of the role it should play in American society.

[16] *Ibid.*, p. 61.

Student Protest

Perhaps there is no greater internal crisis facing institutions of higher learning today than the widespread student unrest which has swept the nation. It reflects a basic malaise at our institutions which inevitably must affect the morale of students, faculty, and administration alike and have profound effects upon the way in which the university performs its traditional tasks. The protests are not just a passing phenomena but increasingly involve more college campuses and more students. During the academic year 1968–1969, 145 institutions became embroiled in violent demonstrations and 379 others were disrupted by nonviolent protests.[17] Nor have the demonstrations ceased in intensity as witnessed by the outbreak of campus violence in 1970 that ultimately saw the tragic death of six college students (four at Ohio's rurally situated Kent State University and two at Mississippi's predominantly black Jackson State College).

Although one can point to the fact that violence and protest on American campuses were known in the past, they never before had the quality of such a sustained movement involving such large numbers. The immediate predecessor of the current movement was the civil rights activities of the 1950s, particularly the students, white and black, who joined together in organizations such as the Student Nonviolent Coordinating Committee to protest segregated conditions in the South. The demonstrations were essentially nonviolent and off campus. By early 1960, similar techniques were used to protest the Vietnam war, capped by the 1962 Washington Peace March. Yet the civil rights and war protest movements of the fifties and early sixties were basically different from the demonstrations that emerged later in the sixties. As described by a staff report to the National Commission on the Causes and Prevention of Violence:[18]

• • •

The two general phases of the movement—before and after 1965—may be viewed as follows: In phase one, the student movement embodied concern, dissent, and protest about various social issues, but it generally accepted the legitimacy of the American political community in general and especially of the university. . . .

In phase two of the student movement, a considerable number of young

[17] *Campus Tensions: Analysis and Recommendations,* Report of the Special Committee on Campus Tensions (Washington, D.C.: American Council on Education, 1970), p. 57.
[18] Jerome Skolnick, *The Politics of Protest,* Staff Report to the National Commission on the Causes and Prevention of Violence (Washington, D.C.: U.S. Government Printing Office, 1969), p. 76.

people, particularly the activist core, experienced a progressive deterioration in their acceptance of national and university authority.

. . .

Increasingly since 1965, student protests have constituted a conscious defiance of university authority, sometimes marked by violence and destruction of property. The inability of college administrations to control a disorder and the call for outside help from police or national guard has almost invariably resulted in violent confrontations. Although the tactics of such groups as the Students for a Democratic Society are often disclaimed by a majority in the student body, their activities seem increasingly expected if not "legitimatized." The strategy of confrontation has been adhered to by radical groups because they feel:[19]

1. Confrontation and militancy are methods of arousing moderates to action.

2. Confrontation and militancy can educate the public.

3. Confrontation, militancy, and resistance are ways to prepare young radicals for the possibility of greater repression.

4. Combative behavior with respect to the police and other authorities although possibly alienating "respectable" adults has the opposite effect on the movement's relationships with nonstudent youth.

5. The experience of resistance and combat may have a liberating effect on young middle-class radicals.

6. The political potency of "backlash" is usually exaggerated.

Parallel to the general student movement but remaining apart from it has been the activities of black student groups. Blacks have not generally identified with radical groups such as the Students for Democratic Society, although their tactics often have been as militant. At the same time, blacks seem more capable of utilizing their demonstrations to obtain specific objectives related to curricula and admission policies. The black student movement more than the white seems to be related to off-campus political forces, the activity of blacks merely a part of the more widespread protests in urban communities. It is because of the brutal social and economic condition of blacks generally that their movement constitutes a serious challenge to the moral authority of the university. Many believe that higher educational institutions have a special responsibility toward the black community. Thus to discipline black protestors who have violated university regulations is a very sensitive undertaking for most college administrations.

[19] *Ibid.*, pp. 81–82.

The problems confronting the universities at the start of a new decade are related to the erosion of authority generally in society. Yet the problems of the university in governing itself are unique. Few institutions are as ill-equipped to deal with the politics of confrontation. Nurtured in a tradition of civility and rational discussion, how do faculty and administration come to terms with the "nonnegotiable demand"? The fact is that governance of institutions of higher learning in general, and public institutions of higher learning in particular, has not been studied systematically. Yet because educational resources of a nation represent a significant national asset, how values are allocated in the university community must be of central concern to political scientists. Education too long has been sheltered by the notion that somehow it must be isolated from the mainstream of politics. Today it has been thrust into the mainstream and perhaps at a time when we have too little systematic knowledge of its governance. Political scientists and academicians from other disciplines must bring their skills of analysis to bear on the problems of the new politics at the university.

15. THE POLITICS OF LAW ENFORCEMENT

Few issues are more explosive today than law enforcement. Reported increases in major crimes, civil riots erupting in city ghettos, and student seizures of university buildings suggest to some the destruction of the America they once knew. Lawlessness and anarchy, they believe, have replaced law and order. Even the phrase "law and order" is interpreted by some as a euphemism to conceal racial bias or antagonism to today's youth or at least its "hippie" element. The press now refers to "law and order" mayoralty candidates to describe those who advocate a get-tough policy against law violators.

That law enforcement should be such an emotional issue can only exacerbate problems which are real enough. Major crimes have increased. Civil riots, whatever their cause or justification, have cost lives and millions of dollars in property damage. And universities have been disrupted. In the following pages we hope to clear through the underbrush of emotionalism to provide a clearer perspective of the issues involved.

THE INCIDENCE AND RATE
OF CRIME

Few will contest the fact that crime today poses a major problem for American society, no matter how twisted the law and order slogan as a campaign appeal has become. Nearly 4.5 million serious crimes were committed during 1968, affecting an average of two people out of every 100 inhabitants. More than 1.7 billion dollars worth of property was reported stolen for the same reporting period. Added to these shocking figures is the overall 32 percent decline in police solutions of crime since 1960. Although the gross figures require interpretation, Table 15.1 portrays a general picture of crime in the United States.

The actual incidence of crime is probably understated by the Uniform Crime Reports of the Federal Bureau of Investigation. Certain types of crimes often are not reported to the police. The President's Commission

TABLE 15.1
National Crime, Rate, and Percent Change

CRIME INDEX OFFENSES	ESTIMATED CRIME, 1968		PERCENT CHANGE OVER 1960	
	NUMBER	RATE PER 100,000 INHABITANTS	NUMBER	RATE
Total	4,466,600	2234.8	+121.7	+ 98.9
Violent	588,800	294.6	+106.5	+ 85.3
Property	3,877,700	1940.0	+124.2	+101.2
Murder	13,650	6.8	+ 51.7	+ 36.0
Forcible rape	31,060	15.5	+ 84.3	+ 64.9
Robbery	261,730	131.0	+143.7	+118.7
Aggravated assault	282,400	141.3	+ 85.8	+ 66.8
Burglary	1,828,900	915.1	+103.8	+ 82.8
Larceny $50 and over	1,271,100	636.0	+151.1	+125.3
Auto theft	777,800	389.1	+138.8	+114.3

SOURCE: Federal Bureau of Investigation, *Uniform Crime Reports*, 1968, p. 5.

on Law Enforcement and the Administration of Justice attempted the first national survey to determine more accurately the amounts and types of crime committed. The commission concluded that the Uniform Crime Reports systematically understate serious crime with two exceptions. Willful homicide cannot very well be ignored and one presumes most cases come to the attention of police authorities. On the other hand, motor vehicle thefts are well reported probably because it is necessary to collect on insurance policies. The principal reasons given for a failure to report crimes are that the matter is essentially a private affair or that the police would be unable or unwilling to do anything about the matter.[1]

Although it is generally accepted that the rate of crime has been increasing, it does not follow necessarily that the possibility of victimization is evenly distributed through the population. Indeed, one of the most significant of crime statistics is the variation in rate of victimization among demographic groupings. As Table 15.2 suggests, the rate of victimization among income levels varies with the type of crime. The

TABLE 15.2
Victimization by Income
(rates per 100,000 population)

| | INCOME | | | |
OFFENSES	$0 TO $2999	$3000 TO $5999	6000 TO $9999	ABOVE $10,000
Total	2369	2331	1820	2237
Forcible rape	76	49	10	17
Robbery	172	121	48	34
Aggravated assault	229	316	144	252
Burglary	1319	1020	867	790
Larceny ($50 and over)	420	619	549	925
Motor vehicle theft	153	206	202	219
Number of respondents	(5232)	(8238)	(10382)	(5946)

SOURCE: The President's Commission on Law Enforcement and Administration of Justice, *Task Force Report: Crime and Its Impact—An Assessment* (Washington, D.C.: U.S. Government Printing Office, 1967), p. 80.

rates of forcible rape, robbery, and burglary are consistently higher for lower-income groups than for higher-income levels. Only for larceny or $50 or more is it clearly shown that the affluent are the more likely victims of crime.

[1] The President's Commission on Law Enforcement and Administration of Justice, *Task Force Report: Crime and Its Impact—An Assessment* (Washington, D.C.: U.S. Government Printing Office, 1967), pp. 17–18.

The pattern of victimization that is brought out in comparing crimes committed against whites with crimes committed against nonwhites is even more striking. The rate of victimization is significantly higher for nonwhites than whites for each of the crime categories other than larceny of $50 or more. Table 15.3 shows the relationships.

TABLE 15.3
Victimization by Race
(rates per 100,000 population)

OFFENSES	WHITE	NONWHITE
Total	1,860	2592
Forcible rape	22	82
Robbery	58	204
Aggravated assault	186	347
Burglary	822	1306
Larceny ($50 and over)	608	367
Motor vehicle theft	164	286
Number of respondents	(27,484)	(4902)

SOURCE: The President's Commission on Law Enforcement and Administration of Justice, *Task Force Report: Crime and Its Impact—An Assessment* (Washington, D.C.: U.S. Government Printing Office, 1967), p. 80.

Other data collected by the President's Commission on Law Enforcement and the Administration of Justice show that men are more likely to be victimized than women, and that crimes against the person are higher for the 20-to-29 age group than others. Property offenses are more commonly committed against older age groups who have had a greater opportunity to accumulate property that may be stolen.

The importance of determining the rate of victimization is twofold. It can be an aid in crime prevention. Presumably if police authorities are aware of who are likely to be victimized and where, then they are in a better position to take preventive measures. But an analysis of victimization has added significance. A general fear of "crime in the streets" pervades middle-class society, a fear that includes a concern for personal safety. Some of the apprehension might be dispelled if the threat to one's security is realistically appraised.

Most individuals who express anxiety over the "crime problem" are fearful of personal injury and, to a much lesser extent, that their property will be taken or damaged.[2] Yet crimes of violence—willful homicide,

[2] *Ibid.,* chap. 6.

forcible rape, aggravated assault, and robbery—constitute less than 15 percent of the crime index. Moreover, much of the public's fear of crime is that the individual will be attacked by a stranger while away from his home or neighborhood. Yet about 70 percent of willful homicides, nearly two thirds of aggravated assaults, and a high percentage of forcible rapes are committed by persons known to the victim, including his family and friends. Only robbery is more likely perpetrated by a stranger to the victim.

Among some segments of the population there is a suspicion that Negroes are likely to victimize whites. Any objective observer has to recognize that racial antagonisms lie behind the support given to many "law and order" candidates for public office. The evidence, however, does not support the belief in widespread interracial victimization. On the contrary, as Table 15.4 suggests, Negroes are the more likely victims of other Negroes, and whites, the more likely victims of other whites.

TABLE 15.4

Victim-Offender Relationships by Race and Sex in Assaultive Crimes Against the Person (Except Homicide)

| | OFFENSES ATTRIBUTABLE TO | | | | |
| | WHITE OFFENDERS | | NEGRO OFFENDERS | | ALL TYPES OF |
	MALE	FEMALE	MALE	FEMALE	OFFENDERS
Victim rate for each 100,000:					
White males	201	9	129	4	342
White females	108	14	46	6	175
Negro males	58	3	1636	256	1953
Negro females	21	3	1202	157	1382
Total population	130	10	350	45	535

SOURCE: The data are taken from the Chicago Police Department for the period September, 1965 to March, 1966. The table appears in the President's Commission on Law Enforcement and Administration of Justice, *Task Force Report: Crime and Its Impact—An Assessment* (Washington, D.C.: U.S. Government Printing Office, 1967), p. 82.

What we are suggesting is that part of the general public's anxiety over crime results from a lack of accurate information. Although data are difficult to collect, some evidence suggests that public views of crime are based on vicarious impressions gleaned from the media—not from experience or witness of a crime. Oftentimes, crime reporting emphasizes the most bizarre and violent criminal acts which instill a fear in the minds of even the least likely victims. If a stereotype of crime is created that associates violent crime with all crime, then the public may become alarmed as they see news accounts of increases in the crime index. A general fear among unlikely victims causes a change in their everyday activities (travel at night, particularly in the city; answering the door when alone) and gives rise to elaborate precautions (purchase of firearms or watchdogs) which would be ludicrous if their anxiety were not so real. One cannot tell the public whether they should be afraid. But one can believe that more factual information might allay somewhat the fears of those who exaggerate the threat posed to their persons or property.

THE SOCIAL AND PHYSICAL ENVIRONMENT OF CRIME

Sociologists have found that the kinds of social relationships that exist in a country determine its level of social control. The more socially integrated a given society, the less there is of crime and other antisocial behavior. Moral and ethical codes are known and accepted in the homogeneous community and behavior patterns conform to the norms established. If this is the case, then the United States is confronted with peculiar problems.[3] It is primarily an immigrant nation and its immigration has been recent enough that a sizable portion of its urban population are the sons and daughters of foreign-born parents, many still living in ethnic enclaves. But the matter of social integration goes beyond racial, ethnic, and religious variations in the population. The United States has been a mobile nation. The push westward across the continent during an earlier age and the population movement today toward regions of economic growth have meant that many of our communities do not possess a stable and indigenous population with long roots in the past. And equally as important as geographic movement has been social mobility, in which class consciousness and class norms have been easily transcended. Regardless of the melting pot theory, the level of social integration in the United States is not as advanced, say, as Great Britain. In supporting the contention that this affects the crime rate, Michael Banton reported that in 1962 the murder rate for the average American city was nine times that of Edinburgh and the number of forcible rapes was seven and a half times greater.[4]

There is some evidence that the implications of the theory of social

[3] Michael Banton, *The Policeman in the Community* (London: Tavistock Publications, 1964), pp. 86–87.
[4] *Ibid.*, p. 2.

integration described above also explain variations in our domestic rate of crime. Consider the case of California, a state recognized for its professionalized police forces, modern correctional system, and generally high level of governmental services. In 1965, California had the highest rate of crimes against property in the nation, twice the national average, and its crimes against the person were one half again greater than the national average. A partial explanation for the high crime rate may be the excellent reporting system that California maintains. But it is probably also the case that its high rate of urbanization and the extremely high rate of immigration to the state have affected the level of social integration within its communities.[5] We are not suggesting any neat indices to predict crime rates but rather are pointing to the complexity of determining crime causes. The makeup of the population, the quality of political and governmental leadership, community attitudes, the professionalization of police forces, and unique regional and state histories undoubtedly all play a part. Thus the Federal Bureau of Investigation suggests that the following conditions may affect the amount and types of crime:[6]

Density and size of the community population and the metropolitan area of which it is a part.

Composition of the population with reference particularly to age, sex, and race.

Economic status and mores of the population.

Relative stability of population, including commuters, seasonal, and other transient types.

Climate, including seasonal weather conditions.

Educational, recreational, and religious characteristics.

Effective strength of the police force.

Standards governing appointments to the police force.

Policies of the prosecuting officials and the courts.

Attitudes of the public toward law enforcement problems.

The administrative and investigative efficiency of the local law enforcement agency, including the degree of adherence to crime reporting standards.

Attempts have been made to explore more closely the correlates of crime. In keeping with the theory of social integration, well-documented evidence points to a higher crime rate for property offenses in cities than in rural communities. The differences between city and countryside, however, extend beyond indicies of crime. The rural community has no criminal subculture. It has no criminal argot, no professional criminal techniques, and no definite criminal progression, at least prior to im-

---

[5] President's Commission on Law Enforcement and Administration of Justice, *op. cit.*, p. 34.
[6] Federal Bureau of Investigation, *Uniform Crime Reports*, 1968, p. vi.

prisonment.[7] In the absence of a criminal culture, criminal acts are more individualistic and less patterned activity.

A second well-documented finding is the variations in crime rates and criminal activities within a city. The highest rates are found in the poorest neighborhoods, those that are physically deteriorating. One standard pattern, referred to as the gradient theory, suggests that crime rates are highest in areas surrounding the central business district and then become progressively lower as one moves outward from the city. The gradient theory holds true for all ethnic and racial groups—that is, the high central-city rate, the low out-city rate. It is in these areas that one may expect a criminal culture to develop and to show continuity. Here there are "socializing" institutions to indoctrinate one to the criminal techniques and codes.

The fact that a recurring pattern of crime rates is found among the geographical areas of a city leads to the next question. What are the social and economic factors associated with high crime areas? Again the statistical evidence reveals a consistent pattern. High crime areas also experience other social and economic problems. Thus one study revealed that delinquency rates were related to school truancy, infant mortality, tuberculosis, mental disorder, decreasing population, high percentage of families on relief, low monthly rents, low rates of home ownership, and a high proportion of overcrowded and substandard dwelling units.[8] Community characteristics of Peoria are compared to delinquency rates in Table 15.5 and one presumes the relationships are not untypical.

Of all the indicators of crime, perhaps none is a more sensitive issue than the correlations that have shown a relationship between nationality and racial groups and the crime index. Earlier a charge of criminal propensities was leveled at the most newly arrived ethnic groups, who, indeed, provided disproportionate numbers to juvenile courts and professional gangs alike. Recently the Negro in particular has been singled out as more prone to criminal activity. Careful analysts point to the harsh social and economic conditions under which Negroes live today as an explanation for his antisocial behavior. Yet obtaining statistical verification for the reasons why crime rates vary among racial groups is an almost hopeless task. How can one find a control group that has suffered the indignities of the Negro? It is known that all nationality and racial groups show both high and low crime rates when in differing environments. The relative difference in rates for all groups, as one moves

7 President's Commission on Law Enforcement and the Administration of Justice, *op. cit.,* p. 141.
8 Clifford R. Shaw and Henry D. McKay, *Juvenile Delinquency and Urban Areas* (Chicago: University of Chicago Press, 1942), pp. 134–163. Reported in President's Commission on Law Enforcement and the Administration of Justice, *op. cit.,* p. 69.

TABLE 15.5
*Community Characteristics of High- and Low-Rate
Delinquency Areas in Peoria[a]*

| | RATE OR AVERAGE[b] | |
| | LOW DELINQUENCY | HIGH DELINQUENCY |
COMMUNITY CHARACTERISTICS	AREA	AREA
Delinquency	0.53	6.58
Church membership	33.45	18.83
Divorce	1.64	3.79
Suicide	0.27	0.51
Residential mobility	6.03	10.39
Proportion of males in population	45.48	52.89
Infant mortality	0.61	2.15
Insanity	0.34	1.14
Total adult crime	1.87	16.73
Relief	0.17	4.88
Average property values	$481.00	$277.00
Average rent	$40.07	$23.10
Home ownership	60.75	30.38
Annual income	$2813.50	$1166.88
Unemployment	0.91	4.50

[a] Based on cases of behavior problems brought before juvenile probation officers, 1930–1937.
[b] The units of measure are either rates based on population proportions or average dollar amounts as in the case of rentals, property values, and annual income.
SOURCE: Clarence W. Schroeder, "Peoria, Illinois," in Clifford R. Shaw and Harry D. McKay, *Juvenile Delinquency and Urban Areas* (Chicago: University of Chicago Press, 1942), p. 396. Reproduced in President's Commission on Law Enforcement and Administration of Justice, *Task Force Report: Crime and its Impact —An Assessment* (Washington, D.C.: U.S. Government Printing Office, 1967), Table 7, p. 70.

outward from the deteriorating portions of the city, may be the more significant statistic.

It is important to note that the various factors found correlated with crime rates are themselves often highly intercorrelated. There are probably only a few basic influences underlying the associations. One could point to groups that are culturally or socially or economically deprived without being too wide of the mark. It is to this gross association that we wish to point. We tend to agree with the complaint of James Q. Wilson that "one might suppose that criminologists would long since have satisfied themselves that lower-income people commit more common crimes, omitting so-called 'white collar' or business crime, than middle-or-upper-income persons. I find to my surprise (and irritation) that this is not the case."[9]

[9] James Q. Wilson, *The Varieties of Police Behavior* (Cambridge: Harvard University Press, 1968), footnote 35, p. 40.

THE SPECIAL CASE
OF ORGANIZED CRIME

Organized crime presents a problem in American society that is not ordinarily conveyed by the muggings, assaults, or robberies to which the slogan "crime in the streets" refers. Its distinctiveness lies in its organization, a private government with its own rules and its own enforcers. That the notion of a crime syndicate or criminal cartel is not fanciful was convincingly shown by the shocking revelations of the investigating committee headed by Senator Estes Kefauver in the early fifties. Control of its operations has received the special attention of federal law enforcing officials, but their efforts have produced at best only minor successes.

The activities of the criminal cartel, variously referred to as "the mob," the "Mafia," the "syndicate," the "outfit," extend into all sections of the country today, including most of our major cities and some of the smaller ones as well.[10] The cartel is divided into 24 groups or "families" each with a membership ranging from 20 to as many as 700 members. Normally only one family controls a city, but five share New York City. The family is headed by a "boss" who directs the operations of the group and enforces its codes. Commonly an elder member of the family serves as a counselor or adviser to the boss who is also aided in his tasks by an underboss and lieutenants who oversee the work of the soldiers in the elaborate structure which is maintained. (See Figure 15.1.) The purpose of the organization is to insulate the boss as much as possible from direct contact with his underlings, particularly the soldiers who may be unaware of their leader's identity.

The 24 families are under the loose, general control of the "commission," whose composition varies. Currently only nine families are represented, but its authority extends to all 24. Although the commission "serves as combination legislature, supreme court, board of directors, and arbitration board, its principal functions are judicial."[11] The commission has final authority over organizational and jurisdictional disputes of its family members.

The operations of the syndicate include both criminal activities and legitimate business interests. The criminal activities are likely those that show a high profit and involve only minimal risk. The goods or services offered are demanded by sizable segments of the population and include gambling, loan-sharking, and narcotics. Neither bootlegging nor prostitu-

[10] This section relies heavily on the President's Commission on Law Enforcement and Administration of Justice, *Task Force Report: Organized Crime* (Washington, D.C.: U.S. Government Printing Office, 1967).
[11] *Ibid.,* p. 8.

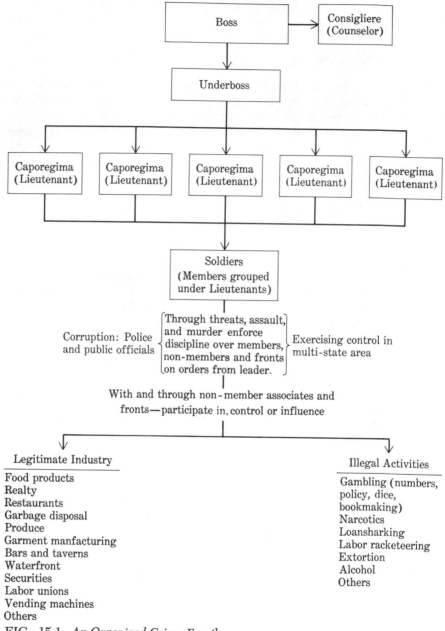

FIG. 15.1. *An Organized Crime Family*

SOURCE: President's Commission on Law Enforcement and Administration of Justice, *Task Force: Organized Crime* (Washington: U.S. Government Printing Office, 1967), p. 9.

tion any longer constitutes a major source of income for the syndicate. Bootlegging requires an investment in plant and equipment that frequently is detected and destroyed. Prostitution is difficult to organize and resulted in the conviction of several syndicate leaders in the thirties and forties.

From the profits illegally gained, the syndicate has branched out into legitimate business but often bring their strong-arm tactics with them. For example, the President's Commission on Law Enforcement and Administration of Justice reported the following cases:[12]

> A restaurant chain controlled by organized crime used the guise of "quality control" to insure that individual restaurant franchise holders bought products only from other syndicate-owned businesses. In one city, every business with a particular kind of waste product useful in another line of industry sold that product to a syndicate-controlled business at one-third the price offered by legitimate business.

The advantages accruing to the syndicate extend beyond their efforts at physical intimidation. Because they seldom pay taxes on their illegal revenue, the gangster element has plentiful capital to pour into their operations. And at times, because of their influence in some unions, they have been able to arrange so-called "sweetheart" labor contracts. Of whatever stripe of influence, the entry of criminal elements into legitimate business and labor organizations is alarming.

According to the President's Commission, organized crime has operated successfully only in cities in which local officials have been corrupted. We see no reason to doubt this judgment if the corruption asserted applies to some but not all of the officials and not necessarily the most prominent ones. The corrupting influence of crime is all the more serious today because of the enormous tasks confronting urban leaders. The mind must boggle at the thought of morally weak officials attempting to deal with the crises in our cities.

LAW VERSUS ORDER

Despite political rhetoric, which commonly associates law with order, conflicting tendencies oftentimes emerge between the rule of law and the maintenance of order in the activities of policemen. The assertion is not intended to imply that there are no important philosophical relations between the two—that is, the quality of the order and the means by which it is achieved—but that as a practical matter the law is often

[12] *Ibid.*, p. 5.

viewed by police as an obstacle confronting them in their assigned tasks. Given the increased amount of political dissent taking ever more radical forms, particularly protests over ghetto conditions whose squalor also breeds the crime and behavior that challenge police authority, the order-maintenance functions of the police are no longer unquestioned and appeal is made for legal and political protection from the police. Under such circumstances, the rule of law and the policeman's order becomes ever more disparate.

To comprehend the dimensions of the conflict between law and order, the social and organizational environment of the police must be understood.[13] The world in which the policeman works is a hostile one. It is he who must respond to the radio call that armed robbery has been committed or that a gathering shows signs of incipient riot conditions or that a street fight between rival teenage gangs has erupted. In other words, his work brings him into association with violence in which his physical safety is at times threatened. But his exposure to violence is unpredictable; therefore he must be taught to be suspicious, that any personal encounter is potentially dangerous. Any wonder, then, that the apprehensiveness of the police is reflected in their professional conduct, for example, in conducting field interrogations of "suspicious characters"?

Because the policeman symbolizes authority in his order-keeping functions, he often finds himself resented by the community he serves. That those who are subjected to field interrogations or arrested for criminal activity show animosity is to be expected. But even the normal law-abiding public may be resentful of the policeman's exercise of authority as he issues traffic summons, controls a crowd at a sports event, or attempts to untangle a traffic snarl on a hot day at evening rush hours. Whether correctly perceived or not, most policemen feel that the public fail to accord them the respect and backing they deserve. A feeling of isolation is engendered in their professional duties which may carry over into their private lives.

Both the element of danger in their lives and the experience of isolation in their work combine to make the police an uncommonly cohesive work force. The exposure to danger requires a cooperation among policemen for their self-protection which is enhanced by their military style of organization and uniforms which are the visible symbols of their comradeship. The mutual feeling of isolation turns the policeman toward his fellow officers not simply in his professional associations but frequently for his social friendships as well. The combination of factors are such that the police constitute a work force whose solidarity is greater than other working crafts.[14]

[13] See Jerome H. Skolnick, *Justice Without Trial* (New York: Wiley, 1966), chap. 3.
[14] *Ibid.*, pp. 52–53.

A dangerous occupation, a sense of isolation in their work, and the solidarity within their ranks combine to make the policeman's task of maintaining order under the rule of law a problematic undertaking. A person confronted with a threat to his personal safety is unlikely to be scrupulous in following the niceties of procedural rules. This is all the more the case if he feels that his work is misunderstood and unappreciated anyway. Moreover, the clannishness within police ranks suggests that fellow officer will back fellow officer, superior will support subordinate, in an attack by any segment of the public against police procedures.

The basic issue involved in reconciling the maintenance of order with the rule of law concerns police discretion. The fact of the matter is that the rule of law is not precise enough to provide effective guidelines for the police should they wish to conform to procedural safeguards, which, of course, is not always the case. Discretion is necessarily involved when, for example, the patrolman decides that he has "probable cause" to make an arrest. Now a police officer believes, with justification, that he is an expert in his craft, which requires him to be knowledgeable about law violators. Yet his insight, perhaps correct in a given case, may be insufficient to meet legal standards. Thus Skolnick reports on a policeman's comments following a narcotic's arrest:[15]

> It's awfully hard to explain to a judge what I mean when I testify that I saw a furtive movement. . . . I can testify as to the character of the neighborhood, my knowledge that the man was an addict and all that stuff, but what I mean is that when I see a hype move the way that guy moved, I *know* he's trying to get rid of something. [Emphasis supplied by the speaker.]

Skolnick then asked the policeman if he had ever been proven wrong. Although conceding that he had, he nevertheless felt he was right often enough to justify a search even if he lacked evidence for an arrest.

The expertise that the patrolman acquires is a consequence of his apprenticeship as a member of a craft. It involves on-the-job training, and all of the uniformed policemen start in this way. Thus there is no lateral entry into the craft—the college graduate, for example, is not immediately commissioned as a lieutenant of police. The fact that it is a craft means, as James Q. Wilson has written, that "there is no body of generalized, written knowledge nor a set of detailed prescriptions as to how to behave."[16] The craft is learned under the hostile environment described earlier, and the knowledge gleaned will govern police judgment in instances which can cause their action to be in conflict with the rule of

15 *Ibid.*, p. 216.
16 Wilson, *op. cit.*, p. 283.

law. "Socialization" to police procedures and practices may actually impair the policeman's ability to comprehend legal norms.

THE TASKS OF THE POLICE

James Q. Wilson has written that the police have been assigned two basic responsibilities, one in which there is no agreement over what constitutes satisfactory performance and the other one which is unlikely to be obtained. The first responsibility is that of order maintenance; the second is that of law enforcement.[17]

When Wilson speaks of order maintenance he is referring to the tasks of policemen in intervening in disputes in which there is either disagreement by the public or the participants over what constitutes acceptable conduct, or there is disagreement over who should be assigned the blame for what is conceded to be unacceptable conduct. An example of the first may be a gathering of young men with long beards and young ladies with stringy hair who are acting out the rites of some new cult. Or it can be a noisy but otherwise harmless drunk, a shouting match between angry spouses, a roisterous party that continues into early morning hours, or any of many occurrences which may annoy others but scarcely label the offenders as criminal types—or suggest a clear way of handling the disturbance. The second type of order-maintenance problems involves a clearer violation of law, but the assignment of blame is much less clear. If the domestic quarrel involves an assault of the husband upon the wife (or vice versa), the attempt to arrest one or the other may bring down the wrath of both upon the officer.

The second task assigned the police is that of enforcing the law against clear violations in which blame can be appropriately assigned, assuming that the guilty party is known. Thus burglary, robbery, arson, homicide, mugging, or purse-snatching present no ambiguous standard to the policeman. His duty is clear. He should prevent the execution of the crime if he is able, and, if called in after the fact, should determine who is the guilty party and arrest him.

The problem confronting the police according to Wilson is over the objectives of order-maintenance and the means of law enforcement. Order-maintenance in a homogeneous community is simple compared to the conflict engendered in an urban community with difference of race and class, each with its own set of norms concerning acceptable behavior. The police who disperse a boisterous crowd of teenagers who have

[17] James Q. Wilson, "Dilemmas of Police Administration," *Public Administration Review*, XXVIII (September–October, 1968), p. 407 ff. This section relies heavily on Wilson's analysis.

gathered in a middle-class residential suburb are unlikely to provoke angry citizen reaction within the community. The community generally accepts the police view of what constitutes unacceptable conduct. But the police who would question teenagers in the central city must proceed with caution. It is customary behavior in the ghetto to hang about the streets in an entirely harmless way. Of course, the activity of the teen-agers may be suspicious. But whatever the case, the incident could spark a disturbance whose spread would be difficult to control. When to inter-vene and when to ignore is not clear, and ghetto residents can and do differ with the police.

The problem of law enforcement raises issues over the techniques involved in apprehending law violators. Most police departments are ineffective in crime detection, as Figure 15.2 suggests. The ability of police to "clear" serious crimes is related to whether the victim can iden-tify the offender. Offenders in homicide, rape, and assault cases fre-quently are known to their victims. The offender in robbery, larceny, burglary, and automobile theft is commonly unknown. Since some crimes go unreported and some police departments are eager to clear crimes by inducing a suspect to confess to crimes he possibly did not commit (the suspect might be quite willing to cooperate because he will be judged cooperative and may be charged with a lesser offense or be recommended

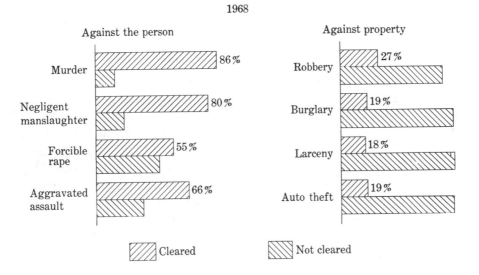

FIG. 15.2. *Crimes Cleared by Arrest*

SOURCE: Federal Bureau of Investigation, *Uniform Crime Reports—1968*, p. 32.

for a minimum sentence, and he probably will not be charged with all the offenses to which he has confessed), the actual number of clearances is probably overstated. To make matters worse, the number of "uncleared" cases has recently been on the rise.

Theoretically it might be possible for the police to improve their record in apprehending law violators. Certainly the modern police department with efficient crime laboratories, careful selection and training of personnel, and wise specialization and deployment of its staff is better able to cope with crime than those not similarly equipped or organized. And perhaps the clearance of crime would be even lower in the absence of a modern, professional organization. Yet the best urban police departments still have a problem of law enforcement on their hands. To achieve a better record involves costs to the community, specifically in loss of freedom, that they have been unwilling to undertake. Indeed, increased effectiveness in the law enforcement functions may cause a loss of effectiveness in the order-maintenance functions. Thus one way to combat crime would be to saturate the high crime areas with patrolmen who would exercise close surveillance over all suspicious persons and activity on their beat. But given the working personality of the patrolman, he undoubtedly would throw his net of suspicion over innocent and guilty alike if they fitted the age, race, or class of likely offenders. The innocent who are subjected to field interrogations indiscriminately will be justly outraged. A decline in the crime rate may be replaced by worsened community relations, possibly a more serious matter.

STYLES IN POLICE ORGANIZATION

According to the Task Force on Police of the President's Commission on Law Enforcement and Administration of Justice, there is little justification for ineffectual organization of American police forces.[18] The Task Force supports its contention by asserting the availability of a "large and authoritative general body of guidance in public administration." That modern management principles should be utilized in running sizable police organizations is readily conceded. Yet to presume that matters of administrative management hold the key to effective police performance, particularly in their order-keeping functions, is to misunderstand the problems surrounding the policeman's tasks. A more realistic appraisal

[18] President's Commission on Law Enforcement and Administration of Justice, *Task Force Report: The Police* (Washington, D.C.: U.S. Government Printing Office, 1967), p. 46.

suggests widespread disagreement over the appropriate role of the police and little information as to the consequences of differing police styles.

The most sophisticated attempt to analyze variations in police behavior has been the seminal work of James Q. Wilson.[19] Based on a study of police systems in eight communities, Wilson isolated three distinctive police styles or strategies—the watchman, the legalistic, and the service. None is found in pure form, nor are all cities of a given style alike in all details or characteristics. Yet each carries some of the flavor of the "ideal" type in which it is placed. If additional communities had been surveyed, other types might have emerged. From this beginning, however, we may hopefully learn more about police administration than might be gleaned from the more pristine approach of traditional public administration.

The watchman style receives its particular distinctiveness from the department's attitude toward order-maintenance functions. Order-maintenance is given priority over law enforcement. But the watchman's style is more than this. In maintaining order, the patrolmen in the watchman's style judges "the seriousness of infractions less by what the law says about them than by their immediate and personal consequences, which will differ in importance depending on the standards of the relevant group—teenagers, Negroes, prostitutes, motorists, families, and so forth."[20] It thus follows that the moral standards enforced in a watchman department will vary in relation to the composition of the population it serves. And while the watchman's style incorporates a system of distributive justice that varies with the police perception of a group's moral standards, all groups will be accorded some leniency in the interpretation of legal standards.

Certain organizational characteristics are associated with departments following a watchman style. Salaries are low. Recruitment is locally based. Entrance requirements are a high-school education or less. Little attention is paid to formal training in police academies. Staff work is not emphasized. Few civilians are employed who, in other departments, commonly provide specialized staff services. Record keeping is poor. Standardized procedures and written rules are not stressed. In short, the watchman style is associated with an organization that violates most modern management principles.

Departments that follow a legalistic style are inclined to treat order-maintenance functions in a law enforcement fashion. Legal prescriptions are applied to offenders without regard to group norms and the personal consequences to the offender. Thus the number of traffic summons, misdemeanors charges, and juvenile arrests will be high. A single stand-

[19] Wilson, *The Varieties of Police Behavior, op. cit.* We are again indebted to Wilson's insightful analysis in this section.
[20] *Ibid.,* p. 141.

ard of legal conduct will be applied to Negroes, whites, juveniles, teen-agers, and upper-income or lower-income groups. In a legalistic style there is no attempt to "privatize" the law.

If the attitude of the legalistic style toward order-maintenance stands in sharp contrast to that of the watchman style, so too are their differ-ences in the organizational patterns associated with each. The informality and clannishness that characterize a watchman style is replaced by depersonalization and reliance on centralized, formal authority in a legalistic department. Entrance qualifications are high, with the college graduate sought after. Salaries are attractive, technical proficiency is valued, and staff specialization advanced. Record keeping is extensive. Training programs are elaborate. The latest in management virtues are thus found in the organization of legalistic departments.

The service police style has attributes of both the other two. The service department will handle its order-maintenance functions infor-mally (the mark of the watchman style) but will take seriously infrac-tions of legal codes (the mark of the legalistic department). Before one reaches the conclusion that the service style incorporates the best from the other styles and points to a possible solution to problems of police organization, it should be noted that it is commonly found in homoge-neous middle-class communities that are not wracked by sharp racial and class cleavages. The community is more likely agreed on a definition of public morality and less likely victimized by serious crime. Thus the department can concentrate on serving its constituency.

The organization of the service department is much like that of legal-istic departments. Service departments also employ modern management practices and value well-trained, courteous policemen. In fact, it is the organization of the service department that prevents its classification under a watchman style that responds not to the conflicting norms of the polyglot city but the near consensus of a homogeneous suburb. The organization of the watchman style could not provide the community services expected by middle-class residents. On the other hand, if one were to transfer a service department intact to a racially mixed commu-nity with a large lower socioeconomic class, the style might change to that of the legalistic department. At least one might wonder whether an informal method of handling street disturbances would meet with the same approbation that occurs in more like-minded suburbia.

A comparison of the effect the alternative styles have on arrest rates in racially mixed communities is revealing of the problems encountered by police. Since the service style is confined to middle-class communities with only a small Negro population, the contrast is between watchman and legalistic cities. Because they emphasize order-maintenance rather than law enforcement, the watchman cities show a lower arrest rate in law enforcement situations than do the legalistic cities. This applies to the rate of both Negro and white arrests. Blacks in some watchman cities complain bitterly of the lack of police protection. Their complaint is that infractions in the Black community are overlooked because policemen presume Negroes have a lower standard of morality. At the same time, watchman cities are more inclined to arrest Negroes for drunkenness or disorderly conduct than the legalistic cities. Such actions, as perceived by the police, are no longer private in character but threaten a breach of the peace. Since the police impute an inferior morality to the Negro, he cannot be restrained by a warning or an appeal for aid from his family, but must be arrested. Such treatment is seen by blacks as discriminatory.

The legalistic cities largely escape Negro criticism of a lack of police protection. Yet because order-maintenance is treated as if it were a law enforcement situation, blacks charge police with harassment and community relations are not noticeably superior. Impersonal but strict law enforcement, untempered by some sense of feeling for the community, is unlikely to generate satisfactory community support. But to depart from the law involves police discretion which has its own dangers. It is relatively hidden from public view and, in a racially mixed community, is likely to produce controversy over what standards to apply to guide police judgment.

THE POLICE AND
THE COMMUNITY

Although police feel isolated in their work, the problem is less that the normally law-abiding are annoyed at law enforcement tactics than that members of minority groups feel they receive inadequate protection and, to a lesser extent, are subject to both harsh and subtle forms of discrimination. Survey following survey has shown that while a majority of the general public believe that the police are doing a good to excellent job, a substantial minority believe otherwise. And Negroes in the surveys are more inclined to be suspicious of the police than whites. In Table 15.6 the problem is seen to be most critical for local law enforcement agencies.

To a degree the police are caught in the conflicting forces that have tended to polarize the larger community. On the one hand, there are those who feel that riots and civil disturbances are merely an extension of a general growth in lawlessness and call for a get-tough policy on the part of the police. On the other hand, there are those who feel that underlying social and economic conditions have created urban unrest and suggest broad-gauged programs to attack the root cause of the cities' malaise. As part of their approach, the latter groups counsel a greater sensitivity to

TABLE 15.6
Ratings of Law Enforcement

| | GOOD-EXCELLENT RATING | | |
| | FEDERAL | STATE | LOCAL |
	%	%	%
Nationwide	76	70	65
By size of place			
Cities	80	67	57
Suburbs	79	71	72
Towns	75	72	65
Rural	71	72	66
By race			
White	75	71	67
Negro	81	63	51

SOURCE: *A National Survey of Police and Community Relations,* Field Surveys V, A Report of a Research Study Submitted to the President's Commission on Law Enforcement and Administration of Justice (Washington, D.C.: U.S. Government Printing Office, 1967), p. 10.

the needs and grievances of the ghetto dweller. The outcome of a mayoralty contest may hinge on which of the two viewpoints gains the upper hand in the community.

Faced by the escalating demands of the two opposing camps, the police cannot ignore the issue of community relations. But when one thinks of improved police-community relations, one thinks immediately, not of the relations of the police with the general public, but of their relations with minority group members. And it is our judgment, after immersion in the literature, that the primary irritant is not police brutality or discrimination, although one cannot discount these factors, but it is the absence of adequate police protection. Thus the U.S. Commission on Civil Rights, in commenting on police-community relations in Cleveland, wrote:[21]

> The complaints of the Negro community against the police department are legion. But the most frequent complaint is that of permissive law enforcement and that policemen fail to provide adequate protection and services in areas occupied by Negroes.

A survey in Harlem showed that 39 percent of the respondents were concerned about crime and criminals, but police abuse was not ranked among the nine most frequently mentioned problems. Polls in Washing-

[21] The President's Commission on Civil Rights, *Task Force Report: The Police, op. cit.,* p. 148.

ton and the Bedford-Stuyvesant area of New York City produced similar results.[22]

The concern of the black community is realistic given the victimization rate of the Negro. Presumably some measure of improved community relations would flow from a greater professionalization of police departments and an initial adoption of a legalistic style for arrests. We are not suggesting that police-community problems would be solved by more strict law enforcement in the Negro community, but, by any objective standards, they deserve greater protection.

The second greatest irritant to Negroes and other minority group members is alleged police brutality and discrimination. It is our judgment that physical abuse, while still a problem in some communities, is nevertheless on the decline.[23] It has been replaced by more subtle forms of discrimination. Surveys reveal widespread sentiment among Negroes that the police verbally abuse them by use of so-called "trigger" words or by manner or attitude otherwise slight them in ways not experienced by white offenders. Similar discontent is evidenced when patrolmen single out Negroes for field interrogations, often with the disrespect blacks already find offensive.

But as we have said before, a relationship exists between effective law enforcement and the feeling of harassment among minority group members. To the police officer effective law enforcement entails preventive action of which the field interrogation is a necessary part. And it is most likely applied against those who the crime statistics say are the most likely offenders. The worst crime areas are in the ghettos and the highest crime rates are among the blacks. If the innocent and guilty alike are treated with suspicion by the police, crime prevention may be aided, but at the cost of worsened community relations. Thus the dilemma posed.

Whether justified or not, the widespread belief in police discrimination by the blacks constitutes a serious problem. It means that riots can break out over relatively routine matters. Indeed most of the civil disturbances of the 1960s arose out of trivial police actions, in many cases the initial incident reported by a Negro complainant. As Robert Fogelson has written, "a confrontation develops because few groups are less willing to hear a reasonable gripe than the police, few are less ready to accept an honest error than the Negroes, and, however much each would prefer to avoid a showdown, neither is secure enough to concede the issue."[24] To

---

22 *Ibid.*
23 For a contrary view, see *A National Survey of Police and Community Relations,* Field Surveys V, A Report of a Research Study Submitted to the President's Commission on Law Enforcement and Administration of Justice (Washington, D.C.: U.S. Government Printing Office, 1967), pp. 148–188.
24 Robert Fogelson, "From Resentment to Confrontation: The Police, the Negroes, and the Outbreak of Nineteen Sixties Riots," *Political Science Quarterly,* LXXXIII (June, 1968), 231–232.

overcome the ingrained hostility which exists between a policeman whose craft outlook stems from his dangerous occupation and the minority member whose views are colored by his brutal economic and social life is not easy.

The point that must be highlighted is that the issue of crime control and crime prevention is larger than the issue of the police and the skills they bring to and develop in their craft. As the police are fond of pointing out, they do not make crime. Ghettos breed crime and until the problems of ghettos are solved in a more meaningful way, crime rates will remain high and relations between police and ghetto dwellers will continue uneasy. In the interim, one can only counsel greater professionalization of police forces and greater sensitivity to minority feelings. Simple expedients of civilian review boards or neighborhood councils are in and of themselves unlikely to produce desired results. Perhaps James Q. Wilson did not overstate the case when he wrote:[25]

> If all big-city police departments were filled tomorrow with Negro college graduates and placed under the control of the neighborhoods they are supposed to control, most of the problems that exist today would continue to exist and some in fact might get worse. The crime rate would not go down; indeed, owing to police timidity about making arrests among people who have a voice in their management, it might go up marginally. Police involvement in conflict and disorder would have no happier outcomes, because most disorder—family or neighbor quarrels—does not involve the community nor would the community necessarily have any better idea how to resolve it than do the police now. Perceived police abuse and harassment might decline in the neighborhood, but since each neightborhood would have its own police, the amount of abuse and harassment perceived by a person from one neighborhood entering a different neighborhood (say a Negro entering a white area, or vice versa) might increase. The conflict between neighborhood residents who want more police protections (small business-men, homeowners, older people) and those who want less (teenagers, transients, young men hanging on street corners) would remain and the police would tend, in the eyes of one group, to serve the standards of the other.

[25] Wilson, "Dilemmas of Police Administration," *op. cit.,* p. 409.

16. URBAN HOUSING

The economic system of this country has been enormously successful in providing housing for middle- and upper-income groups. Part of the reason for this success is the political system's strategic underwriting and reinforcement of the economic system in the area of housing. The combined strength of the economic and political systems, however, has been insufficient to deliver adequate and sound housing to sizable segments of the lowest socioeconomic sector of the society. This chapter will examine urban housing, governmental programs and responsibilities in and affecting urban housing, and state and local governmental organization in housing and urban renewal. Special emphasis will be placed on the politics of housing, especially the nature of interest group and political party activity in this field.

SUBSTANDARD HOUSING

As of 1960, there were eleven million substandard or overcrowded housing units in the United States—or 16 percent of the total housing inventory. In 1969, twenty million Americans lived in housing units considered to be below minimum standards required for human habitation. Metropolitan areas contain approximately four million units of substandard and overcrowded housing, plus millions of additional dwellings that are deteriorating and in violation of local codes. However, somewhat contrary to what might be expected, unsound housing is not concentrated exclusively in urban areas or in central cities of urban areas—in fact, proportionately more substandard housing exists in rural and "suburban"[1] areas than in urban and central city areas respectively (see Table 16.1), possibly because of the absence of housing and other regulatory codes in many rural and suburban communities. Nevertheless, the peculiar nature of city housing (its visibility and the population density associated with it) and the political ramifications of unsound

TABLE 16.1
*Unsound Owner-Occupied Housing in
Metropolitan Areas by Region, 1960*

	WHITE AND NONWHITE		NONWHITE	
	UNSOUND UNITS AS A PROPORTION OF TOTAL UNITS IN:			
	CENTRAL		CENTRAL	
REGION	CITY	SUBURB	CITY	SUBURB
United States	11%	16%	33%	51%
Northeast	10	10	32	32
North Central	11	16	31	47
South	13	21	38	64
West	7	14	19	33

SOURCE: Advisory Commission on Intergovernmental Relations, *Metropolitan Social and Economic Disparities: Implications for Intergovernmental Relations in Central Cities and Suburbs* (Washington, D.C.: U.S. Government Printing Office, January, 1965), p. 183.

[1] "Suburban" refers to all portions of the metropolitan area (SMSA) not part of the central city, discussed as the "suburban circle" theory in Chapter 12, and to be distinguished from the more popular conception (or the "upward class mobility" theory) of suburbia.

housing has clearly made the city housing "problem" more pressing than that in rural America or in the "suburbs."

Substandard housing is located in metropolitan areas in all parts of the nation, with the South in particular having more than its share (Table 16.1). A relatively low 10 percent of the owner-occupied housing units in the Northeast are unsound, and in western cities an even smaller proportion of such housing falls in this category. Using the incidence of substandard owner-occupied units as the measure, housing conditions for the poor do not vary along central city-suburban lines in the northeastern section of the country, while in the north central, southern, and western regions, areas outside the central city but still within the metropolitan area have proportionately fewer sound housing units than do cities. In all parts of the United States and spread throughout the metropolitan area, nonwhites are considerably less likely than whites to enjoy decent housing, as can be seen in Table 16.1. Unsound owner-occupied dwellings inhabited by metropolitan area nonwhites ranges from one fifth (the lowest) to a high of nearly two thirds of all housing in this class, depending on the region or portion of the metropolitan area examined. One third of the in-city housing units owned by nonwhites are substandard; outside of cities half of such dwellings fall in this category.

At the same time, most housing in the central city is not owner-occupied but rental in character.[2] Here the statistics are even more illuminating. About one third of the rental units in metropolitan areas are substandard, and this figure rises to well over 50 percent for nonwhites (Table 16.2). The incidence of unsound nonwhite rental housing is found at staggering levels in all regions of the United States, both in and outside metropolitan area central cities.

These figures more than suggest that housing is an acute problem, particularly for the nonwhite minority. However, our primary purpose is not to call attention to the problem, but to outline some of its dimensions so that the reason for the emergence of urban housing as a political issue (and it has so emerged) will become clearer. Urban housing first became a nationwide issue during the Depression and has gained increasing recognition in national and local councils since that time. Although the degree of success attached to housing programs for the poor has been limited, over the years both public and private resources have been mobilized to seek solutions to the housing problem, especially, more recently, in Negro ghettos. Two key national commissions—the National Advisory Commission on Civil Disorders and the National Commission

[2] In the suburbs on the other hand, three quarters of the housing units are owner-occupied. Advisory Commission on Intergovernmental Relations, *Metropolitan Social and Economic Disparities: Implications for Intergovernmental Relations in Central Cities and Suburbs* (Washington, D.C.: U.S. Government Printing Office, January, 1965), p. 182.

TABLE 16.2
Unsound Renter-Occupied Housing in
Metropolitan Areas by Region, 1960

	WHITE AND NONWHITE		NONWHITE	
	UNSOUND UNITS AS A PROPORTION OF TOTAL UNITS IN:			
	CENTRAL		CENTRAL	
REGION	CITY	SUBURB	CITY	SUBURB
United States	33%	36%	56%	70%
Northeast	30	25	54	55
North Central	35	36	55	66
South	37	44	61	82
West	26	27	42	49

SOURCE: Advisory Commission on Intergovernmental Relations, *Metropolitan Social and Economic Disparities: Implications for Intergovernmental Relations in Central Cities and Suburbs* (Washington, D.C.: U.S. Government Printing Office, January, 1965), p. 189.

on Urban Problems—issued reports in the late 1960s stressing the poor condition of housing for the disadvantaged and urging immediate remedial action.[3] Congressional and executive branch action in 1968 and 1969 is further evidence of the mounting national concern with low-income housing. In the Housing Act of 1968, Congress called for the construction and rehabilitation of 26 million housing units over the next ten years, which goal is to include six million dwellings for "low and moderate income families" (the somewhat guarded term used by national authorities to identify or alternatively to keep from identifying the group the national government would like to reach).

THE POLITICAL SYSTEM
AND HOUSING PRODUCTION

All rhetoric aside, the building industry has been producing at an average rate of 1.5 million housing units per year (1959–1968). It is instructive to note that if this rate were projected for the years 1969–1978, only 15 million units would be constructed, not the 26 million Congress set as the objective; and even this projection may exceed actual production if 1969's predicted drop from the average 1.5 million figure is to be representative of the coming decade. Further, nearly all of the housing

[3] See *Report of the National Advisory Commission on Civil Disorders* (New York: Bantam Books, 1968); and National Commission on Urban Problems, *Building the American City* (Washington, D.C.: U.S. Government Printing Office, 1968).

currently being provided (including private units assisted by government programs) is for middle-to-upper-income groups; only a small portion of the total production is made available to low-income families currently housed in substandard dwellings.

Why is it that the homebuilding industry has been so effective in serving certain social classes and not others? In a general sense, the reason is that large numbers of low-income families cannot afford decent and particularly new housing units. Builders build for those who can pay, not for those who cannot. And unlike others responsible for a basic service—such as doctors—builders do not provide housing for those in need and pass along the costs to those who can afford to pay. More significant and somewhat startling, government efforts designed to bring sound housing within the grasp of American families of modest means have affected virtually only the middle- and upper-income sectors of the public. The Federal Housing Administration (FHA) and Veterans Administration (VA) programs, initiated by the national government in the 1930s and 1940s respectively, have directly or indirectly assured the middle class of decent housing—and on attractive terms. FHA- and VA-guaranteed loans at government-pegged interest rates have significantly broadened the middle-class housing market and bolstered the building industry in its quest to serve this market. In addition, the pump-priming secondary market activities of the Federal National Mortgage Association (Fannie Mae)[4] have further strengthened the building industry and expanded this industry's ability to meet middle-class housing needs. Upper-income segments of the population have been helped, although somewhat indirectly, by the "carryover" and institutionalizing effects of these government actions—that is, conventional loans or loans not backed by the government, including those to upper-income groups, are higher (as a percentage of the total value of the home) and the interest rates lower, and funds for such loans more readily accessible because of the economic patterns set by government mortgage policy. As this demonstrates, the housing industry and the national government have in reality joined forces to increase the capacity of the homebuilding business; but this alliance has had a broadly differential effect among the various class levels in the economy. Later, we shall review other governmental programs which have an impact on housing for the disadvantaged, particularly activities directed specifically at the lower strata of the social system.

Another factor is important in this respect. The building industry is inhibited in the production of low-cost housing for the poor as well as for

[4]   Fannie Mae was restructured in the Housing Act of 1968, and made a government-sponsored private corporation. A new government corporation—Government National Mortgage Association (Ginnie Mae)—was established by the same legislation to assume some of Fannie Mae's previous responsibilities.

others because of the structure of the industry itself. The homebuilding field is dominated by the small builder, operating within a relatively small geographical area, and doing only a limited business. Throughout this land there are over 100,000 homebuilders. By far the vast majority are each responsible for no more than $5 million worth of contracts per year, and a sizable proportion are found in the under $500,000 a year category.[5] The largest of the homebuilding firms is Levitt and Sons, now a subsidiary of International Telephone and Telegraph, which had $123 million worth of business in (fiscal) 1968. Following on Levitt's heels is Del C. Webb of Phoenix ($112 million); and a large gap separates the two volume leaders from the third, the Centrex Corporation of Dallas, whose sales are in the $60-to-$70 million range. In all, on the basis of the most recent figures, only 22 building companies do over $20 million of business annually, and less than 60 of the 100,000-plus housing producers are in the $10-million-or-over category. The housing industry then is to be distinguished from other major industries in America, in which $1 to $2 billion in sales each year are not uncommon and where an annual sales total of $500 million or more is typical among the larger firms. And without the introduction of mass-produced, off-site-constructed housing in this country, it would appear that builders can make only limited strides toward large-scale operations. Currently, housing is put up on-site, one house and one element at a time, with a wide array of high-priced subcontractors doing most of the work (this includes plumbing, roofing, electrical, dry-wall, heating, and numerous other subcontractors), which means that building costs are high and volume low. Without economies of scale, which could reduce housing costs by one quarter or more, it is doubtful if much new housing will find its way to low-income families who need it. In all likelihood, with government at its side, the middle class will continue to be able to absorb the economic consequences—the costs—of the building industry's internal structure; and upper classes in the future as at present will reap the side-benefits of the government-builder-middle-class coalition's public policies, while at the same time having little difficulty in meeting the high costs imposed by the industry's structure and operating methods.

The housing industry is an economic force—or part of the institutional apparatus of the economic system. Yet, to an extent, the housing portion of the economic system is organized the way it is because of the character of the political system. Certainly, national government programs have had a significant impact on builders, and the nature of the effect has been both to expand the industry's capability and in the last analysis to reinforce the industry as it is now and has been organized in the past. But in this respect the more important part of the political system—the part that directly and immediately structures the organizational foundation of the

[5] "Here Come the Giants," *Professional Builder* (August, 1968), 87–88, 90.

building industry—is local government. Public regulation of housing and related activities is largely, almost exclusively, a local matter in the United States, meaning that this sort of power is in the hands of numerous, independent governments, found in limited geographical settings, and containing small populations (see Chapter 9).

To be exact, over 14,000 local governments have the building regulation authority in this country; this includes planning, zoning, subdivision regulation, building codes, housing codes, and a local building-permit system. Not all local governments exercise all of these powers, however, and the content and patterns of administration and organization of each activity vary considerably from jurisdiction to jurisdiction.[6] Of a total universe of 18,000 local governments that might be assumed to have building regulation control, the incidence of this kind of regulatory power is as follows:[7]

	NUMBER OF GOVERNMENTS WITH ACTIVITY
Planning board	10,717
Zoning ordinance	9,595
Subdivision regulation	8,086
Building code	8,344
Housing code	4,904
Any of these or a local building permit system	14,088

Building and land-use regulatory authority is widely found in urban-type jurisdictions throughout the United States. Among municipalities and townships in the 5,000-or-above population category, about 3,900 of the some 4,000 governments, or nearly 97 percent of the total units in this population class, have some form of building regulation. (See Table 16.3.) Further, as is evident in Table 16.3, the public regulation of building is characteristic of both metropolitan and nonmetropolitan governments with a minimum population of 5,000—even in townships outside of metropolitan areas, which of all the groups of governments in Table 16.3

6   The content of building and related land-regulation controls is by no means uniform among local governments. Further, the organizational structure within which building and land regulations are administered follows no single pattern, and any number of local departments may have responsibility for these functions. Often, a buildings department will have code enforcement and building-permit authority and a planning commission will have some control over planning, zoning, and subdivision regulations. Additional agencies that may be involved in building and land regulation include a licenses and inspections department and a health department.

7   Allen D. Manvel, *Local Land and Building Regulation* (Washington, D.C.: National Commission on Urban Problems, 1968), p. 4.

TABLE 16.3
Municipalities and New England–Type Townships[a]
of 5,000 or More Population with
Building Regulation Activities, 1968

	TOTAL GOVERNMENTS (1967)	GOVERNMENTS WITH REGULATIONS	
		NUMBER	PERCENT OF TOTAL
Total	4067	3931	96.7
Within SMSA's	2382	2317	97.3
Municipalities, 50,000+	314	314	100.0
Municipalities, 5,000–49,999	1303	1303	100.0
Townships of 5,000+	765	700	91.5
Outside SMSA's	1685	1614	95.8
Municipalities, 5,000–49,999	1352	1333	98.6
Townships, 5,000+	333	281	84.4

[a] New England–type townships are townships with municipal responsibilities. Such
units are found in the six New England states and New Jersey, New York, Ohio,
Pennsylvania, and Wisconsin.
SOURCE: Allen D. Manvel, *Local Land and Building Regulation* (Washington, D.C.:
National Commission on Urban Problems, 1968), p. 27.

are least likely to have building regulations, over 80 percent of the
governments are engaged in building regulation activities.

Building and land-use governmental authority then is a thoroughly
decentralized matter. Decentralization of governmental power nevertheless in and of itself does not tell us much, and, in fact, this is not really
the question under consideration. From the standpoint of the structure of
the housing industry, what is more important is the substantive nature of
the regulations over building from community to community. For instance, although we have already suggested that this is not true, it would
be entirely possible for all or substantially all localities to have uniform
and nonrestrictive building regulations, and such a pattern would certainly have an effect on the building industry. Nationally recognized and
professionally recommended codes, for example, are in existence and
could theoretically be used by local governments. Model building codes
(governing new construction) have been formulated by various organizations; the major model building codes are the Southern Standard
Building Code, the National Building Code, and separate codes of the
Building Officials Conference of America and the International Conference of Building Officials. This is not to say that the "model" codes are all
consistent with one another and therefore uniform, or that they are all

nonrestrictive; they are not. But at the same time, their widespread use would add an element of uniformity and nonrestrictiveness to local building regulations. And if large-scale operations and modern building practices were to be encouraged or at least allowed by local governments, local building codes would have to be somewhat uniform and nonrestrictive. Yet, the facts of the matter are that less than one sixth of all local governments have a building code that conforms to a model code and has been kept up to date.[8] Further, local building codes are frequently restrictive, sometimes in the extreme. To illustrate, many local governments prohibit the use of plastic pipe (requiring the more expensive metal variety instead) and preassembled electrical wiring and plumbing systems in housing. The effect has been the clear inhibition of quantity housing production; additionally, big corporations with a national field of operations considering new product areas have been deterred from entering the housing business because the substantive content and notable variety in local building codes limit the potential profitability of housing ventures compared to high-volume alternative investments. Techniques of standardization, industrialized housing, and assembly-line processes cannot be used in residential construction because of the presence of a whole host of nonuniform and restrictive building regulations at the community level. A builder in the metropolitan area of Cleveland must comply with 50 different codes; homebuilders in Chicago must cope with the same number of independent regulatory controls over building; and 30 distinct building codes stand firmly in the way of more economical construction in the Minneapolis region. Conditions in local building regulation then contribute substantially to the current structure of the housing industry, and no change is in sight.

Zoning is another regulatory authority of local government which can have a major impact on building and housing. The zoning power, which controls the specific use of land, lot size, and population density, has more influence on land development than any of the other regulatory measures. And as building codes and along with the other regulatory activities, zoning serves to fragment the housing market and thus has the same effect on the building industry. In fact, zoning is one of the most cherished local functions, particularly in the suburbs of the metropolitan area, where it is the key general-purpose governmental mechanism for advancing the middle-class values of physical, social, and economic homogeneity. Because of the decentralized location of the zoning authority in the political system and because of its uneven application in communities, zoning discourages virtually all but small-scale building endeavors. Further, typical local zoning restrictions on density (limiting

[8] *Ibid.*, p. iii (foreword by Paul H. Douglas, Chairman of the National Commission on Urban Problems).

development to low densities) and lot size (limiting development to high minimums) make big housing undertakings impractical for large segments of the urban and metropolitan area.

All evidence points to the conclusion that local government regulatory controls in housing directly or indirectly account in large part for the conditions in the building industry and the high cost of housing. Existing policies of local government in this area however do not survive without the support of influential elements in the local community. It is also correct to surmise that communities, in part as a result of pressures from the various interests dependent on present land-use and building regulation assignments in the political system, will not readily relinquish authority in this field. We shall return to the question of the role of local government in housing later in the chapter, in a discussion of proposed strategies by which governmental regulatory control over housing and land-use might be restructured, mass production of housing facilitated, and low-cost housing advanced to the poor. In the meantime, we shall examine national urban housing policy, particularly as this policy affects localities and their governments, and the politics of housing, including a review of the dominant interest groups in and the position of the two political parties on urban housing policy.

NATIONAL URBAN HOUSING POLICY
AND LOCAL GOVERNMENT

The national government has taken significant action which has tended to set the tone of the more activist aspects of urban housing policy—that is, the aspects of housing policy that have given the governments of the nation direct responsibility for community housing (this is to be contrasted with housing *regulatory* functions). At the subnational level, local government as opposed to state government has had the primary authority for carrying out urban housing policy, including housing programs aided by the national government. In view of federal assistance in the urban housing area, urban housing has been largely a national government-local government affair. Only relatively recently have state governments begun to demonstrate an interest in urban housing. Major housing efforts were launched by New York, Connecticut, New Jersey, and Maryland in the 1960s; otherwise, states have commonly restricted their participation to the delegation of urban housing powers to local governments. In this section, we shall first discuss national housing legislation and then analyze how the programs or requirements established by this legislation have operated in or affected communities and their local governments. We shall examine each such program, beginning with those set up in the earliest legislation, before going on to more recent national action.

Housing Act of 1937: Public Housing

The first national housing legislation directly involving local government in an ongoing national urban housing program was the Housing Act of 1937. The key feature of this enactment was its introduction of public housing as a more or less permanent activity of local and national government. Public housing refers to the provision, ownership, and management of residential dwelling units by government for the needy poor, to be distinguished from governmental housing measures (of the FHA and VA variety) in which the government performs a facilitative or stimulatory function by underwriting or guaranteeing loans for middle- and low-income families. Although not the first or only example of public housing in the United States, the housing initially authorized by the 1937 act formed the foundation of what was to become the major domestic public housing program in the nation.

The objectives of this legislation were twofold: to increase the number of jobs and assist in alleviating recurring unemployment (through the resulting construction work generated), and to clear slums and eliminate unsafe and unsanitary housing inhabited by poor families. The values underlying the legislation were of an economic and social welfare nature: public housing was seen as a means to stimulate the economy and to assure decent housing for the disadvantaged. Additionally, one of the social welfare assumptions behind the legislation was that improved housing would contribute importantly to a decrease in the incidence of social deviancy and disorganization in slums, a belief at best only partially realized in practice. Significantly, the 1937 enactment did not openly emphasize the values of community planning or private business involvement, although some site planning and private contractors would necessarily be a part of public housing processes; furthermore, the act did not grant any meaningful role in housing planning and execution to affected citizens, since citizen participation was not an element of the original concept found in national housing legislation.

Support for the 1937 program was widespread, but far from universal. As reflected in the congressional vote, it would appear that city constituencies were strongly behind public housing, with rural populations outside the South and other areas represented by Democrats opposed. Public housing was backed by a liberal Democratic administration, and the powerful majority Democratic party in Congress led by its northern liberal wing cast a sizable percentage of its votes for public housing. Senate Republicans were narrowly against the measure; a minority liberal

GOP faction in the upper house sided with the Democrats, and House Republicans were united in opposition. (See Table 16.4.) It should be pointed out that the idea of the government (even at the local level) building and operating housing projects for low-income groups was and still is a controversial political issue, frequently setting off heated ideological debates. In fact, the conflict surrounding public housing is undoubtedly one of the reasons why this program has been given such limited funds over the years; conservatives, who have nearly always viewed government housing with considerable alarm, have been able to contain and restrict the public housing effort. In addition, the business community, while standing ready to embrace certain private enterprise-oriented concepts such as urban renewal, has shown little if any sympathy with public housing; many segments of the private sector to this day are unequivocally against public housing. The political base of public housing in 1937 was therefore largely liberal and Democratic.

PUBLIC HOUSING
AND THE COMMUNITY

The means of implementing national public housing policy affects local institutions in a basic way and conforms in broad outline to the spirit of the American political system. The program was not to be executed directly by the national government—this method was used in the early days of the New Deal but eventually discarded—but by local government with federal assistance. After state governments, usually through enabling legislation, authorize communities to develop public housing, localities create public housing authorities or what are known as local housing agencies (LHAs) to administer the program. The national government then advances loan and subsidy aid to community housing authorities which construct, own, and run government housing projects.

Presently, well over 1,500 public housing authorities are located in communities throughout the country. Technically, most of these authorities are independent of general-purpose government in the locality; in fact, they are usually governments in and of themselves (that is, special districts). A persistent and troublesome concern of numerous political scientists and public administration experts has been what is considered an excessive fragmentation of public power over the various matters of a governmental character at the local level; and according to the standard judged important by these scholars, public housing authorities are at least contributing guilty forces. The existence of these autonomous units of government within municipalities and counties certainly does not add to the unity and central direction that public administration orthodoxy and conventional wisdom in political science believe essential.

Initially, one of the more immediate reasons for placing the public housing function outside general-purpose local government was the fear that within city government this vital activity would be more directly subject to political influence. Of course, when many public housing authorities were first established, the chances of machine dominance of municipal government were substantially greater than would be the case today. In defense of their independent status, it is sometimes argued that public housing authorities do have key links with general-purpose governments, and that under these circumstances such authorities should not be too harshly judged if indeed they should be criticized at all.[9] Supporting evidence for this position can be cited, as often the chief executive and/or governing body of a municipality or county government appoints members of the local housing agency board. Further, the general-purpose community government will have considerable formal and informal control over the location of public housing sites, and this can be pointed to as an additional check on the housing authority's independence. Finally, if the objective of public housing is the provision of more sound dwelling units for the poor, and if the desirability of integrating housing under a single head or council with general responsibilities in the community is determined by this criterion (and not uncritically accepted as an article of faith), it is a matter of some question as to whether public housing should be assigned to city hall. In many cities public housing has become essentially Negro housing—and what is more important, low-income Negro housing. As a result, finding sites and vacant land which can be used for public housing has become and still is a political issue of some magnitude.[10] This issue has been an especially intense one where the local authority has attempted to place public housing in a lower-middle-class ethnic neighborhood; in actuality, the publicly proposed location of government-owned housing in or near nonpoor neighborhoods of either race (including blacks) or of any ancestral background (including Anglo-Saxon) will draw middle-class fire. City governments are understandably sensitive to majoritarian pressures—meaning middle-class white influence—on matters such as public housing which have at best lower-class constituencies, and are therefore unlikely to expand significantly housing opportunities for blacks; and this holds even if larger sums of money were appropriated for public housing. Housing authority units that are governed by an appointed body, while definitely not immune to such pressures, are less susceptible to stampeding majorities than are popularly elected city officials.

[9] See Advisory Commission on Intergovernmental Relations, *The Problem of Special Districts in American Government* (Washington, D.C.: U.S. Government Printing Office, May, 1964), p. 73.
[10] See Martin Meyerson and Edward C. Banfield, *Politics, Planning, and the Public Interest* (New York: Free Press, 1955).

Public housing has not been particularly successful in achieving what might reasonably be seen as the program's objectives in communities. Waiting lists numbering into the thousands of persons are not uncommon in some cities, as is discussed in greater detail later. The recent trend toward the development of high-rise public housing projects has caused some communities sociological pain, since it appears that these structures are not particularly well-suited for low-income families. Spiraling costs and vandalism have made some localities increasingly dependent on national government subsidies and support and have forced a few authorities to boost rents to such a point that they are hardly consistent with the income of the residents, let alone the goals of public housing.

Housing Act of 1949: Urban Renewal

BACKGROUND TO THE LEGISLATION   After World War II several developments in metropolitan areas were of growing concern to many Americans, especially downtown central-city businessmen and related interests. These developments included: the decline and deterioration of the center core of the city, population movement out of the city and into the suburbs of the metropolitan area, the initial stages of business decentralization into the fringe areas, and the concentration of the poor and nonwhite in the city's close-in areas.

Action of some major dimensions was required, or so it seemed to those concerned. Central-city economic leaders staked out a strategy, the first step of which was to form an organizational mechanism that could serve as the nucleus of an effort to moderate, arrest, and perhaps reverse some of the trends characteristic of the postwar city. Working through the local chamber of commerce was a possibility, but this alternative was typically discarded because this traditional business organization's membership base was too broad and its interests too narrow for it to be an effective vehicle to serve the desired end. Instead, special civic action groups were initiated with the avowed goal of improving and revitalizing the downtown core of the central city. Examples were the Greater Philadelphia Movement (GPM), the Allegheny Conference on Community Development in Pittsburgh, the Central Area Committee of Chicago, Civic Progress in St. Louis, and the Civic Conference in Boston.[11]

The dominant forces in these organizations were core-city bankers, industrialists, department store executives, members of prominent law firms, and other key representatives of the local economic power structure. These were interests that were deeply affected and increasingly

11 Edward C. Banfield and James Q. Wilson, *City Politics* (New York: Random House, 1963), p. 267.

negatively impressed by the economic and social conditions in the central core. The immediate agenda was to promote action directed toward changing the city's image, making it more attractive to residents of the metropolitan area and to potential investors, and encouraging physical redevelopment of the central-city core area.

In some instances the attainment of these goals necessitated a significant reform of the local political climate (Philadelphia), while elsewhere the existing political organization found it expedient to adjust its operations to accommodate downtown redevelopment pressures (Pittsburgh). The Greater Philadelphia Movement became a unifying instrument for the foes of machine politics, emerging in the late 1940s and early 1950s as a rallying point of a Democratic reform movement. In a timely although unconventional alliance with such liberal forces as the local Americans for Democratic Action and intellectually inclined Democrats, the GPM succeeded in crushing the long-dominant Republican machine, hoisting to power bluebloods Joseph S. Clark and Richardson Dilworth on the city Democratic ticket. Along with Clark, Dilworth, and their professional entourage, GPM interests controlled important city planning and redevelopment activities throughout the 1950s. The Greater Philadelphia Movement and its allies also served to upgrade the city's stature and public image while muscling through an unparalleled physical renewal program. The redevelopment-minded downtown businessmen in GPM worked most effectively with the central-city mayor—both Clark and Dilworth were reform mayors—a coincidence of interests, as a matter of fact, noted in other cities undergoing downtown face-lifting.[12]

We believe that this background illustrates the nature of the foundation that was being built in American communities in the postwar period and stimulated national concern in the area of city redevelopment and slum clearance. The fact of the matter is that big-city businessmen were not particularly exercised by the New Deal housing legislation which was primarily intended to be an economic measure which provided government housing for the poor. Now that city business investments were seriously threatened, a reemphasis in national housing and city development policy and a reordering of objectives seemed imperative. The direct or indirect influence of powerful local interests in shaping legislation in Washington should not be discounted in any analysis of American politics.

THE LEGISLATION   The most important part of the 1949 legislation was the urban development section, or what became known as the "Title I"

---

[12] Urban redevelopment linked Mayor Richard Lee's New Haven administration with downtown businessmen for example. [Robert A. Dahl, *Who Governs?* (New Haven: Yale University Press, 1961), chap. 10.] It served the same end in Pittsburgh under Mayor David Lawrence.

(after its title in the act) program. Other sections of this legislation covered public housing, mortgage insurance, and planning.

The objectives of the Housing Act of 1949 were to clear slums, stimulate housing production, and provide "a decent home . . . for every American family." The values behind this enactment are to be compared and contrasted with those in the 1937 legislation. The economic and social welfare values were generally carried over from 1937. However, two additional values were incorporated into the 1949 act: planning and private enterprise involvement. Specifically, the legislation called for some degree of community planning in redevelopment and housing with the goal of clearing slums and improving the environment of the city; further, the act provided for maximum private business participation in the revitalization of American cities.

The identification of the objectives and values of this housing legislation is helpful in gaining insight into the partisan support and opposition patterns associated with the enactment. The most important factor in this respect is that the Housing Act of 1949 had considerable support in some traditionally conservative quarters. For example, upper-chamber co-sponsors of the bill were Senator Robert A. Taft, prominent Republican leader from Ohio, Senator Allen Ellender, conservative Democrat from Louisiana, and Senator Robert Wagner, liberal Democrat of New York. Neither before nor since has a major controversial piece of (what was widely considered to be) social legislation enjoyed such broad political endorsement. The favorable stance of northern Democrats was, of course, not unexpected, as this position is consistent with the liberal Democratic attitude on social policy generally. In all, Senate and House Democrats and Senate Republicans voted for the bill; the one dissenting group was the House GOP. (See Table 16.4.) The partisan voting behavior on the 1949 legislation is discussed in greater detail under The Politics of Housing: Political Parties, later in this chapter.

URBAN RENEWAL AND COMMUNITIES

The means by which the urban redevelopment program was to be implemented followed the pattern established under public housing: it was to be a local effort. As a result of the 1949 action of the national government, many communities created local public agencies (LPAs), called redevelopment or renewal authorities (for example, the Boston Redevelopment Authority and the Yonkers, N.Y., Urban Renewal Agency). Local government participation in the national urban redevelopment program is typically authorized through state enabling legislation; presently, well over 600 localities have urban redevelopment and renewal projects which have received or are currently operating with federal assistance.

Unlike public housing authorities, most urban redevelopment authorities are not considered to be sufficiently independent of general-purpose governments in the community to qualify as special districts.[13] In this sense, these authorities then operate as subordinate units within the general political and governmental processes in the locality. If the general-purpose local governing body serves as the local public agency, the legal nature of the relationship between urban renewal and other local public functions is clear: the responsibility over redevelopment as well as other activities rests in a single body. In addition, redevelopment may be delegated to the local housing authority or be set up as a special district.[14] In these two cases some integration of redevelopment with general-purpose government programs can be expected in view of the federal requirement that the governing body of every community anticipating national urban renewal assistance must approve proposed renewal projects before they are submitted to Washington for funding.

Nevertheless, political reality has dictated a somewhat independent role and status for local redevelopment authorities across the United States, an organizational position incidentally not too sharply differentiated from that of the legally autonomous local public housing authority. Urban renewal agencies have been at best selectively responsive to local political pressures, a posture permitted because of the administrative isolation of urban renewal from the broader political processes in the community. At least in their early years, urban renewal authorities were dominated by local and federal administrators and city business interests whose main objective was to clear slums from central business district areas. The independent local boards which administered the urban renewal program either within or without the city government usually were well manned by representatives of the local business community, a pattern much less typical of the local housing authority. This method of representation coupled with a powerful administrative bureaucracy clothed with condemnation authority and backed by federal resources allowed the urban renewal program to progress toward the achievement of its objectives in a way that has frequently drawn the admiration and respect of other agencies and departments in local government.

At the same time, the consequences of this kind of operation have caused urban renewal to come under heavy fire from scholars and others

---

13 U.S. Bureau of the Census, *Census of Governments, 1967;* Vol. 1, *Government Organization* (Washington, D.C.: U.S. Government Printing Office, 1968), pp. 297–457.
14 Greer classifies LPAs into three categories: subagencies of a city government, part of a housing and redevelopment agency, and separate entities. See Scott Greer, *Urban Renewal and American Cities* (Indianapolis: Bobbs-Merrill, 1965), p. 11.

representing both the conservative[15] and liberal[16] points of view. Conservatives have been ideologically opposed to urban renewal since its inception in 1949, while many liberals have turned against the program in view of its effects on the Negro minority and its emphasis on providing upper-income housing. Urban renewal has been tagged "Negro removal" by some, and has come under sharp attack from the left in this light. Many of the program's liberal critics are troubled because neighborhood social systems have been disrupted, adequate housing is not guaranteed to the dispossessed poor, and few of those displaced can afford the high-price housing of the redeveloped area under urban renewal. Without the freedom that comes from organizational and policy independence, it is doubtful that urban redevelopment authorities would have been able to muster much support and initiate much of a program at all. As it has turned out in practice, with the rise of additional "independent" forces in community politics such as community action agencies and model cities organizations, urban renewal has slowly grinded to a halt in a number of communities; and the program's direction has changed in others. As long as the urban renewal function had limited visibility—and this was facilitated by independent administration—the program was technically successful. Opening urban renewal to public debate and numerous community pressures was bound to curtail the activity as it was initially administered.

The detailed workings of urban renewal are as follows: Once established, the local public authority plans the redevelopment of a particular subneighborhood area, secures the necessary local and national government approvals, acquires the land and improvements in the approved project area through condemnation or otherwise, razes or clears the land where necessary, prepares the land for disposition, and then sells the land at low cost to private developers who construct buildings and facilities for private use in accordance with certain governmentally set standards and stipulations (some portion of any project area may be used for public housing, a "public" use).[17]

Although the financing of urban renewal programs is complicated— essentially, two thirds of the difference between what it costs the locality to acquire, clear, and prepare the land for disposition and what is paid to

[15] See Martin Anderson, The Federal Bulldozer, A Critical Analysis of Urban Renewal, 1949–1962 (Cambridge: MIT Press, 1964).
[16] See, for example, Nathan Glazer, "The Asphalt Bungle," Book Week, Washington Post, January 3, 1965; and Herbert J. Gans, "The Failure of Urban Renewal," in James Q. Wilson (ed.), Urban Renewal (Cambridge: MIT Press, 1966), pp. 537–557.
[17] For a concise discussion of urban renewal and how it operates, see William L. Slayton, "Report on Urban Renewal," Statement of Commissioner, Urban Renewal Administration, before the Subcommittee on Housing, Committee on Banking and Currency, U.S. House of Representatives, November 21, 1963, pp. 398 ff.

the locality by private developers for the land is made up in the form of a grant from the national government—in actuality, the cash contribution of the national government amounts to more than two thirds of all cash given by the local and national governments because of noncash aid provided by the local government (which is, incidentally, counted twice, as part of the gross project cost and the local contribution).[18]

As this suggests, both the local and national governments have important roles to play in urban renewal; and as indicated previously, the state government passes enabling legislation to permit communities to engage in urban redevelopment activities. States may also assist local renewal efforts in other respects. Upon the publication of Martin Anderson's *The Federal Bulldozer* in 1964, some controversy developed over whether urban renewal was a federal or local activity. By virtue of the title of his work as well as the substance of his book, Anderson views urban renewal as a federal program; by contrast, the National Association of Housing and Redevelopment Officials, which represents local redevelopment agencies, sees urban renewal as basically a local matter.[19]

One final comment on the 1949 legislation is in order. Urban renewal has not turned out to be a social welfare program, and this is true notwithstanding the intent of the legislation or any of its sponsors. In the light of its accomplishments, it is better described as a business and middle-to-upper-income housing program. By providing the legal power and financial subsidies, governments in this country have in effect underwritten the preferences of influential local interests through urban renewal.

Housing Act of 1954:
Broadening Urban Redevelopment

After becoming President in 1953, Dwight D. Eisenhower appointed an Advisory Committee on Housing to recommend a course of action in housing for the new administration. The committee was composed of manufacturers, industrialists, and real estate interests, among others, and in its report it urged the abolition of the public housing program, an expansion of FHA, and a broadening of redevelopment efforts. The advice of the Eisenhower housing panel was important in two respects: first, if accepted, it would require a modification of national urban housing and redevelopment policy; and second, it tended to confirm the suspicions of some observers that businessmen saw the private enterprise-

18 For details on the financing of an urban renewal project, see Ashley A. Ford and Hilbert Fefferman, "Federal Urban Renewal Legislation," in James Q. Wilson (ed.), *Urban Renewal, op. cit.*, p. 95. This article also presents a summary of urban renewal legislation from the time of the program's origin to 1960.
19 See "Federal Bulldozer's Fallacies," *Journal of Housing*, April, 1965.

oriented redevelopment program taking the place of the social welfare-type public housing program. Nearly the entire business community had always opposed direct government subsidy to the disadvantaged for housing, which was likened to a form of socialism. Some of the same business interests, however, favor other kinds of government assistance, including urban renewal grants, which they frankly view in a different light. The Republican administration, in any event, appeared to reflect some of the committee's thinking in its actions and proposals (in public housing, for instance), and advanced some of the ideas of this group in its housing package submitted to Congress in 1954.

Specifically, the Housing Act of 1954

1. introduced the term and newly defined concept of "urban renewal," broadening the earlier legislation's concentration on urban redevelopment to include rehabilitation and conservation as well as slum clearance;

2. expanded FHA by extending the government-guaranteed loan program to the rehabilitation of existing units in urban renewal areas and to the construction of new housing for persons displaced by redevelopment;

3. required each community participating in urban renewal, public housing, and the low-income FHA programs to comply with a seven-point Workable Program for Community Development, including codes and ordinances (building, housing, and zoning regulations), comprehensive community planning, neighborhood analyses, adequate administrative organizations, financing, housing for displaced persons, and citizen participation; and

4. authorized grants for urban planning, a provision popularly known as the "701" program, so-named after that section in the 1954 act.

The 1954 legislation represented a major step in the national housing policy area, and some of its provisions no doubt startled a number of more conservative Republicans who had expected the new administration to press for a return to the free market in housing and for a rollback in the housing agenda for the mid-1950s. In point of fact, it does seem that the Republican administration was strongly influenced by political conservatism in the housing area, but by a new kind of conservatism. Neither urban renewal nor urban planning as administered in practice in communities can be considered "liberal" programs, nor do either have a social welfare flavor, except perhaps on a high theoretical plane. Both urban renewal and urban planning at the community level have been oriented toward the interests of the business sector, usually the larger of the local businesses; and, not uncommonly in the past, both functions have been administered by boards dominated by businessmen, with the real estate community enjoying a disproportionate voice in both areas. Channeling federal funds to local urban renewal or planning agencies is not likely to work to weaken the power position of business in community politics; indeed, it may strengthen it. As suggested above, the same cannot be said of public housing.

Localities have been affected by the Workable Program for Community Development requirement. The theory behind the "Workable Program," as it is known, is that communities must "put their own houses in order" before additional federal funds would be spent. And it was assumed that if the stipulations of the Workable Program were not being met on the surface of it that the local house was not in order. So, for example, if a local government did not have a zoning ordinance or a housing code, it could not continue to participate in the specified federal assistance programs. Thus, communities hurried to take the necessary action to fulfil Workable Program requirements; and this gave community planning and the codes and ordinances areas quite a boost. Cities that failed to enact the required codes and ordinances were ruled ineligible for housing aid (Houston, which to this day has no zoning or housing code, is an example). It was not until the Housing Act of 1968 that a key housing assistance program was not linked to the Workable Program provision.

Hindsight suggests that the existence on paper of the various codes and ordinances in the housing and land-use area, a comprehensive plan, neighborhood blight analyses, an adequate administrative organization, sufficient financing, housing for displaced persons, and citizen participation was in reality no proof of a community's commitment to a rational housing and land-use policy. Little in-depth analysis went into determining whether a city was carrying out such a policy, only whether it met the checklist Workable Program requirements. This is an important point to students of federalism in America, since one of our system's assumed merits is that it allows for considerable local diversity to satisfy local needs, as interpreted locally. Certainly more important than whether a city has a particular code or ordinance is whether that city is achieving the objectives which that code or ordinance is intended to achieve; or whether a city without zoning ordinance is any worse off than a typical city with one. Performance standards, based on land-use and housing attainments, may be preferable federal measures of community activities.[20] In this light, cities like Houston may qualify for federal housing aid; for instance, Houston is characterized by the widespread use of deed restrictions (which serve some of the same objectives as zoning), a building code, a fire code, a street plan, and subdivision control.

Before leaving the Workable Program, it is further instructive to note

[20] In a thoughtful work on the regulation of land use, Babcock significantly raises the question of the effect as opposed to the simple presence of land-use controls. Richard F. Babcock, *The Zoning Game* (Madison: The University of Wisconsin Press, 1966), p. 28.

that although cities apparently reported that this requirement was being fulfilled, the execution of urban renewal programs raises some questions in this area. For example, one review of Newark's urban renewal activities concluded that the reason for the program's success was "limited" participation in the urban renewal process; this authority, in fact, speculated that a "sudden increase" of popular interest might have turned routine proposals into "controversial issues."[21] Whether genuine, as opposed to the mere appearance of, citizen participation in urban renewal in Newark and other major American cities would have led to an alleviation of the conditions contributing to the near revolutionary big-city riots in the mid-1960s will probably never be known.

LATER HOUSING LEGISLATION: EXPANDED NATIONAL GOVERNMENT COMMITMENT

The enactments of 1937, 1949, and 1954 set forth the basic framework within which national and much local housing action developed. Summarizing the major aspects of national housing legislation through 1954, housing policy provided for public housing, urban renewal, FHA assistance for low-income families, and a community planning grant program.

In 1956, national legislation was amended to authorize federal assistance for the relocation of persons removed from their homes and businesses by urban renewal and for general neighborhood renewal planning. The 1959 congressional enactment further broadened redevelopment planning and federal funds were made available for community-wide renewal planning—specifically for the preparation of a Community Renewal Program (CRP). The CRP was to identify areas of existing and future decay in the city, including rehabilitation and conservation areas, propose a course of action, and set priorities. Legislation in 1959 additionally permitted the use of urban renewal powers and resources to assist urban colleges and universities to expand and eliminate physical decay around their campuses. Later, hospitals were made eligible for renewal benefits.

In 1961, a new provision was written into the housing legislation: section 221-D-3, believed at the time to be an important advance in the low-income housing area. The 221-D-3 program was designed to encourage nonprofit and limited return profit organizations to build and rehabilitate housing for low- and moderate-income families. The principle behind this program was that it was to lead to the creation of a whole

21 Harold Kaplan, *Urban Renewal Politics* (New York: Columbia University Press, 1963), p. 164.

new substructure of housing sponsors, builders, and investors who would be dedicated to the construction and rehabilitation of low-income housing. Sponsors might include churches, labor unions, and universities. The program was to be carried out through the use of federally guaranteed loans, bearing below-market-interest-rates (BMIR) under certain circumstances. Despite the general optimism surrounding the enactment of the 221-D-3 program, many fewer units have been built or rehabilitated under the legislation than was originally anticipated (about 50,000 units were completed by mid-1968).

Legislation in 1964 and 1965 authorized direct federal loans and grants to improve housing in blighted areas and federal rent payments to the poor. The Demonstration Cities and Metropolitan Development Act of 1966 introduced the "model cities" concept, the central feature of which was the advancement of federal planning and implementation funds to communities for the purpose of developing a coordinated and comprehensive attack on the physical and social problems of the most deprived of slum neighborhoods. Under the Housing Act of 1968, 1 percent loans could be made to low-income citizens to buy and rent standard housing, with the difference between the market interest rate (which the lender receives) and 1 percent being made up by a subsidy from the national government.

This completes a description of the key provisions of the major national housing acts and of the operation of some of the programs authorized by this legislation. One must be careful not to confuse legislation on the books with action in the community. The establishment of a housing program does not necessarily mean that funds will be provided to carry out a program. Further, and more important, the availability or spending of public funds does not necessarily mean that housing for the deprived will be forthcoming. For example, public housing waiting lists in the larger cities run into the thousands of persons; in the late 1960s, the National Commission on Urban Problems pointed out that there were 193,000 persons on the waiting lists of the 50 largest cities alone.

THE POLITICS OF HOUSING:
INTEREST GROUPS

A number of interests are vitally concerned with housing, especially legislative action and governmental activities in this field. The relevant interests are organized and seek to influence governmental action affecting housing at all levels in the political system, but particularly at the national and local levels where the major housing and land-use powers are located. The politics of housing is probably unusually complex because of the wide distribution of public authority over building and land-use, and because of the large variety of interests directly or indirectly dependent on the housing industry and government activities in housing. Among the various segments of the economic and political systems with basic interests in housing are residential builders and developers, realtors, mortgage bankers and brokers, building and construction trades unions, local government building, housing, and other codes officials, local public housing and urban renewal officials, national government officials responsible for the administration of housing programs, and housing and building materials manufacturers and suppliers and other dependent businesses. Most of these forces are organized through their respective trade, business, or other associations, which serve political as well as service, educational, public relations, and standard-setting ends. It is the political activities of these associations that we will be discussing in the following paragraphs, and not their more commonly publicized functions however useful they may be to their members and to the general public. In this light, these organizations will be viewed as interest groups, whether they represent governmental or private interests (some term the governmental-type "public" interest groups).[22]

In the private sector two groups—builders and realtors—stand out as being the most important interests organized for the purpose of influencing the direction of public policy in housing and shaping the attitudes of the American public on housing matters. Congressional legislation makes direct provision for the representation of private housing interests on the board of directors of the Federal National Mortgage Association, specifically naming the homebuilding industry (builders), the real estate industry (realtors), and the mortgage lending industry. The relative significance of the mortgage banking community in shaping national housing policy—especially in structuring the monetary posture of the national government which affects this policy—should not be underrated; nevertheless, this segment of the housing industry has quite broad interests and is not organized for political action to the extent that builders and realtors are in the housing legislative and administrative areas.[23]

[22] The literature of political science treats extensively the role of business trade associations as interest groups. See, for example, Harmon Zeigler, *Interest Groups in American Society* (Englewood Cliffs: Prentice-Hall, 1964), chap. IV, and Edwin M. Epstein, *The Corporation in American Politics* (Englewood Cliffs: Prentice-Hall, 1969), pp. 70–74. Labor unions are also commonly seen in the literature as performing interest group functions. Less frequently recognized are organizations of local and state government officials, which also serve as interest groups at least within the context of the national government.

[23] Mortgage bankers, who originate and service real estate loans, are represented nationally by the Mortgage Bankers Association of America. Mortgage brokers and investors may also belong to this association. Mortgage investors (those who invest in real estate and hold mortgages) include savings and loan associations (whose busi-

Both builders and realtors have organizations which can serve as their political spokesmen at the key influence points in the American federal system—that is, at the national, state, and local levels. The builders' resources are basically their prestige and concentrated wealth, both of which can be impressive assets in transmitting their point of view to public policy-makers and administrators. Realtors are the less professional of the two and appear to draw principally on their enormous numbers and organizational strength throughout the entire United States in the development of their political strategy.

As used here, "builder" refers to general contractors who construct residential dwelling units, usually of the detached, single-family variety. In this sense, the term "builder" is synonymous with homebuilder or housebuilder. Builders use subcontractors in the electrical, plumbing, roofing, and other areas; and subcontractors are not considered builders as such, even though builders may perform some subcontracting functions. Builders may also be developers, if they acquire and prepare land for subdivision in addition to constructing the housing on the land. Often, the terms "builder" and "developer" are used interchangeably because of the frequent integration of the two functions in the same firm, although the two activities are technically distinct from one another. Occasionally, residental builders do commercial construction work; as an example, high-rise apartment and office building construction may be done by the same company. "Realtor" refers to real estate brokers, dealers, agents, and sales personnel (and the firms they represent or own) engaged in the business of bringing the buyer and seller of real estate together through contract, for which service a commission or fee is charged.

Builders are organized at the national level through the National Association of Home Builders (NAHB), composed primarily of single-family homebuilders, but also apartment contractors, materials manufacturers, realtors, and other business firms. The NAHB is a well-financed, professionally staffed, and authoritative spokesman for some 50,000 member companies and local builder organizations, and has its headquarters in Washington, D.C. In addition, builder associations are found in most major metropolitan and urban areas, as well as at the state level in some instances. Local organizations may represent builders primarily from a particular local government jurisdiction such as a municipality (for example, the Minneapolis Home Builders Association), from a submetro-

---

ness is investing in real estate) and commercial banks. Savings and loan associations are organized into the United States Savings and Loan League and the National League of Insured Savings Associations; commercial banks are represented in Washington and elsewhere by the American Bankers Association and the Independent Bankers Association of America. As this suggests, there is some intraindustry competition. Any of these groups plus others may take a stand on public policy in the housing area.

politan area encompassing two or more jurisdictions (for example, the Suburban Maryland Home Builders Association, which has members in two counties outside of Washington, D.C.), or from an entire metropolitan area (for example, the Home Builders Association of Metropolitan Pittsburgh). Homebuilder organizations may also be found in state capitals (for example, the New York State Builders Association). This vast organizational structure, patterned after the decision-making process in the political system, is relevant from both a political and economic standpoint. It permits the effective mobilization of economic resources for collective action consistent with the interests of the members and their dependencies, and has helped make builders respected and powerful participants in national and local legislative and administrative councils.

The nation's largest builders are now represented separately from NAHB in the Council of Housing Producers. Created in 1968 to assist in meeting national housing objectives, the council currently counts among its members a relatively small number of major building firms engaged in a number of housing activities; members include such giants as Levitt and Sons, Boise Cascade, and the Centrex Corporation. The council seeks to expand market and sales opportunities for its constituents, and has a particular interest in fulfilling the demand for low- and moderate-income housing in urban areas. To this end, the organization unequivocally supports efforts to overcome local government and related obstacles to more efficient housing production; for instance, it has urged the intercession of a "higher authority" than the city or county to create the environment needed for the development of low-cost housing for Americans.

Council of Housing Producer members consider themselves professionals in the housing industry, distinguished by their management, production, and marketing skills and highly educated staffs. Although the NAHB favors the same general goals that the council does, the contrasting nature of the constituency bases of the two groups could cause them to drift apart as critical national and local policy questions (concerning factory-produced housing, for example) are raised in future years.

Realtors also are organized at all levels of government in the American political system and prepared to represent and defend the interests of their members in a variety of ways. The broadest-based organization of realtors is the National Association of Real Estate Boards, composed of some 1,500 subnational board members. Locally, as in the homebuilding field, real estate boards may include members within a single governmental jurisdiction, a submetropolitan area covering more than one government but not an entire metropolitan area, or an entire metropolitan region. Examples of each, respectively, are the Prince Georges County Board of Realtors (Maryland), the Main Line Board of Realtors (drawing members from a number of suburban jurisdictions near Philadelphia), and the Greater Baltimore Metropolitan Board of Realtors. Boards of realtors are important political interest groups which seek to influence public policy, legislation, and administrative actions in the real estate, land-use, and housing areas.

In general, builders can be expected to take a more liberal stand than realtors on public policy matters, probably because builders are considerably more directly dependent on positive government action to bolster and stimulate the housing market than are realtors. The NAHB supports virtually all national legislation and administrative actions in the housing area, including low-income housing and open occupancy proposals; the National Association of Real Estate Boards, at the same time, has opposed public housing and open occupancy legislation. It should also be noted that organized builders have a more intense interest in housing, building code, and land-use policy at both the national and local levels than do realtors; this means that builders play a more aggressive part in housing and land-use policy-making and administration processes than do realtors. Locally, builders associations work for simplified and uniform codes and ordinances affecting housing development and construction, although this effort appears to be tempered by the building industry's adjustment to existing regulations and to some extent by its dependency on the current land-use and housing administration practices in local government.

Labor is also directly affected by governmental housing policy. The building occupations in the country are politically represented primarily through the Building and Construction Trades Department of the AFL-CIO at the national level. The building and construction trades are also organized in the same union in localities and in states through councils which serve local and state constituency bases and which protect labor's interests in local governments and state legislatures. Building and construction trades include electricians, plumbers, bricklayers, and other skilled occupational groups which perform work in the housing and building industries. It seems as though the power of organized labor in housing is felt in a more formal manner in Washington and in a more informal way locally and in state capitals (that is, in the latter instances public policy makers take into account the effect of possible actions in housing on the laboring man without unions necessarily exerting direct pressure or testifying in public hearings). Generally, it is safe to say that while labor unions recognize the magnitude of the country's housing problem, they tend to support national subsidization as opposed to cost-cutting in housing the poor, presumably reasoning that greater government outlays are preferable to the possible elimination of jobs in construction.

No discussion of the interest groups in housing would be complete

without an examination of the organized public officials and administrators and government agencies responsible for the execution of housing
policy, programs, and regulations. Most meaningful in this respect are the
various public interest groups which represent local government housing
officials and departments. National government administrators, who certainly help set the tone for housing policy in the nation, may also belong
to or otherwise work closely with these public interest groups.

Local government building code officials are organized through three
major groups: the Building Officials' Conference of America (BOCA),
the International Conference of Building Officials (ICBO), and the
Southern Standard Building Codes Conference. These organizations have
developed model codes (discussed previously), including building codes,
which can be adopted by localities if desired. It is not an insignificant
point that at present the primary source of model codes is associations of
officials who administer the codes and who are subject to the pressures
and interests of local forces who may be dependent on somewhat restrictive codes. In fact, such interests may have some effect on determining
the nature of the provisions of the model codes. The National Commission on Urban Problems has recommended the creation of a new and
perhaps more independent body—to be called the National Institute of
Building Sciences—to formulate standards in the codes area.

The basic organization of local government housing officials outside
the building codes function is the National Association of Housing and
Redevelopment Officials (NAHRO) which represents agencies and individuals with responsibilities in housing code administration, public housing, urban renewal and redevelopment, and model cities.

The NAHRO is administered by a 35-member board of governors
which is representative of seven regions and 26 local, metropolitan, and
statewide chapters of housing and redevelopment employees. This association has what is probably the most liberal constituency of all of the
Washington-based local-government public interest groups, and its policy
positions tend to reflect this philosophical orientation. NAHRO publishes
the *Journal of Housing*, which has become the professional organ of the
more progressive and socially directed of the housing forces in this country and which is sometimes an outlet for federal officials in various
subbureaucracies within the U.S. Department of Housing and Urban
Development. The existence of an expansion-minded and talented staff in
this organization tempts one to conclude that NAHRO's relative influence
over public policy in housing at the national level will rise in the future.
The association is credited with the initiation of a new federal codes
enforcement grant program (under which funds are made available to
local governments), passed in the Housing and Urban Development Act
of 1965.

In terms of basic causes of government action in housing, interest groups and public bureaucracies are probably more responsible than political parties for making and carrying out housing policy in the current age. Nevertheless, political parties must play a role in the housing decisional process given the nature of our political system. We shall next review political parties.

THE POLITICS OF HOUSING: POLITICAL PARTIES

Political parties are important to the analysis of housing policy because their national representatives are called upon to take action in housing in the legislative and administrative areas. Understandably, considering their different constituencies,[24] the two parties have not always agreed on matters related to housing.

To examine the parties' positions, it is useful to analyze each party's component parts. In the national Republican party there are three significant groups: House Republicans, Senate Republicans, and administration Republicans. Similarly, the Democratic party is divided into northern and southern wings. The most consistently liberal of these groups has been the northern Democrats and the most consistently conservative, the House Republicans. All of the others—including southern Democrats, Senate Republicans, and administration Republicans—fall in between these two.

As can be seen in Table 16.4, GOP Representatives voted overwhelm-

TABLE 16.4
Congressional Voting, by Party,
Selected Housing Enactments

	DEMOCRATS						REPUBLICANS			
	HOUSE		SENATE				HOUSE		SENATE	
			ALL		NORTHERN					
	Y	N	Y	N	Y	N	Y	N	Y	N
				(PERCENTAGES)						
Housing Act of 1937	79	21	88	12	98	2	1	99	47	53
Housing Act of 1949	85	18	94	6	100	0	18	82	69	31

SOURCE: *Congressional Record.* In the House, votes are taken from motions to recommit; in the Senate, from final passage. All figures are calculated on the basis of those voting.

[24] V. O. Key, Jr., *Politics, Parties, and Pressure Groups,* 5th ed. (New York: Crowell, 1964), pp. 214–218.

ingly against the Housing Act of 1937, which contained the controversial public housing program. One Republican representative—Congressman Wolverton of Camden, New Jersey—sided with the Democratic majority, breaking the otherwise solid Republican opposition to the enactment. When the somewhat less controversial 1949 legislation was being considered, the House GOP lined up against federal housing again, this time by an 82 to 18 percent margin. More recently, House Republicans, in the same tradition, were recorded heavily in opposition to the rent supplement section of the 1965 housing legislation. In the Senate on the other hand, the Republican party has advanced a more liberal position, splitting evenly on the 1937 bill and supporting the 1949 enactment by a respectable margin. Administration Republicans appear to lean in the direction of the liberal GOP senators, as is reflected in the Eisenhower housing proposals in the 1950s and the Nixon administration housing programs in the late 1960s and early 1970s. Differences within the Republican party on housing can be accounted for essentially by the wider and more diversified constituencies and audience that must be appealed to by Senate and administration Republicans. House Republicans are more typically responsible to rural and small-town populations, and less to urban concentrations.

The conflict within the Democratic party over housing does not seem to be as great as that that characterizes the Republicans. Opposition among Democrats in Congress to the 1937 and 1949 legislation almost certainly was based in the southern camp (according to the figures in Table 16.4, this is clearly correct for Senate Democrats). Yet, it would also appear that the Democratic party members from either the North or South usually voted for this housing legislation. Since Democratic administrations have strongly backed liberal housing bills, this means that the Democratic party in general has been to the left of the Republican party when it comes to major national housing enactments. Democrats have been more inclined than Republicans to pass housing legislation placing the national government prominently in housing, giving equal support to both social welfare and private enterprise types of housing measures. Republicans have been most aggressive in fostering the latter kind of policy.

EFFECT OF GOVERNMENT ACTION
IN URBAN HOUSING: AN OVERVIEW

One is led to speculate as to the consequences of the various forms of national, state, and local government assistance, regulation, and other activity for housing, particularly for low-income families in urban areas.

First, it is reasonably evident that public housing and urban renewal programs have eliminated more dwelling units than these programs have provided for the poor. (See Table 16.5.) Second, other government

TABLE 16.5
Public Housing and Urban Renewal Statistics, to 1968

Public housing units built	707,000
Dwelling units eliminated by public housing and urban renewal	724,000
Deficit (units eliminated over units built)	18,000

SOURCE: Calculated from figures presented in National Commission on Urban Problems, *Building the American City* (Washington, D.C.: U.S. Government Printing Office, 1968), pp. 81–82.

action seems to have cut sharply into the supply of housing for low-income residents. For instance, the federal interstate highway program has destroyed 330,000 units, many of which were inhabited by the disadvantaged. Recent statistics show that about 48,000 dwellings a year have been demolished under local code enforcement, and that another 26,000 units are eliminated by other state and local government action each year.[25] As in urban renewal and public housing, most of these units that were destroyed by state and local government were in all probability occupied by lower income citizens. Even if one were to add the 100,000 or so moderate-income housing units built and operated privately but assisted by special federal government programs to the public housing total, the deficit of housing constructed for the lower socioeconomic groups over that eliminated by all levels of government is enormous. In this light, two broad courses of action are presented next.

Douglas Commission Recommendations

In 1965, President Lyndon B. Johnson appointed the National Commission on Urban Problems to study the urban housing problem and to make recommendations based on this study. The panel was known as the Douglas Commission, after its chairman, former Senator Paul H. Douglas of Illinois. After the completion of a series of surveys and some exhaustive analyses, the commission called for:

[25] Michael Sumicrast and Norman Farquhar, *Demolition and Other Factors in Housing Replacement Demand* (Washington, D.C.: Homebuilding Press, 1967), p. 19.

1. An increase in the supply of new housing units each year to the 2.0 to 2.25 million range, including at least 500,000 dwellings a year for low and moderate income persons.
2. The administration of land-use controls, such as zoning, in larger local government jurisdictions.
3. The creation of larger general-purpose local governments, to cover a minimum population of 50,000.
4. The decentralization of certain city government functions to the neighborhood level.
5. The elimination of local planning boards, or at least a transfer of their administrative-type activities to elected officials.
6. The institution of nonrestrictive statewide building codes and their required use for entire metropolitan areas if local governments do not act voluntarily.
7. The establishment of state housing agencies.
8. The discontinuation of state and local referenda requirements for public housing and urban renewal.
9. Preparation of development guidance programs by communities, which would state the purpose of land-use controls.
10. A deemphasis on the property tax.

In general, the Douglas group found that the powers of state and local governments have often conflicted wtih the welfare and interests of the poor, especially in housing, have substantially added to the costs of housing, and have in effect confined Negroes largely to the central city of metropolitan areas. The commission also pointed to the weaknesses of the various federal efforts in housing.

Although the commission's findings were well-researched and thoroughly documented, its heavy reliance in the recommendations on local and particularly state governments[26] to bring about change in urban housing and land-use strikes us as being a bit unrealistic. For it is precisely these authorities—state and local governments—that are to some significant extent the causes of the present conditions in the housing area. In view of this, we advance another alternative.

An Alternative Strategy

The initial stimulus for change in housing policy must come, we believe, from outside state and local government. The national government has the constitutional authority to regulate interstate commerce; under this authority, it would be entirely legally possible to enact a national building code of a nonrestrictive and uniform variety and based

[26] Nearly every one of the major recommendations of the commission would require some state action, and most would necessitate local action.

on performance standards, thus permitting local and regional variations where circumstances require.

It is true that the national government does not now have the political power (as opposed to the legal authority) to take this action, as all of the major interest groups in housing such as the National Association of Home Builders, the AFL-CIO, the National Association of Housing and Redevelopment Officials, and local building and housing agencies could be expected to oppose any such move, vigorously. Therefore, a new interest has to be created, one that stands to gain meaningfully from the development of such a code and from the mass-production consequences that should flow from a national code. This interest is the segment of the big business community that could expand or diversify into the housing field. Already there is evidence that a number of large corporations, including some of the currently fading conglomerates, are prepared to step decisively into housing if a nationwide scale of operations can be sustained. The recent organization of several building industry giants in the Council of Housing Producers suggests that the first phase of an interest realignment in housing is well underway.

Barring federal action, the support of conventional and ideological local interests should be enlisted to strike at the heart of high-cost and segregated housing in the United States—that is, community building codes and zoning ordinances. In housing, local government has frequently become a class instrument which has the singular objective of enhancing the economic power position and status of the higher socioeconomic groups, serving thereby to exclude the less fortunate classes from the suburbs. In all likelihood, the elimination of restrictive building codes and zoning practices in the suburbs will not open these areas to large numbers of Negroes, but would assure a greater choice of housing by lower income families at prices set by the free market and not artificially by government land-use and building regulations.

17. CITY AND REGIONAL PLANNING

■■■■■■■■■

URBAN PLANNING IN
A POLITICAL ENVIRONMENT

Urban planning is a political issue, and it is becoming more political with the passing of each day. By this we mean to say not only that there is general agreement in our communities now that planning is a proper function of government, a political institution, but also that there is considerable conflict over just what government should do in the way of planning for the future.

Prior to recent decades urban planning as a function of government was not characteristic of American localities. Planning now is widely accepted as a responsibility of public authorities. At the same time, communities are not always of one mind as to what constitutes good planning; thus arises a significant dimension of politics in a functional area many prefer to think of as nonpolitical. Politics in this sense means conflict—that is, conflict over the values, priorities, and means of implementation that should govern the determination of community policy over planning.

Planning as such as not new: various forms of planning can be traced to ancient times.[1] Furthermore, planning is clearly part of the American economic tradition. But this does not necessarily mean that planning by government has deep historical roots in our society. What planning has been found in this country has been done largely in the private sector and has usually been of a limited nature. In fact, in several respects government planning seems to run directly counter to the American-adopted Lockean doctrine of the preeminence of private property.

Still, outlooks have been changing in recent years, and now it appears that metropolitan citizens are increasingly willing to see important planning powers placed in their local governmental institutions. This trend is quite noticeable, and it has a number of implications for the local community and the academic disciplines which make it their business to understand that community. The most significant effect is that planning is now more "political" than when planning was purely a private matter. In the past, what decisions were made over the areas with which planning is concerned were made or at least registered in the private marketplace; now these decisions are more likely to be made by public agencies. Given this shift in the decision-making process, and in view of the fact that various elements in the community may disagree over what constitutes the nature of proper planning decisions, planning is currently much more of an appropriate subject for political inquiry than was the case some years ago.

The politics of planning includes more than decisions seen in a narrow perspective. Decisions may reflect or even constitute public policy; and at both the academic and community level more individuals appear to be more greatly interested in planning and land-use policy, a cause and an effect of particular decisions. This kind of emphasis has led, in turn, to a more detailed examination of the governmental structure within which specific planning decisions are made and broader public policy generated. It has become apparent that different sorts of administrative arrangements have differential effects in the decision and policy areas. As

[1] See Lewis Mumford, *The City in History* (New York: Harcourt, Brace and World, 1961).

a result, competing community groups may support different administrative patterns in planning, hoping thereby to structure the political process so that the appropriate land-use decisions and planning policy will be the consequence. This adds another feature to the politics of urban planning.

THE NATURE OF PLANNING

In the general sense, planning is the establishment of goals and the selection of a course of action which will achieve the desired ends. Of course, this type of planning is conducted in various quarters and has little specifically to do with the subject of this chapter. Planning as we understand it here is community planning; since nearly all planning done in this country is found in urban areas, we may also refer to this type of planning as urban planning. Defined, community or urban planning is the establishment of policy and guides for a locality setting forth desired land-use patterns for the future. Practically speaking, this is what planning is at present in communities, although some are beginning to challenge the land-use concentration or emphasis of contemporary planning.

Currently, there is some confusion even among professional planners as to what planning is all about. Undoubtedly, much of this confusion stems from the resistance of American local government institutions and the political process generally to accepting or absorbing planning in its ideal state. Some have in this light attempted to make the academic study of planning more consistent with reality while others have steadfastly continued to adhere to idealistic conceptions of planning which have little relevance in actual situations in this nation. The intellectual discipline of urban planning is now in a transitional stage; it is in the process of moving from an abstract matter to a more practical field, anchored in an American political and economic setting.

Urban planning is sometimes termed physical or land-use planning, and land-use planning is descriptive of the essence of community planning in the United States. The product of the community planning process may similarly be considered a land-use plan—that is, a plan that contains the desired land-uses of a private or public nature. Not uncommonly, professional planners view the land-use plan or land-use sections of a community plan as only part of the planning function, using "land-use" to refer to the private uses of land, thus excluding public uses such as community facilities and transportation; some cities employ this distinction in the administration of planning.

The plan that emerges from the planning process may also be called (in addition to a land-use plan) a general plan, master plan, comprehensive plan, or a development plan.[2] The particular terminology will vary by community and state. "City" planning means both the planning process in a particular city and the general field encompassed by community planning; city planning, in other words, could take place in suburbs or elsewhere, even though the area involved is not technically a city. "Regional" planning and "metropolitan" planning are frequently used interchangeably in this country to refer to planning found in the context of an entire metropolitan area (city and surrounding suburbs) or region (perhaps extending beyond a metropolitan area, but not too far). Some now use "regional" to take into account the geographical area that includes more than one state and a number of metropolitan as well as rural areas.

LAND-USE TOOLS, CONTROLS, AND INFLUENCES

Since urban planning is concerned basically with land and its use, it is necessary to consider the kinds of authority and powers associated with planning as well as the other influences that affect land development in communities. A land-use tool is a governmental power used to carry out desired future development policies; a land-use control is a governmental power designed to guide, structure, and direct land development; and a land-use influence is a governmental power or private force that affects the nature of land development. A land-use influence is the broadest of the three terms and would include any power found in the first two categories. A land-use tool and control are the same if the governmental power in question is employed to implement desired future development policies; even if the power is not so used, it is still a land-use control. In other words, to be characterized as a tool, a governmental power that controls land-use must implement an agreed upon policy setting forth future development aims. A land-use control, then, can be a tool but it does not have to be. Thus narrowing down our three concepts, we can concentrate on land-use controls and influences.

Land-use controls include the following governmental powers: zoning, subdivision regulation, and official map.

Zoning is a statutory means by which a government regulates private land and building development within its borders. The legal foundation of zoning is the police power of the state governments. The police power

---

[2] For a technical discussion and definitions of plans and planning by professors of city planning, see F. Stuart Chapin, Jr., *Urban Land Use Planning*, 2nd ed. (Urbana, Ill.: University of Illinois Press, 1965), especially pp. 355–359, and T. J. Kent, Jr., *The Urban General Plan* (San Francisco: Chandler, 1964), esp. pp. 18–22.

is one of the most basic powers of government, generally inherent in sovereign authority and referring to the right to take action to promote the public health, welfare, safety, and morals. Within the American context, the police power is exercised by states and means the regulation of persons and property consistent with the public interest and constitutional or legal guarantees. In the case of zoning, state governments have typically delegated this authority to local governments through state enabling legislation, permitting localities to adopt and administer a zoning ordinance.

In the zoning ordinance is found the categories of land-use allowed in the community, which may include residential, commercial, and industrial. Not all communities provide for all of these uses; these are just the major possibilities. Residential uses often are further subdivided into more specific classes, such as single-family and multifamily or town houses, detached units, garden apartments, high-rise apartments, and so on. Different classes of permitted commercial and industrial uses will also be part of the typical community's zoning ordinance. In any one or more of these categories a locality's ordinance may make certain stipulations concerning minimum lot sizes (from 3,000 square feet in Phoenix, Arizona, for instance, probably the lowest minimum residential lot area in the nation, up to five or more acres, minimum sizes found in some New York and Philadelphia suburbs, for example), minimum house size, maximum area of a lot to be covered by a building, maximum population densities, maximum building heights, provision of offstreet parking, the specific nature of industrial activity allowed (perhaps regulated through performance standards for noise, smoke, and the like), and numerous other matters. Recent zoning innovations that are becoming more popular include planned unit development, planned community zones, cluster zoning, density zoning, and contract zoning, all of which are theoretically intended to introduce greater flexibility into land development and broader standards into the zoning process. The newer zoning ideas apply mainly to residential zones and represent an attempt to deemphasize the stress on the single-family detached residence on large lots removed from other uses and, in some instances, to integrate the traditionally separate districts (residential, commercial, industrial) into a single development pattern.

Each community with a zoning ordinance will have both a text incorporating in written form the provisions of that ordinance and a map depicting the sections of the text that govern land-use on each lot regulated by the ordinance. Much of the controversy surrounding local land-use decision-making processes is focused on proposed or requested changes in the zoning map—called rezonings—and not in the text. In some categories of use covered in the zoning text, the ordinance may provide for special exceptions, or uses not typical of the category in question but specified in the text as acceptable if approval of the appropriate authority is secured (the location of a dentist's office or an electric power substation in a residential zone are examples). Community zoning ordinances will also provide for a variance, or a use not consistent with the legally required use, which is requested and approved on the basis of the fact that the stipulated use would be an "unnecessary hardship" on the owner (unusual terrain conditions might cause such a hardship).[3]

That zoning is a major land-use control and often a land-use tool is not open to serious question. At the same time, as professional planners are prone to point out, it may have only temporary usefulness in carrying out land-use plans or objectives. Over the long-run, zoning is heavily subject to economic market pressures and may not serve community goals (such as the preservation of open space through large-lot zoning) that are not compatible with these pressures.

Another key land-use control is subdivision regulation. The subdivision regulation power is designed to control development in large tracts of land as zoning sets the tone for the use of particular lots. Subdivision regulations cover site design and layout and include standards by which the locality can assure that proposed developments conform to the general existing or planned physical patterns in the area, provide the necessary streets and sidewalks, and make appropriate contributions or dedications of public facilities and land sites for public use. The subdivision authority may regulate such matters as width of streets, length of blocks, and frontage along major streets and may require dedications (without compensation) or cash contributions in lieu of dedications for public purposes such as land for schools and parks. The agency responsible for subdivision control commonly has wide discretion in the execution and administration of these land-use regulations. The role of the subdivision regulation power in shaping urban development, particularly in the suburbs, is greater than is generally suspected and warrants systematic research.[4]

The official map is the least significant of the three land-use controls being discussed; but it is nevertheless a means by which localities can

[3] The planning field does not contain a good, basic text on zoning; and zoning is scantily treated in the planning literature. The best detailed, technical description of zoning is found in Donald H. Webster, *Urban Planning and Municipal Public Policy* (New York: Harper & Row, 1958), chap. 8, a book now out of print. For a zoning casebook, see Charles M. Haar, *Land-Use Planning* (Boston: Little, Brown, 1959). See also William I. Goodman and Eric C. Freund (eds.), *Principles and Practice of Urban Planning* (Washington, D.C.: International City Managers' Association, 1968), chap. 15.

[4] For a statistical summary of subdivision control practices in communities, see International City Management Association, *The Municipal Year Book 1969* (Washington, D.C., 1969), pp. 233–259.

regulate land use within their jurisdiction. The official map is an ordinance that shows proposed and existing streets, water mains, drainage rights of way, parks, playgrounds, and perhaps other public uses and utilities. In many cities the official map applies only to streets. The primary purpose of the official map is to reserve land and rights of way for future public needs and requirements and to keep this land from being developed. Placing a land area on the map, however, does not guarantee that the land will be given to or taken by the municipality without compensation to the owner. The law may require the locality to acquire the land in question or institute condemnation proceedings within a stipulated period of time after the land is put on the map; otherwise, the owner may have the right to develop the property.

Before leaving land-use controls, it could be argued that a community plan or community planning more broadly should be considered such a control. Certainly, a comprehensive plan or the entire planning process could have some effect on structuring land use within a locality. However, it must be pointed out that a plan as such does not have the "force of law"—that is, a plan need not be followed by public officials or private citizens as it serves only an advisory function in the land-use decision-making process.

A number of other public as well as private forces and powers affect the nature of land development and use in communities; these forces and powers will be classed as land-use influences. Among the most important public or governmental activities that affect land use are highways and sewer lines. The location of highways—particularly the arterial variety—and public sewers in the undeveloped portions of the metropolitan area can literally dictate community development patterns. Without highways an area is unlikely to develop, and with highways, development is likely to follow. In the light of the average American's dependence on the automobile for transportation, it would seem natural that the availability of highways would greatly influence land-use. Sewers have a similar effect on development, but for different reasons. The existence of a public sewer system can have a significant bearing on development costs: the absence of sewers means that the developer must provide septic tanks for each home or facility in the subdivision or build a sewage system for the subdivision, an extremely costly venture. In addition, the extension of sewers into an area is often seen as a means of securing changes in zoning from low density, large lot, and residential to high density, small lot, and nonresidential; at least this is the way it has worked out in practice. In the case of both highways and sewer lines these governmental powers may work at cross-purposes with land-use controls and in fact be the main determinants of how land will be used, at least initially, in the newly developing areas of the metropolitan region. Furthermore, these powers are seldom viewed and almost never administered as functions that have meaningful land-use consequences. Their operation is virtually exclusively judged on the basis of technical criteria (transportation of persons and things and disposal of sewage) having little if anything to do with land-use impact.

Other governmental powers that influence land-use are water lines, urban renewal, mass transit (especially rail transportation), parks and open space, public housing, building and housing codes, and public improvements of various types. The principle here is that land development and population settlement patterns follow public facilities and are affected by public regulations. Otherwise, land-use is influenced by a broad range of private actions, with the decisions of large corporations on location of their plants and office buildings being crucial inputs into community land-use schemes.

Planning Administration

Urban planning is primarily a local government function in the American political system. State governments are involved in urban planning essentially through the passage of state enabling legislation, which allows local governments to engage in planning and sets forth the general framework within which the local community may administer planning programs. In addition, some states provide assistance to localities out of state funds, act as conduits for the distribution of federal planning funds to communities, and conduct planning studies of their own, sometimes under contract with local governments. The national government does not do planning as such for urban areas, but has served to stimulate community planning throughout the nation, basically through the Housing and Urban Development Department's urban planning assistance program.

As can be seen in Table 17.1, about three fifths of all local governments in the United States and about two thirds of metropolitan area local governments have planning boards or commissions. And, as might be expected, planning boards are found in nearly all cities with a population of 50,000 or more, and in over 90 percent of the municipalities inside and outside metropolitan areas in the population range of 5,000 to 50,000. Furthermore, about three quarters of American municipalities above 5,000 have a published master plan.[5]

Slightly over one half of the local governments in the country have the zoning power—more have planning boards than zoning. Metropolitan area municipalities are more likely, however, to have a zoning ordinance

[5] Allen D. Manvel, *Local Land and Building Regulation* (Washington, D.C.: National Commission on Urban Problems, 1968), p. 31.

TABLE 17.1
Local Governments with Planning Boards, 1968

TYPE OF GOVERNMENT/ LOCATION/ POPULATION GROUP	PROPORTION WITH PLANNING BOARD
Total	59.6%
In SMSAs	65.2
Outside SMSAs	55.4
County governments	52.3
In SMSAs	80.0
Outside SMSAs	48.1
Municipalities	66.8
In SMSAs	67.7
50,000 or more	98.4
5,000–49,999	92.9
Under 5,000	54.9
Outside SMSAs	66.0
5,000–49,999	91.8
Under 5,000	56.5
New England-type townships	49.4
In SMSAs	57.1
5,000 or more	79.1
Under 5,000	45.7
Outside SMSAs	43.0
5,000 or more	79.3
Under 5,000	37.9

SOURCE: Allen D. Manvel, *Local Land and Building Regulation*
(Washington, D.C., U.S. Government Printing Office, 1968),
p. 24 (adapted from Table 2).

than a planning board, as almost 75 percent of the municipal governments in metropolitan areas possess the zoning authority. Altogether,
9,600 local governments have zoning ordinances; and somewhat over 8,000
administer subdivision regulations.[6]

It is instructive to note that although metropolitan-wide planning is
common, the key planning powers are located in the municipalities and
suburban governments in the metropolitan area. Even in the metropolitan
governments in Dade and Davidson counties, the zoning authority is
divided between the local and metropolitan units, with municipalities
frequently exercising this power within their borders.

Within communities the planning function typically is controlled by an

[6]   *Ibid.*, p. 4.

independent planning commission. This means that the planning commission is generally independent of the chief elected and appointed officials of the general-purpose local government; and although the planning commission is normally not an autonomous unit of government, planning commissioners usually hold office for terms not coinciding with those of the members of the local governing body. The initial reason for the use of the independent commission in planning was that the Standard City Planning Enabling Act (1928) called for such an arrangement (states patterned their enabling legislation on planning after this model), and probably more basically because the reformer-business-professional community, whose views were incorporated in the model legislation, wanted it that way. A fear of "politics" being mixed with planning was the primary motivation. We shall return to the matter of the independent administration of the planning agency later in the chapter.

Typically, a planning commission has the responsibility for preparing, revising, up-dating, and adopting the comprehensive plan for the community as a whole as well as neighborhood master plans, renders advisory opinions and recommendations on proposed changes in the zoning map, drafts and recommends proposed amendments and additions to the zoning text, administers community subdivision regulations (probably the average commission's most powerful function, though it is seldom described as such), prepares and maintains the official map, and has advisory referral jurisdiction over some capital budget expenditures planned by local government departments.

With the exception of subdivision regulation administration, the critical powers in the land-use and planning areas are found in the local governing body or in other governments, including special districts and the state, and not in the planning commission. The governing body may also adopt plans, has considerable authority to implement these plans, normally has the final decision of rezonings, is the only local board with the power to enact zoning, subdivision, and official map ordinances, and approves capital improvement plans and budgets of subordinate departments and agencies. The state highway department administers the major roads system in the metropolitan area, enjoying in the process a traditional independence somewhat free of immediate gubernatorial, legislative, and community constraints. Special district governments, isolated from local general-purpose units, may be given the chief responsibility in the community for one or more of the public activities that affect land-use policy in the locality; special districts may control sewer, water, mass transit, public housing, urban renewal, and other functions, depending on the area involved. As this clearly demonstrates, the actual planning and land-use decision-making process is highly decentralized and fragmented, almost to an extreme degree.

METROPOLITAN PLANNING

Metropolitan planning is in its early stages in this country. Normally, metropolitan planning is done on an entire metropolitan-wide basis, but it may cover only a portion of a metropolitan area. Presently there are about 400 metropolitan planning commissions; and in 1964, the year of the latest comprehensive survey, 150 of the then 212 SMSAs had some form of metropolitan planning.[7] The average metropolitan planning agency was established in the mid-1950s and has a 12-member commission, somewhat larger than the planning boards in big cities and quite a bit larger than planning commissions in smaller cities.

Metropolitan planning commissions include multijurisdictional agencies, city-county agencies, and county agencies. In the first category are planning commissions whose authority spreads across two or more localities (usually counties), councils of governments, and regional transportation boards; about one half of these organizations serve a population of more than 500,000. The city-county agencies have planning responsibility for a county and the central city within the county, typically serving a population of less than 250,000. The power of county planning boards extends over a single county, frequently containing less than 250,000 persons, while multijurisdictional agencies have the broadest geographical authority and are the most recently formed of the three types.

In general, metropolitan planning agencies have limited authority—mainly the right to adopt plans and review certain projects and proposals of local governments within their boundaries; unlike local planning commissions, few metropolitan boards administer subdivision regulations or make rezoning application recommendations. The average metropolitan agency was created under state enabling legislation by local government action, although some were established by special acts of the state legislature, interstate compact, and joint-excrcise-of-powers statutes.

Metropolitan planning organizations report that they receive their chief support from chambers of commerce, citizens planning and development groups, and the League of Women Voters. Business—particularly the real estate community—is normally well-represented on metropolitan

---

[7] The major surveys of metropolitan planning are U.S. Housing and Home Finance Agency, *1964 National Survey of Metropolitan Planning* (Washington, D.C.: U.S. Government Printing Office, 1965); U.S. Housing and Home Finance Agency, *National Survey of Metropolitan Planning* (Washington, D.C.: U.S. Government Printing Office, 1963); Graduate School of Public Affairs, State University of New York at Albany, *1968 Survey of Metropolitan Planning* (Albany, 1968); and Mary E. Snyder and Joseph F. Zimmerman, *The 1967 Survey of Metropolitan Planning: Emerging Trends* (Albany: Graduate School of Public Affairs, State University of New York at Albany, 1967).

planning boards. In a 1964 study, we found that 28 of the 40 members of the three metropolitan planning commissions of one region were businessmen and that 18 of the 28 were in real estate (developers, builders, and the like).

FUNCTIONAL AREA PLANNING:
URBAN RENEWAL AND TRANSPORTATION

Whether conducted at the metropolitan or local level, comprehensive community planning is not the only kind of planning done in localities. In fact, the sort of planning in which plans are most likely to be implemented is not of the comprehensive nature but is found in specific functional areas such as urban renewal and highways.

Urban renewal planning takes place in redevelopment project areas covering only a small part of a city; and even though the city planning commission will usually review urban renewal plans, renewal planning is in reality the primary responsibility of the local urban redevelopment authority. In this case, plans are carried out by the agency that makes the plans in the first place, and urban renewal bodies have considerable authority in executing renewal plans. Herein lies the success (the implementation ability) of urban renewal planning—that is, this planning is done for specific areas, plans are implemented by the organization doing the planning, and that agency has execution powers. Other reasons for the effectiveness of urban renewal planning include the influential clientele base the urban renewal authority has had in the local big business and real estate development community, and the ability to draw upon goals that are readily understandable and agreeable to most Americans and to use criteria that can be measured in precise and quantifiable terms. The objective of urban renewal is to eliminate substandard housing, and renewal planners can easily determine the number of substandard dwellings in a proposed project area. Comprehensive planning lacks the characteristics of urban renewal planning described in this paragraph.[8]

Highway planning is another example. This planning is largely a function of the state government, and the concentration of power in the state highway department to execute highway plans is unparalleled among state and local government agencies. As with urban renewal, the highway planners are also the implementers of the highway program, and the roads activity is backed by powerful business and user groups, giving highways an unusually strong political base. Further, the need for roads

[8] For a discussion of the problems faced by comprehensive planners, see Alan A. Altshuler, *The City Planning Process, A Political Analysis* (Ithaca: Cornell University Press, 1965), part two.

is generally granted among members of the public, and statistics on current highway usage can be simply collected and marshaled as justification for more highways.

Comparing functional area planning in urban renewal and highways with comprehensive planning, the following generalizations can be advanced:

1. Urban renewal and highway planners use generally acceptable and somewhat specific goals and measurable standards by which the existing degree of goal attainment can be determined; comprehensive planners must rely on broader objectives (a better community, a more liveable environment) and lack precise criteria.

2. Urban renewal and highway planning affect rather narrow geographical areas; comprehensive planning covers entire communities.

3. Urban renewal and highway agencies are supported by influential constituent interests; comprehensive planning is usually not (not actively anyway).

4. In urban renewal and highways, planning and implementation powers are located in the same organizational structure; in comprehensive planning, the planning agency is not the prime implementation body.

As time goes on, it is true that urban renewal and highway planning are being moved into broader planning and political channels. Now, Community Renewal Program (CRP) planning encourages localities to develop renewal activities on a community-wide scale, and federal money is available for such efforts. In the same vein, the federal highway legislation of 1962 required each metropolitan region in the United States to have a continuing, comprehensive transportation planning process in operation by mid-1965. This process would in turn take into account general development planning and land-use considerations in metropolitan areas, thereby, hopefully, expanding the horizons of highway planning and programming. Other national and state enactments have served similar ends in urban renewal, highways, and other specific functional areas.

Another type of functional area planning emerging to some extent in local governments is that found in the social fields. This may include manpower, employment, welfare, poverty, health, and related services planning. Some community action agencies and model cities administrators are engaged in social planning, although the existence of a wide variety of public and private organizations with implementation powers in social programs makes this effort a trying one at best. Often (as in model cities) social planning is done for specific neighborhood or clientele groups and not for the community as a whole, as in other forms of planning. Some professional planners are convinced that social planning should be integrated with and become a part of the comprehensive physical or land-use planning process; so far, this kind of thinking has had little impact on local planning commissions.

NEW-TOWN PLANNING

Under the new-town concept, population concentrations are to be created in an orderly fashion outside of highly congested urban areas, functioning perhaps as satellite communities for metropolitan centers.[9] New towns have been popular in some nations in various parts of the world; for example, in Great Britain, about 20 new towns have been developed since the passage of the New Towns Act of 1946. Unlike, however, new-town planning elsewhere, in the United States this planning is largely in private hands.

In fact, the basically private nature of new-town planning in America could make this form the most successful comprehensive planning done here. The two most prominently mentioned new towns in this country are Columbia, Maryland, and Reston, Virginia, both suburbs of Washington, D.C. Both communities have been planned and developed by private profit-making firms—the Rouse Company for Columbia and Gulf-Reston, Inc.—and both have been financed by private capital. New-town planning does not necessarily include provision for the creation of any new units of general-purpose government, as both Columbia and Reston have been developed within the planning and zoning processes of their respective county governments. Incidentally, local governments are infrequently prepared to absorb, guide, and direct comprehensive new-town development, and are commonly found in a position of reacting to rather than structuring such proposals. In this light, the primary stimulus for new-town planning has come from the private and not the public sector.

Whether new-town planning and development will be widely accepted in the United States cannot be determined at this time; an increasing emphasis on urban population decentralization and the growing commitment by larger corporations to undertaking community development of some scale suggest an affirmative answer. One point should be stressed in this respect: ideas about new-town planning coming from experiences abroad can only at great risk be considered transferable in their totality to this country. Here, land-use powers are shared by public and private authorities, with the latter having the edge; and what functions the government does have in the planning and land-use area are exercised largely at the local level, and then in a politically dispersed fashion.

[9] The classic work on new-town planning is Ebenezer Howard's *Garden Cities of Tomorrow* (Cambridge: MIT Press, 1965).

PLANNING: THE IDEAL AND THE REAL

Ideally, urban planning serves the broadest of community interests. However, what constitutes the general community interest in land-use is far from a settled question. And the American political system insofar as it affects planning, zoning, and land-use matters is so ordered that no single authority can determine what shall be done to effect that community interest even if it were known. In fact, the nature of the political system encourages the formation of interest groups which, in turn, through interaction with public officials, more or less decide what the community interest is and how it shall be achieved. Given then the actual behavior of the political system, it is quite likely that specific interests will dominate the land-use policy processes—and do so for rather narrow ends. This means that planning and zoning policy will become what dominant local groups want it to be, and not what it might ideally be.[10]

In this light, we put forth the following considerations:

1. Comprehensive urban planning hardly exists in both a meaningful and ideal form in metropolitan areas.

2. Where urban planning is meaningful (carried out, translated into action), it does not exist in its ideal form.

3. Zoning and not planning is the key land-use activity.

4. Zoning is primarily a suburban matter, used by communities to exclude unwanted land-uses—namely high-density residential, commercial, and industrial development—thus promoting economic and social segregation.

5. Plans are a chief means by which zoning preferences are justified.

6. The existence of the independent planning commission inhibits the use of zoning in the ways outlined in point 4.

Now let us examine each of these points. We have demonstrated that urban planning "exists" in the metropolitan area; we have also shown that most communities in urban America have both planning boards and plans. Yet, this tells us little about the actual nature of planning. Questions naturally arise: What does the planning board *really* do? Are plans actually adopted? Is so, by whom? Is the adopting agency prepared to implement plans, even if it had the power? Are plans being implemented? By not raising these questions and seeking the answers, we lay the groundwork for two possible eventualities: (a) planning will not be absorbed into the local political system because it is not "real"—that is, it has no powerful agency or officials supporting it, no operational objec-

10 This is the urgent message of Richard Babcock's remarkable book *The Zoning Game* (Madison: University of Wisconsin Press, 1966).

tives, no action program, and no political foundation; or (b) planning will be "used" by influential local groups for their own purposes—to clothe private interests with legitimacy and an aura of professionalism.

In practice, both of these developments have typified the actual situation found in planning at the community level. At least until very recently if not at present, urban planning has been an academic matter and not taken seriously by administrators, policy-makers, and interest groups who have the power to influence land-use. In reality, few plans are ever carried out and most are probably not adopted by the public officials who have important control over land-use. As noted, the decentralized character of our political system makes it difficult for decision-makers to act on the basis of a comprehensive community plan.

Nevertheless, there are areas where plans of the comprehensive variety have been and are being implemented [characteristic of (b) above]; and these are commonly areas that are predominantly residential and where the local government is dominated by middle or upper income classes. Frequently, these areas are to be found in the suburbs of the metropolitan region, but they may also be located in the "suburban-type" sections of a city. Such localities are homogeneous in class structure and often see planning as a means of preserving existing residential living patterns, usually of a relatively low-density nature.

However, the key land-use function in such communities is zoning, while planning is of secondary importance at best. And zoning is employed to exclude high-density residential uses (apartments, houses on small lots) and certain if not all types of commercial-industrial development. These communities make their zoning and planning decisions in the light of what they perceive to be the interests of the locality, which locality may be one of 50 to 400 or more similar jurisdictions in the metropolitan area.

Various zoning practices have led to the exclusion of certain land-uses and therefore certain forms of socioeconomic development. Large-lot zoning, prohibitions on multifamily housing and mobile homes, and the establishment of minimum house sizes are particularly relevant in this respect. The National Commission on Urban Problems reported large-lot zoning to be a "common and widespread practice" in a number of major metropolitan areas.[11] For example, 25 percent of metropolitan area municipalities with 5,000 or more in population require all single-family residential development to be on lots of one-half acre or more. As more undeveloped land within the suburbs comes under the legal jurisdiction of local governments controlled by exclusionary-minded middle-to-upper-income residents, greater segments of the metropolitan land area will be

11 National Commission on Urban Problems, *Building the American City* (Washington, D.C.: U.S. Government Printing Office, 1969), p. 214.

zoned for large-lot development. So, for instance, the suburban Philadelphia township of Willistown recently rezoned 60 percent of its land
area from commercial and small-lot residential to single-family residential
with a lot size minimum for each house of four acres. Significant portions
of the New York and Cleveland metropolitan regions as well have been
zoned for lower-density residential use as suburbanites have moved
outward from the central city.

The meaning of large-lot zoning and other comparable zoning and
land-use control actions is high-cost housing. And it follows that housing
in high price ranges is available only to higher socioeconomic families.
The economically disadvantaged cannot afford such housing, and their
living opportunities are thereby restricted to certain sections of the
metropolitan area, often a few neighborhoods in the central city. Zoning
and related land-use regulatory powers cause this to happen. To the
extent that plans support zoning, urban planning is also responsible. This
is where comprehensive planning has been most "effective."

The National Commission on Urban Problems argues that the current
structure of local government in metropolitan areas has much to do with
the absence of decent housing for many persons in low-income brackets.
Among this panel's recommendations was one questioning the usefulness
of the independent planning commission and urging state legislatures to
permit local governments to abolish their planning boards. The reasoning
of the commission was that planning is essentially a "political" matter and
consequently that planning decision-making powers logically belong to
professional planners who are directly responsible to the governing body
or a chief executive of the government (and not to the planning commission). It is not at all clear, however, that the dissolution of the independent planning board will lead in the direction of providing standard
housing for low-income families. If anything, it is likely to accelerate the
move in the opposition direction.

Let us take a more detailed look at the independent planning commission. The arguments for the independent administration of the planning
function are:

1. Planning should be separated from politics.

2. Planning should be independent of partisanship.

3. Planning is too complex a subject for the governing body.

4. Planning differs from all other local activities and therefore deserves
special organizational status.

5. Planning is long range, while elected officials have short-range
perspectives.

6. An independent planning commission will attract better qualified
persons.

Those against the independent planning commission contend that:

1. Planning is political and therefore should be placed under politically responsible leaders.

2. Plans must be implemented to be effective, and planning should be located under elected officials who have the power to implement plans.

3. Planners and elected officials must develop a dialogue and close working relationships; and this cannot be done so long as planning is under the jurisdiction of an independent commission.

4. Planning should be integrated administratively with other local government functions which affect planning.

5. Although there may have been reason to fear the corrupting influence of politicians and elected officials in the past, the quality of such officials has improved over the years, and now planning should be subject to their direction.

6. No factors distinguish planning from other local government activities to the extent or in a manner that would justify treating planning differently (from other functions).

7. The independent planning commission has not worked out the way its proponents hoped it would.

These arguments, pro or con, likely boil down to reasons for doing what those who are most knowledgable in the planning area "sense" to be right for planning. In the 1920s, most experts in planning were convinced that the independent commission was best: circumstances dictated this position. Today, we are in a period of changing values, and an important part of the professional planning community believes some other arrangement to be best—that is, to advance the cause of planning.

In the final analysis, it would not be possible to discuss the advisability of keeping or abolishing the independent planning commission outside of a particular community setting at a given time. Then, one would have to set objectives for planning and measure the probable effectiveness of the independent planning commission in attaining these objectives. From what has been said, the objective that is being achieved by zoning and planning is the isolation of economic groups from one another, high-priced housing, and a sharp curtailment of possible housing choices for lower-income groups. The "means" has been suburban governing bodies which enact and apply zoning ordinances so as to exclude unwanted land-uses, and plans that reinforce and legitimate this action. Now the question is: Do independent planning commissions facilitate this process?

The answer to this appears to be a resounding "No!" In a large number of suburban communities, the conflict over planning and zoning is between the real estate interests and citizens associations, the former including large landowners, developers, builders, and zoning attorneys, and the latter, residential neighborhood citizens who live in single-family detached homes on medium-to-large-sized lots. Real estate interests lean toward the free market mechanism as the vehicle of determining land-use, while the citizens associations feel that zoning (government) should control land-use. Our study of suburban planning and zoning decision-makers in two communities revealed differences in attitude on the part of real estate and citizens associations representatives in this and other respects. Significantly, the free market bias of real estate forces has not prevented them from serving on local planning commissions, and in fact has probably had the opposite effect. That the real estate community has had important representation on planning commissions, especially in the past, has been well documented.[12] We have found such interests to have been the single most powerful group on suburban planning commissions in the past in any event. Although in more and more suburban communities the citizens association point of view is the dominant one on both the governing body and the planning commission, the planning commission appears to be the last of the two to fall into citizens hands. This would seem to make sense since the governing body is elective and likely to fall prey to citizen domination; while the independent status of the planning commission has allowed the real estate interests greater opportunity for representation on this board and therefore in planning.

Real estate interests in the suburbs have worked against virtually all of the zoning practices that now characterize the typical suburb; they have opposed large-lot zoning and fought restrictions against high-density residential and commercial development. If the current objective of urban planning is diversified and varied land-use throughout the suburbs of the metropolitan area, and not economic and residential segregation, then the part of the suburban interest group structure most likely to effect that end is to be found among real estate businessmen. If we want to open up the presently controlled metropolitan land and housing market, this segment of the local community will do it. By eliminating their last stronghold in the suburbs—the independent planning commission—we will not bring about this change, given the reality of politics. Housing for lower-income groups outside the city will not come so long as citizens associations control suburban land-use policy.

In the long run, only a change in the decision-making structure in the metropolitan area is likely to affect suburban land-use, planning, and zoning policy. No one can be positive that even this would change land-use policy as suburbs may have considerable voice over some new structure (say a metropolitan government). Anything short of a removal of key land-use powers from local government influence will probably prove inadequate. Some federal legislation is now directed toward broadening the framework within which local land-use decisions are made (for

12 Robert A. Walker, *The Planning Function in Urban Government* (Chicago: University of Chicago Press, 1950), pp. 150–152.

example, the Demonstration Cities and Metropolitan Development Act of 1966). Some believe that certain state action can lead to suburban land-use policy changes, and this position is presented next.

STATE AND URBAN PLANNING

Richard Babcock has called on state governments to set forth standards by which local land-use decisions can be judged—that is, standards in which the interests of the state and metropolitan area as a whole would be taken into account.[13] Localities would then have to consider these factors and explain once a decision on land use (zoning) is made how the action fulfilled the criteria. These standards would include the effect on metropolitan transportation, state highways, and natural resources. The National Commission on Urban Problems also sees the state governments playing an important part in reversing the direction of certain undesirable local actions in land-use and housing. To date, with a handful of exceptions, states have shown little interest in assuming traditionally local responsibilities in land-use regulation and control. Increasing suburban representation in state legislatures (assisted by the "one-man one-vote" court decision) will not enhance the prospects of broadening the role of states in local land-use and housing matters. Properly structured metro-politan-wide land-use control decision-making processes, encouraged through appropriate federal legislation and inducements, are more apt to break down some of the current practices and open the metropolitan area housing market to wider segments of the urban population. Ultimately, the private market must be given a chance to operate unencumbered by unreasonable and ill-conceived public regulations.

[13] Babcock, *The Zoning Game, op. cit.*, p. 160.

18. URBAN TRANSPORTATION

The urban dimension of transportation is frequently stressed in public policy today. This has not always been the case in this country, and in fact it has only been in recent decades that national decision-makers have begun to view transportation in this light. For years, the nation was concerned with bringing farm goods and products from rural areas to markets, and much of public policy in the past has been directed toward facilitating this process. However, with the concentration of industry, commerce, and populations in urban and metropolitan regions, the transportation of persons and goods has become increasingly an urban issue. Now, transportation within metropolitan areas (or intraurban transportation) and from one urban area to another (or interurban transportation) are of vital importance to large numbers of public officials and private citizens.[1]

We shall begin this chapter by briefly introducing the student to the subject of transportation and then examining transportation trends. We shall then review the responsibilities of the private and public sectors in transportation, including the activities of the different levels of government in this functional area. Finally, we shall turn our attention to a long-neglected aspect of this topic—the politics of transportation. A wide variety of groups at every level of our governmental system have significant transportation interests at stake, and these organized forces affect what will and will not be done both publicly and privately in transportation. In this connection, we shall consider the role of the two major political parties and any other influences that have an important bearing on public transportation policy.

All three levels of government in the American political system perform important functions in transportation, and there is considerable interrelatedness among the levels in some specific program areas. For this reason, it is necessary to consider transportation policy at the national as well as the state and local levels; only through a study of transportation actions in national and nonnational units is it possible to understand fully actions at either level and to picture broadly the urban transportation process.

THE NATURE OF TRANSPORTATION

Transportation is defined as the means by which people, materials, commodities, goods, services, and other items, whatever their nature, are moved or transmitted from place to place. In this sense transportation covers virtually all forms of movement. Stationary activities, physical structures and facilitates, and natural environmental features may, however, affect transportation or be affected by it and therefore should be seen for our purposes here in terms of their relationship to transportation. Among the more relevant of these stationary matters and clearly influences on transportation are, for example, parking facilities, transportation control mechanisms such as traffic lights, and housing and building patterns near transportation stations.

Transportation can take place in a number of different ways and by means of various modes. The methods of transportation would include

---

1 The best and the most comprehensive work on urban transportation is Wilfred Owen, *The Metropolitan Transportation Problem* (rev. ed.; Washington, D.C.: The Brookings Institution, 1966).

automobiles, buses, rail rapid transit, other rail transit including the railroad, airplanes, trucks, boats, and foot. This does not cover all the forms of transportation, especially broadly defined, and excludes, particularly, transport by pipe and wire, not to be discounted at least as competitors to some of the more traditional modes.

Of special importance in urban transportation are automobiles, buses, and rail transport of certain kinds. Automobiles include private passenger cars as well as business and government vehicles, while buses mean both the electric trolley and motored variety. Rail rapid transit refers to high-speed urban mass transportation taking place in vehicles operating on rail tracks; not all rail transit is rapid, nor is all rapid transit necessarily rail. Rail rapid transit would include subway, elevated, and surface transportation systems as well as any combination of these systems. Although rail rapid transit has particular applicability within urban and metropolitan areas, a rail rapid system may also be used to link urban areas to one another and provide transportation from any type of area to another. Other rail transit of interest in urban areas includes commuter railroad operations and other urban rail transit such as the streetcar, interurban rail transport, and the cable car. These are the forms of transportation of greatest concern to us in this chapter. At the same time it must be noted that other transportation should not be overlooked; for example, air and truck transport are important features in the urban transportation picture, particularly in the sense that the industries representing these transport forms play a key part in shaping public transportation policy affecting urban areas. At least politically then if not in other respects, the various transportation categories are interdependent and in this light should not be seen entirely separate from one another.

THE PURPOSE OF TRANSPORTATION

Certainly it can be stated generally that the nation wants a transportation system that will transport whatever needs moving from one place to another in the most efficient, effective, and economical way possible. We can further assume that the American public expects to have a public policy that is most consistent with the achievement of this objective. Although somewhat abstract and broad, this goal undoubtedly serves as a constraining force on public officials and private interests who decide or influence transportation policy.

The tendency in recent years has been for specific governmental functions to be considered and judged from a more comprehensive point of view than has been commonly the case in the past; and transportation is no exception to this. In transportation what this means is that there have been pressur s brought to bear on decision-makers to broaden the considerations that go into determining what action is to be taken. Ultimately, the matter comes back to the question of objectives, which may be in a transitional state in transportation, or at least within some sections of the transportation field. More to the point, some believe that transportation should be used to shape future urban growth and development patterns, and not simply "serve" the transportation needs of the public in the traditional sense. In any event, it has become apparent that transportation facilities affect such factors as land-use and population movement; it is a small step to consider harnessing transportation as an instrument of directing growth and future development. Practically speaking, Congress in national highway legislation in 1962 and 1968 seemed to be taking notice of this modern notion when it required the expansion of the highway planning process. This and other public action which could be cited suggests the addition of another dimension to the "goals" of transportation.

MASS TRANSIT VS. THE AUTOMOBILE

Within the urban context, it is possible to transport individuals by mass forms of public transportation—that is, by rail or bus, termed mass transit, or by the private automobile. As can be readily observed throughout the country, the urban transportation system is presently dominated by the automobile, although mass transit does move large numbers of persons during the rush hours in the morning and at night. Transportation and planning experts outside of highway departments frequently recommend a shift in urban transportation policy away from the currently heavy dependence on the automobile and in the direction of a substantially beefed-up mass transit system. For example, it is argued that rail rapid transit vehicles can move up to 60,000 persons per hour, while automobiles operating on expressways can carry only 2,000 to 3,000 individuals per lane an hour; buses can transport more persons each hour than cars but not as many as rail rapid transit vehicles. These and related statistics have turned a number of students of urban transportation into critics of the existing transportation network in the metropolitan area.

However one should consider, in addition, the costs of one as opposed to another transportation scheme: the expenses of both a public and private nature of the various means of transport should be related to the benefits accruing from these means. Also to be examined in this respect are the particular techniques to be used—and their feasibility—in the raising of funds for transportation, especially for new systems which call for large public capital outlays. Under any circumstances, cost comparisons between mass transit and automobile transportation are difficult to advance without making a number of simplifying and perhaps unrealistic assumptions; but any determinations made here necessitate a study of both capital and operating costs as well as all governmental and non-governmental expenditures associated with the transportation means in question. Along these lines, an initial obstacle to the development of rail rapid transit systems in metropolitan areas is the expense factor. Costs of constructing subways in the downtown sections of larger cities can run as high as $30 million or more a mile; and this is exclusive of the money needed for rolling stock, equipment, maintenance, and administration. In view of the relatively few rail rapid transit operations in the United States at present, sharply escalated public outlays would have to be forthcoming if any basic changes are to be made toward rail rapid systems. It might be added that urban transportation cost calculations have become more of a political matter of late, with different interests citing different statistics on the same subject, usually designed to sway the public in one direction or another.

TRANPORTATION TRENDS

As noted, the automobile enjoys a position of unparalleled superiority in the urban transportation network. More generally, the automobile and other motored vehicles, especially the truck, have been the single most important force in setting the tone for contemporary transportation trends. Nothing more meaningful can be said about transportation at present or in recent years than that the effect of the motored vehicle can hardly be overestimated: the car is the central element.

In the modern era transportation can be traced to the stream railroad and the electric streetcar. Prior to the twentieth century, the nation had both, and by the early 1900s the streetcar was the dominant form of public transportation in and near urban areas, not only serving as a transit instrument but shaping development as well. The interurban railroad in the early years prospered along with the streetcar, linking population concentrations and influencing population settlement as did the streetcar.

With the emergence of the automobile and its mass production, the whole nature of our transportation was drastically altered. With the rise of the motor vehicle, we have witnessed the virtual disappearance of the streetcar, the steady decline of public mass transportation in urban areas, the economic deterioration of the public transit industry, and a weakening of the position of the railroads. While transportation used to be essentially a public matter, it is now basically a private concern. And in the public policy area governmental actions on the whole have seemingly accelerated the movement to the private automobile, serving to underwrite a vast and costly highway system. Specific figures on automobile, bus and rail transit, railroad, and trucking trends follow.

AUTOMOBILE[2]   The number of passenger car registrations increased substantially between 1940 and 1968—from 27.5 million to nearly 83 million. Four out of five American families own automobiles, and the proportion of families with cars is up from 60 percent in 1950. In upper-income groups most families own two cars: 62 percent of the families with an income of $15,000 or more possess two or more automobiles, as do over 40 percent of those in the $10,000 to $15,000 range. In metropolitan areas, the car is used more than any other means to go to work. Ninety percent of all suburban workers drive to their jobs, compared to just over two thirds of those in central cities; moreover, 65 percent of the suburbanites and slightly less than one half of central-city residents drive to work alone, meaning that a large proportion of commuter automobiles in urban areas contain only the driver.

BUS AND RAIL TRANSIT   Public bus and rail transit has not fared as well as the automobile in the last quarter of a century. Significantly, considerably fewer persons now use public transit compared to 1945; specifically, in 1945, public bus and rail transit vehicles carried over 23 billion passengers, and this was down to 8.2 billion in 1967, a rather noticeable decline (Table 18.1). The general downward trend was characteristic of transit operations on a year-to-year basis from 1945 to 1966; interestingly, a slight increase in total numbers of passengers was found in 1967 over 1966. The drop in passengers has been greatest in the surface rail or streetcar and the trolley coach (electric bus) categories, while the subway-elevated rail and motor bus classes have largely stabilized in terms of numbers of passengers in the 1960s. In fact, more persons used the subway and elevated transit systems in 1967 than in 1966; and this accounts entirely for the rise in the grand total in 1967 (all other transit experienced passenger losses between 1966 and 1967).[3]

RAILROAD   Although statistics show that their freight business and revenue are up, railroads have been steadily losing money and riders in the passenger area over the last decade or two. At the same time, the railroad industry reports that commuter revenues are at an all-time high and that there has been a boost in the number of commuter passengers recently.[4]

---

[2]   The source of statistics in this paragraph is American Manufacturers Association, *Automobile Facts and Figures 1969* (Detroit, 1969).
[3]   American Transit Association, *1968 Transit Fact Book* (Washington, D.C., 1968).
[4]   Association of American Railroads, *Yearbook of Railroad Facts, 1969 Edition* (Washington, D.C., 1969).

TABLE 18.1
Public Transit Ridership Figures, 1945–1967
(*all figures in millions*)

	NUMBER OF PASSENGERS BY TYPE OF TRANSIT					
	RAIL			TROLLEY	MOTOR	
		SUBWAY &		COACH	BUS	GRAND
YEAR	SURFACE	ELEVATED	TOTAL	(ELECTRIC)		TOTAL
1945	9,426	2,698	12,124	1,244	9,886	23,254
1950	3,904	2,264	6,168	1,658	9,420	17,246
1955	1,207	1,870	3,077	1,202	7,250	11,529
1956	876	1,880	2,756	1,142	7,043	10,941
1957	679	1,843	2,522	993	6,874	10,389
1958	572	1,815	2,387	843	6,502	9,732
1959	521	1,828	2,349	749	6,459	9,557
1960	463	1,850	2,313	657	6,425	9,395
1961	434	1,855	2,289	601	5,993	8,883
1962	393	1,890	2,283	547	5,865	8,695
1963	329	1,836	2,165	413	5,822	8,400
1964	289	1,877	2,166	349	5,813	8,328
1965	276	1,858	2,134	305	5,814	8,253
1966	282	1,753	2,035	284	5,764	8,083
1967	263	1,938	2,201	248	5,723	8,172

SOURCE: American Transit Association, *1968 Transit Fact Book* (Washington, D.C., 1968), p. 6.

TRUCKING   Unlike railroads, the trucking industry in America is strong. In 1968, there were close to 17 million publicly and privately owned trucks in the country. Counting only private vehicles, 4.5 million trucks were registered in 1944, and by 1960 that figure had soared to over 11 million. About a million new trucks are registered each year (exclusive of government vehicles), and the number of truck vehicle miles traveled each year moved sharply upward from 1944 to 1967.[5]

The Future of Transportation

The automobile will continue to be an important transportation means for years to come, although changes may be made in the size and nature of the engine of the car as well as in transportation control devices which might affect these vehicles. Buses will likely begin to use special highway lanes reserved just for that purpose as time goes on, thereby making bus

[5] American Trucking Associations, Inc., *American Trucking Trends 1968* (Washington, D.C., 1968).

transit more competitive with rail rapid transit than has been true in the past. Subway and other rail rapid transit operations can be expected to be developed in more American cities in the future, and to be expanded in some of the cities that now have such systems. The monorail (single rail, elevated) has been discussed in some quarters and tried on an experimental basis in this country; but to date, this concept has failed to show much promise, especially from a cost point of view.

Helicopters and commuter airplanes are employed at the present time within metropolitan areas and surrounding regions as means of transporting persons into and out of cities, and the use of these and similar air vehicles will undoubtedly be on the upswing in future years. Any number of other changes—such as moving sidewalks and ground-effect machines —designed to take us into a new transportation era may mark the American transportation landscape in the years to come.

TRANSPORTATION: THE PUBLIC AND PRIVATE SECTORS

Transportation in the United States is largely a private responsibility: most automobile, bus, railroad, airline, and truck vehicles or systems are privately owned. Of the major forms of transportation, only the rail rapid transit systems are completely a governmental activity. The rail rapid transit networks of Boston, Philadelphia, New York, Chicago, and Cleveland—the only such systems in the nation today—are owned and run by government, in each case by local government (usually, public authority). In addition, the new rail rapid transit systems underway in San Francisco and Washington, D.C., will also be operated by government at the local level.

City buses are partly in public and partly in private hands. Of all urban transit systems, 9 percent are owned by government, but this segment of the industry carries 62 percent of the urban transit revenue passengers, meaning that a number of big-city bus operations are publicly owned.

Generally, however, governments are important in transportation in two basic respects: as builders of highways and as regulators of various forms of transportation. All three levels of government contribute to the financing of the expensive highway network blanketing the nation, and state and local governments construct, maintain, and own the country's highways. Highways are funded largely through special highway user taxes, and in 1969, all units of government received an estimated $18.4 billion in highway taxes. Another key function of the public sector is the regulation of transportation; governments regulate all transportation in one way or another but have particularly significant powers in specific areas of concern to metropolitan Americans. Additionally, local governments operate the major airports of the nation; and all levels of government perform research, experiments, and promotional work in transportation. We shall now look at the transportation functions of each level of government.

National Government

While a number of federal agencies such as the Interstate Commerce Commission, the Department of Housing and Urban Development, and others have important transportation responsibilities, the key programs in this area are found in the newly created Department of Transportation. Of this department's six major operating divisions, those most directly concerned with urban transportation and with assisting state and local governments in transportation are the Federal Highway Administration, the Federal Aviation Administration, and the Urban Mass Transportation Administration.

The Federal Highway Administration has authority over the federal highway program, highway and motor carrier safety, and highway beautification; and part of the Highway Administration is the powerful Bureau of Public Roads (BPR), previously in the U.S. Department of Commerce. The Bureau of Public Roads administers the federal highway assistance activities, and in the process works basically through state governments.

Federal highway aid efforts are divided into two general categories: the interstate system and the "ABC" program. The interstate system was authorized by national highway legislation in 1944, although for all practical purposes, it can be traced to 1956 when Congress advanced the necessary financing to embark on this highway program in a major way. Formally called the National System of Interstate and Defense Highways, this highway network when completed will encompass 42,500 miles of freeways, connecting nearly all of the central cities of the country's metropolitan areas and carrying 20 percent of the nation's traffic. (See Figure 18.1.) So far, Congress has authorized over $50 billion in federal funds for the interstate program, making it one of the most expensive domestic government undertakings in American history. The final federal contribution will probably exceed the currently authorized amount by as much as $5 to $10 billion by 1972, the scheduled completion date, if anything can be learned from past experiences in highway financing.

Ninety percent of the cost of interstate highways is provided by the national government, and 10 percent comes from the states. The federal portion is raised through a special highway trust fund, established by the

Federal-Aid Highway Act of 1956 (prior to 1956, highway funds came from general appropriations). The chief trust fund source is the motor fuel tax (4 cents a gallon in 1969); the national government draws upon this fund for other state highway assistance as well.

The Federal-Aid Road Act of 1916 marked the beginning of the national government's state highway aid activities, and important state road building programs followed this enactment. Although the initial federal assistance was to be used for intercity highways, in the late 1920s, some federal funds were authorized for urban highways; and in the Federal-Aid Highway Act of 1944, more federal dollars were allocated to urban roads.

The "ABC" program is composed of federal aid in three classes of state highways: primary, secondary, and urban extensions. The primary system includes nearly 270,000 miles of main highways and streets (the interstate system's 42,500 miles are technically part of this); the secondary system covers farm-to-market and feeder roads, totaling over 642,000 miles of state, county, and local highways; and the urban extensions are the urban portions of the other two systems. Money authorized for the three categories is divided as follows: 45 percent for primary, 30 percent for secondary, and 25 percent for urban highways. Unlike the situation in the interstate system, "ABC" funds are used by states to rebuild and upgrade existing highways and can be used to develop arterial routes into major expressways and freeways. For eligible projects the national government advances 50 percent of the costs in the ABC program, with the states or the states and local governments providing the other 50 percent.

Highway planning and safety have been stressed by national authorities in recent years. For instance, the national government stipulates that the states must use a portion of their federal money for highway planning, research, and development. More specifically, the Federal-Aid Highway Act of 1962 essentially made it mandatory that states and localities establish a continuing, comprehensive, cooperative transportation planning process in the larger of the urban areas by mid-1965. This process was to be carried on by state and local governments for the purpose of coordinating highway and other transportation planning and developing long-range highway plans and programs which take into account the effects of highways on future urban land use. Furthermore, under the Federal-Aid Highway Act of 1968, each state must consider in its highway planning the social, economic, and environmental impact of new highways and examine the consistency of proposed highways with local comprehensive planning objectives. In the safety area, according to federal legislation enacted in 1966, the states are required to have highway safety programs in operation.

The national government exercises reasonably close supervision and

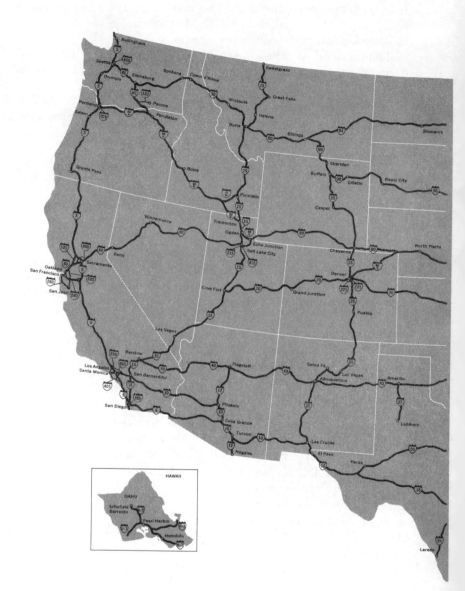

FIG. 18.1. *The National System of Interstate and Defense Highways*

control over federally assisted state highway activities, in part by setting standards for construction, contracting, and personnel practices. This is another illustration of the important role played by federal officials in a state-administered function through a major grant program. Altogether, in 1967, funds from the national government accounted for 40 percent of all public spending on highway construction.

Some of the national government's air transportation responsibilities are administratively located in the Department of Transportation's Federal Aviation Administration. This agency has authority over air traffic control and, of concern to us, administers the federal airport aid program. Congressional legislation in 1946 initially set up an airport grant-in-aid program under which funds were provided directly to localities; incidentally, this was one of the earliest of the direct national-local government grant activities. In the year for which the most recent figures are available—fiscal 1970—Congress appropriated $30 million for local airport assistance. A new and vastly expanded federal airport grant program is currently being considered by the Nixon administration and Congress.

Control over federal mass transportation is found in the Urban Mass Transportation Administration of the Department of Transportation. The national mass transportation program began with the enactment of the Housing Act of 1961 and was substantially broadened with the passage of the Urban Mass Transportation Act of 1964. In urban transportation, federal funds have been made available to local governments for capital improvement purposes, including the acquisition of new transit system equipment and the modernization of facilities, demonstration, research, and development, technical studies, managerial training, and university transportation research. The national government distributed about $134 million in grant funds under the urban mass transportation program in fiscal year 1968. Most recently, the Nixon administration has proposed a somewhat broader federal urban mass transportation effort calling for the expenditure of $300 million in 1971 and progressively higher sums for the fiscal years up through 1975.

State Government

State government transportation activities are generally found in three administrative areas: highways, public utility regulation, and aviation control.

STATE HIGHWAYS   The interest of the state governments in the nation's transportation system is heavily concentrated in highways. In 1969, state governments collected nearly $10 billion in highway receipts (exclusive of federal and local government highway funds), over half of the $18.5 billion worth of proceeds from all highway sources in the country.

States construct and maintain highways under their jurisdiction, including interstate, primary, and other roads. As indicated, states receive federal highway assistance, and states may use federal funds for highway construction, rebuilding, expansion, and planning, as permitted; federal money is not, however, to be used for maintenance, an entirely state and local government responsibility. For a period of time some states like Pennsylvania and New Jersey embarked on important turnpike construction programs, but with the passage of the financially attractive federal interstate highway legislation in 1956, states have engaged in little turnpike construction activity.

At the state level, the highway function is administered by a state highway department or roads commission, normally enjoying considerable independence from the direct control of the governor; one recent study classified all but 13 of the 50 state highway departments as independent agencies.[6] The relatively small number of "dependent" highway departments were limited largely to the urban-industrial states. A dependent agency is one in which the governor is free to name his own highway chief without certain restrictions. Not uncommonly, state highway boards have administrative and policy-making duties, and certain economic and geographical interests may be represented on highway commissions by law or custom, seemingly adding to the relative autonomy of the roads agency in the general political scheme of things.

The bulk of state highway revenues come from the motor fuel gallonage tax; in 1968, over $5 billion of the over $8 billion of state highway tax revenues could be traced to this source, with most of the difference being made up by state motor vehicle registration fees. Consistent with current federal practice, states normally segregate highway receipts from general revenue, and most states—28 to be exact (1969)—have adopted constitutional provisions prohibiting the diversion of state gasoline and motor vehicle taxes for nonhighway purposes. In fact, in 1967, only 8 percent of all road revenues in states were used for other than highway matters, down substantially from the proportion found in the 1930s and early 1940s. The state of New Jersey serves as a major exception to the general rule, and in 1967 spent almost 44 percent of its highway revenues for nonhighway public uses.

As suggested above, states have become increasingly involved in new forms of highway planning and highway safety activities. States must use at least 1.5 percent of their annual allotment of federal highway funds for planning and research work; and state highway administrators now operate in somewhat broader channels in planning the roads program, particularly in urban areas where close working relationships have been developed between the state highway agency and metropolitan planning

6   Robert S. Friedman, "State Politics and Highways," in Herbert Jacob and Kenneth N. Vines (eds.), *Politics in the American States* (Boston: Little, Brown, 1965), pp. 422–423.

bodies in some parts of the country. Highway safety programs have been set up in all states, and some states such as New Hampshire and Wyoming now have highway safety coordinators operating directly out of the governor's office.

A few states have recently created state departments of transportation, following the federal pattern. For instance, New Jersey, New York, and Wisconsin presently have such departments; the New Jersey Department of Transportation has highway, commuter railroad, and aviation responsibilities. Part of the theory behind the establishment of departments of transportation is that they will promote the coordination of major transportation program activity for the state as a whole, allowing for the development of a wider base on which transportation priorities can be considered and transportation funds allocated. In view of the enormous independent power base of the typical state highway department, one is led to speculate as to whether an administrative reorganization will affect the political foundation of the highway function in state government. Experience to date suggests that this effort will have few immediate political consequences, meaning that for the indefinite future highway funds will be used for highway purposes and not for mass transit and the like.

PUBLIC UTILITY REGULATION States have long regulated private business in the public utility area, normally delegating this matter to a public utility or public service commission (also, possibly, a corporation, railroad, or commerce board). The commission's regulatory authority will extend to any number of intrastate transportation utilities such as trucks, buses, street railways, interurban railroads, and aviation. State public utility commission members may be appointed by the governor (32 states), elected directly by the voters (14 states), or appointed by the state legislature (as in Virginia and South Carolina). Two states break with the typical practice and have utilities agencies headed by a single director rather than a commission (Rhode Island and Oregon).

AVIATION CONTROL The regulation of intrastate aviation may fall under a separate state aeronautics department or commission, although as can be seen in the previous paragraph, some states have given this authority to a public utilities commission. The control of interstate aviation as well as other forms of interstate transportation is within the jurisdiction of the Interstate Commerce Commission, a federal regulatory board.

Local Government

Local governments have significant transportation powers in the areas of highways, mass transit, and airports.

American municipalities, counties, townships, and towns have local road and street construction and maintenance authority. In city government this responsibility is often found in a department of public works or a department of streets, administered by a department head or commission as at the state level. In counties, townships, and towns, the roads function is assigned either to the governing body or to a highway commissioner, superintendent, or other officer. Local governments have a tendency to attempt to shift the highway activity upward in the governmental structure. What this means is that localities try to have as many roads as possible designated as part of the state system, and the smaller of the local units (townships) frequently press the county into taking over their roads.

Municipalities, counties, and townships collected an estimated $3.2 billion in highway funds in 1969, not an unimportant portion of all such receipts nationwide. Because of federal and state aid granted local governments, localities spend considerably more than they collect: in 1969, the figure was over $5 billion.

Some local governments regulate privately owned urban transit companies, normally a function of the state government. Further, communities are increasingly responsible for the operation of mass transit systems; and now, as noted, publicly owned transit carries most of the passengers transported by urban transit systems. Governmentally owned transit may be administratively located in a municipal department or public authority created by state or local governments.

As has been pointed out, all rail rapid transit systems are owned by local government. This includes operations in the five cities that have had such systems for some time and in the two cities that are currently developing rail rapid transit. A few other cities including Atlanta, Seattle, and Baltimore are in the process of planning new rail rapid transit systems. Commonly, rail rapid transit is under the control of an agency outside the general-purpose municipal government, usually a special district or public authority. The Boston system is administered by the Massachusetts Bay Transportation Authority; in New York, rail rapid transit is run by the New York City Transit Authority and more broadly by the Metropolitan Transportation Authority; in Chicago, it is under the Chicago Transit Authority; in Philadelphia, the Southeastern Pennsylvania Transportation Authority; and in Cleveland, the Cleveland Transit System is operated by the Cleveland Transit Board. The San Francisco and Washington systems will be within the jurisdiction of the Bay Area Rapid Transit District and the Washington Metropolitan Area Transit Authority respectively. The latter agency is unique among organizations with authority over rail rapid transit in that it is an interstate compact, having been approved by the legislatures of Maryland and Virginia, the District of Columbia, and the Congress of the United States.

The trend has been in the direction of public ownership of municipal and urban bus transit systems. It is probably not unfair to observe that many private bus firms look forward to the day that they can sell out to local government at what they consider to be a reasonable price. The transit industry in general is in a state of sharp economic decline, reporting progressively escalating deficits with the passing of each year; transit firms, for instance, lost over $66 million in 1967. Bus transit therefore can be expected to be a more visible part of local government responsibilities in the future.

The third area of local government transportation interest is air transport. Nearly all of the major airports of the nation are owned by local government (including special districts or authorities), although some are privately or federally run. The responsibility for airport facility administration varies by locality, as either an agency of the general-purpose local government, such as the Department of Airports in the City of Los Angeles, or a special unit of government, such as the Massachusetts Port Authority, may exercise this control.

THE POLITICS OF
URBAN TRANSPORTATION

Transportation has seldom been treated in a basically political manner, except in the most general and vaguest of senses. This is unfortunate, for it overlooks the essence of the field at least as far as public policy is concerned. The roots of domestic public policy in the United States can often be traced to organized interests which have something to gain or lose by the enactment of one or another public policy. So, in transportation, government at all levels largely responds to pressures from the more powerful of the private and public forces which have an important stake in this vital segment of the American economy. Public transportation policy then tends to be reflective of the relative influence position of the various affected elements in the private transportation industry, transportation users, and organized public officials. We shall now examine each of the major groups concerned with urban transportation policy.

Interest Groups in Transportation

The key interests in urban transportation are the automobile, oil, rubber, trucking, railroad, transit, airline, and highway construction industries, motorists, and state and local highway, transit, airport, aviation, and public works officials and departments. Not mentioned (but not because they are unimportant) since they are not organized into interest groups are federal government administrative, legislative, and judicial officials and departments, the general public, and political parties. National government officials are not simply registrants of the will of others: they have some independent influence over transportation policy. The role of the general public is hard to gauge, although it is an understatement to indicate that the organized interests, public officials, and political parties will claim to speak for this unorganized force. The position of the political parties in transportation is reviewed in the next section of the chapter.

At the national level, the automobile industry is organized through the Automobile Manufacturers Association, the oil industry is represented by the American Petroleum Institute, the rubber industry by the Rubber Manufacturers Association, the trucking industry by the American Trucking Associations, Inc., railroads by the Association of American Railroads, transit by the American Transit Association, the airline industry by the Air Transport Association of America, and the road construction industry by the American Road Builders' Association and the Associated General Contractors of America. Motorists are represented politically by the American Automobile Association, state highway departments by the American Association of State Highway Officials, municipal transit systems by the American Transit Association (as are private transit companies), municipal airports by the Airport Operators Council International, Inc., state aviation regulation agencies by the National Association of State Aviation Officials, and state and local government public works officials by the American Public Works Association. Other organizations which serve essentially as coalitions of transportation groups and which have an important effect on the public transportation policy-making processes are the National Highway Users Conference, the Automotive Safety Foundation, and the Transportation Association of America. Any number of other interest groups are concerned with transportation policy —such as the National League of Cities, the United States Conference of Mayors, the Automotive Electric Association, the National Association of Motor Bus Owners, the National Parking Association, and the National Association of Regulatory Utility Commissioners—but these groups either have interests broader than transportation or have interests or members more directly and powerfully represented by other organizations in the transportation area.

The "big three" private forces with interests in highway policy are the auto, oil, and rubber industries. These industries are represented both by their own trade associations and by the National Highway Users Conference and the Automotive Safety Foundation, although both of these latter groups have constituents in addition to the big three industries.

The Automobile Manufacturers Association is the national organization of motor vehicle makers; its members include the General Motors

Corporation, Ford Motor Company, Chrysler Corporation, American Motors Corporation, Checker Motors Corporation, Kaiser Jeep Corporation, Mack Trucks, Inc., Walter Motor Truck Company, White Motor Corporation, International Harvester Corporation, and Warner and Swasey Company. Automobile manufacturers are primarily interested in highway and automobile-related policy in the national government, but the association has field representatives who watch state and local government activity which might affect the interests of the industry and who testify before nonnational government legislative committees. The Automobile Manufacturers Association works with other organizations involved in transportation such as the Highway Research Board of the National Academy of Sciences.

The oil industry's chief political arm at the national level is the American Petroleum Institute, which has some 10,000 company and individual members throughout the United States, including the large oil firms. Rubber interests are defended by the Rubber Manufacturers Association which represents about 190 private companies including the major rubber corporations. Like the automobile and oil interests, the rubber industry has a permanent Washington staff.

Together, the automobile, oil, and rubber industries are major contributors to the National Highway Users Conference and the Automotive Safety Foundation. The Users Conference considers one of its objectives to be the support of the federal-state highway program—and this is undoubtedly its key goal. To this end, the conference opposes diversion of highway funds to nonhighway uses and favors the trust-fund approach as the means of financing the national highway program. The Users Conference, however, does not lobby in the technical sense; nevertheless, its viewpoint and political base are well known and widely respected in transportation circles. There are also state highway user organizations which work to protect highway funds and generally promote the highway cause in state capitals.

The American Trucking Associations, Inc., is the national organization of the trucking industry, operating basically as a federation of state trucking groups. Structured politically along points of the decision-making process in the federal system, organized truckers are primarily concerned with national and state trucking regulation and highway policy. The railroad industry is represented by the Association of American Railroads, and the major railroads of the nation are members of this group. It should be noted that the railroad industry directs its attention not only to railroad policy matters (particularly in the Interstate Commerce Commission), but also to public policy which could affect the competitive position of railroads in the transportation picture. What this means in practical terms is that rail interests will often take stands on proposed or existing highway and trucking policies. For instance, railroads commonly favor higher taxes on trucks and fight the relaxation of truck weight and size limitations by governments at both the national and state levels. Present transportation policy found in American governments is clearly one of the chief causes of the bleak economic condition of the American railroad industry. Governments have not underwritten the railroads the way they have in effect the automotive and trucking industries through the highway program.

The American Transit Association is the trade organization for the urban transit industry, and its membership roster includes all the rail rapid transit systems in the nation (also represented by the Institute for Rapid Transit) plus the major publicly and privately owned bus operations. The transit industry strongly supports greater federal urban mass transportation assistance, and is convinced that a transit trust fund (like the highway trust fund) should be created at the national level as a vehicle to providing expanded and long-term mass transit aid to localities.

The Air Transport Association of America is the big airline companies' voice in Washington. Of current interest to local governments, this group backs a broadened airport and airways grant program. This industry's weight could be decisive in determining future federal policy in this area.

The two construction industry representatives in Washington are the American Road Builders' Association and the Associated General Contractors of America, although the former is more particularly concerned with highway transportation policy. Highway contractors are also organized at the state level where they, as in Washington, can be expected to support expanded outlays for state roads.

The American Automobile Association is the major motorists' political agent in national councils. Tracing its origin to 1902, this organization is composed of 820 affiliated motor clubs and branches, serving 11 million members. Its public policy objectives include the promotion of highway expenditures and the use of special motorist taxes exclusively for highway purposes. The American Automobile Association boasts that it was instrumental in securing passage of the first federal highway aid legislation in 1916 and that it "played a leading role" in the 1956 enactment which funded the interstate system. Along with the auto, oil, and rubber industries, the American Automobile Association belongs to the National Highway Users Conference.

State highway departments are organized through the American Association of State Highway Officials. Recognized by some as a prime force in setting national highway policy, this organization has behind it both the professional expertise and the political clout of the influential state highway agencies.

Municipally owned airports are represented by the Airport Operators Council International, Inc., which has 131 member air terminals, including, for instance, the Port of New York Authority (an interstate compact agency which runs Kennedy, LaGuardia, and Newark airports), the Massachusetts Port Authority (Logan Field in Boston), and the local Department of Aviation of Los Angeles. This organization has lobbied in Washington for a substantially stepped-up federal airport aid program, claiming that an additional $14 billion is needed for airport construction and expansion over the coming ten years. The council also believes that the new federal funds should be placed in a special trust fund, apparently suggesting that what is good for highways is also good for airports. Another organization which includes municipal airport officials is the American Association of Airport Executives.

State government aviation regulatory body interests are protected by the National Association of State Aviation Officials, an organization of state aeronautic departments and commissions. Some state and local highway and related transportation officials or agencies belong to the American Public Works Association which in addition represents federal administrators, consulting engineers, equipment manufacturers, contractors, and others.

Judging the relative political importance of these organizations in the public transportation policy area is no simple task. The power wielded by each group would depend to a considerable extent on the particular issue involved and the degree to which the organization considered its interests affected. However, some generalizations can be advanced.

From the standpoint of state and local government, there are three major policy issue areas of significance at the national level: highways, airports, and mass transit. Let us examine each.

In highways, the "big three" industries probably provide the basic political backbone for the national and state highway programs since it is "their" products that have been offered and accepted as tax sources for these programs. Certainly, all three worked for or at least consented to the enactment of the 1956 highway legislation which set the tone for current highway and transportation policy. At the same time, one should not overlook the organized truckers, motorists, highway contractors, or state highway officials in any discussion of the political base of highway policy. Since all of these groups agree on the fundamentals of highway policy, it is not possible to determine with precision the exact influence of each; nor is it necessary for purposes of public policy analysis. No one can deny that together these interests form an impressive coalition. Its record has been a good one.

The national government has been providing federal airport funds to localities over the past 25 years; yet, the amount of that assistance has been limited by Washington standards. One of the reasons for this has been the absence of a strong clientele base which wants airport aid expanded. However, in view of the economic growth of the airline industry[7] and the increasing use of air transportation, one can expect federal policy changes in this area. The various air transport interest groups such as the Air Transport Association and the Airport Operators Council International are not in complete accord on the nature of federal policy they want, but they will get a bill out of Congress which will advance billions instead of the present millions for air transport improvement, and the money will probably be protected through some means (such as a trust fund). Again, as in highways, these funds will come from the air industry and its customers.

The politics of mass transit differs from the politics of highways and air transportation. The reason for this is that there are no important industrial or user interests in mass transit as in highways and air transport. In fact, the only industry that has a serious stake in transit is in a severely declining economic state, hardly in a position to bargain with hard-pressed public officials or to present itself or transit riders for taxation. In this light, no major spending legislation can be anticipated in mass transit; and whatever money is advanced by Washington to local governments will not come from a protected source.

Political Parties

Essentially, the political parties will support whatever the key interest groups can agree upon in transportation, of course, within the limits imposed by public opinion. If a particular policy is unacceptable to either of the two major parties it will likely be unacceptable to the other; similarly, what is acceptable to either party in transportation will probably be acceptable to the other. In this sense, the interest groups in transportation are not dependent on one or the other parties as tends to be the case in some other issue areas.

At the national level, for example, both political parties in Congress supported the highway legislation in 1956 by wide margins; both parties will likely vote by large majorities an expanded federal air transportation bill in the early 1970s; and both Republicans and Democrats will probably consent to a moderately broadened national mass transit policy.

In the state capitals, one study has found that Republicans are associated with higher roads outlays relative to other spending than are Demo-

---

[7]   In the decade from 1958 to 1968, the revenue passenger miles flown by the airlines jumped from 31 billion to nearly 114 billion. Air Transport Association of America, *1969 Air Transport Facts and Figures* (Washington, D.C., 1969), p. 26.

crats. At the same time, this analysis concluded that partisanship was not correlated with the diversion of highway funds to nonhighway uses. In addition, the study reported that the economic development status of the state and the administrative location of the highway function in state governments appeared to affect highway expenditures.[8]

[8] Thomas R. Dye, *Politics, Economics, and the Public: Policy Outcomes in the American States* (Chicago: Rand McNally, 1966), pp. 159, 163, 171–173.

19. POVERTY
AND
COMMUNITY
POLITICS

The idea of governmental support for the needy poor has never been part of the doctrines of either Lockean individualism or Puritan self-reliance, which enjoy deep and enduring roots in the American political tradition. In reality, American governments at all levels have been slow to respond to any but the most extreme form of disaster or misfortune experienced by disadvantaged citizens. This nation's welfare philosophy has been based on the concept that the private institutions of the family, charity organizations, and churches have the primary responsibility for providing for the poor as well as the physically and mentally handicapped. Only when the resources of private sources are exhausted, the theory has it, should government step in, with the national government being called upon as a last resort. Following this philosophy, state and local governments have carried a significant portion of the country's public welfare burden; prior to the New Deal they had virtually the total governmental responsibility for the needy. Also, traditional welfare policy of public and private agencies has been premised on the assumption that assistance of a material variety (food, clothing, money, shelter) dispensed to those in need by sympathetic amateurs and (later) trained professionals characterized the appropriate response of the middle class to the plight of the poor.

Breaking somewhat with tradition, the national government in the 1930s became a prominent and in some respects independent participant in the public welfare policy and administrative processes of the United States, enacting social security and other legislation in this field. The New Deal's action on the welfare front signaled an end to state and local government dominance of public welfare; but new national government policy continued the material emphasis of welfare programs, parting from the past only by substituting professionals for amateurs in welfare administration. Later, this element of the traditional welfare philosophy came under stinging attack, as new forces began to challenge the conventional material and professional aspects of welfare administration. The recent history of welfare programs will be presented in the following section, in which we shall treat the current posture of state and local government in welfare and the role of the national government in shaping welfare policy in the entire federal system.

DEVELOPING WELFARE POLICY

Significant national government involvement in welfare was marked early in the Depression period by direct federal grants to states (and through states to localities) for general relief. This approach, however, was soon scrapped, and in 1935, Congress passed the sweeping, revolutionary Social Security Act which introduced a social insurance system for the first time on a national scale. While social security is often popularly equated with the old-age retirement program, the Social Security Act initiated other activities as well. Since its original enactment, social security legislation has been expanded substantially as the two major political parties have scrambled to gain credit for raising benefits and broadening coverage. Mounting pressures from welfare professionals and assorted welfare bureaucracies and organizations throughout the country have also led to the addition of costly amendments to social security legislation.

The national social security legislation has three key provisions: old-age insurance, unemployment compensation, and public assistance. Each aspect of this legislation has important effects on state and local government and will be reviewed. Under the old-age insurance program, both employers and employees must contribute to a special fund from which payments are made to insured workers during retirement, to survivors of insured workers, and to those who become permanently and totally disabled. Old-age insurance provisions have been widened considerably over the years, recently to include medical care for the aged—or medicare, a controversial proposal vigorously fought by organized medicine. As noted in Chapter 2, although the old-age insurance program is administered exclusively by the national government, it undoubtedly has affected subnational public institutions by cutting down on state and local welfare rolls.

In unemployment compensation, employers contribute to a state insurance fund which is used to pay workers who are out of a job (the portion contributed by employers to the national government is used for administration). Unemployment compensation is mostly a state-administered function, but it was national legislation that made it financially attractive for states to enter the field in the first place (a tax was essentially delegated to them); by national law, the federal government could collect the entire tax and administer the whole program—that is, if states do not act (they all have). In state governments an employment security department or commission or a labor, or a labor and industry department exercises administrative authority over unemployment compensation.

Finally, the social security legislation authorizes grants to states for public assistance to the aged (for general purposes and medical care), the blind, the totally and permanently disabled, and dependent children—the so-called categorical assistance programs. In 1965, Congress added the Medical Assistance Program—medicaid—to its numerous welfare activities. Under this effort, the national government makes grants to states to cover medical assistance for welfare recipients, a program incidentally which has proved to be an increasingly and unpredictably expensive undertaking for the states.

While general assistance (or general relief) for the needy regardless of age is solely within the province of state and local governments, categorical aid is a shared intergovernmental responsibility; at present, the federal government finances the bulk of the outlays in the categorical assistance programs. In the late 1960s, the National Advisory Commission on Civil Disorders and Governor Nelson Rockefeller of New York among others urged the national government to take on general relief assistance as well; federal activity in this area would not be unlikely in this light.

An important conflict between conservatives and liberals over the financing of medical care for the needy aged should be briefly mentioned. Liberals including organized labor and welfare interest groups have lobbied for the extension of the insurance concept to medical care assistance for the aged, where benefits are paid more or less as a matter of right; while conservatives including organized doctors (American Medical Association) have supported the granting of federal money to states for this purpose. In the early 1960s, conservatives secured passage of the Kerr-Mills bill (named for its Senate and House legislative sponsors respectively), which authorized federal grants to states to provide medical assistance for the indigent aged (conservatives probably saw this legislation at least in part as a means of heading off attempts to place such assistance under the social security insurance program, a much bolder and more costly step). Regardless of this early victory by the conservatives, the issue was finally resolved in favor of the liberals as Congress enacted the medicare program in the mid-1960s, in which aged medical care was to be financed on an insurance basis for insured workers as part of the social security system.

The various public assistance and general assistance functions are administratively assigned to state and local (city, county, township) public welfare departments. A number of states have combined welfare with other activities; thus welfare is sometimes administered in health and welfare departments or in social services agencies. In the national government, the Department of Health, Education, and Welfare has the responsibility for the social security-welfare functions.

Related to the welfare function in state and local governments are the various public health programs. Health activities are less directed toward a particular clientele (poor, aged) than much of welfare, but at the same time, because of the differential impact of disease on and the general health conditions of the various socioeconomic classes in American communities, health as a function of state and local government tends to have a sizable and disproportionate lower-status service constituency. State and local health functions include: communicable disease prevention and control, sanitation and food inspection, maternal and child hygiene, mental health treatment, the operation of hospitals, air and water pollution, collection of vital statistics (birth, death, sickness), and health education. Many health matters are intergovernmental in administrative assignment, with all levels of government having some authority in most health fields; as in welfare, federal participation in public health has sharply escalated in recent years. In state and local government, health is normally separated administratively from welfare, a functional responsibility of a department or board of health at both the state and local levels. In the national government, the health function is theoretically integrated with welfare—in the Department of Health, Education, and

Welfare (in fact, health and welfare programs in Washington are sub-stantially independently administered as well, even though both are subordinated to the same overarching organizational hierarchy).

Although there was considerable resistance in some circles to the federal government moving decisively in welfare in the 1930s, by the 1960s, a general consensus on welfare seemed to prevail in the nation. No longer was an aggressive federal role in this field seriously questioned in most quarters. Nevertheless, as the old conflict had subsided, a new one of some basic dimensions began to emerge in the early 1960s and by the middle- and late-1960s was in full bloom. Old welfare policies built on the concept of bestowing material benefits on the poor and on striving lower-middle classes and administered by welfare professionals in vari-ous bureaucratic structures were being challenged by an unlikely com-bination of young (largely upper-middle class) liberals, middle-class intellectuals (black and white), the New Left, and unorthodox conserva-tives, linked only by their collective skepticism of traditional welfare practices. The more politically significant of the challengers along with some sympathetic federal administrators formed the nucleus of a group that was to advance and carry out a new national welfare approach. Basically, this group reasoned that the problems and nature of the poor in the 1960s differed from the situation in the 1930s, and that the new poor must be given the means (not just the end-products of money, housing, and the like) by which to lift themselves from the poverty cycle. The needed means included education and the political and economic power by which the interests of the poor could be advanced and protected. Existing welfare policy as applied to the most visibly disadvantaged subculture in the 1960s—the urban Negroes—seemed to be making the poor wards of the state, perpetuating and deepening the dependency of the needy blacks on the political power structure; in short, it was a kind of middle-class welfare colonialism. The new approach was most clearly incorporated in the operation of the national war on poverty, explained in the following paragraphs.

NEW WELFARE POLICY:
THE WAR ON POVERTY

Depending on one's standards, in the early 1960s somewhere between 30 and 50 million individuals in the United States were in the poverty class, with the nonwhite and aged accounting for a disproportionate share of this number. And what appeared to add to the significance of these figures was that the poverty-stricken, possibly for the first time in the history of the nation, were not terribly visible and maybe not understood by large segments of the nonpoor middle-class American society. Because of profound social and political changes of the 1930s, 1940s, and 1950s—the most important of which were the sharpened social class differences and increasing class awareness and isolation brought about in part by segregation in residential living patterns and enhanced by the decentralized (or localized) nature of metropolitan area governments—a whole urban "underclass" had arisen in metropolitan slums by the 1960s, a class not recognized by most Americans. This "other America" was the section of the country's class structure that although in need was overlooked and essentially by-passed by the lower-middle-class-directed social legislation and the security-minded middle-class institutions (labor unions, liberal government bureaucracies), a part of the nation's social structure that was literally "beyond the welfare state."[1] And from a political standpoint, it was the black portion of the underclass that mattered.

Having been uncovered by enterprising social analysts and private foundation activists, the new poor quickly stimulated the moral consciences and political sensitivities of certain governmental and party leaders who called for a reexamination of the country's social welfare system. The upshot of this was the Democratic party's flashy election-year passage (over Republican outcries and opposition) of the Economic Opportunity Act of 1964, which contained the national "war on poverty."

The new poverty legislation was not merely another welfare bill, not simply another relatively innocuous effort by Democratic politicians to expand their party's political base in the liberal-intellectual community. Its implications went far beyond that. In fact, in view of the way the legislation was carried out in practice, the war on poverty will likely prove to be the *single most important domestic measure in the modern era.* This is so, in part, because of the philosophy implicit (or so it could be interpreted) in the legislation but more realistically because of the political base the act in effect delegated to national and local poverty program administrators, policy-makers, and partisans. Furthermore, the significance of the war on poverty is not limited to poverty and welfare, or to the poor and the nonwhites in slums. Its lessons range additionally to the nature of the structure and processes of the local political systems in this country and perhaps in the academic sense to the operation of political systems in general. The information pouring in from the effects of the war on poverty has left political scientists and other scholars of the local community with little option but to revise some basic notions about local political behavior and about the characteristic activity of local governmental systems. For the first time in America, students of local

---

[1]   Michael Harrington, *The Other America* (New York: Macmillan, 1964), p. 160.

government have been able to observe, if not participate in, in some form or another, a sort of revolutionary social and political change (the impact of political change in the Depression was felt largely at the national level). Consequently, we now have a clearer understanding, for example, of the relationships between certain middle- and upper-middle-class leaders and economically deprived elements in the society, and of the public policy implications and economic and political meaning of the interaction among various types of groups and interests in the local power structure.

Financially and politically, the most important aspect of the war on poverty is the community action program, although the economic opportunity legislation encompasses a number of additional activities as well (discussed later). The community action program is particularly relevant to local government because of its organizational location in the local community, the power and resources assigned to it at the community level, and its effects on the distribution of influence in local political institutions.

Title II of the Economic Opportunity Act defined a community action program as an activity that "mobilizes and utilizes in an attack on poverty" the resources of communities or neighborhoods, and that "provides services, assistance, and other activities of sufficient scope and size to give promise of progress toward the elimination of poverty or a cause or causes of poverty. . . ." The poverty measure provided that community action programs could be administered by a governmental or private nonprofit agency (or a combination thereof) at the local level, and that such programs were to be developed, operated, and administered with the "maximum feasible participation" of the residents in the areas and members of the groups served—that is, the poor. As it worked out, it was the organizational and maximum feasible participation features that caused so much attention to be focused on the poverty effort and that have been objectively so significant. In the last analysis, both aspects of the legislation were but parts of one basic matter—the nature and composition of the political groups and interests that would be given positions of influence in the policy and administrative processes of the community action programs. Since community action programs were to be established in numerous communities throughout the land, both provisions' practical effects were at least potentially great. In a slightly different sense, the question raised and perhaps to be answered by these two points was whether private or public—that is, governmental—interests would control community action programs at the local level, with the public sector representing the status-quo-directed political power structure (hindsight and not necessarily the language of the legislation allows us to make this analysis).

On the organization of community action programs, the legislation was essentially neutral, although privately run programs were possible. In other words, either public or private community action programs were theoretically acceptable. In enacting this provision, Congress was apparently demonstrating no preference for one over the other organizational assignment of the function and presumably assumed that whether the program in any particular community would be operated by a public or private institution would depend on the specific circumstances and the special requirements or needs in the locality. At the same time, perhaps there was more meaning to the organizational option permitted by Congress, as in all of the other comparable major national-local grant-in-aid functional areas in the "urban-poor" category (public housing, urban renewal, model cities), federal administrators have little discretion concerning which local organization is to be the recipient of federal resources—that is, in these fields, money and other assistance go to local *public* institutions, meaning local government.

The history of the 1964 enactment sheds some light on the organizational consideration. The poverty proposal was basically designed in the executive branch of the national government, specifically by a task force headed up by Sargent Shriver, the first national administrator of the entire war on poverty. One of the concerns of the Shriver committee was that local governments were not always as broadly based as might be desired, an especially important matter in the South (where it was assumed there was discrimination against Negroes). Further, the Shriver task force reasoned that since no unit of local government had complete responsibility for welfare and related functions (education, employment services and manpower development), no single local government or public agency could assure the needed centralization and coordination.[2] In addition, politically a factor, neither the National League of Cities which represents 14,000 municipalities nor the United States Conference of Mayors which represents the powerful large-city mayors in the country opposed the organizational option in the bill (the politically weaker National Association of Counties and individual mayors urged local government control of the community action program).

The critical nature of the private-option provision of the law becomes clearer with an examination of the actual operation of community action programs. As can be seen in Table 19.1, the community action agencies which run the programs at the local level have been largely privately controlled, infrequently found administratively in local governments. Although the national administrators of the Office of Economic Opportunity (which has authority over the poverty legislation in Washington)

[2] Advisory Commission on Intergovernmental Relations, *Intergovernmental Relations in the Poverty Program* (Washington, D.C.: U.S. Government Printing Office, April, 1966), pp. 25–26.

have consistently denied it, the typical organizational arrangement in the administration of the community action program in cities and counties suggests that national executive branch officials came down firmly on the "antigovernment" and "antiestablishment" side of the local political structure, forming implicitly an alliance with local blacks and upper-middle-class whites who were dissatisfied with the conservative and bureaucratic way-of-life which dominates so many local governments and welfare agencies.

TABLE 19.1
Community Action Program Sponsors

	1965	1966	1967
Local government	21.6%	20.6%	20%
Private nonprofit agency	73.9	79.4	80
Total	100.0%	100.0%	100%

SOURCE: Advisory Commission on Intergovernmental Relations, *Intergovernmental Relations in the Poverty Program* (Washington, D.C.: U.S. Government Printing Office, 1966), p. 28; and Office of Economic Opportunity (1967 figures).

The second most crucial aspect of the poverty legislation's community action program has been that requiring the maximum feasible participation of the poor in local programs. In the 1964 act, Congress did not specify any standard by which this provision could be definitively interpreted. However, in 1966, Congress amended the Economic Opportunity Act, stipulating that the poor must comprise one third of the local membership on community action agency boards. In actuality, the poor have constituted only a minor force in the administration of the community action program, even though "representatives" of the poor (not the same as poor) officially comprise one third or more of community action agency governing bodies.[3] Additionally, the turnout of the poor in community action agency elections has been startlingly low—for example, in a recent year in Philadelphia, 20,000 out of an eligible 480,000 voted for delegates to that city's poverty board; and the participation rate in elections in Cleveland, Kansas City, Missouri, Los Angeles, and Boston in no instance exceeded 5 percent of those qualified to vote.[4] However, it is not the *actual* involvement of the poor that counts here; the legal stipula-

[3] United States Conference of Mayors, *Economic Opportunity in Cities, Local Anti-Poverty Programs* (Washington, D.C., January, 1966), p. 32.
[4] Sar Levitan, "Is this Poverty War 'Different'?" in Sar Levitan and Irving Seigal (eds.), *Dimensions of Manpower Policy: Programs and Research* (Baltimore: Johns Hopkins University Press, 1966), pp. 55–56.

tion that the poor be represented is in and of itself potentially meaningful and has had important political consequences. The fact of the matter is that this requirement clothed spokesmen and "representatives" of the poor with a political status and legitimacy that they otherwise would not have had. Without this legitimacy and the federal money that went with the community action agencies, it is unlikely that the community action program would have been taken seriously in many local communities. Of course, when this is coupled with the fact that most of the some 1,100 community action programs were administered outside the framework of local government, it is not difficult to see that the foundation for an all-out attack on local government and particularly its welfare policies was laid by the national legislation. This set of circumstances in reality permitted the emergence of a new conception of welfare and poor assistance in the nation. And this new conception was that the poor must organize and do battle with the powers that could do something to change the conditions of the poor. As is true in all major revolutions, however, it was not the poor who did the organizing or who were in the main active in community action programs: it was the "name" of the poor that was invoked as a means of restructuring the distribution of influence in the local community and of changing public policy. Whether this "revolution" succeeded in these respects is a matter of question, but it did cause conflict, intensify racial antagonisms in the community, awaken Americans to a matriarchally controlled subculture,[5] and probably had much to do with creating the conditions that led to the riots of the mid-1960s in hundreds of United States cities. And all of this was done essentially through a coalition of middle-class intellectuals and disaffected members of the white upper-middle class at the national and local levels on one hand and the economically deprived in local communities on the other. This sort of alliance is the stuff of modern political change: it has now reached local government in America.

Local power structures were so troubled by community action agencies that in 1967 Congress, responding largely to local pressures, granted local governments the right to assume control of the dreaded community action programs, although the administrative regulations by which this congressional mandate was to be carried out inhibited local governments from moving to gain control of these programs. Nevertheless, the 1967 amendment to the economic opportunity legislation seemed to signal the beginning of the end for community action programs, at least as they had operated in the past.

[5]   For a dramatic public revelation of the internal structure of the Negro family, see U.S. Department of Labor, *The Negro Family* (Washington, D.C.: U.S. Government Printing Office, 1965), especially pp. 30–34. This is known as the Moynihan report (after its author Daniel Patrick Moynihan).

The conservative posture of the American electorate in 1968, the election of Richard M. Nixon that same year, and President Nixon's appointment of Daniel P. Moynihan as the new administration's urban affairs adviser appeared to spell final defeat for the community action approach to the conditions and problems of the poor. In fact, Moynihan, who helped shape the war on poverty in the early 1960s, had turned into one of the community action program's sharpest critics by the end of the 1960s.[6] Moynihan was most disturbed by the community action program's "conflict" base, arguing convincingly that most Americans find conflict distasteful and deeply value order, stability, and continuity. The Nixon confidant further pointed out that government had nothing more than a theory when it initiated the community action concept, that the major beneficiaries of the program were not the poor but professionals, and that social scientists prominent in the development and administration of the community action program seemed bent on reform and social change, frequently wandering afar from their scholarly disciplines.

Other antipoverty programs affecting state and local governments and growing out of the 1964 economic opportunity legislation are Job Corps, Neighborhood Youth Corps, Volunteers in Service to America, Head Start, and Neighborhood Legal Services. Job Corps and Neighborhood Youth Corps are both designed to assist the disadvantaged in the 16-to-21 age group—young men and women who are out of school and out of work. Job Corps facilities include centers for men, centers for women, and conservation camps, and are normally located away from the community of the corpsmen being trained and educated. Although the Job Corps program may be run by the state or local government level (as well as by the national government, private profit-making businesses, and nonprofit organizations), state and local government agencies have only a few Job Corps camps under their direct control; state governors do, however, possess the veto power over the location of Job Corps centers in their states (as of 1968, no governor had used this authority).

Job Corps has been indirectly relevant to local governments in the sense that it has helped train urban youth and therefore relieved local government in metropolitan areas of certain law enforcement and manpower development duties, and further in that it has served to tie a number of large blue-ribbon national corporations (Burroughs Corporation, Philco Corporation, Brunswick Corporation, AVCO Corporation) to a key government social program, which has tended to stimulate the interest of these firms in urban affairs generally and has led them to put some of their enormous resources to work in urban areas, often in cooperation with local governments. The Nixon administration drastically

[6] Daniel P. Moynihan, *Maximum Feasible Misunderstanding* (New York: Free Press, 1969).

curtailed Job Corps operations in 1969, fulfilling a Republican campaign promise.

The Neighborhood Youth Corps is based on the principle of community or local training and counseling, is available to young people in need in their own neighborhoods, and is, as might be expected, an administrative activity of local government in most cases (a few state governments also operate Neighborhood Youth Corps programs as well). As in Job Corps, state governors may veto specific Neighborhood Youth Corps proposals, and this authority has been used in several instances. Volunteers in Service to America (VISTA) is the domestic version of the Peace Corps, providing for the recruitment of persons to serve in one of a number of possible local poverty activities such as community action agencies and Indian reservation and migrant worker programs. The gubernatorial veto is part of the VISTA effort and has been exercised by some governors. Head Start is a child development program in which federal grants are authorized to communities to prepare and administer preschool curricula for children from economically and culturally deprived homes, and is normally implemented by or in conjunction with the local school system. Neighborhood Legal Services are now an independent part of the national poverty package, and through these services, disadvantaged residents are given legal assistance in a variety of areas, including tenant-landlord relationships and contractual obligations with local business firms. Where local governments have proprietary operations in or serving low-income sections (public housing), they could ultimately be affected by expanded legal aid to the poor in their boundaries. Neighborhood Legal Services should also favorably affect the workload of law enforcement agencies in city government.

The governor of each of the states is granted by the national poverty legislation an absolute veto over the establishment of a Job Corps camp or center and VISTA assignments, and a conditional negative over community action programs and Neighborhood Youth Corps projects (originally the veto in the latter two cases was absolute, but this was changed in 1965). As noted, the gubernatorial veto has been used (in all programs but Job Corps); and two considerations appear to have accounted for most of the state chief executive objections: race and radicalism. Actually, both of these factors are part of a single matter: fear of excessive political change. In the South, gubernatorial vetoes suggest that this fear frequently manifests itself in terms of a threat to the present power relationships between whites and Negroes (that is, the proposed programs were seen as giving an edge to Negroes); while the use of the negative in the North has been more a result of the concern over the radical views of possible sponsoring organizations. Essentially, northern vetoes have been based on the desire to preserve the status quo in the economic sense; to the extent that race is simply reflective of an economic conflict—and this is largely the case—there is little philosophically to separate the southern from the northern vetoes.

A number of new national poverty- and welfare-related activities in addition to the 1964 War on Poverty characterized the legislative agenda of the 1960s. The national government's Manpower Development and Training Act of 1962 (funds are provided for training workers), Elementary and Secondary Education Act of 1965 (money is made available to states and localities for general education purposes, with the emphasis being on poor areas), and Public Works and Economic Development Act of 1965 (where assistance is given to economically depressed areas) are illustrative of this agenda, and all of these laws affect the poverty picture and authorize the granting of federal resources to state and local governments or organizations. Finally, the Demonstration Cities and Metropolitan Development Act of 1966 represents a substantial expansion of national social activities. The most pertinent portion of this legislation in this respect is the "model cities" provision, discussed next.

The Model Cities Program

Model cities is both an extension of (in principle) and a departure from the national war on poverty. That is, under model cities the national government advances funds to localities for the purpose of fighting poverty, in this instance in urban slums; however, unlike the community action agency which may be public or private, the local model cities administering organization must be local government (in nearly all instances it is, in fact, city government). Model cities was in reality the power structure's response to the community action program, and certainly an element of parity was involved in the enactment of this legislation. Even at the national level, model cities—although compatible in substance with the entire antipoverty effort and especially the community action program—was delegated not to the more radicalized Office of Economic Opportunity but to the politically safe national Department of Housing and Urban Development.

In addition to the city-hall control feature, the basic concepts in model cities are citizen participation and comprehensive and coordinated deprived neighborhood development. In model cities, citizen participation was stressed from the beginning, the idea having been drawn from and structured in practice on the experience under the 1964 poverty legislation. Each local model cities organization—formally known as the City Demonstration Agency (CDA)—was to have a board composed at least in part of residents from the neighborhood of the city being assisted. This board, however, again unlike the typical situation in the community action agency, is purely advisory, as the city government has final responsibility for the decisions made in model cities.

The model cities program additionally emphasizes the development of the most deprived neighborhood in the community, and this development is to take place on a comprehensive (including manpower, education, housing, health, recreation, welfare, transportation, and so forth) and coordinated (through the model cities agency) basis.

In model cities, the national government provides communities with both planning and implementation grants. As of late 1968, over 100 cities had received model cities planning grants, and by late 1969, some cities had begun to carry out their programs with federal implementation funds. So far, local model cities agencies are treading lightly in the political sense, apparently preferring to remain in the more stable discussion stages and somewhat fearful of disturbing the existing state of things (the community action program has made a deep impression on some model cities administrators).

STATE AND LOCAL
GOVERNMENT SUPPORT OF WELFARE

Welfare service levels and expenditures vary considerably by state and locality, and this is true even in the federally aided categories. On the average, the more urbanized and industrialized sections of the country have been more generous to the poor than the less urbanized and less industrialized areas—measured in terms of state and local government welfare activity. Or put another way, welfare outlays are greater in big cities and urban-industrial states than in smaller cities and rurally dominated states. For example, Richard Dawson and James Robinson have reported a correlation between the degree of urbanization, industrialization, and ethnicity on one hand and welfare efforts on the other at the state level—that is, states with greater urbanization, industrialization, and concentrations of ethnic groups have made more extensive welfare efforts than other states.[7] Thomas Dye further points out that the nature and extent of social and economic development (urbanization, industrialization, income, and education) has more of an effect apparently on welfare policy in state government than do certain "political" factors (apportionment of state legislatures and the degree of party competition in legislative bodies).[8] More specifically, liberal welfare policies—that is,

[7]   Richard E. Dawson and James E. Robinson, "The Politics of Welfare," in Herbert Jacob and Kenneth N. Vines (eds.), *Politics in the American States* (Boston: Little, Brown, 1965), pp. 399–400.
[8]   Thomas R. Dye, "State Legislative Politics," in Jacob and Vines, *Politics in the American States, supra,* pp. 155–156, 163–164, and 199–200.

higher average expenditures in unemployment compensation and other welfare areas—are related to more equitable representation and greater two-party competition in state legislatures, but such policies are even more strongly correlated with greater degrees of urbanization and industrialization and higher income and educational levels. This suggests that state public policy (here in welfare) is essentially a by-product of more important underlying economic forces, as perhaps is political structure in the last analysis.[9]

In a somewhat different vein, at the local level, it would appear that a centralized political structure might lead to greater expenditures in some federally aided welfare areas. For example, one study shows that more federal poverty funds (calculated on a per poor family basis) were advanced to Chicago than to the other of the very largest American cities.[10] And, consistent with what would be expected, Chicago was found to have a more centrally directed political system than the other cities in the study. Presumably, a greater degree of centralization of power encourages the emergence of a cohesive influence center which has the ability to wring resources out of Washington in a way that a more dispersed structure could not.

A CLOSING COMMENT:
WELFARE AND POLITICAL ALIGNMENTS

This chapter has pointed out, we hope, that welfare is not a static concept. Attitudes toward welfare change as times and conditions change. Further, it should be clear by now that it is not possible to view welfare and poverty except as part of the broader political processes. In other words, we cannot simply see the poor as a group that should be assisted by the middle class, as contemporary morality might suggest. The poor are within a political system, as are those who would help them; and neither can be understood properly independently of the patterns of conflict and interrelationships of that system. For instance, the poor may become instruments of political and social change, or vehicles to the advancement of the political aspirations of a party, or professional administrators and others; thus, not only the "needs" of the poor but the drives, motives, and interests of those who have wider or other objectives

[9] Fenton argues persuasively that political variables (specifically the degree of issue-orientation in the political system) may have an important impact on welfare policies. See John H. Fenton, *Midwest Politics* (New York: Holt, Rinehart and Winston, 1966), esp. p. 230.
[10] J. David Greenstone and Paul E. Peterson, "Reformers, Machines, and the War on Poverty," in James Q. Wilson (ed.), *City Politics and Public Policy* (New York: Wiley, 1968), pp. 286–289.

in helping the poor become suitable and virtually necessary topics for political analysis and inquiry. This kind of untraditional examination, nevertheless, should not serve to obscure the possible positive and healthy consequences of the efforts of the nonpoor to aid deprived citizens. The benefits may be immense indeed from the point of view of the disadvantaged, and they may in effect perform a social function in the society at large by their stabilizing tendencies.

INDEX

"ABC" program, 420, 421

Adrian, Charles R., 196 n.

Advisory Commission on Intergovernmental Relations (1959), 35, 38, 225

AFL-CIO, 41, 64, 142, 256, 391

AFL-CIO American Federation of Teachers, 279

AFL-CIO Building and Construction Trades Department, 385

Age, and voter turnout, 53

Agger, Robert E., 262 n.

Agricultural assistance and regulation, administration of, 32, 33

Air Transport Association of America, 429, 431, 433

Airport Operators Council International, Inc., 429, 432, 433

Alabama, 50, 129, 149

Alaska, 47, 193, 289

Alienation, in American society, 54

Allegheny Conference on Community Development, 255, 372

Allen, Ivan, 246

Almond, Gabriel, 262 n.
Altshuler, Alan A., 249 n., 403 n.
American Association of Airport Executives, 432
American Association of State Highway Officials, 429, 431
American Automobile Association, 429, 431
American Bar Association, 165, 170
American Dental Association, 257
American Federation of State, County, and Municipal Employees, 256
American Institute of Architects, 257
American Institute of Planners, 257
American Medical Association, 257, 438
American Mercury, 213
American Motors Corporation, 430
American Petroleum Institute, 429, 430
American Public Works Association, 429, 432
American Revolution, 19
American Road Builders' Association, 429, 431
American Transit Association, 429, 431
American Trucking Associations, Inc., 429, 431
Americans for Democratic Action, 373
Anaconda Company, 61
Anderson, Martin, 376 n., 377
Anglican church, and county government, 194
Anglo-Saxon law, 93
Anne Arundel County (Md.), 234
Anton, Thomas J., 102, 102 n.
Appalachia, economic plight of, 7
Appalachian Regional Development Act (1965), 33
"A real division of powers," 207
Aristotle, 22, 201
Arizona, 149
Arkansas, 129, 323
Arlington County (Va.), 195, 273
Articles of Confederation, 18, 19–20, 208
Associated General Contractors of America, 429, 431
Association of American Railroads, 429, 430
Association of Bay Area Governments of San Francisco, 227
Atlanta, 187, 259, 262, 427

Automobile Manufacturers Association, 429, 430
Automotive Electric Association, 429
Automotive Safety Foundation, 429, 430
AVCO Corporation, 445
Ayres, Richard E., 48 n.

Babcock, Richard F., 379 n., 406 n., 411, 411 n.
Baker v. *Carr,* 38
"Balkanization," of metropolitan political systems, 206, 227
Baltimore, 29, 32, 150, 152, 153, 157, 234, 236, 427
Baltimore County, 195, 234
Baltimore Municipal Court, 150, 152–153, 157
Banfield, Edward C., 178, 178 n., 215, 217 n., 245, 245 n., 249 n., 250, 250 n., 371 n., 372 n., 411
Banton, Michael, 341, 341 n.
Barr, Joseph, 247
Barrett, Edward L., Jr., 155 n.
Baton Rouge, 238, 239
Bay Area Air Pollution Control District, 233
Bay Area Rapid Transit District, 427
Bedford-Stuyvesant, 357
Beer, Samuel, 107, 107 n.
Berger, Bennett M., 274, 274 n.
Big City Politics, 245
Bill of Rights, 20
Blair, George S., 194 n.
Boise Cascade, 384
Bollens, John C., 199 n., 222 n., 229 n.
Booth, David A., 238 n.
Boston, 203, 211, 246, 374, 419, 443
Boston Development Authority, 374
Bowen, William G., 48 n.
Brinkley, David, 37
British Parliamentary system, 107
Brown v. *Board of Education of Topeka,* 322
Brunswick Corporation, 445
Buchanan, William, 63 n., 119 n.
Budget-making, 307–311
Building Officials Conference of America, 366, 386
Building regulatory authority, 365–367, 368
Bureau of Public Roads, 420

Bureaucracy, at state level, nature of, 109–111
Burke, Edmund, 22, 139
Burkhead, Jesse, 318 n.
Burroughs Corporation, 445
Business, in city political life, 253–255

California, 27, 29, 103, 151, 170, 183, 186, 232, 233, 342
California superior courts, 151, 154
Campbell, Angus, 53 n., 84 n.
Canada, 242
Cannon, "Uncle Joe," 127
Career officials, 110–111
Carroll County (Md.), 234
Cartier, Richard F., 278 n.
Cater, Douglass, 66, 66 n.
Caucus, role in state legislature, 125–126
Cavanagh, Jerome, 246, 247
Central Area Committee of Chicago, 372
Central city, 11–12, 265, 266, 267, 268, 269, 273, 275, 351, 360, 361, 372–373, 375
Centralization, political roots of, 38–41
Centrex Corporation, 364, 384
Chapin, F. Stuart, Jr., 395 n.
Charter Party (Cincinnati), 257
Checker Motors Corporation, 430
Chicago, 25, 34, 232, 249, 250, 367, 419, 427, 448
Chicago Transit Authority, 427
Chrysler Corporation, 430
Cincinnati, 257
Citizens for a Better City (Falls Church, Va.), 257
Citizen's role, in contemporary democracy, 45
City, politics of, 244–263
    and class-based conflict, 252–253
    and community power structure, analysis of, 258–263
    and interest groups, role of, 253–258
    and mayor, vulnerability of, 246–247
    and political systems, decentralization of, 247–250
    and population characteristics, 250–253
    and urban riots, 245–246
City Demonstration Agency, 447
City government, types of, 182–192

Civic Conference (Boston), 372
Civic duty, 53–54
Civic groups, in city political life, 253, 255
Civic Progress (St. Louis), 372
Civil proceedings, in state and local courts, 160–162
Civil service system, as factor in city politics, 189–190, 248–249
Clark, Joseph, 178, 373
Cleveland, 175, 232, 258, 356, 367, 408, 419, 427, 443
Cleveland Metropolitan Park District, 232
Cleveland Transit Board, 427
Closed primary, 89
Code administration, 31, 32
Coke, James G., 281 n.
Coleman, James S., 262 n.
Columbia (Md.), 405
Commission in Intergovernmental Relations (1955), 35, 38, 138, 288, 289, 292
Commission-form county government, 194
Committee on Political Education, 256
Communist parties, European, 71
Community Action Agency, 246
Community action programs, 34, 36
Community power structure, analysis of, 258–263
Community Renewal Program, 380, 404
Conant, James C., 277 n., 316
Confederacy, 74
Conference of Mayors, 36
Congress of Cities (1967), 246
Congress on Racial Equality, 257
Congressional Quarterly, 246
Connecticut, 27, 61, 88, 129, 137, 183, 193, 368
Conservatives, American, attitude toward intergovernmental relations, 38–41
Constituent-unit principle, 231, 232–233
Constitutional Convention, 19–20
Converse, Philip E., 47 n., 53 n., 84 n.
Cooley, Thomas M., 25 n.
Corty, Floyd, 240, 240 n.
Corzine, John, 182 n.
Council of Housing Producers, 384, 391
Council of State Governments, 36, 103

Council-manager government, 177–178, 187, 190–192
County government, 193–196
County-unit dominant government, 174
Courts, state and local, 147–172
  appellate courts, 151, 154–155
  inferior courts, 149–150
  civil proceedings, 160–162
  criminal proceedings, 155–160
  judges, selection of, 168–172
  structure and jurisdiction, 149–155
  trial courts of general jurisdiction, 150–151
Crime, correlates of, 342–344
Criminal proceedings, 155–160
  decision to charge, 156–157
  felony cases, 158
  guilty plea, 158–160
  misdemeanors, 157–158
Crouch, Winston W., 232 n.
Curley, James, 90

Dade County (Fla.), 32, 195, 236, 400
Dade County League of Municipalities, 241
Dahl, Robert A., 11 n., 13 n., 44, 44 n., 45 n., 46 n., 250 n., 373 n.
Dallas, 229, 364
Dan Smoot Report, 213
Danielson, Michael N., 182 n., 217 n.
Davidson County (Tenn.), 193, 238–239, 400
Dawson, Richard, 448, 448 n.
Decentralizationists, 206–208, 211–216
Delaware, 88, 229
Delaware County (Pa.), 274
Democracy, classical theory of, 42–43
Democracy, territorial, 18
Democracy, Rouseauean/Jacobin, 18
Democratic government, theory of, 18
Democratic party, 5, 49, 50, 73, 74, 76, 77, 78, 85, 89, 90, 116, 117, 140, 165, 178, 189, 247, 250, 251, 257, 273, 274, 276, 280, 369, 373, 374, 387, 388, 433, 440
Demonstration Cities and Metropolitan Development Act (1966), 36, 226, 234, 381, 411, 447
Denver, 233, 236
Department of Airports in the City of Los Angeles, 428, 432

Departments of community development, 32
Derge, David R., 121, 121 n., 122
Detroit, 175, 227, 246, 247
Detroit Recorders Court, 157–158
Dillon, John F., 25 n.
Dillon rule, 291–292
Dilworth, Richardson, 178, 373
Dinerman, Beatrice, 232 n.
Direct primary, 88–91
District of Columbia, 300, 322, 427
Dobriner, William M., 266 n., 273 n.
Douglas Commission, 389–390
Douglas, Paul H., 367 n., 389, 390
Downing, Randall G., 170 n.
Dual sovereignty, 20–21, 24–25
Duncombe, Herbert Sydney, 194 n.
Duval County (Fla.), 192, 238
Dye, Thomas R., 178 n., 216 n., 217 n., 230 n., 307, 307 n., 434 n., 448, 448 n.

East Baton Rouge Parish (La.), 238, 239–240
Eastern states, and organized labor, power of, 61
  and political competitiveness, 84
  and post-Civil War immigration, 9
  and state legislatures, composition of, 121
  and voter perceptiveness, 85
Easton, David, 13 n., 14 n., 147
Economic determinism, 176–177
Economic development, and state public policy, 307
Economic differences, and city politics, 252
Economic Opportunity Act (1964), 440, 441, 443, 445, 447
Economic structure, and social structure, 7–10
  and state politics, 9–10
Edinburgh (Scotland), 341
Education Act (1965), 301
Education, and voter turnout, 52
Educational system, and lay public, 316–317
Eighty-eighth Congress, 36
Eisenhower, Dwight D., 117, 322, 377, 388
Elazar, Daniel J., 18 n.

Elementary and Secondary Education Act (1965), 322, 447
Eliot, Thomas H., 316, 316 n., 317 n.
Ellender, Allen, 374
El Paso, 257
Epstein, Edwin M., 382 n.
Erie County (N.Y.S.), 195
Essex County (N.J.), 195
Eulau, Heinz, 63 n., 119 n.
Evers, Charles, 50
Executive power, nature of, 93–94

Fabricant, Solomon, 306 n.
Fairfax County (Va.), 273
Falls Church (Va.), 257
Far western states, fiscal capacity of, 295
  and tax effort, 300
Farquhar, Norman, 389 n.
Faubus, Orville, 322
Fayette (Miss.), 50
Federal agencies, influence in city government, 248
Federal Aviation Administration, 420, 424
Federal Bulldozer, The, 377
Federal Bureau of Investigation, 337, 342
Federal grants-in-aid, 300–303
Federal Highway Administration, 420
Federal highway legislation (1962), 404, 415
Federal Housing Administration, 363, 369, 377, 378
Federal National Mortgage Association, 363, 382
Federal tax base, use of, for state tax purposes, 289
Federal-Aid Highway Act (1956), 420, 421
Federal-Aid Highway Act (1962), 234, 421
Federal-Aid Highway Act (1968), 421
Federal-Aid Road Act (1916), 421
Federalism, and centralization, at national level, 25, 26–28, 30, 37–41
  and centralization, at state level, 27–29
  and classical thought, 22–23
  and closeness of government to citizens, 23–24
  creative, 26

Federalism (Continued)
  definition, 17
  historical roots of, 18–22
  and national government, prestige of, 26–28
  and New Deal, 2
  philosophy of, 18, 21–22
  political roots of, 38–41
  and power, assignment of, to local, national, and state levels, 24–35
  and states, future of, 37–41
  as territorial democracy, 18
Federalist Papers, 20, 58
Fefferman, Hilbert, 377 n.
Fenton, John, 84, 84 n., 449 n.
Ferguson, LeRoy C., 63 n., 119 n.
Fester, James W., 113 n.
Field, John Osgood, 252 n.
Fifteenth Amendment, 46, 49
Finances, and allocation of funds, 303–307
  and budget-making, 307–311
  interstate variations, 294–300
  local tax systems, 290–294
  nontax revenue, sources of, 300–303
  state tax policies, 287–290
  state tax revenue, 288
Fiscal capacity, 294–300
Fisher, Glen W., 306 n.
Florida, 50, 240
Fogelson, Robert, 357, 357 n.
Ford, Ashley A., 377 n.
Ford Motor Company, 430
Forrestal, James, 95
Forty-fifth Annual Congress of Cities, 245
Founding Fathers, 21, 23, 39, 209
Fourteenth Amendment, 46, 49
Fowler, Edmund P., 252 n., 254 n.
France, 329
Francis, Wayne L., 64, 83, 83 n., 84 n., 105, 105 n., 106, 124, 124 n., 128, 128 n., 129, 142 n., 144, 144 n., 145, 145 n.
Freund, Eric C., 347 n.
Friedman, Robert S., 425 n.
Friedrich, Carl, 69
Functional area planning, 403–404

Galveston, 192
Gans, Herbert J., 376 n.

General government controls, resistance to, 113, 115
General Motors Corporation, 430
General-purpose governments, 175, 179
Geography, as determinant of state economy, 6–7
Georgia, 47, 50, 129, 229
Gerrymandering, 79, 82, 124–125
Gift tax, 289
Gilbert, Charles E., 274 n.
Glazer, Nathan, 376 n.
Goldrich, Daniel, 262 n.
Goodman, William I., 397 n.
Goodnow, Frank, 109, 109 n.
Governmental expenditures, comparison of, 27
　total (1967), 284
Governmental form, 173–182
Governor, authority of, sources of, 102–104
　functions, 94–96
　and legislative decision making, 143–144
　vulnerability of, 116–117
Governor, as management leader, 107–116
　administrative operations, 107–109
　gubernatorial control, limits of, 111–116
　and state bureaucracy, 109–111
Governor, as policy leader, 96–107
　extralegal resources, 96, 97, 98–100
　formal powers, assessment of, 104–107
　gubernatorial authority, index of, 104–106
　legal-institutional resources, 96–97, 100–104
　personal resources, 96, 97–98
Graham, Milton, 241
Grass-roots democracy ideology, in suburbs, 275–276
Great Britain, 329, 341
Great Depression, 79, 301, 305, 360, 436, 441
Greater Baltimore Metropolitan Board of Realtors, 385
Greater Miami Dade County, 240–241
Greater Philadelphia Movement, 255, 372, 373
Greek city-state, 207
Greenstone, J. David, 250 n., 449 n.

Greer, Scott, 214 n., 232 n., 241 n., 281 n., 375 n.
Grimes, Alan P., 194 n. 196 n.
Grodzins, Morton, 24, 24 n., 215, 215 n.
Gulf-Reston Corporation, 405
Gulick, Luther, 209 n.

Haar, Charles M., 397 n.
Hamilton, Alexander, 18 n., 19, 189
Hamilton, John A., 162 n.
Hanson, Royce, 225, 225 n.
Harford County (Md.), 234
Harlem, 356
Harrington, Michael, 440 n.
Harris, Robert, 306 n.
Harris poll, 246
Hartley, David K., 29 n.
Hauser, Philip M., 203 n., 267 n., 268
Havard, William C., Jr., 240, 240 n.
Hawaii, 47, 183, 186, 300
Hawkins, Brett W., 238 n.
Hazard, Geoffrey C., 155 n.
Head Start, 445, 446
Health and hospitals, state and local expenditures for, 305–306
Herman, Harold, 217 n.
Higher public education, 34–35
Highways, state and local expenditures for, 305–306
Hobbes, Thomas, 22
Hodge, Patricia Leavey, 203 n., 267 n., 268
Home Builders Association of Metropolitan Pittsburgh, 384
Home-rule charters, 195
Homo Civicus, 44
Homo Politicus, 44
Housing, low-cost, 363–364
Housing Act (1937), 369–370, 374, 388
Housing Act (1949), 372–374, 376, 377, 388
Housing Act (1954), 377–380
Housing Act (1968), 362, 379, 381
Housing and Urban Redevelopment Act (1965), 226, 386
Houston, 229, 379
Howard, Ebenezer, 405 n.
Hudson County (N.J.), 195
Huntington, Samuel P., 207 n.

Idaho, 149
Illinois, 84, 121, 126, 183, 186, 300, 315, 389

Immigration, to U.S., 9, 78, 79, 137
Income, and voter turnout, 52
Income tax, corporate, 285, 288
Income tax, personal, 285, 288–289, 292
Indiana, 84, 88, 230
Indigent defendants, and justice, quality of, 158, 163, 164, 165
Ingraham, Page L., 28 n.
Inheritance Tax, 289
Institute for Rapid Transit, 431
Intellectuals, and attitudes toward state government, 37–40
Interest groups, and government housing policy, 381–387
builders, 382–384
labor, 385
public officials, 386–387
realtors, 382, 384–385
Interest groups, and government transportation policy, 428–433
Interest groups, in state and local government, 4–5
Intergovernmental relations, strategy of, 35–36
Intergovernmental Relations Act (1968), 36
International City Managers' Association, 5
International Conference of Building Officials, 366, 386
International Harvester Corporation, 430
International Telephone and Telegraph Company, 364
Interstate Commerce Commission, 420, 426, 430
Interstate highway system, 32, 420–421
Intrastate public utilities, regulation of, 31
Iowa, 329
"Iron law of oligarchies," 68

Jackson, Andrew, 93
Jackson County (Mo.), 170
Jackson State College, 333
Jacksonian era, 108
Jacksonville (Fla.), 192, 238, 240
Jacob, Herbert, 66 n., 76 n., 425 n., 448 n.
Jefferson, Thomas, 22, 206, 207, 208
Jefferson Parish (La.), 195
Jencks, Christopher, 326, 326 n., 329 n.

Jensen, Merrill, 276 n.
Jewell, Malcolm, 120, 120 n., 133 n.
Job Corps, 445, 446
Johnson, Lyndon B., 322, 389
Jones, Harry W., 155 n.
Journal of Housing, 386
Judges, state and local, selection of, 168–172
Judicial activism, 148
Judicial decision making, in state and local courts, 162–168
Judicial delay, 155, 161–162
Justice of the peace, 149
Juvenile Delinquency Act (1968), 36

Kaiser Jeep Corporation, 430
Kansas, 183
Kansas City (Mo.), 443
Kaplan, Harold, 380 n.
Kaufman, Herbert, 107, 107 n., 108–109, 109 n., 112, 249 n.
Kefauver, Estes, 345
Kelley, Stanley, Jr., 48 n.
Kenosha, 259
Kent, T. J., Jr., 345 n.
Kent State University, 333
Kentucky, 47, 300
Kerner, Otto, 245 n.
Kerner Commission, 245, 246
Kerr, Clark, 68, 68 n., 331 n., 352 n.
Kerr, Norman D., 280 n.
Kerr-Mills bill, 438
Kessel, John H., 178 n.
Kestnbaum Commission, 35
Key, V. O., Jr., 38, 38 n., 73, 73 n., 74, 90, 90 n., 142, 142 n., 387 n.
Kimbrough, Ralph B., 313 n.
Ku Klux Klan, 323
Kurnow, Ernest, 306 n.

Labor, in city political life, 253, 256
Labor, and government housing policy, 385
Lakewood Plan, 222
Land development and regulation contract, 222, 223
Land-use regulation, 180, 186, 228, 276–277, 280–283, 365–367, 368, 395–399, 400, 406, 407–408, 409, 410
Lasswell, Harold, 12, 12 n.
Latin-American civic organizations, 257

Law enforcement, 336–358
  crime, incidence and rate, 337–341
  crime, social and physical environment of, 341–344
  law vs. order, 336, 340, 347–350
  organized crime, 345–347
  and the police, 350–358
Law and order, 336, 340, 347–350
Lawrence, David, 373 n.
Lawyers, as legislators, 121–122
League of Women Voters, 58, 214, 402
LeBlanc, Hugh L., 85 n., 137 n., 141
Lee, Richard, 246, 250, 373 n.
Legal sanctions, function of, 13
Legislative decision making, 135–144
  and constituence, influence of, 139–141
  and gubernatorial influence, 143–144
  and legislative output, 144–146
  and party, influence of, 135–139
  and pressure groups, 142–143
Legislative role playing, 132–135
  and external sources, influence of, 133–134
  and internal sources, influence of, 134–135
Legitimacy, and political stability, 144
Levitan, Sar, 443 n.
Levitt and Sons, 364, 384
Licensing of occupations and professions, 31
Liebman, Charles S., 217 n., 281 n.
Limited-function government, 182
Lindberry, Robert L., 252 n., 254 n.
Lindsay, John, 247
Lipset, Seymour M., 53 n., 72, 72 n., 262 n.
Little Rock (Ark.), 323
Lobbies, most effective, by state, 64
Local government, activities, 31–32
  and building industry, 364–368
  and transportation, 426–428
Local government, 173–201
  city government, 182–192
  county government, 193–196
  definition, 175
  expenditures and revenues, 186
  and governmental form, 173–182
  and municipal reform movement, 177–178
  New England town government, 182–186

Local government (Continued)
  and public education, 200–201
  school government, 182–186
  special districts, 198–200
  by state, 184–185
  township government, 197–198
Local-state activities, 34–35
Lockard, Duane, 28 n., 215, 215 n., 274 n.
Locke, John, 22, 393, 435
Los Angeles, 161, 222, 232, 246, 247, 249, 428, 443
Los Angeles County, 222
Louisiana, 50, 129, 193, 374

Maass, Arthur, 201, 207 n., 209 n., 210 n.
McClure machine, 274
Machiavelli, Niccolo, 259
Mack Trucks, Inc., 430
McKay, Henry D., 343 n.
Madison, James, 21, 58, 206, 208
"Mafia," 345–347
Magistrate, urban, 149
Main Line Board of Realtors, 384–385
Maine, 183, 196, 300
"Mallory Rule," 157
Manitoba, 242
Manpower Development and Training Act (1962), 447
Manvel, Allen D., 252 n., 365 n., 367 n., 399 n., 400
Martin, Roscoe, 207, 209 n., 222 n., 225, 225 n., 278 n., 279 n.
Marxist parties, 71
Maryland, 27, 29, 179, 186, 234, 235, 368
Maryland-National Capital Park and Planning Commission, 231–232
Mass media, influence of, 24
Massachusetts, 20, 27, 90, 183, 196, 427, 428
Massachusetts Bay Transit Authority, 211, 247
Massachusetts Port Authority, 428, 432
Masters, Nicholas A., 317 n.
Mayor, vulnerability of, 246–247
Mayor-council government, 6, 174, 187–190
Medicaid, 437
Medical Assistance Program (1965), 437

Medicare, 437–438

Melting pot theory, 341

Membership in organizations, and voter turnout, 53

Men at the Top, 262

Metropolitan agencies, 34

Metropolitan areas, growth of, 180–182

Metropolitan Capital Improvement District of Denver, 233

Metropolitan Corporation of Greater Winnipeg, 242

Metropolitan districts, examples of, 232–233

Metropolitan government, 179–182

Metropolitan government, decentralization of, 202–218

and decentralizationists, 206, 207, 208, 211–216

and governmental structure, 203–206

and metropolitanists, 206, 207, 208–211

Metropolitan planning, 402–403

Metropolitan reorganization, strategies of, 219–243

annexation, 228, 229–230

city-county consolidation, 237–240

city-county separation, 236

contract plan, 221–223

councils of government, 221, 223–227

extraterritorial jurisdiction, 227–228

informal cooperation, 221

metropolitan federation, 240–243

metropolitan planning commission, 233–234

metropolitan transportation planning board, 234–235

special district, 231–233

urban county, 235–236

Metropolitan Sanitary District of Greater Chicago, 232

Metropolitan Transit Authority (New York State), 427

Metropolitan Washington Council of Governments, 225, 227

Metropolitan Water District of Southern California, 232, 233

Metropolitan-wide government, 174, 212

Meyerson, Martin, 250 n., 371 n.

Miami, 236, 243

Miami-Dade County Chamber of Commerce, 241

Michels, Robert, 68, 259

Michigan, 84, 183, 315

Middle Atlantic states, and legislative partisanship, 137

state party unity, 126

Middletown, 259

Mideastern states, and fiscal capacity, 295, 296

Midwestern states, and composition of state legislatures, 121

county government, 193

legislative partisanship, 137

organized labor, power of, 61

political competitiveness, 84

post-Civil War immigrants, 9

sectional politics, 75

state party unity, 126

Mid-Willamette Valley Council of Governments, 227

Milbrath, Lester W., 67, 67 n.

Mill, C. Wright, 45

Mill, John Stuart, 207

Miller, Warren E., 47 n., 53 n., 84 n.

Milwaukee County (Wisc.), 195

Minneapolis, 246, 249, 267, 387

Minneapolis Home Builders Association, 383

Minnesota, 84, 125, 183, 186, 230

Minnesota Municipal Commission, 230

Mississippi, 50, 145, 149, 287, 300, 323

Missouri, 121, 168, 169, 170, 230, 300

Missouri plan, for selection of judges, 168–170

Mitau, G. Theodore, 306 n., 329 n.

Mobility, geographic, and social stability, 341

Mobility, social, and social stability, 341

Model building cities codes, 366–367

Model cities, 36, 381

Model cities program, 447–448

Montana, 61, 149

Montgomery County (Ala.), 273

Mormon Church, 61

Morrill Act (1862), 326, 331

Morris (Ill.), 262

Mosca, Gaetano, 259

Mountain states, and legislative partisanship, 137

Moynihan, Daniel Patrick, 444 n., 445, 445 n.

Mumford, Lewis, 209 n., 343 n.

Muncie (Ind.), 262

Municipal bus transit, 427–428
Municipal Manpower Commission, 248, 252
Municipal reform movement, 189–190, 373
Municipality of Metropolitan Seattle, 232, 233
Municipality of Metropolitan Toronto, 241

Naftalin, Arthur, 246
Nagel, Stuart S., 163 n., 164, 164 n., 165 n., 167 n., 170, 170 n., 171 n.
Nashville, 193, 238, 239, 240, 241
Nassau County (New York State), 195
National Academy of Sciences, 430
National Advisory Commission on Civil Disorders, 245, 361, 437
National Association for the Advancement of Colored People, 257
National Association of Counties, 227, 443
National Association of Home Builders, 383, 384, 385, 391
National Association of Housing and Redevelopment Officials, 377, 386, 391
National Association of Motor Bus Owners, 429
National Association of Real Estate Boards, 384, 385
National Association of Regulatory Utility Commissioners, 429
National Association of Social Workers, 248
National Association of State Aviation Officials, 429, 432
National Building Code, 366
National Capital Region Transportation Planning Board, 235
National Commission on Urban Problems, 362, 381, 386, 389, 390, 407, 408, 411
National Council on the Causes and Prevention of Violence, 333–334
National Education Association, 248, 256, 279, 313
National Governors Conference, 36
National Highway Users Conference, 429, 431
National League of Cities, 36, 227, 245, 247, 429, 442

National-local activities, 33–34
National Parking Association, 429
National political system, as "external environment," 14–15
National Service to Regional Councils, 227
National-state activities, 32–33
National System of Interstate and Defense Highways, see Interstate highway system
Nebraska, 125, 183, 186, 238
Nebraska Youth Corps, 446
Negroes, and access to elective office, 44–45, 121
  and activist organizations, 257
  alienation of, 54
  and black curricula in public schools, 318
  and central city, 265, 273
  and city government, 245–246
  and coalition of the disadvantaged, theory of, 258
  and community action programs, 442, 443, 444
  and crime rates, 11–12, 343–344
  and de facto segregation in public schools, 323, 325
  and housing, 40, 360, 361, 371, 376, 390, 391
  and justice, quality of, 164
  and metropolitanism, 218
  and the police, 353, 354, 355, 356–358
  political awareness of, 61
  and power relationships in the South, 446
  and racial integration in public schools 322–326
  and rate of criminal victimization, 339–340
  as source of cheap labor, 78
  and student protest, 333, 334
  in the suburbs, 213–214, 269
  and voting, 15, 49–52
  and welfare policy, 439
Neighborhood citizens associations, 253, 256
Neighborhood Legal Service, 445, 446
Neighborhood Youth Corps, 445
Neustadt, Richard, 98, 98 n.
Nevada, 289
New Deal, 2, 79, 370, 373, 436

New England, and county government, 193
and legislative partisanship, 137
and fiscal capacity, 295, 296
and state party unity, 126
New England town government, 182, 183, 186, 187, 196
New Federalism, 30
New Hampshire, 95, 183, 196, 426
New Haven, 44, 246, 250
New Jersey, 27, 32, 129, 197, 368, 425, 426
New Jersey Department of Transportation, 426
New Left, 439
New Mexico, 147
New-town planning, 405
New Towns Act of 1946 (Great Britain), 405
New York City, 175, 189, 247, 249, 326, 345, 357, 408, 419, 427
New York City Transit Authority, 427
New York State, 27, 28, 29, 32, 63–64, 88, 103, 124, 151, 183, 197, 300, 368, 374, 384, 426, 427, 437
New York State Builders Association, 384
New York State supreme court, 151
Newark, 380
Newburyport, 262
Nineteenth Amendment, 46
Nixon, Richard Milhous, 30, 388, 424, 445
"No-fault," automobile insurance, 162
Norfolk County (Va.), 193
North Carolina, 50, 186
North Central states, and substandard housing, 361
North Dakota, 183
Northeastern states, and metropolitan suburbanization, 203, 266
and sectional politics, 75
and substandard housing, 361
and urban-suburban socioeconomic status, 267
Northern states, and de facto segregation in public schools, 323, 325
and political competition, 76
and Republican sectionalism, 79
and war on poverty, 447–448
Nutter, Ralph H., 160 n.

Occupation, and voter turnout, 52
Office of Economic Opportunity, 37, 442, 447
Official map, in land-use control, 395, 397–398
Ohio, 32, 84, 137, 183, 374
Ohio Univeristy, 37
Oklahoma, 66
Oklahoma City, 229
Old-age insurance, 437
Omaha, 247
"One-man, one-vote," 38, 124
One-party states, 77–78
Ontario, 241
Open primary, 89, 90
Orange County (Calif.), 232
Oregon, 149, 300, 426
Organized labor, power of, 61
Ostrom, Vincent, 216 n.
Owen, Wilfred, 413 n.

Padberg, Judge, 169
Parent Teachers Association, and suburban education, 279–280
Pareto, Vilfredo, 259
Party mavericks, 90–91
Party system, and centralization, 38
Paterson (N.J.), 258
Patterson, Samuel, 66, 66 n., 120, 120 n., 133 n.
Peace Corps, 446
Pennsylvania, 27, 129, 137, 183, 197, 229, 274, 292, 425
Peoria (Ill.), 343
Personal wealth, and state budget, 10
Peterson, Paul E., 250 n., 449 n.
Philadelphia, 178, 189, 211, 255, 257, 262, 274, 372, 373, 384, 385, 396, 408, 419, 427, 443
Philco Corporation, 445
Phoenix, 229, 247, 364, 396
Physical planning, comprehensive administration of, 31
"Piggyback," tax, 294
Pittsburgh, 34, 203, 247, 255, 372, 384
Plains states, and tax yield, 295
Planning and zoning, as basis for region-wide institution, 210–211
Plato, 207
Plea bargaining, 160

Police, and community, 355–358
and law enforcement, administration of, 31, 32
organization of, 352–355
and social environment, 348–350
Police brutality, 157
Political affiliation, as factor in judicial decision making, 164–167
Political conflict, in state and local government, 4–6
Political efficacy, 53–54
Political executives, 110
Political interest groups, 55–67
and group theory of politics, 58–59
lobbying, at state level, 63
in state and local government, 59–63
Political participation, and democratic governance, 67–69
and political interest groups, 55–67
and power elites, 44–45
and voting, 46–55
Political parties, in city political life, 257
and legislative decision making, 135–144
and politics of housing, 387–388
and transportation policy, 433–434
Political parties, functions of, 55, 58, 70, 71, 72
and ideology, 71–72
interdependence of national, state, and local organizations, 73
and political interest groups, 61–63
Political parties, at state level, 70–91
autonomy of, 72–75
and divided party control, 79, 82–83
and interparty difference, 79, 84
and intraparty cohesion, 79, 80, 83, 84
and national elections, 73–74
and nominations, 87–91
organization, 85–87
and two-party competition, 75–79
and voter perceptions, 84–85
Political practices, American, fundamental rules of, 6
Political science, methodology in, 1, 10–11, 12, 13, 15–16, 45–46
and state and local politics, analysis of, 10–16, 214–216
Politician, skills required of, 44

Politics, definition, 12
and power relationships, 12–16
Politics-administration dichotomy, 109–111
Population, in metropolitan area, 202–203
Populists, 78
Port of New York Authority, 232, 432
Portland (Ore.), 247
Post-Civil War era, and immigration to U.S., 9
Presidential election (1956), 54
Presidential election (1964), 322
Presidential election (1968), 445
President's Advisory Committee on Housing, 377, 378
President's Commission on Law Enforcement and the Administration of Justice, 157, 337–338, 339, 347, 352
President's Commission on Registration and Voting Participation, 47
Press, in city political life, 253, 256
Pressure groups, and legislative decision making, 142–143
Presthus, Robert V., 250 n., 262, 263, 263 n.
Prewitt, Kenneth, 63 n.
Prince Georges County (Md.), 273, 274, 384
Prince Georges County Board of Realtors, 384
Princess Anne County (Md.), 193
Professional organizations, in city political life, 253, 257
Progressive movement, 88
Prohibition, 287
Property tax, 285, 290–292, 296
Public assistance, 437
Public education, control of, 31, 182, 200–201, 314–317
controversies over, 317–322
cost of, 312–316
and public schools, political structure of, 314–317
and racial integration, 322–326
in suburbs, 277–279
Public health programs, 31, 438
Public higher education, 326–335
finances, 331
federal grants and influence, 331–332

Public higher education (*Continued*)
    political structure, 329–331
    student protest, 333–335
Public housing, 34, 231–232, 370–374
Public Works and Economic Development Act (1965), 447
Puritan Church, 196
Puritan ethic, 435

Rail rapid transit, 427
Ranney, Austin, 76, 76 n.
Ransone, Coleman, 94, 94 n., 95, 95 n.
Realtors, and politics of housing, 382–385, 410
Reapportionment, 38, 79, 82, 124–125
Regional development commissions, 33
Regionalists, *see* Metropolitan government, and Metropolitanists
Regional Planning Council (Baltimore), 234
Religion, as factor in politics, 44–45
Religious background as factor in judicial decision making, 165, 167
Republican party, 5, 10, 41, 73, 76, 77, 78, 79, 89, 116, 117, 137, 165, 247, 251, 257, 258, 273, 274, 276, 280, 370, 373, 374, 378, 387, 388, 433, 440, 446
Residence, and voter turnout, 53
Reston (Va.), 405
Reynolds v. *Sims*, 38
Rhode Island, 27, 129, 183, 193, 229, 426
Rice indexes of cohesion and likeness, 136
Riesman, David, 326, 326 n., 329
Riker, William, 26, 26 n.
Riverside County (Calif.), 232
Robinson, James E., 448, 448 n.
Rock Creek park, 273
Rockefeller, Nelson, 437
Rocky Mountain states: tax yield, 295
Roman Empire, 208
Roosevelt, Franklin D., 2, 117
Rosenberg, Maurice, 161 n.
Rosenthal, Alan, 280 n.
Rouse Company, 405
Rousseau, Jean Jacques, 207
Rubber Manufacturers Association, 429, 430
Runciman, W. G., 259 n.

Rural resident, dependence of, on government, 9–10
Rusk, Jerrold G., 47 n.

Sachs, Seymour, 306 n.
Safe Street Act (1968), 36
St. Louis (Mo.), 170, 232, 236
Salem (Ore.), 227
Sales tax, 285, 287–288
Salisbury, Robert H., 178 n., 317 n.
San Antonio, 257
San Bernardino County (Calif.), 232
San Diego County (Calif.), 232
San Francisco, 63, 211, 229, 233, 236, 419, 427
San Francisco Bay Area Rapid Transit District, 211, 233
Sayre, Wallace S., 249 n.
Schattschneider, E. E., 45, 45 n., 63 n.
Schlesinger, Joseph, 100 n., 104, 105
Schmandt, Henry J., 222 n., 229 n.
Schnore, Leo F., 265 n., 266 n.
Schrunk, Terry D., 247
Scott, Stanley, 182 n.
Seattle, 232, 233, 427
Sectional politics, weakening of, 75
Seigal, Irving, 443 n.
Service contract concept, 222–223
"701" program, 378
Sex, and voter turnout, 53
Sharkansky, Ira, 307, 307 n., 309 n.
Shaw, Clifford R., 343 n.
Shay's Rebellion, 20
Shriver, Sargent, 442
Silver Spring (Md.), 187
Skolnick, Jerome, 333 n., 334 n., 348 n., 349, 349 n.
Slayton, William L., 376 n.
Slums, and crime, 11–12
Smallwood, Frank, 241 n.
Smith, Robert G., 199 n.
Snyder, Mary E., 402 n.
Social class, and city politics, 177–181, 252–253
Social control, as function of social relationships, 341–342
Social integration, theory of, and crime rate, 341–342
Social Security Act (1935), 436–437
Socialist parties, European, 68–71
Socioeconomic status, and voter turnout, 52

Sofen, Edward, 241 n.
Sorel, Georges, 259
Sorenson, A. W., 247
Souraf, Frank, 71, 71 n.
South, and black-white power relationship, 446
  and city-county consolidation, 237
  and community action programs, 442
  and county government, 193–194
  and Democratic party, monopoly of, 78
  economy of, 7
  governor, power of, 126–127
  and metropolitan federation, 237
  and Negroes, as source of cheap labor, 78
  and public schools, administration of, 314
  and public schools, integration of, 322–323
  and race relations, politics of, 44, 74, 78–79
  and restrictive election laws, 49–52
  and sectional politics, 75
  and student protest, 333
  and substandard housing, 361
  and urban-suburban socioeconomic status, 30, 267, 268
  and war on poverty, 446, 447
South Carolina, 50, 88, 126–127, 426
South Dakota, 149, 183, 186
Southeastern Pennsylvania Transit Authority, 211, 427
Southeastern states, and fiscal capacity, 295
Southern Standard Building Code Conference, 366, 386
Southwestern states, and annexation, 230
  and extraterritorial regulatory authority, 228
  and urban population concentration, 203
Sovern, Michael I., 161 n.
Soviet Union, 301, 318
Speaker, of U.S. House of Representatives, 127
Special district government, 182, 198–200, 231–233
Special-purpose governments, 175, 179, 198
Spoils system, 108

Springfield (Mass.), 258
Sputnik, 301, 318
Standard City Planning Enabling Act (1928), 401
Standard metropolitan statistical areas (SMSAs), 203, 204, 205, 402
State education associations, 64–65
State government, and transportation, 424–426
State government, and urban housing, 368
State government activities, 31
State legislatures, and committees, 128–129
  and leadership posts, 126–128
  and party, role of, 125–126
  and rules of procedure, 129–132
State legislatures, composition of, 121–125
  functions of, 119–120
  and legislative decision making, 135–144
  and legislative role playing, 132–135
  organization and procedures, 125–132
State and local government, attitudes toward, 29
  "demise" of, 2
  differences among, 6–10
  depoliticization of, 5–6
  and political conflict, 4–6
  powers, growth of, 60
  and professional expertise, reliance on, 5–6
  and reapportionment, 38, 79, 82, 124–125
  responsibilities of, 2–6
  study of, 1–16
  tax policies, 287–290, 294–300
States, classification by index of centralization in decision making, 130, 131
"States rights," 38–41
Staunton (Va.), 191
Stenvig, Charles S., 246
Stokes, Carl, 258
Stokes, Donald E., 53 n., 84 n.
Student protest, 257, 333–335
Student Nonviolent Coordinating Committee, 257, 333
Students for a Democratic Society, 334
Subdivision regulation, 31, 32, 395, 397
Suburban circle theory, 265, 267–274

Suburban Maryland Home Builders Association, 384
Suburban politics, and land-use, 276–277, 280–283
  and middle-class polity, 274–283
  and population trends, 265–266
  and public education, 276–280
  and suburban circle theory, 265, 267–274
  and upward class mobility theory, 265
Sumicrast, Michael, 389 n.
Supervisor-form county government, 194
Supervisors Inter-County Committee (Detroit), 227
Sutthaff, John, 278 n.
Swanson, Bert E., 262 n.
Syed, Anwar, 26 n., 209 n.
"Syndicate," see "Mafia"
Syracuse, 159, 247
Syracuse City Court, 159

Taft, Robert A., 374
Tax bases, segregation of, among governmental levels, 285
Tax effort, 294–300
Tax Foundation, Inc., 103
Tax policies, local, 290–294
Tax policies, state, 287–290, 294–300
Tax sharing, 292–294
Taxation, progressive, 285, 287
Taxation, regressive, 285, 287
Tennessee, 50, 129
Tenth Amendment, 301
Texas, 183, 186, 230
Tiebout, Charles M., 216 n.
Tillman, "Pitchfork Ben," 88
Toronto, 240, 241, 242, 243
Township government, 197–198
Trade-union government, 68–69
Transportation, as basis for region-wide institution, 210–211
Transportation, and automobile vs. mass transit, 415–416, 417, 419
  nature of, 413–414
  politics of, 428–434
  and public sector, 419–428
  purpose of, 414–415
  trends, 416–419
Transportation Association of America, 429

Trucking industry, 418
Truman, David, 58, 59, 59 n.
Twain, Mark, 2
Twenty-third Amendment, 46
221-D-3 program, 380–381

Unemployment compensation, 32–33, 437
Uniform Crime Reports, 337, 358
U.S. Census Bureau, 175, 269
U.S. Chamber of Commerce, 238
U.S. Civil War, 75, 326
U.S. v. Classic, 49
U.S. Commission on Civil Rights, 50, 356
U.S. Conference of Mayors, 247, 429, 442
U.S. Congress, 2, 15, 21, 29, 36, 41, 117, 121, 125, 127, 175, 198, 199, 300, 301, 362, 369, 374, 378, 380, 382, 415, 420, 424, 427, 433, 437, 442, 443, 444
U.S. Constitution, 18, 20, 21, 23, 37, 46, 208, 301
U.S. Department of Agriculture, 33, 223
U.S. Department of Commerce, 33, 295, 420
U.S. Department of Health, Education, and Welfare, 37, 438–439
U.S. Department of Housing and Urban Development, 34, 36–37, 227, 386, 399, 420, 447
U.S. Department of the Interior, 33
U.S. Department of Transportation, 420, 424
U.S. Internal Revenue Service, 289
U.S. Soil Conservation Service, 223
U.S. Supreme Court, 14, 38, 39, 49, 79, 93, 124, 323
University of Michigan Survey Research Center, 53, 54
University of Minnesota, 246
Upward class mobility theory, 265
Urban Development Corporation, 28
Urban dweller, dependence on government, 9
Urban housing, 359–391
  and building industry, 362–368
  and government action, effect of, 388–391
  and interest groups, 381–386

Urban housing (*Continued*)
national policy, and local government, 368–370
and political parties, 387–388
public housing, and the community, 370–374
and substandard housing, 360–362
and urban renewal, 34, 252, 372–381, 403–405
Urban image, in state government, 27–29
Urban-industrial states, and governor's formal powers, 104
Urban Mass Transportation Administration, 420, 424
Urban planning, 392–411
administration of, 399, 408–409
evaluation of, 406–411
and land-use tools, controls, influences, 395–399
and metropolitan planning, 402–403
nature of, 394–395
and new-town planning, 405
and state-government, role of, 411
and transportation, 403–405
and urban renewal, 403–405
Urban renewal, 34, 252, 372–381
and Housing Act (1949), 372–374, 376, 377
and Housing Act (1954), 377–380
and urban planning, 403–405
Urban riots, 245–246
Utah, 61

Vanlandingham, Kenneth E., 149 n.
Ventura County (Calif.), 232
Vermont, 183, 300
Veterans Administration, 363, 369
Vietnam, 23–24, 333
Vines, Kenneth N., 66 n., 76 n., 425 n., 448 n.
Virginia, 86, 89, 186, 193, 230, 235, 236, 300, 323, 426, 427
Virtue, Maxine B., 149 n.
Volunteers in Service to America, 445, 446
Voters, knowledgeability of, 70–71
Voting, as political participation, 46–55
and absentee voting, 48
and age requirements, 46–47
and election-day procedures, 48
and literacy requirements, 48, 50

Voting (*Continued*)
and party, influence of, 54–55
and psychological involvement, 53–54
and registration systems, 47–48, 49
and residence requirements, 48
socioeconomic correlates, 52–53
voter turnout, 47, 49
"white primary," 49–50
Voting Rights Act (1965), 50–52

Wagner, Robert, 374
Wahlke, John C., 63 n., 119 n., 132, 132 n., 133 n., 139 n., 140, 140 n., 141, 142, 142 n.
Wald, Patricia, 158
Waldo, Dwight, 109 n.
Walker, Jack L., 45 n.
Walker, Robert A., 410 n.
Wallace, George, 47, 54
Walsh, William, 247
Walter Motor Truck Company, 430
War on poverty, 439–448
community action programs, 441–447
Ward-based electoral system, 251
Warner and Swasey Company, 430
Warren, Earl, 170
Warren, Robert, 216 n.
Washington, D.C., 29, 36, 38, 39, 40, 41, 178, 187, 190, 211, 227, 231, 233, 235, 269, 273, 274, 357, 375, 383, 384, 405, 419, 427, 431, 433, 442, 448
Washington Metropolitan Area Transit Authority, 211
Washington Metropolitan Bay Area Transit Authority, 427
Washington Peace March (1962), 333
Washington (State), 67, 89, 149
Washington Suburban Sanitary Commission, 233
Watershed projects, 223
Watson, Richard A., 170 n.
Watson, Tom, 78
Watt, Graham, 192 n.
Watts riots, 246
Webb, Del C., 364
Webster, Daniel, 20
Webster, Donald H., 397 n.
Welfare, and community action programs, 441–447
and model cities program, 447–448

Welfare (*Continued*)
  and political alignments, 449–450
  state and local expenditures for, 305–306
  state and local support of, 448–449
  and war on poverty, 439–448
Welfare, housing, and health groups, in city politics, 253, 256–257
Welfare colonialism, 439
Wells, H. G., 201
Weltanschauung, 71
West Virginia, 289
Western states, and annexation, 230
  county government, 193
  legislative partisanship, 137
  metropolitan suburbanization, 203, 266
  substandard housing, 361
  urban-suburban socioeconomic status, 230, 267, 268
Westchester County (New York State), 195
White Citizens Council, 323
White Motor Corporation, 430
"White primary," 49–50
Why Johnny Can't Read, 318
Wilhern, York, 113 n.
Williams, Oliver P., 217 n., 251 n.
Williston (Pa.), 408
Wilmington (Del.), 203
Wilson, James, 2, 178, 178 n., 249 n., 250 n., 252 n., 254 n., 344, 344 n.,

Wilson, James (*Continued*)
  349, 349 n., 350, 350 n., 353, 353 n., 358, 358 n., 372, 376 n., 377 n., 449 n.
Winnipeg, 240, 242
Wirt, Frederick M., 274, 274 n.
Wisconsin, 42, 84, 183, 197, 288, 291, 315
Wolfe, Arthur C., 47 n.
Wolfinger, Raymond E., 252 n.
Wood, Robert C., 207, 209 n., 210, 210 n., 217 n., 274 n., 277 n.
Workable Program for Community Development, 378, 379, 380
Workmen's compensation, 31
World War II, 229, 326, 327, 331, 372
Wright, Deil S., 111, 111 n., 113
Wyoming, 149, 426

Ylvisaker, Paul, 209 n., 210, 210 n., 211
Yonkers, New York, Urban Renewal Agency, 374
Yorty, Sam, 246, 247
Youngstown (O.), 319
Youngstown Sheet and Tube Company v. Sawyer, 93

Ziegler, Harmon, 66 n., 279 n., 382 n.
Zimmerman, Joseph F., 402 n.
Zisk, Betty H., 63 n., 68 n.
Zoning, 31, 32, 180, 367–368, 395–397, 399–400, 406, 407–408, 409, 410

71 72 73 74   7 6 5 4 3 2 1